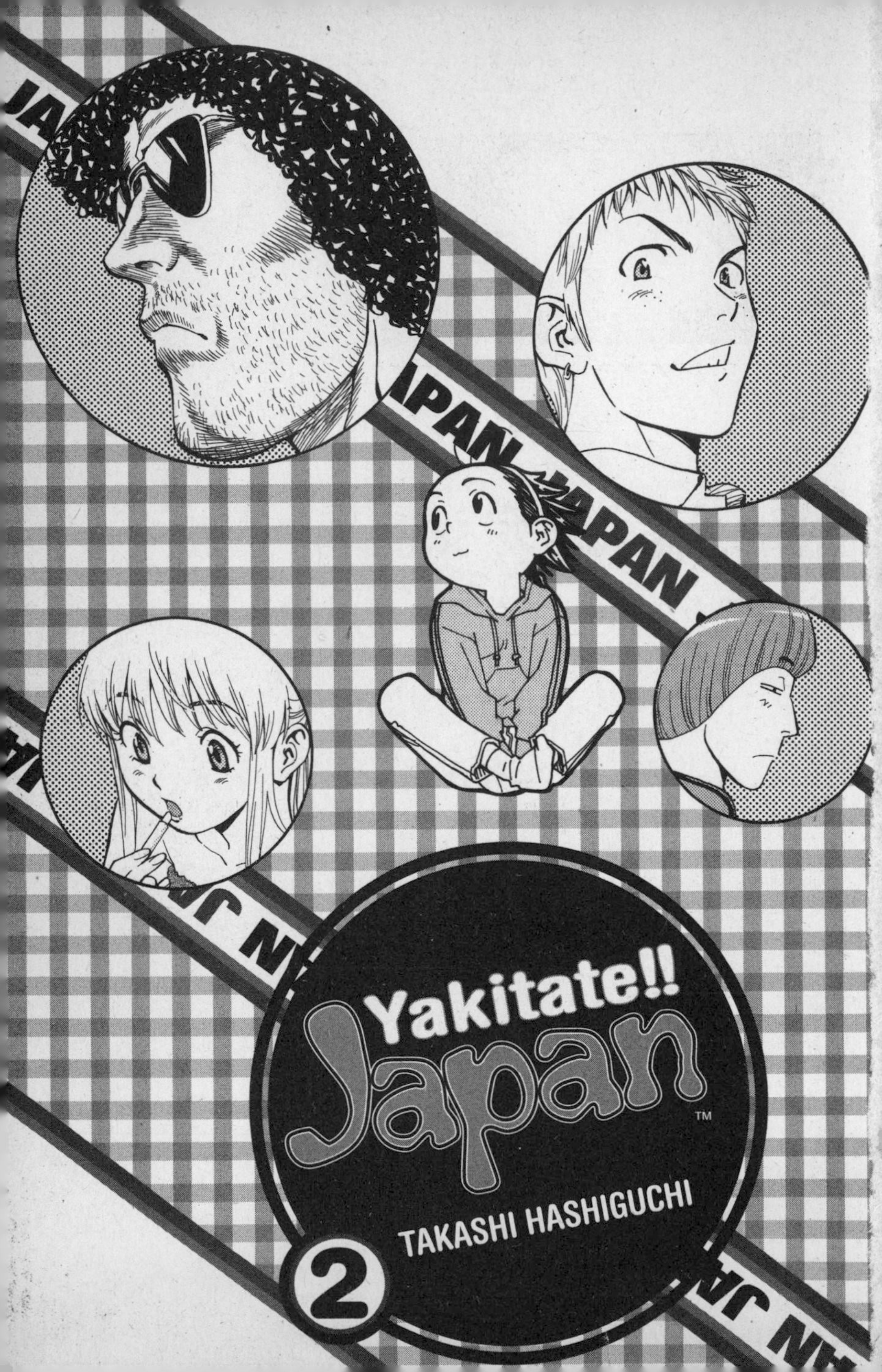
Yakitate!!
Japan™
TAKASHI HASHIGUCHI
2

YAKITATE!! JAPAN
2
VIZ Media Edition

★The Story Thus Far★

There are many national breads: France, Germany, and England all have their namesake loaves. But Japan has no bread to call its own—no "Ja-pan" to carry the baked-goods banner. Faced with this dire situation, a boy named Kazuma Azuma decided to make Japan's signature bread and headed for the bright lights of Tokyo, bringing his 55 experimental bread recipes with him. His goal: pass the employment examination at Pantasia Bakery's flagship store, where only first-class bread makers are allowed to work.

Using his "Hands of the Sun"—exceptionally warm hands perfectly suited to kneading bread dough—Kazuma had no problem advancing to the final exam round. But disaster struck when a scheming colleague named Kawachi ruined Kazuma's chances of passing. However, thanks to the intervention of Pantasia baking scion Tsukino, both Kazuma and Kawachi were hired at the South Tokyo branch of the bakery. Their first job is to make a "MARE-velous" bread...but what does that even mean?!

CONTENTS

Research Assistance: Aruru Sugamo, Andersen Aoyama, Shikishima-sei Pan (Pasco).

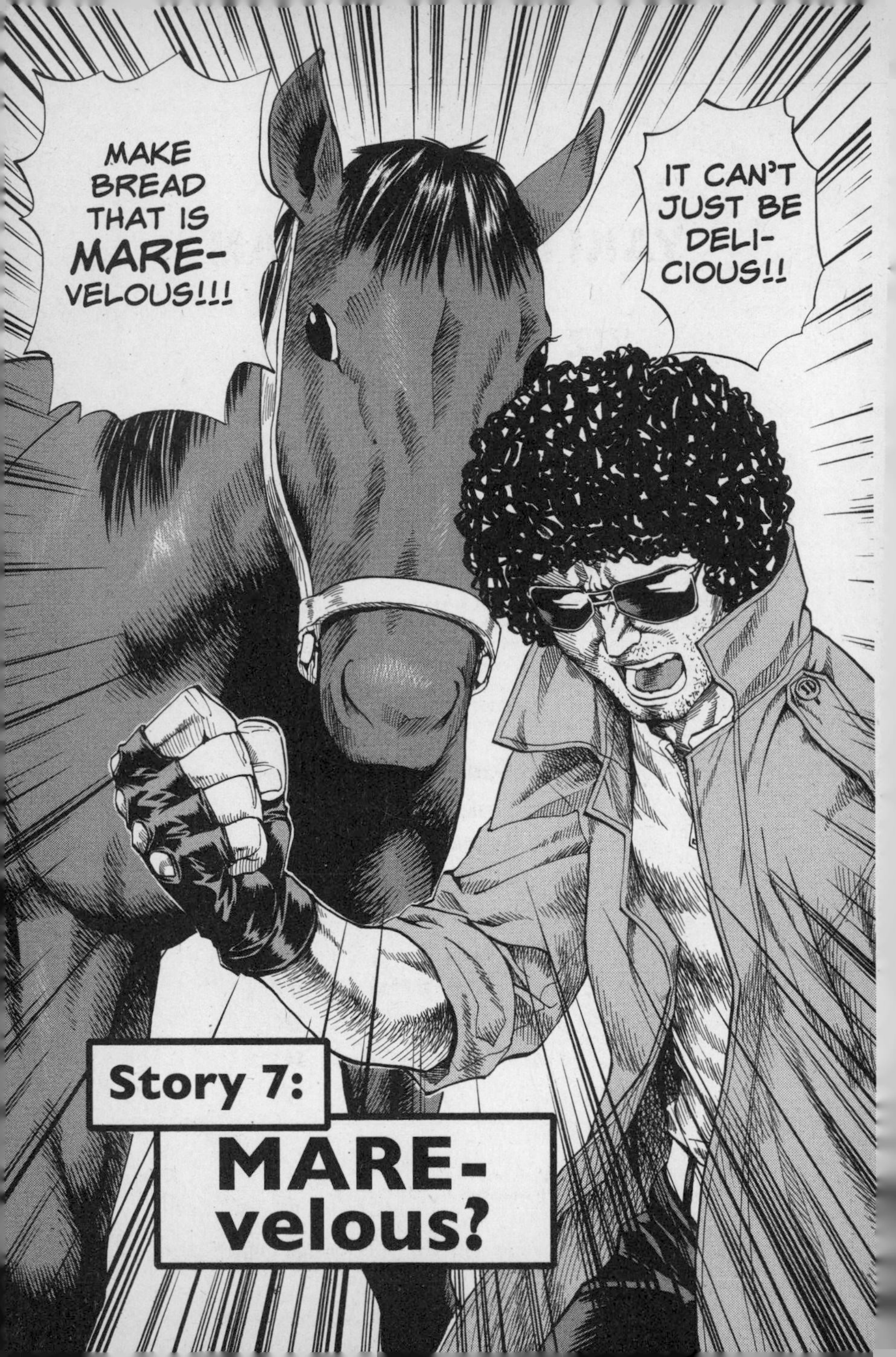
IT CAN'T JUST BE DELI-CIOUS!!
MAKE BREAD THAT IS MARE-VELOUS!!!
Story 7:
MARE-velous?

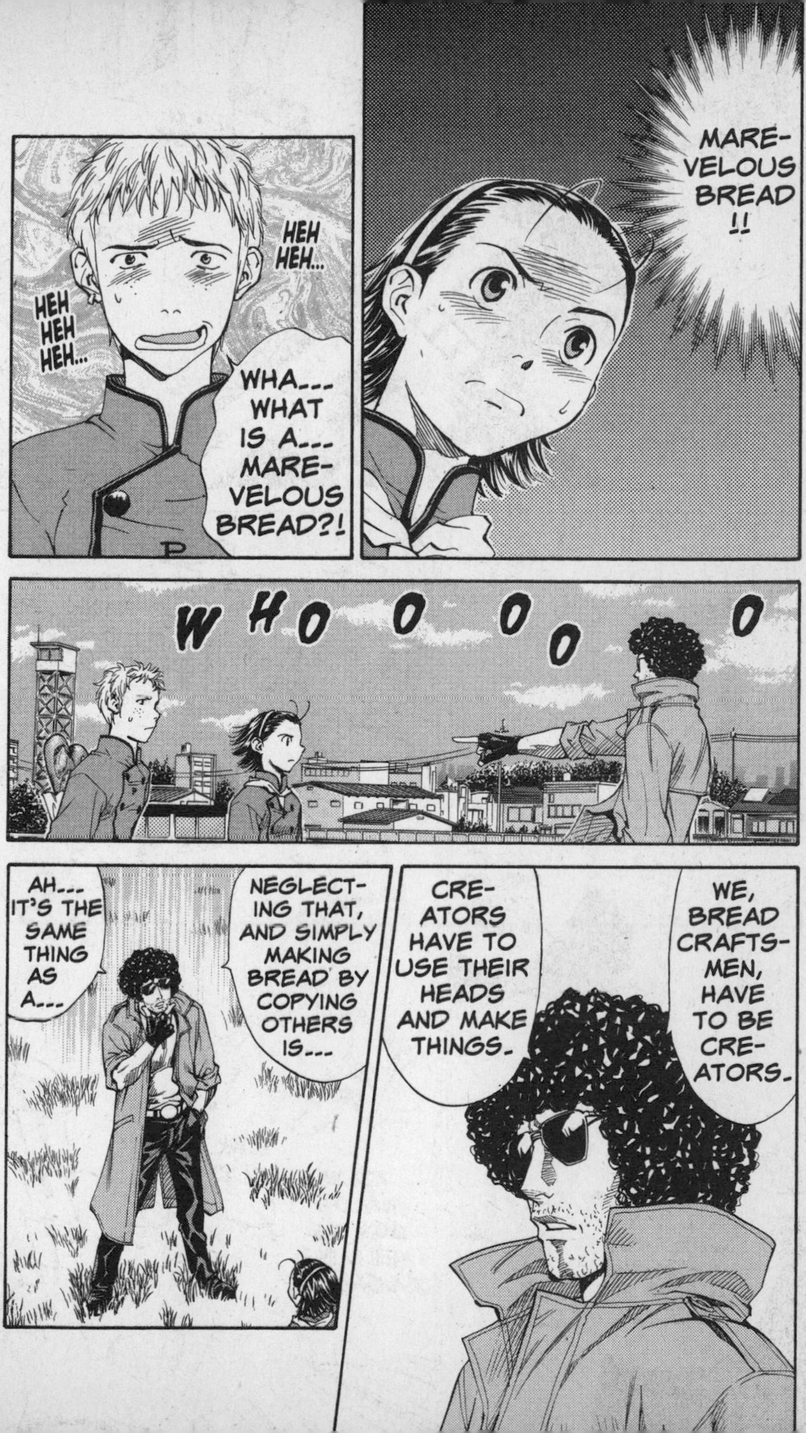
MARE-VELOUS BREAD !!
HEH HEH...
HEH HEH HEH...
WHA... WHAT IS A... MARE-VELOUS BREAD?!
WHOOOOOO
WE, BREAD CRAFTS-MEN, HAVE TO BE CRE-ATORS.
CRE-ATORS HAVE TO USE THEIR HEADS AND MAKE THINGS.
NEGLECT-ING THAT, AND SIMPLY MAKING BREAD BY COPYING OTHERS IS...
AH... IT'S THE SAME THING AS A...

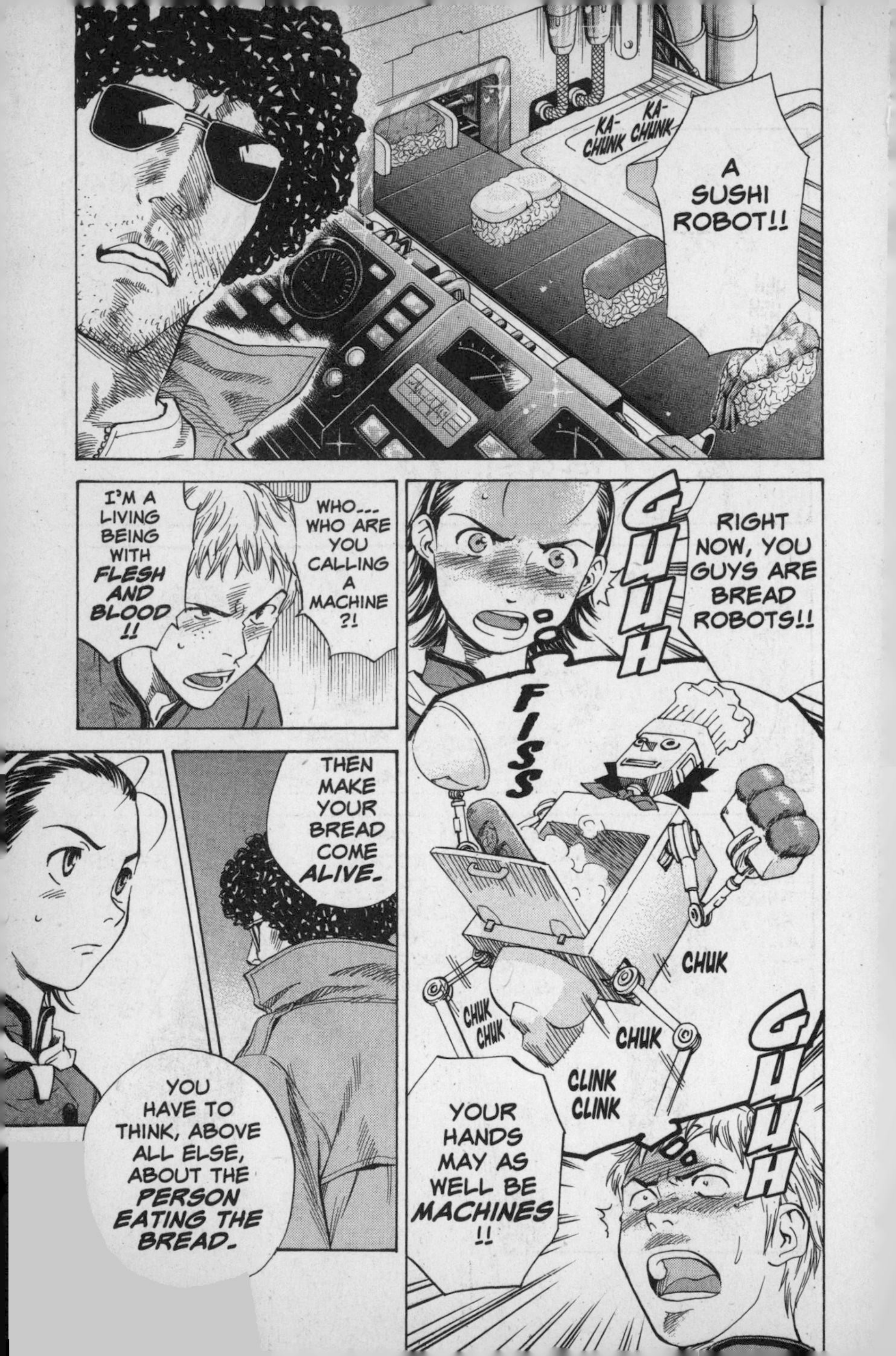
KA-CHUNK
KA-CHUNK
A SUSHI ROBOT!!
GUUUH
RIGHT NOW, YOU GUYS ARE BREAD ROBOTS!!
FISS
WHO... WHO ARE YOU CALLING A MACHINE?!
I'M A LIVING BEING WITH *FLESH AND BLOOD*!!
CHUK
CHUK CHUK
CHUK
CLINK CLINK
GUUUH
YOUR HANDS MAY AS WELL BE *MACHINES*!!
THEN MAKE YOUR BREAD COME *ALIVE*.
YOU HAVE TO THINK, ABOVE ALL ELSE, ABOUT THE *PERSON EATING THE BREAD*.

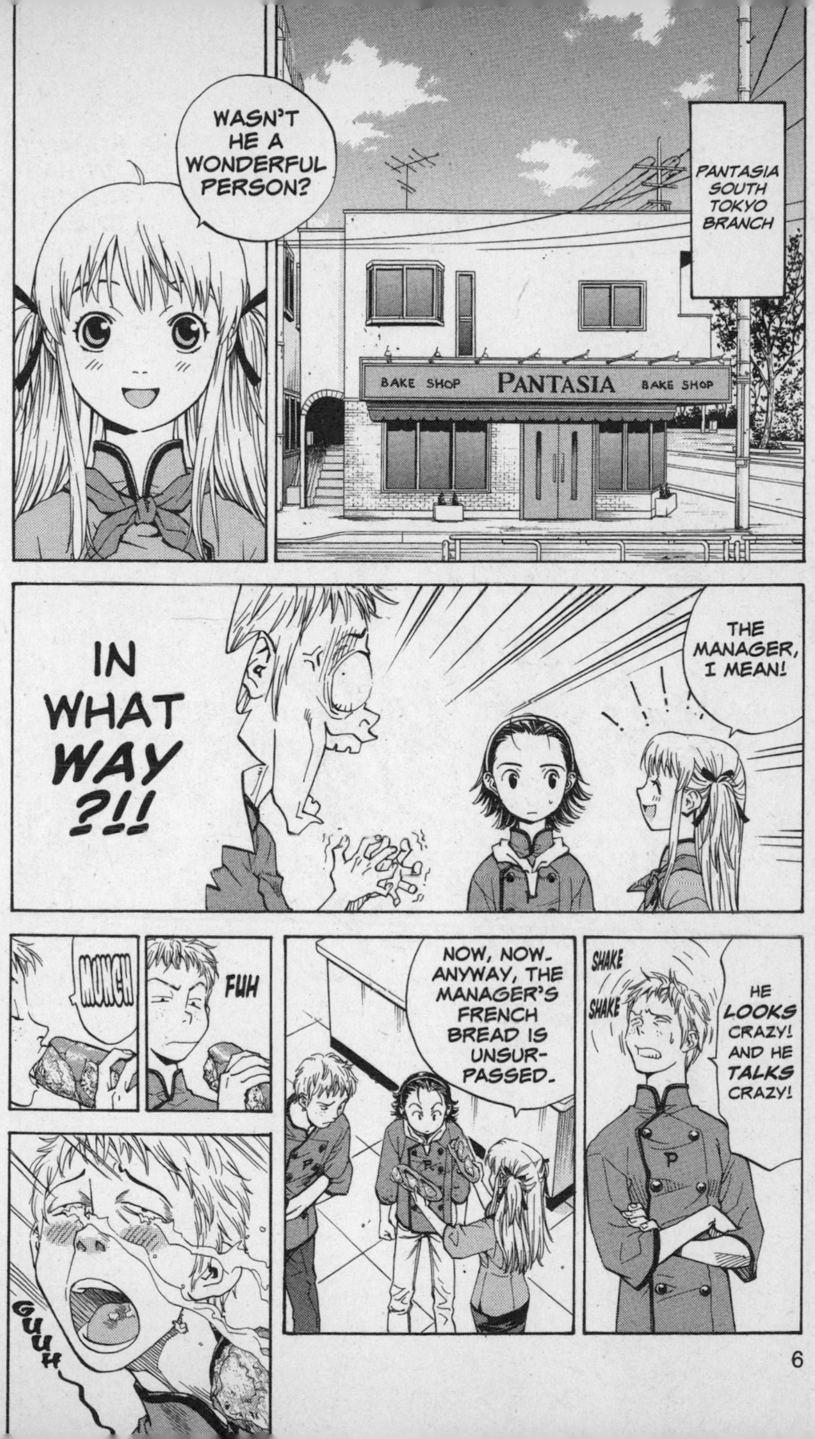
PANTASIA SOUTH TOKYO BRANCH
BAKE SHOP PANTASIA BAKE SHOP
WASN'T HE A WONDERFUL PERSON?
THE MANAGER, I MEAN!
IN WHAT WAY ?!!
SHAKE SHAKE
HE LOOKS CRAZY! AND HE TALKS CRAZY!
NOW, NOW. ANYWAY, THE MANAGER'S FRENCH BREAD IS UNSURPASSED.
FUH
MUNCH
GUUH

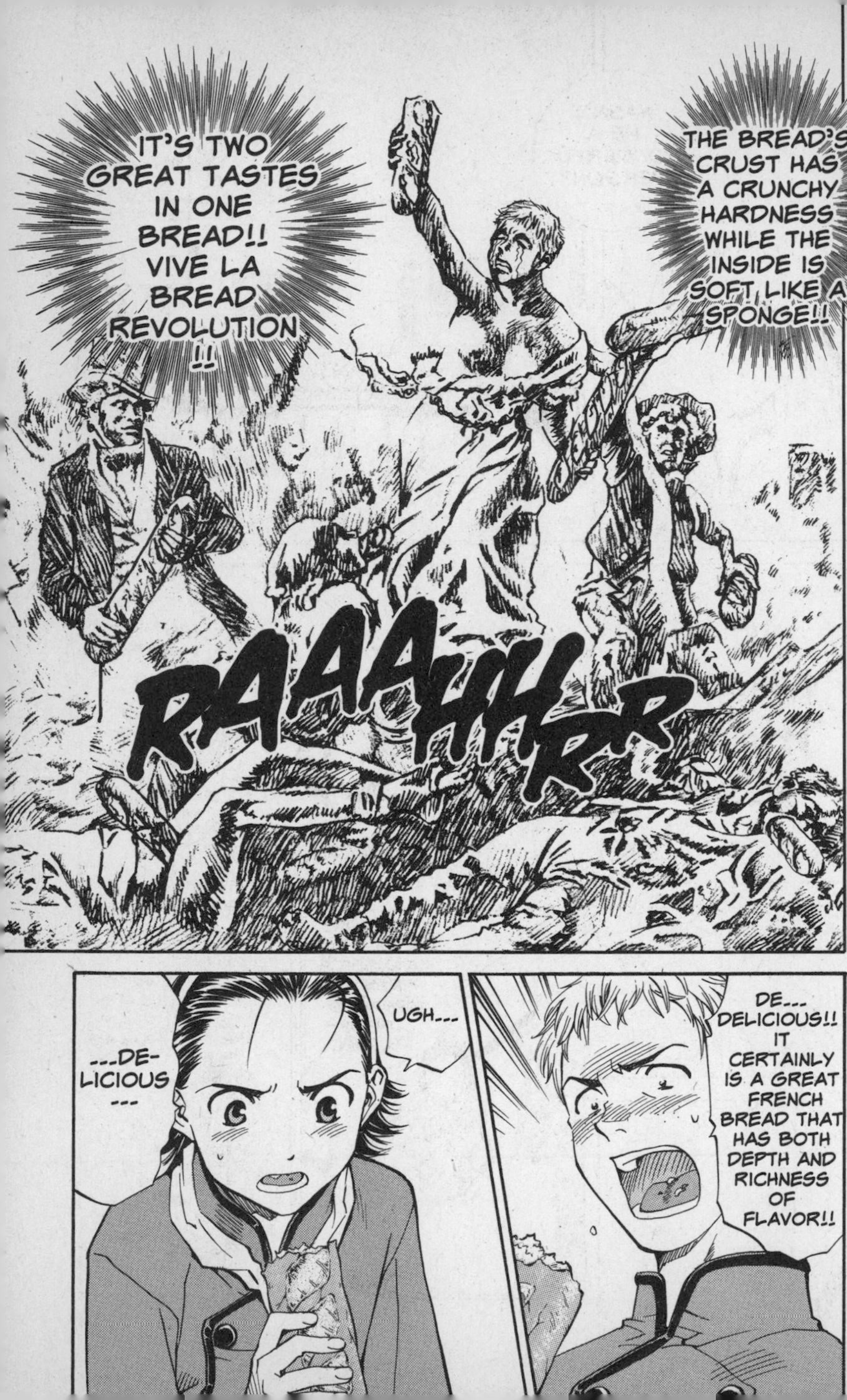
THE BREAD'S CRUST HAS A CRUNCHY HARDNESS WHILE THE INSIDE IS SOFT LIKE A SPONGE!!
IT'S TWO GREAT TASTES IN ONE BREAD!! VIVE LA BREAD REVOLUTION!!
RAAAHHRR
DE... DELICIOUS!! IT CERTAINLY IS A GREAT FRENCH BREAD THAT HAS BOTH DEPTH AND RICHNESS OF FLAVOR!!
UGH...
...DE-LICIOUS...

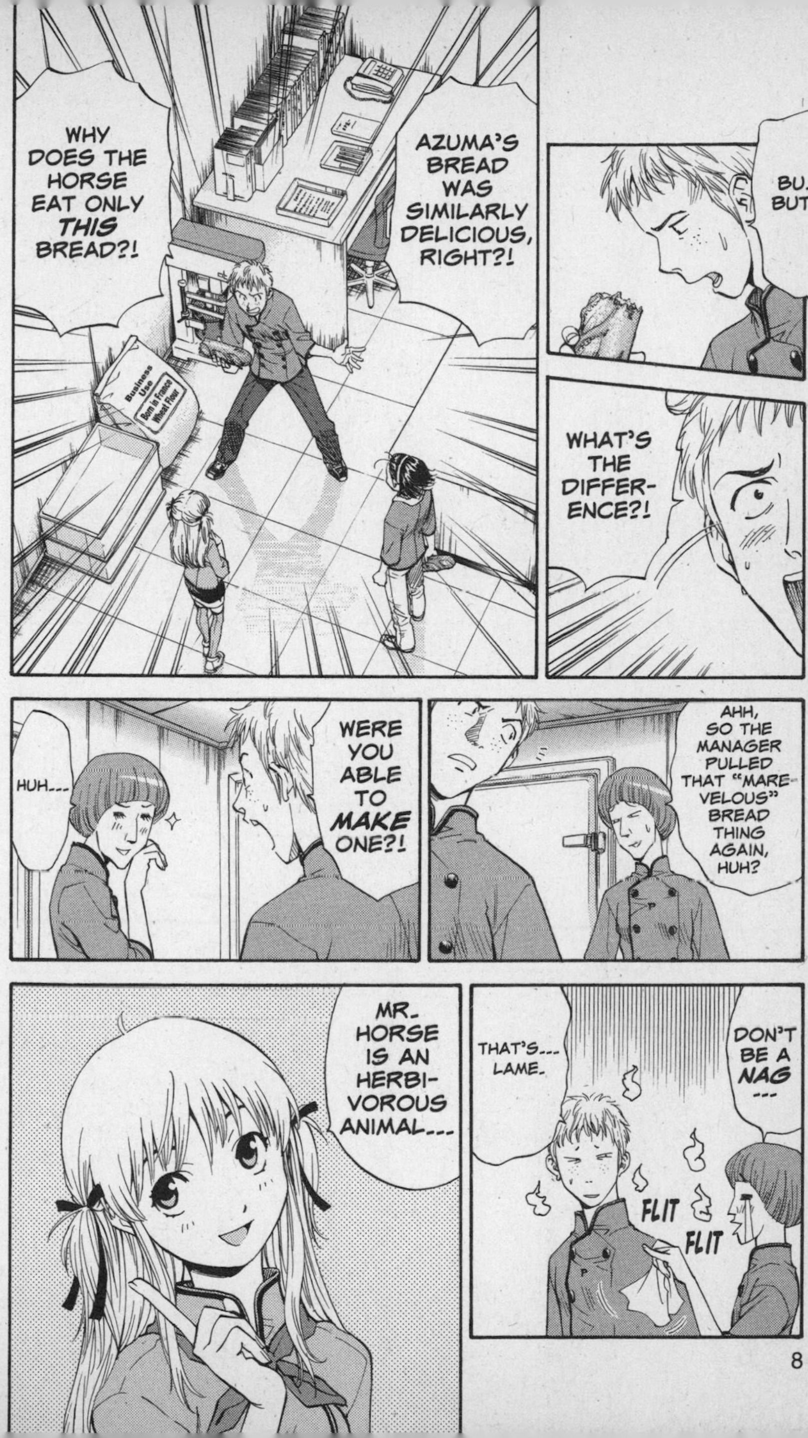
BU... BUT...
WHAT'S THE DIFFERENCE?!
AZUMA'S BREAD WAS SIMILARLY DELICIOUS, RIGHT?!
WHY DOES THE HORSE EAT ONLY *THIS* BREAD?!
Business Use
Born in France Wheat Flour
AHH, SO THE MANAGER PULLED THAT "MARE-VELOUS" BREAD THING AGAIN, HUH?
WERE YOU ABLE TO *MAKE* ONE?!
HUH...
DON'T BE A *NAG* ...
THAT'S... LAME.
FLIT
FLIT
MR. HORSE IS AN HERBIVOROUS ANIMAL...

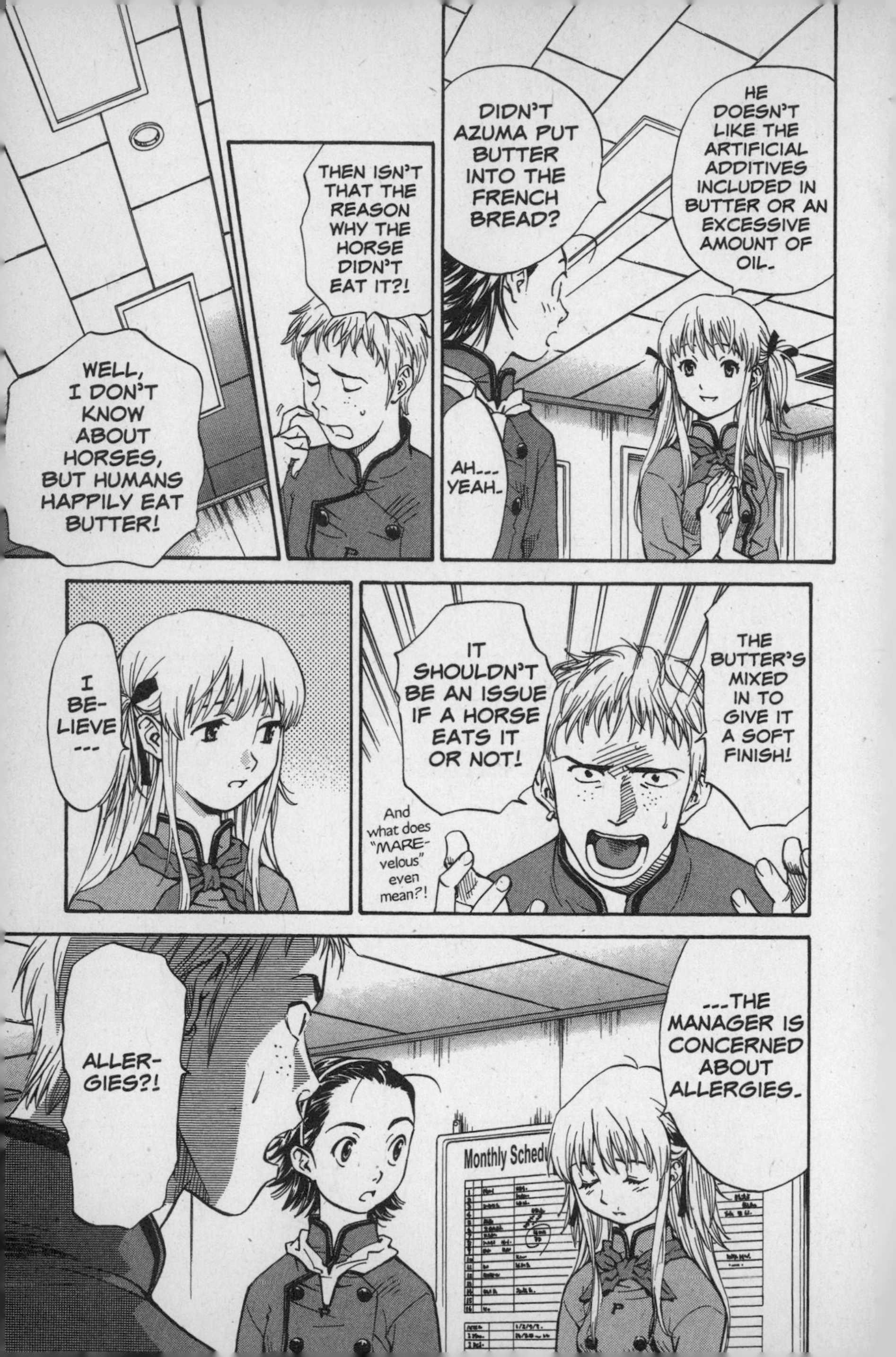
DIDN'T AZUMA PUT BUTTER INTO THE FRENCH BREAD?
HE DOESN'T LIKE THE ARTIFICIAL ADDITIVES INCLUDED IN BUTTER OR AN EXCESSIVE AMOUNT OF OIL.
AH... YEAH.
THEN ISN'T THAT THE REASON WHY THE HORSE DIDN'T EAT IT?!
WELL, I DON'T KNOW ABOUT HORSES, BUT HUMANS HAPPILY EAT BUTTER!
THE BUTTER'S MIXED IN TO GIVE IT A SOFT FINISH!
IT SHOULDN'T BE AN ISSUE IF A HORSE EATS IT OR NOT!
And what does "MARE-velous" even mean?!
I BE-LIEVE...
...THE MANAGER IS CONCERNED ABOUT ALLERGIES.
ALLER-GIES?!

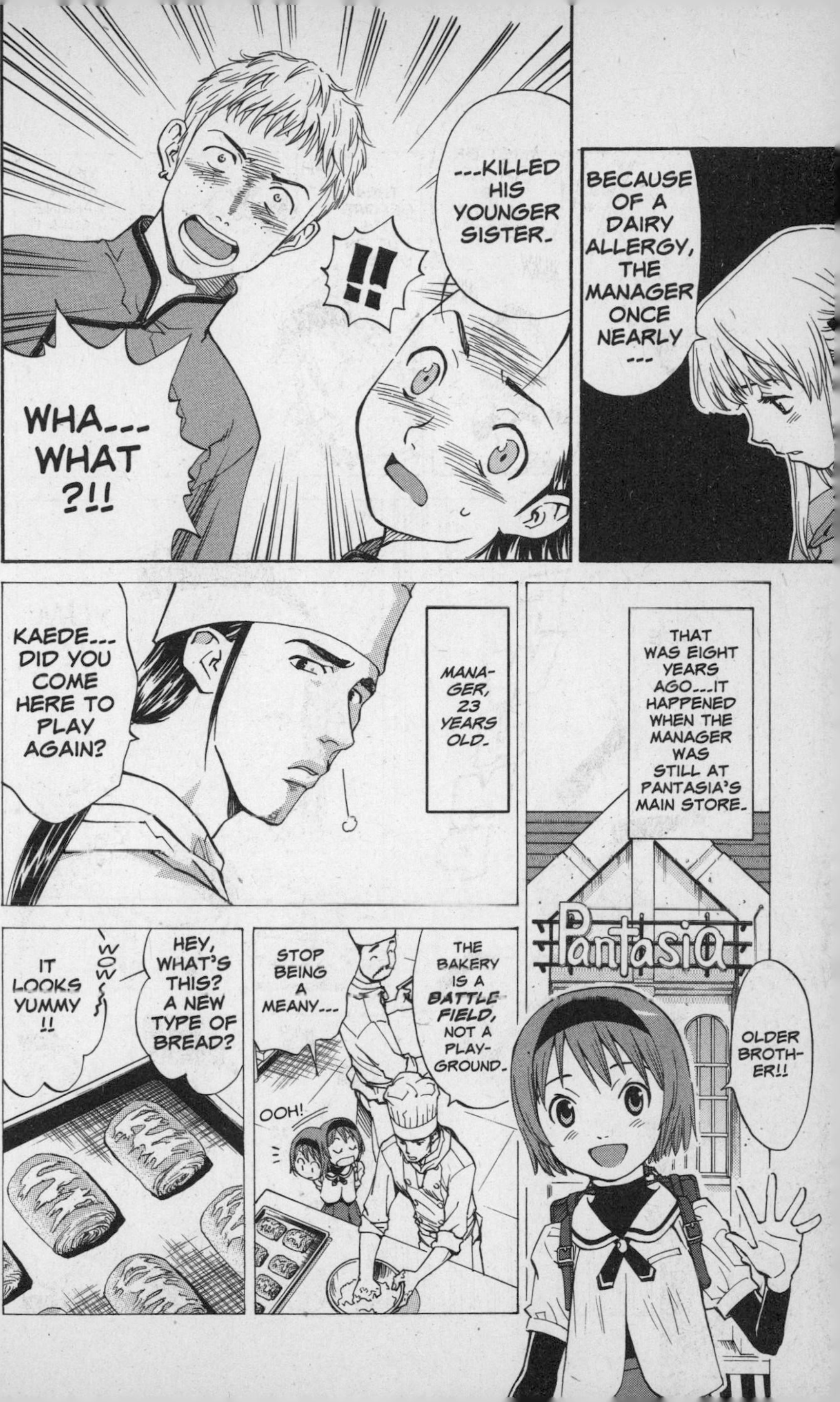
BECAUSE OF A DAIRY ALLERGY, THE MANAGER ONCE NEARLY...
...KILLED HIS YOUNGER SISTER.
!!
WHA... WHAT ?!!
THAT WAS EIGHT YEARS AGO...IT HAPPENED WHEN THE MANAGER WAS STILL AT PANTASIA'S MAIN STORE.
Pantasia
OLDER BROTHER!!
MANAGER, 23 YEARS OLD.
KAEDE... DID YOU COME HERE TO PLAY AGAIN?
THE BAKERY IS A *BATTLEFIELD*, NOT A PLAYGROUND.
STOP BEING A MEANY...
OOH!
HEY, WHAT'S THIS? A NEW TYPE OF BREAD?
WOW~
IT LOOKS YUMMY !!

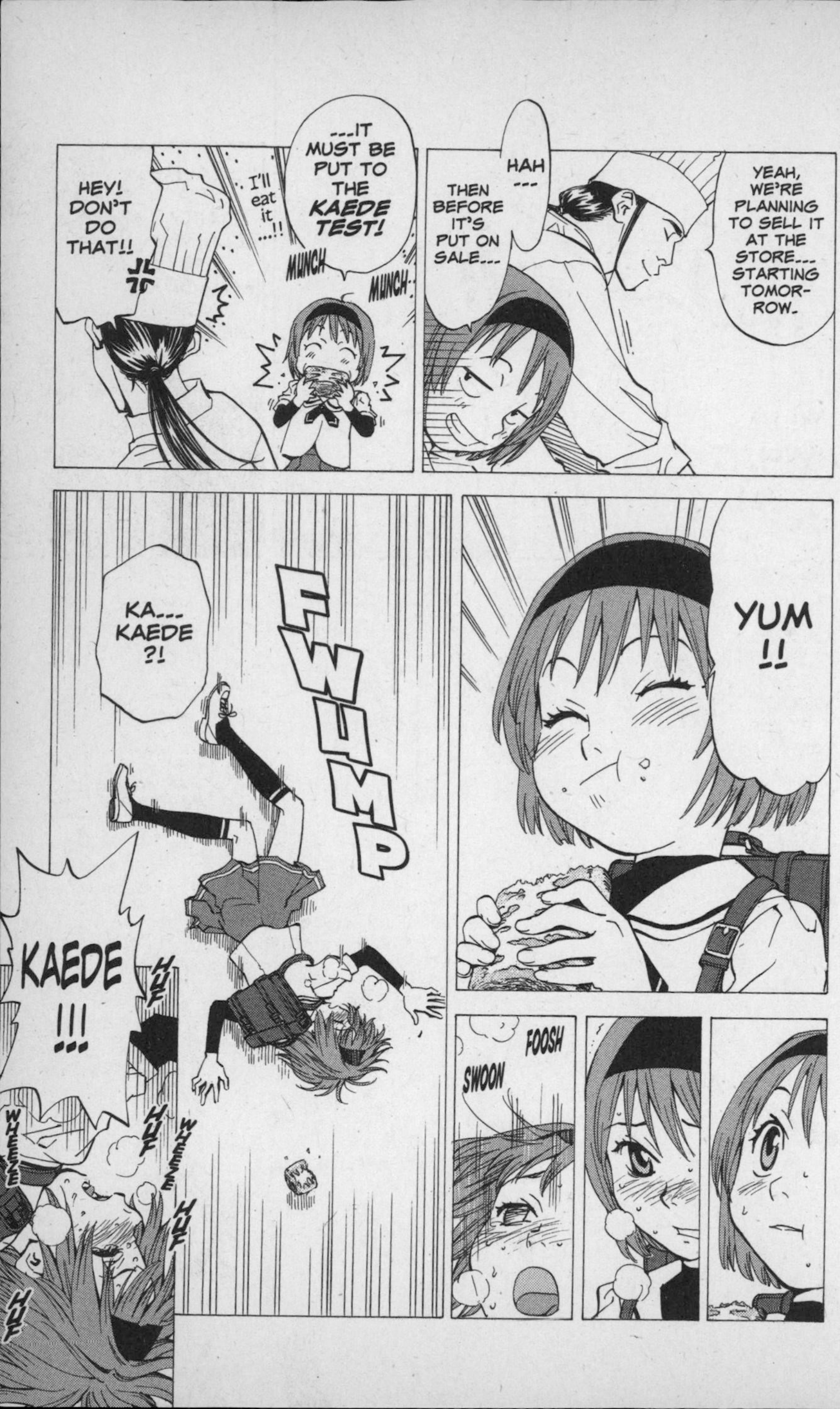
YEAH, WE'RE PLANNING TO SELL IT AT THE STORE... STARTING TOMORROW.
HAH...
THEN BEFORE IT'S PUT ON SALE...
...IT MUST BE PUT TO THE KAEDE TEST!
MUNCH
MUNCH
I'll eat it ...!!
HEY! DON'T DO THAT!!
YUM !!
FOOSH
SWOON
FWUMP
KA... KAEDE ?!
HUF
KAEDE !!!...
HUF
WHEEZE
HUF
WHEEZE
HUF

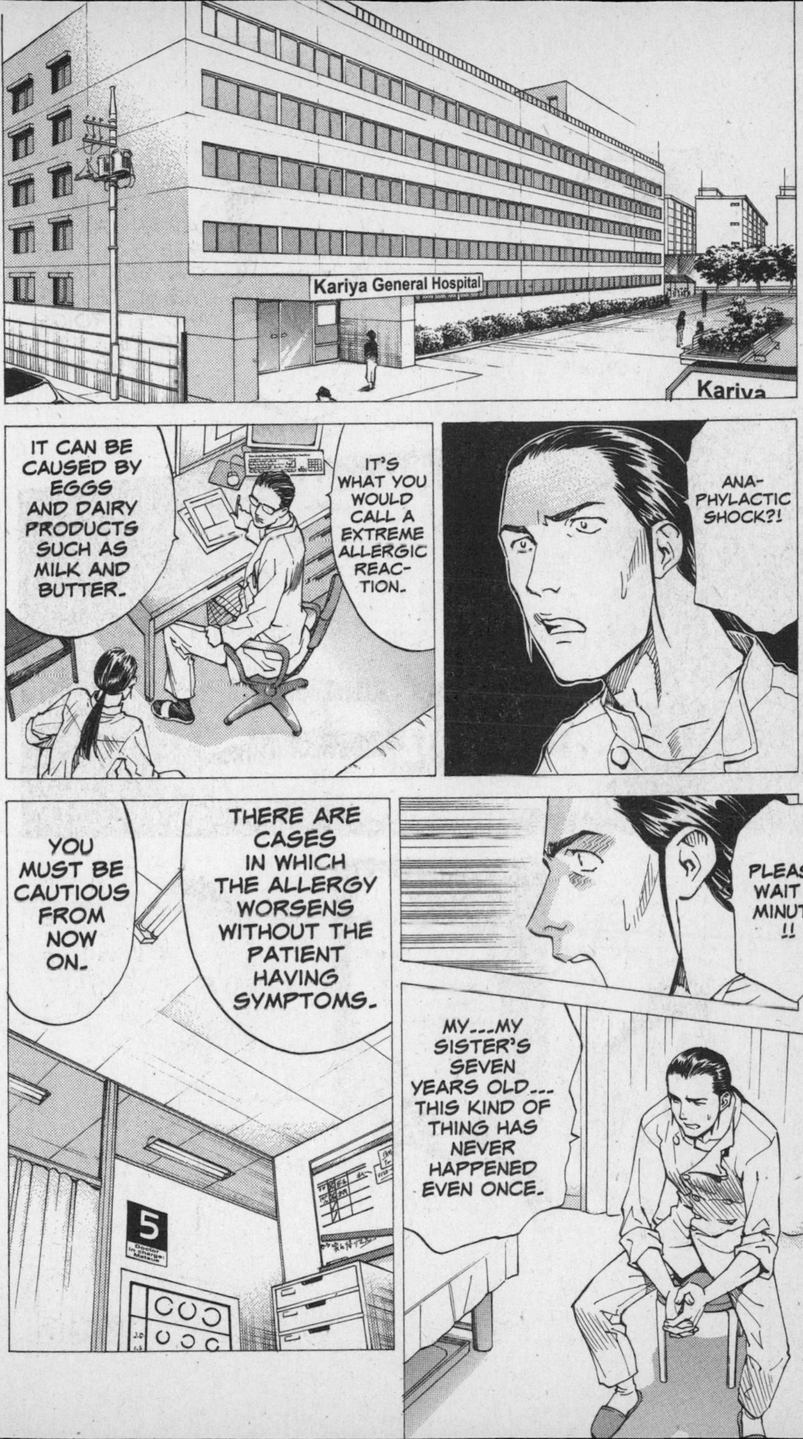
Kariya General Hospital
Kariya
ANA-PHYLACTIC SHOCK?!
IT'S WHAT YOU WOULD CALL A EXTREME ALLERGIC REAC-TION.
IT CAN BE CAUSED BY EGGS AND DAIRY PRODUCTS SUCH AS MILK AND BUTTER.
PLEASE WAIT A MINUTE !!
MY...MY SISTER'S SEVEN YEARS OLD... THIS KIND OF THING HAS NEVER HAPPENED EVEN ONCE.
THERE ARE CASES IN WHICH THE ALLERGY WORSENS WITHOUT THE PATIENT HAVING SYMPTOMS.
YOU MUST BE CAUTIOUS FROM NOW ON.
5

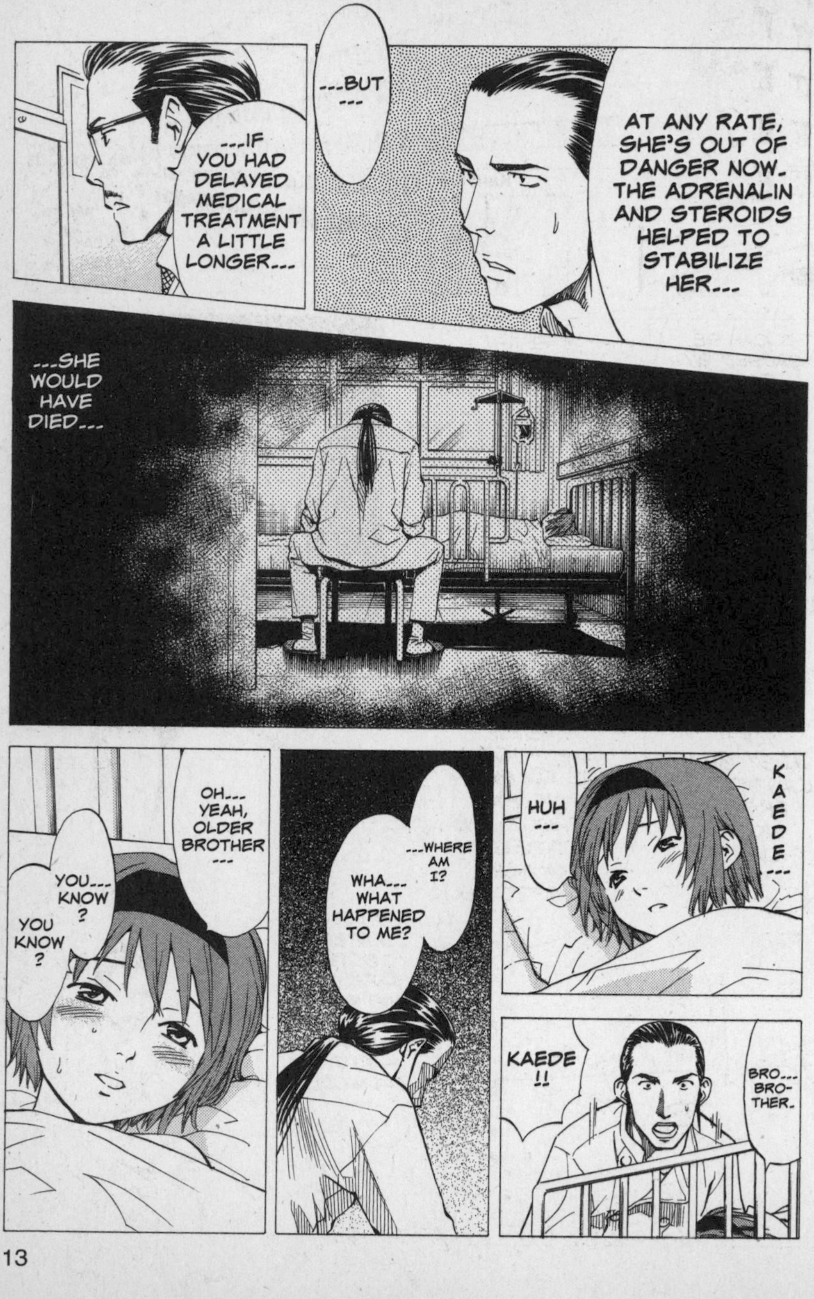
AT ANY RATE, SHE'S OUT OF DANGER NOW. THE ADRENALIN AND STEROIDS HELPED TO STABILIZE HER...
...BUT ...
...IF YOU HAD DELAYED MEDICAL TREATMENT A LITTLE LONGER...
...SHE WOULD HAVE DIED...
KAEDE...
HUH ...
BRO... BRO-THER.
KAEDE !!
...WHERE AM I?
WHA... WHAT HAPPENED TO ME?
OH... YEAH, OLDER BROTHER ...
YOU... KNOW ?
YOU KNOW ?

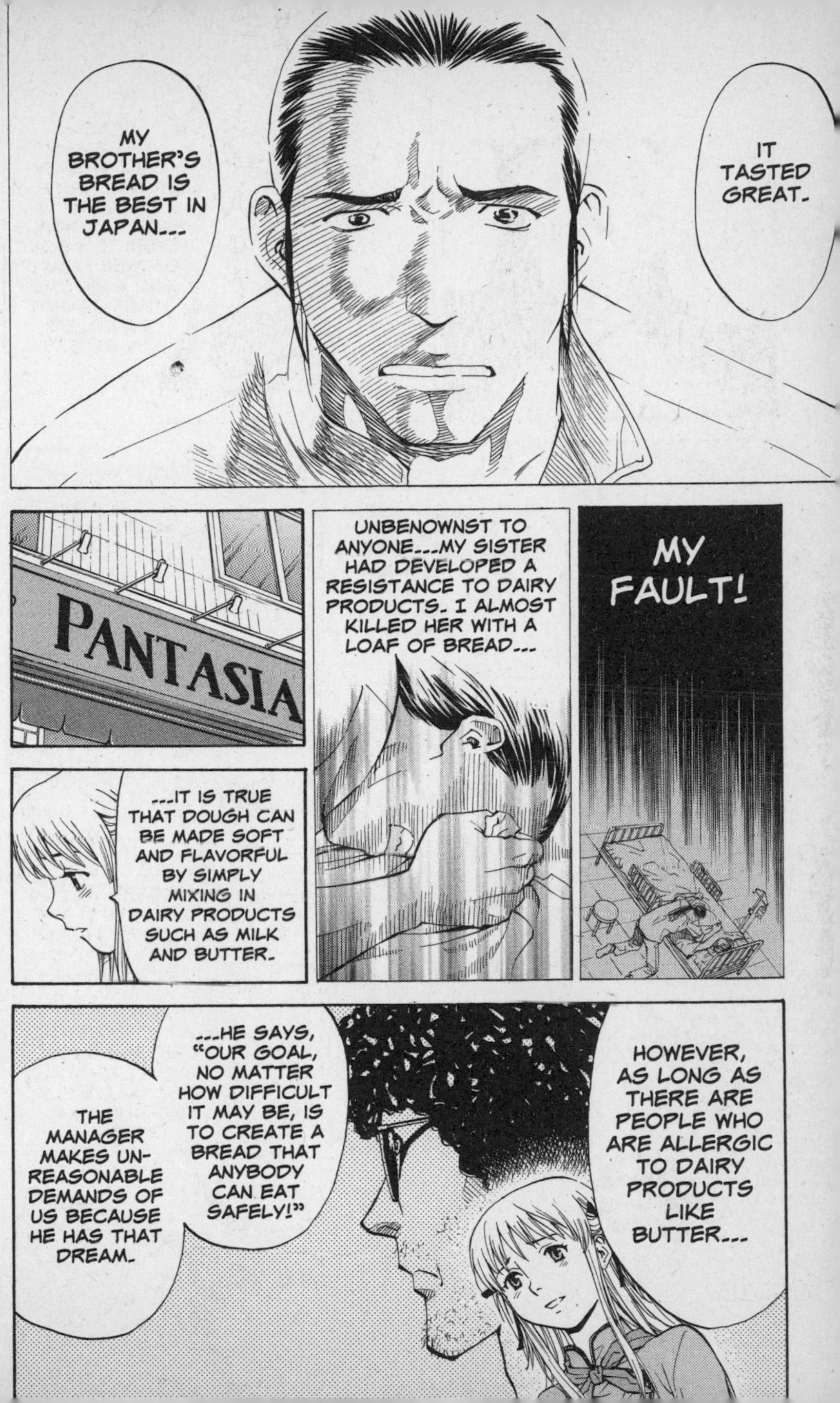
IT TASTED GREAT.
MY BROTHER'S BREAD IS THE BEST IN JAPAN...
MY FAULT!
UNBENOWNST TO ANYONE...MY SISTER HAD DEVELOPED A RESISTANCE TO DAIRY PRODUCTS. I ALMOST KILLED HER WITH A LOAF OF BREAD...
PANTASIA
...IT IS TRUE THAT DOUGH CAN BE MADE SOFT AND FLAVORFUL BY SIMPLY MIXING IN DAIRY PRODUCTS SUCH AS MILK AND BUTTER.
HOWEVER, AS LONG AS THERE ARE PEOPLE WHO ARE ALLERGIC TO DAIRY PRODUCTS LIKE BUTTER...
...HE SAYS, "OUR GOAL, NO MATTER HOW DIFFICULT IT MAY BE, IS TO CREATE A BREAD THAT ANYBODY CAN EAT SAFELY!"
THE MANAGER MAKES UN-REASONABLE DEMANDS OF US BECAUSE HE HAS THAT DREAM.

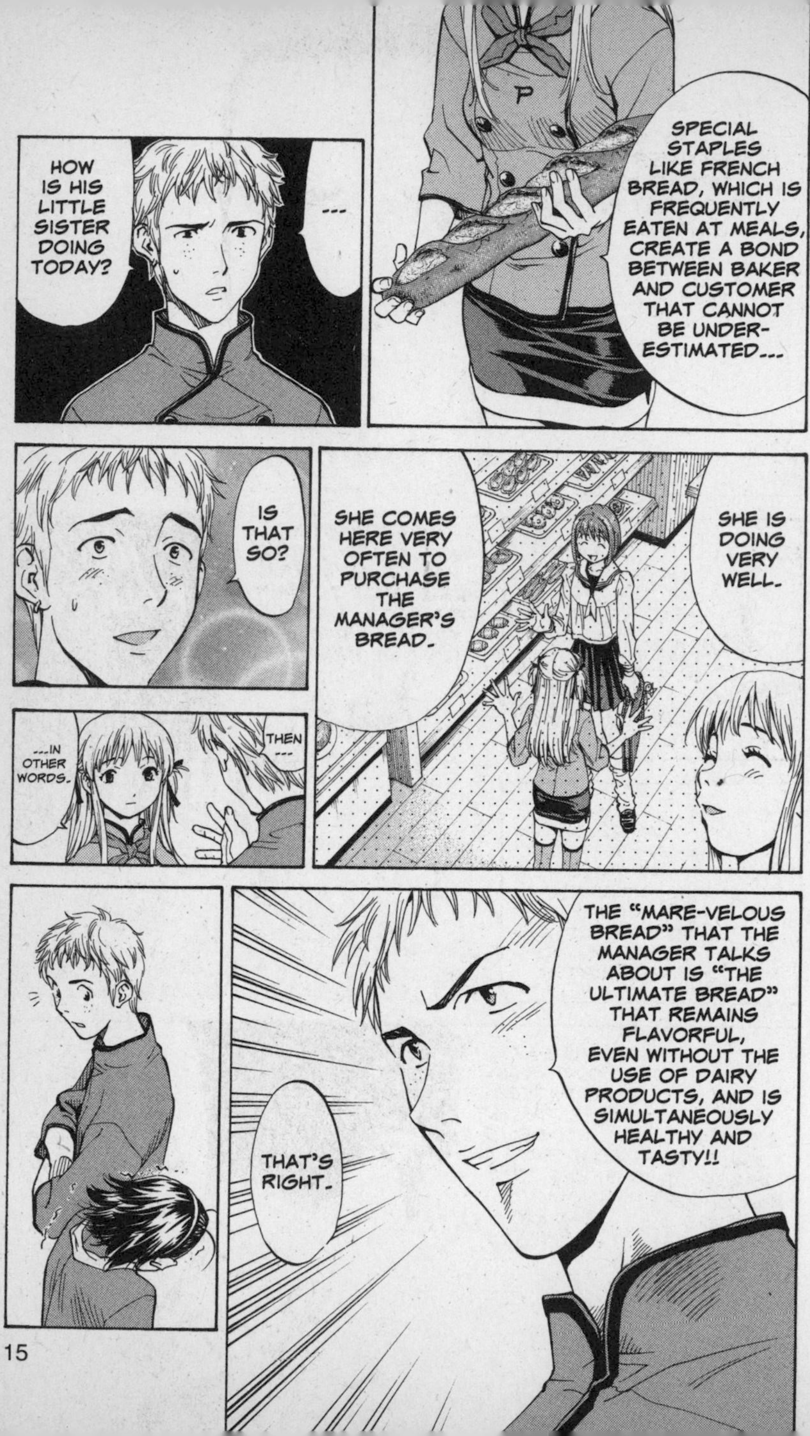
SPECIAL STAPLES LIKE FRENCH BREAD, WHICH IS FREQUENTLY EATEN AT MEALS, CREATE A BOND BETWEEN BAKER AND CUSTOMER THAT CANNOT BE UNDER-ESTIMATED...

HOW IS HIS LITTLE SISTER DOING TODAY?
SHE IS DOING VERY WELL.
SHE COMES HERE VERY OFTEN TO PURCHASE THE MANAGER'S BREAD.
IS THAT SO?
THEN ---
---IN OTHER WORDS.
THE "MARE-VELOUS BREAD" THAT THE MANAGER TALKS ABOUT IS "THE ULTIMATE BREAD" THAT REMAINS FLAVORFUL, EVEN WITHOUT THE USE OF DAIRY PRODUCTS, AND IS SIMULTANEOUSLY HEALTHY AND TASTY!!
THAT'S RIGHT.

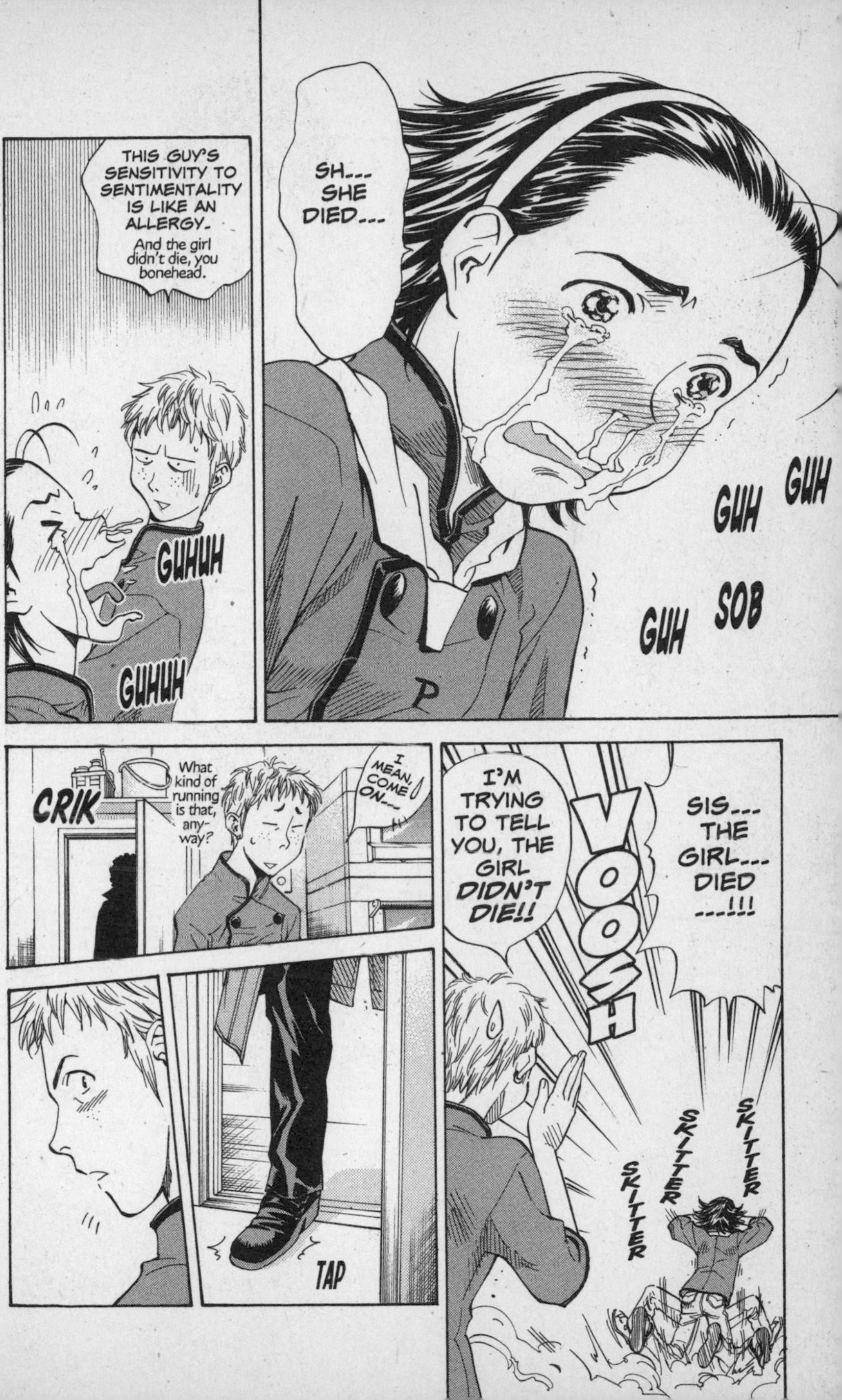
SH... SHE DIED...
GUH
GUH
SOB
GUH
THIS GUY'S SENSITIVITY TO SENTIMENTALITY IS LIKE AN ALLERGY.
And the girl didn't die, you bonehead.
GUHUH
GUHUH
SIS... THE GIRL... DIED ...!!!
VOOOSH
I'M TRYING TO TELL YOU, THE GIRL DIDN'T DIE!!
SKITTER
SKITTER
SKITTER
I MEAN, COME ON...
What kind of running is that, anyway?
CRIK
TAP

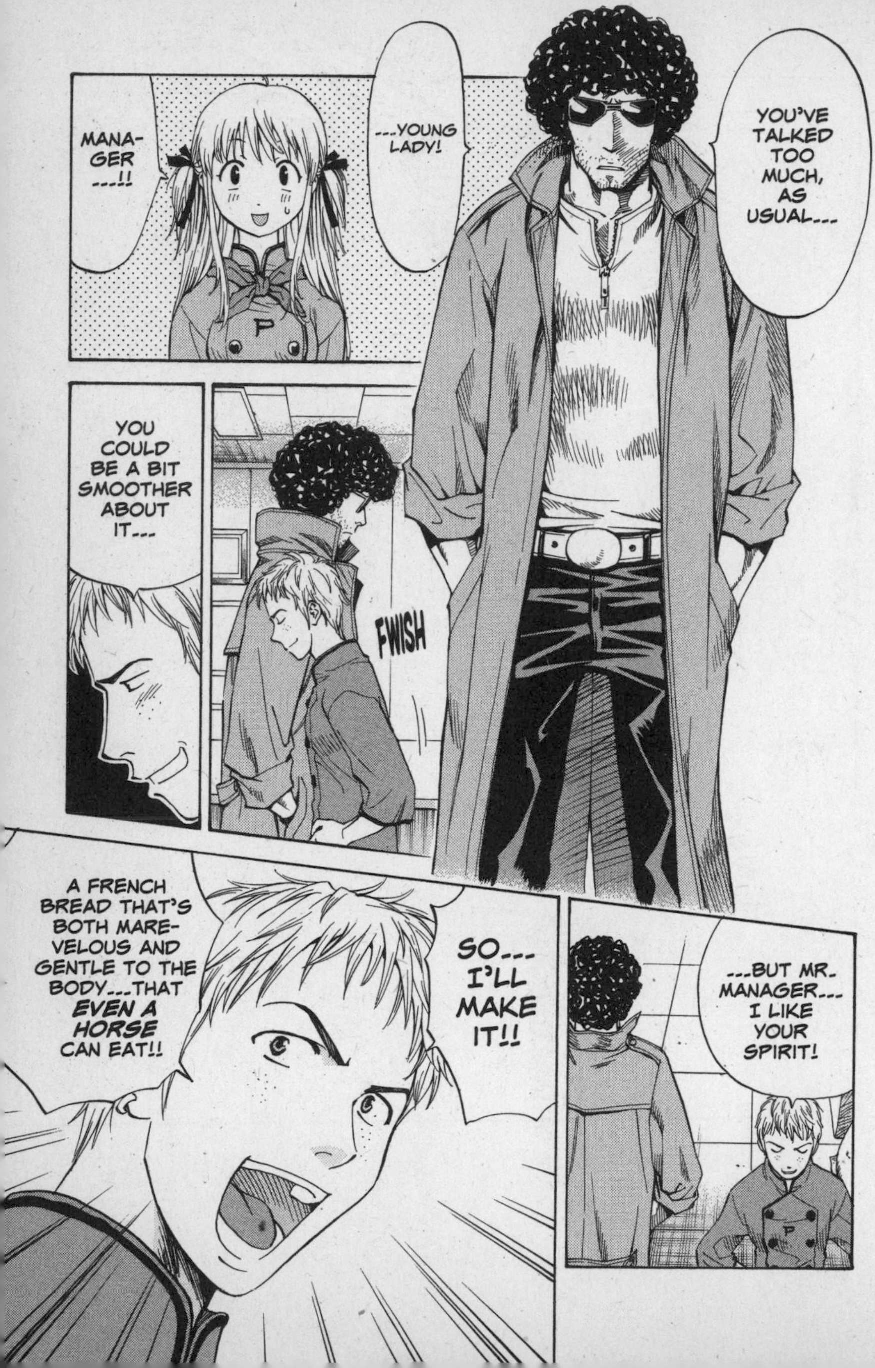
YOU'VE TALKED TOO MUCH, AS USUAL...
...YOUNG LADY!
MANA-GER ---!!
FWISH
YOU COULD BE A BIT SMOOTHER ABOUT IT...
...BUT MR. MANAGER... I LIKE YOUR SPIRIT!
A FRENCH BREAD THAT'S BOTH MARE-VELOUS AND GENTLE TO THE BODY...THAT *EVEN A HORSE* CAN EAT!!
SO... I'LL MAKE IT!!

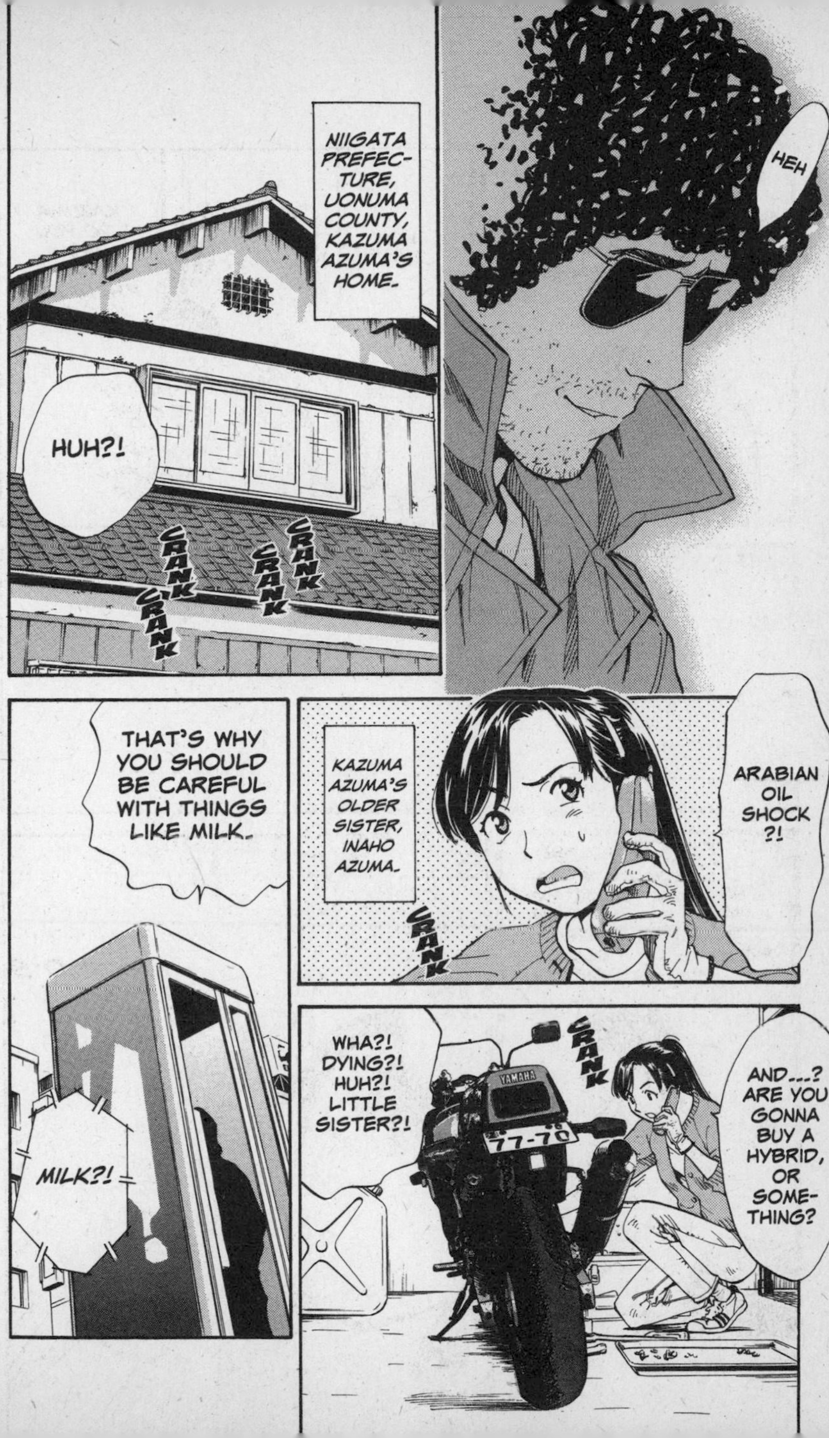
HEH
NIIGATA PREFECTURE, UONUMA COUNTY, KAZUMA AZUMA'S HOME.
HUH?!
CRANK
CRANK
CRANK
CRANK
ARABIAN OIL SHOCK?!
KAZUMA AZUMA'S OLDER SISTER, INAHO AZUMA.
CRANK
AND...? ARE YOU GONNA BUY A HYBRID, OR SOMETHING?
CRANK
WHA?! DYING?! HUH?! LITTLE SISTER?!
THAT'S WHY YOU SHOULD BE CAREFUL WITH THINGS LIKE MILK.
MILK?!

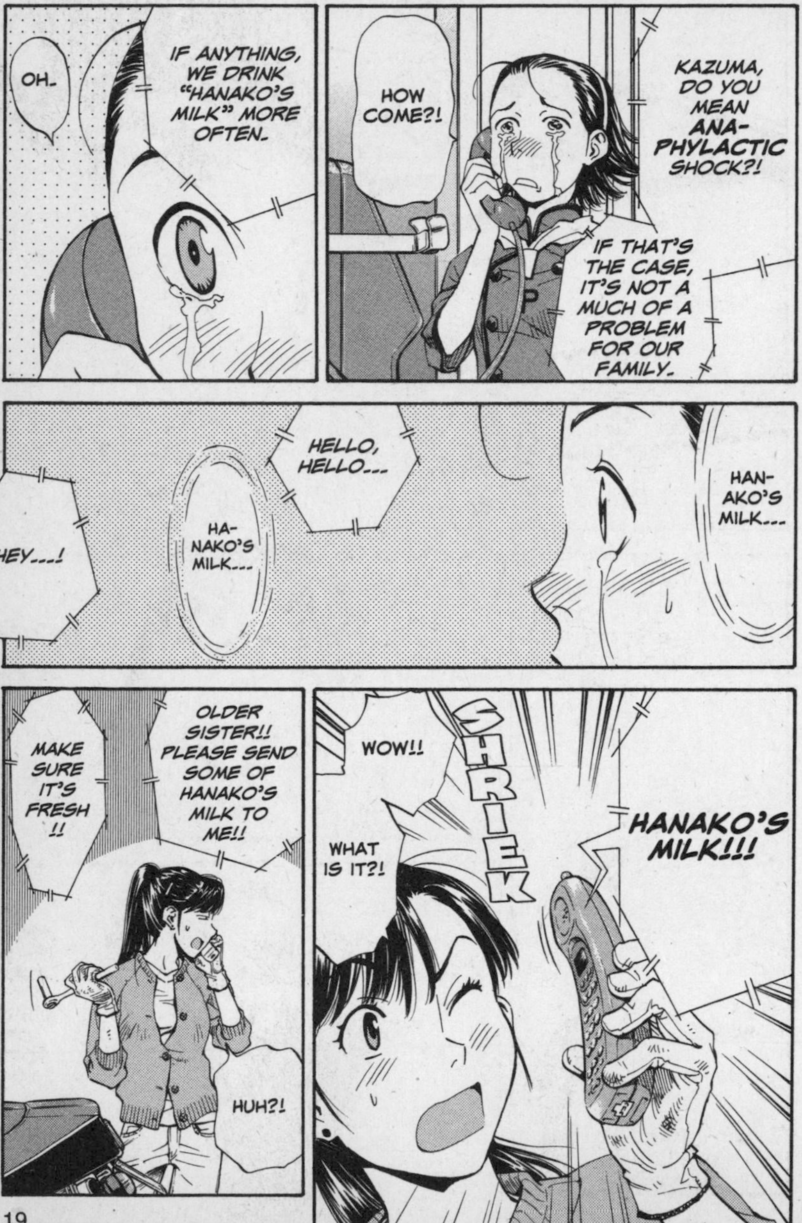
KAZUMA, DO YOU MEAN ANA-PHYLACTIC SHOCK?!
HOW COME?!
IF THAT'S THE CASE, IT'S NOT A MUCH OF A PROBLEM FOR OUR FAMILY.
IF ANYTHING, WE DRINK "HANAKO'S MILK" MORE OFTEN.
OH.
HAN-AKO'S MILK...
HELLO, HELLO...
HA-NAKO'S MILK...
HEY...!
SHRIEK
WOW!!
HANAKO'S MILK!!!
WHAT IS IT?!
OLDER SISTER!! PLEASE SEND SOME OF HANAKO'S MILK TO ME!!
MAKE SURE IT'S FRESH !!
HUH?!

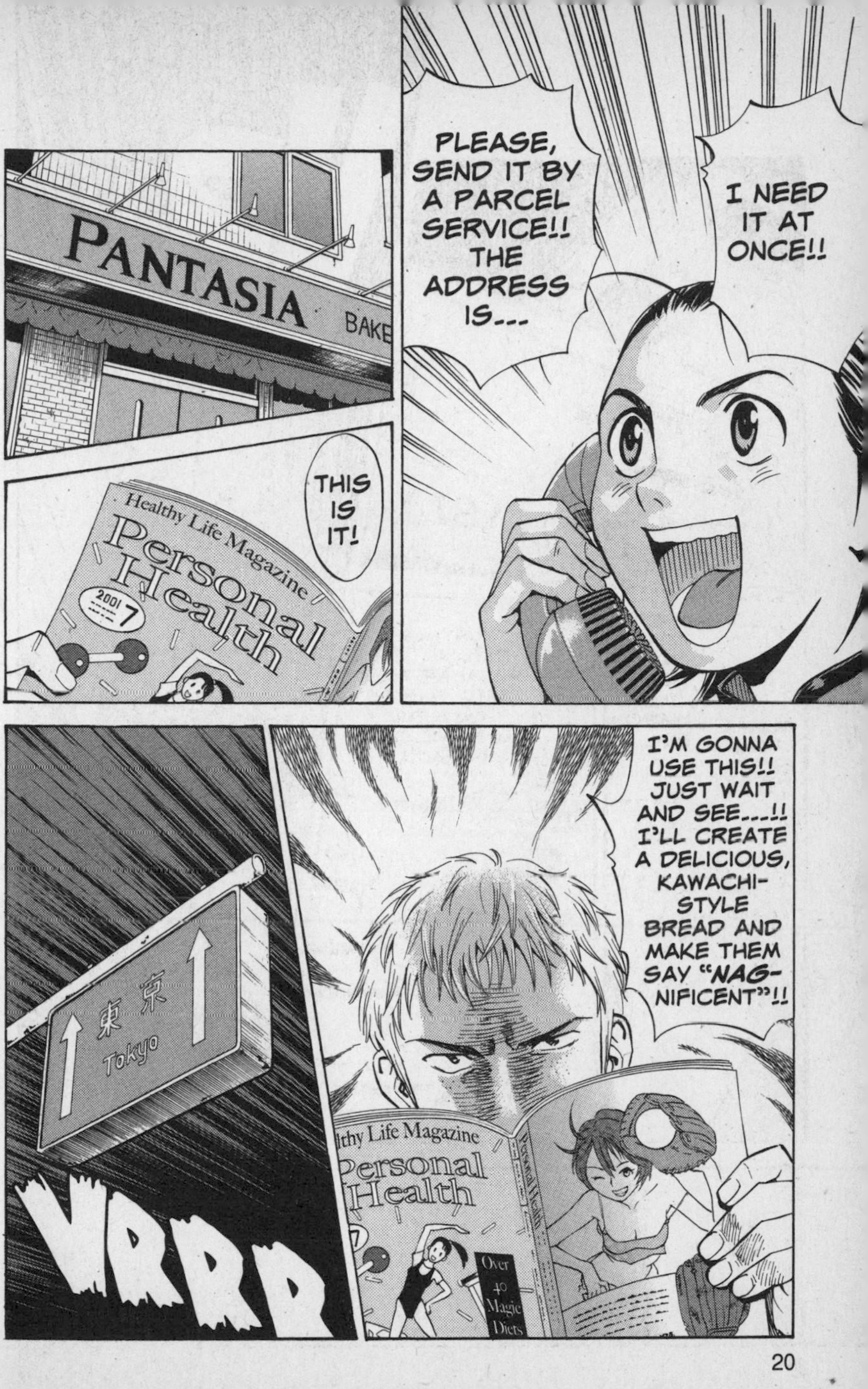
I NEED IT AT ONCE!!
PLEASE, SEND IT BY A PARCEL SERVICE!! THE ADDRESS IS...
PANTASIA
BAKE
Healthy Life Magazine
Personal Health
2001 7
THIS IS IT!
I'M GONNA USE THIS!! JUST WAIT AND SEE...!! I'LL CREATE A DELICIOUS, KAWACHI-STYLE BREAD AND MAKE THEM SAY "NAG-NIFICENT"!!
lthy Life Magazine
ersonal Health
Over 40 Magic Diets
東京
Tokyo
VRRP

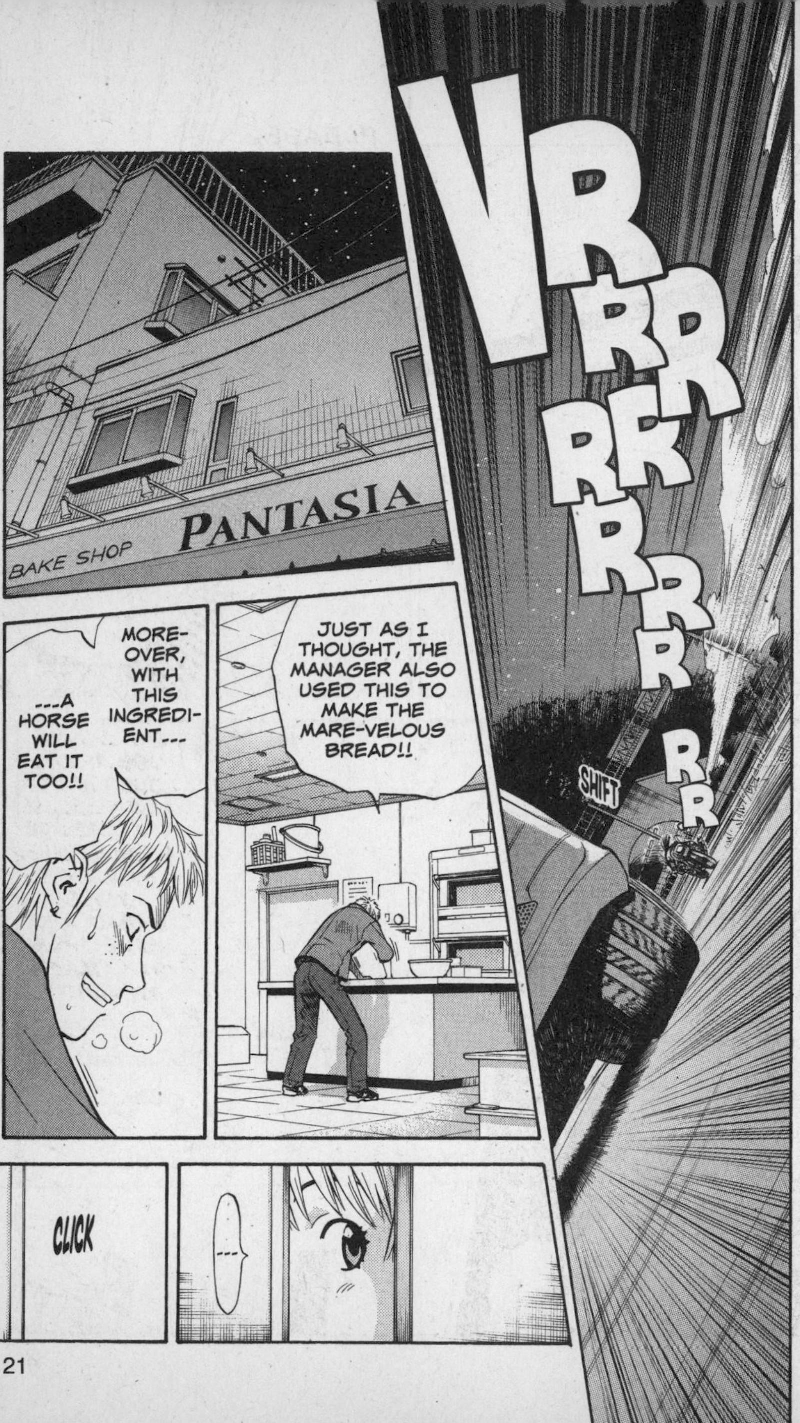

VRRRRRRRRRRR
SHIFT
BAKE SHOP PANTASIA
JUST AS I THOUGHT, THE MANAGER ALSO USED THIS TO MAKE THE MARE-VELOUS BREAD!!
MORE-OVER, WITH THIS INGREDI-ENT---
---A HORSE WILL EAT IT TOO!!

CLICK

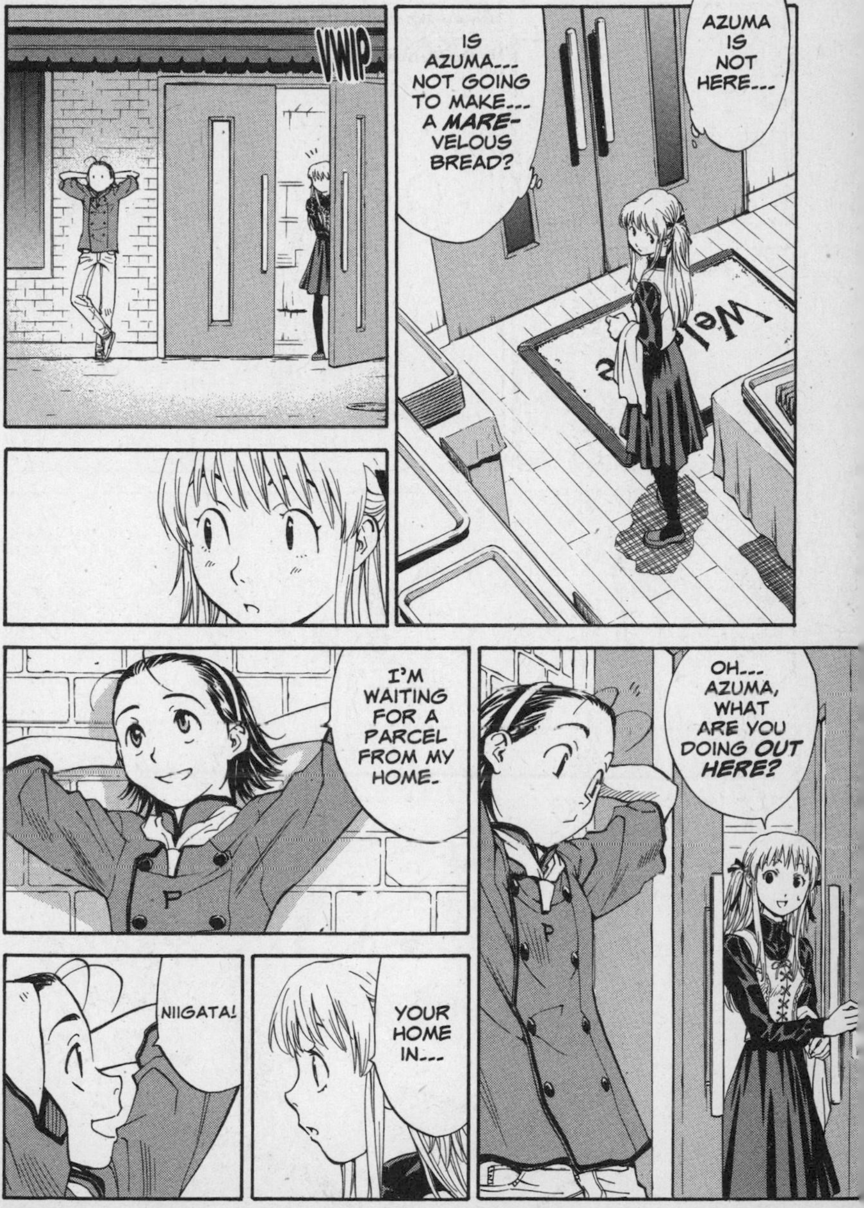
AZUMA IS NOT HERE...
IS AZUMA... NOT GOING TO MAKE... A MARE-VELOUS BREAD?
VWIP
OH... AZUMA, WHAT ARE YOU DOING OUT HERE?
I'M WAITING FOR A PARCEL FROM MY HOME.
YOUR HOME IN...
NIIGATA!

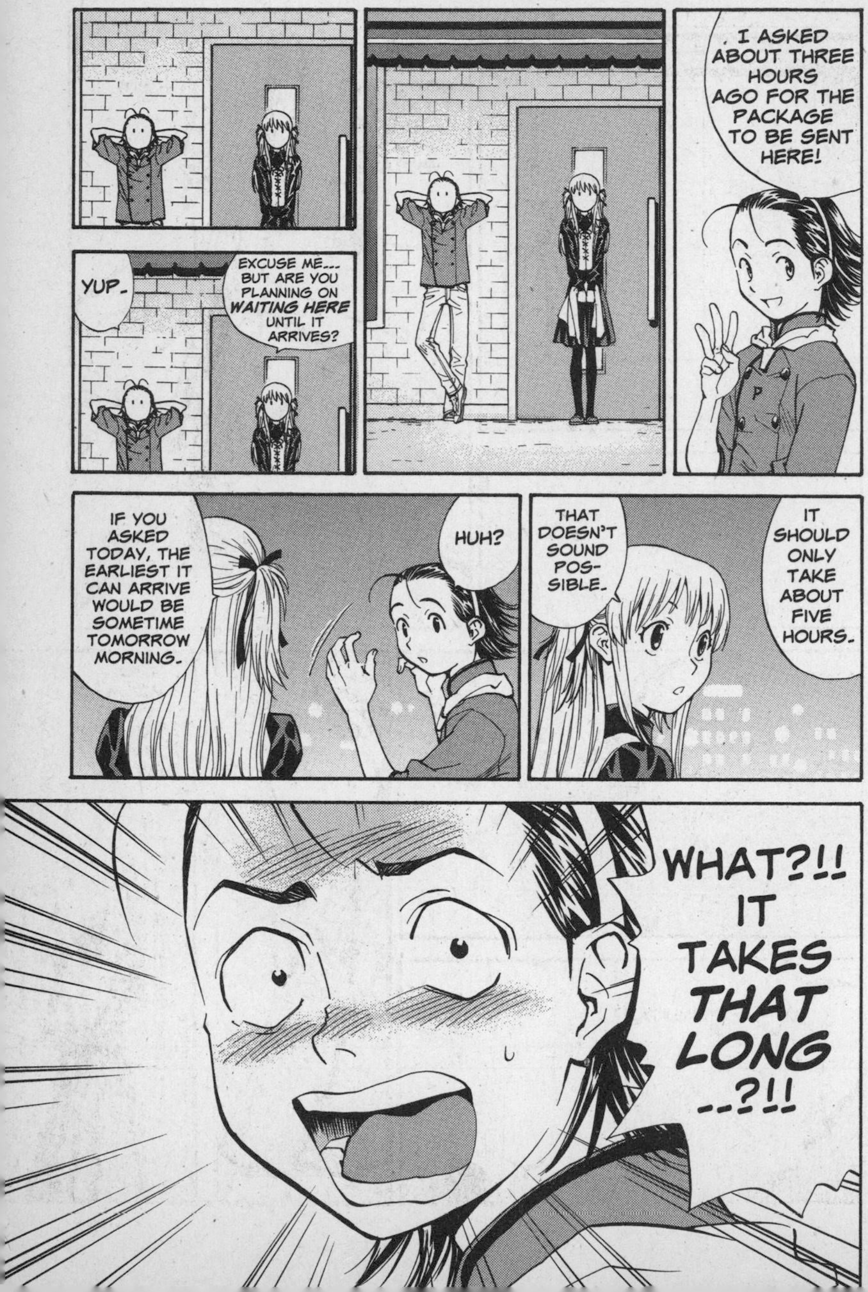
I ASKED ABOUT THREE HOURS AGO FOR THE PACKAGE TO BE SENT HERE!
EXCUSE ME... BUT ARE YOU PLANNING ON *WAITING HERE* UNTIL IT ARRIVES?
YUP.
IT SHOULD ONLY TAKE ABOUT FIVE HOURS.
THAT DOESN'T SOUND POS-SIBLE.
HUH?
IF YOU ASKED TODAY, THE EARLIEST IT CAN ARRIVE WOULD BE SOMETIME TOMORROW MORNING.
WHAT?!! IT TAKES *THAT LONG* ...?!!

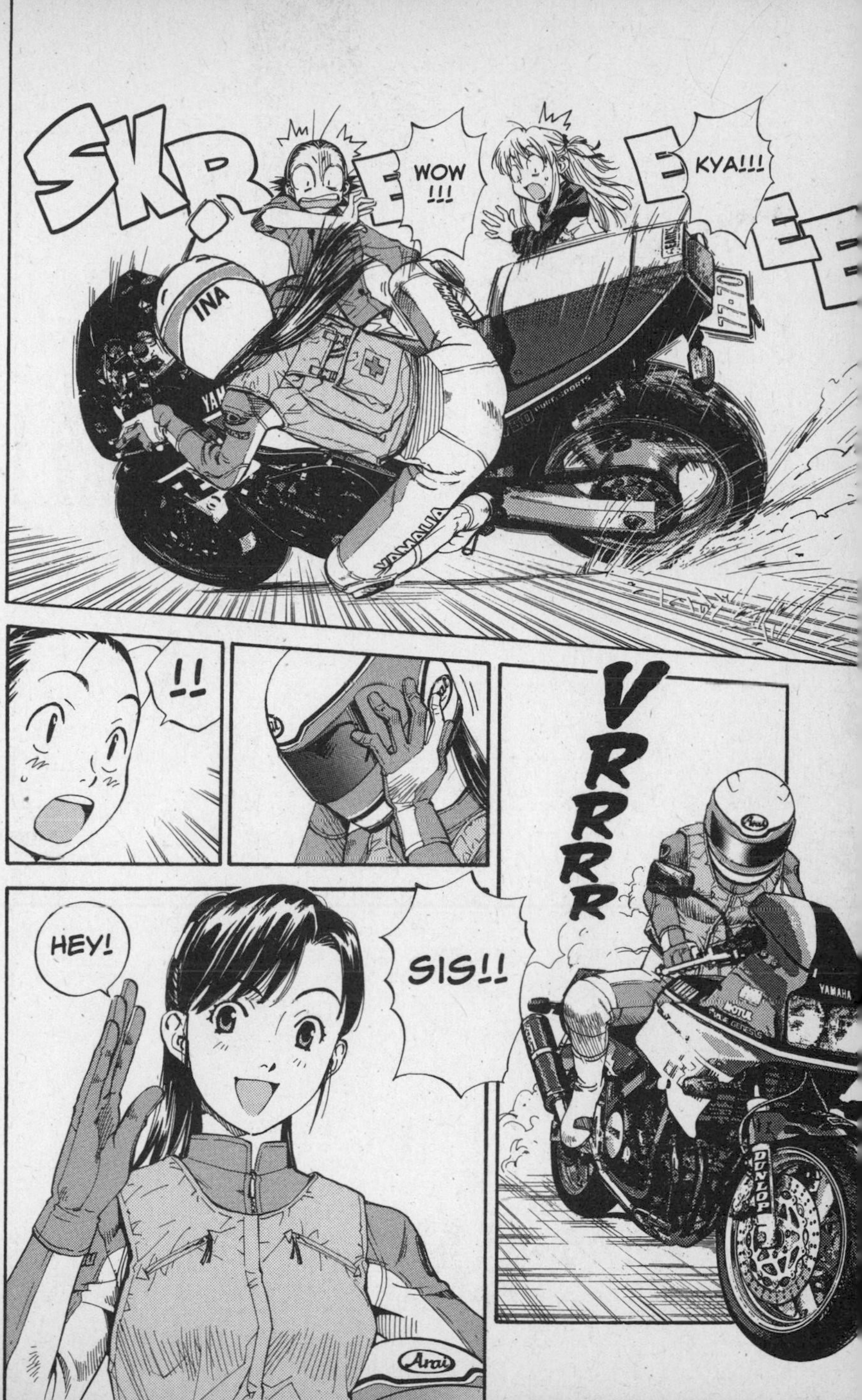
SKREEEE
KYA!!!
WOW !!!
VRRRR
!!
SIS!!
HEY!

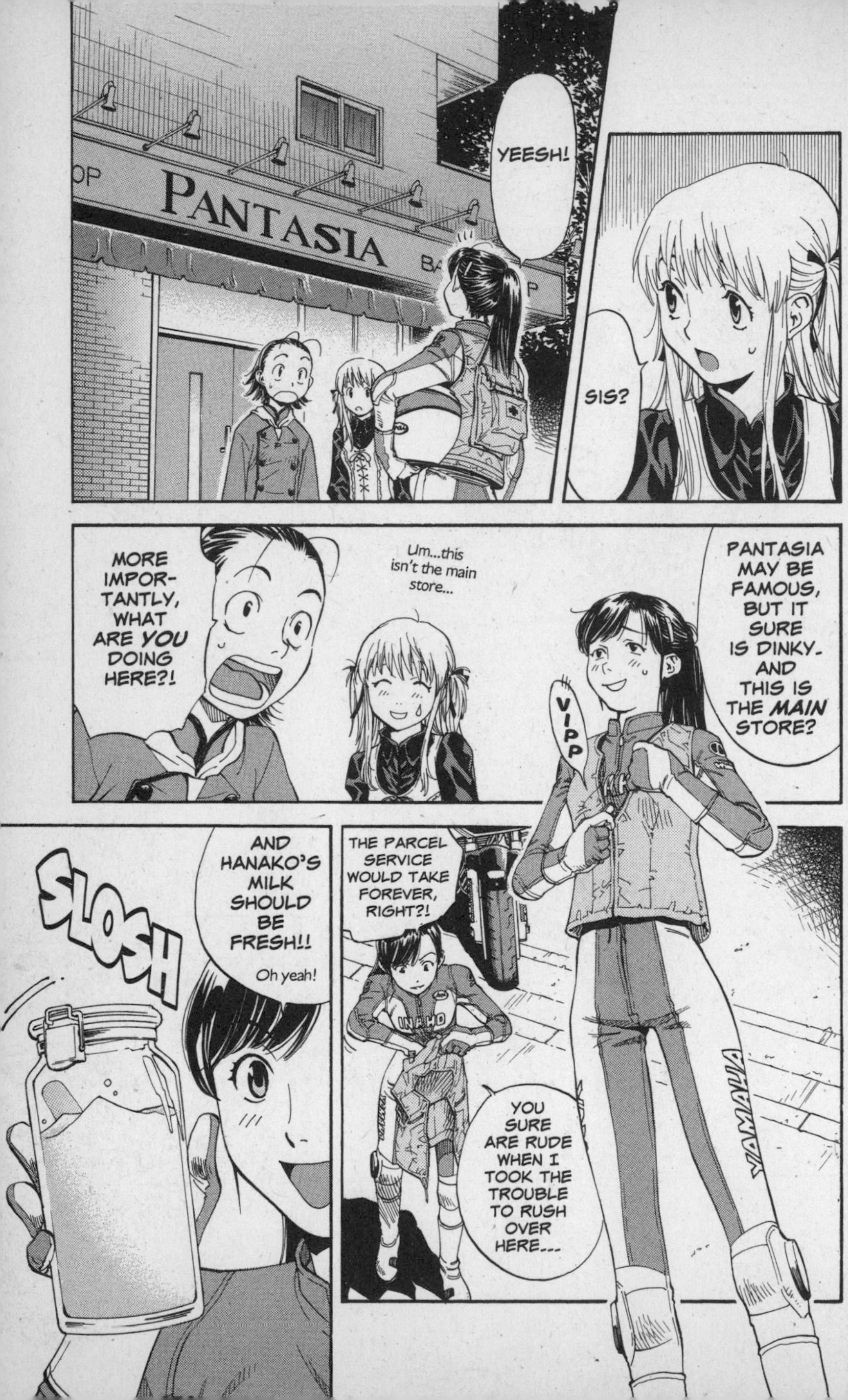
SIS?
PANTASIA
YEESH!
PANTASIA MAY BE FAMOUS, BUT IT SURE IS DINKY. AND THIS IS THE *MAIN* STORE?
VIPP
Um...this isn't the main store...
MORE IMPOR-TANTLY, WHAT ARE *YOU* DOING HERE?!
YOU SURE ARE RUDE WHEN I TOOK THE TROUBLE TO RUSH OVER HERE...
THE PARCEL SERVICE WOULD TAKE FOREVER, RIGHT?!
AND HANAKO'S MILK SHOULD BE FRESH!!
Oh yeah!
SLOSH

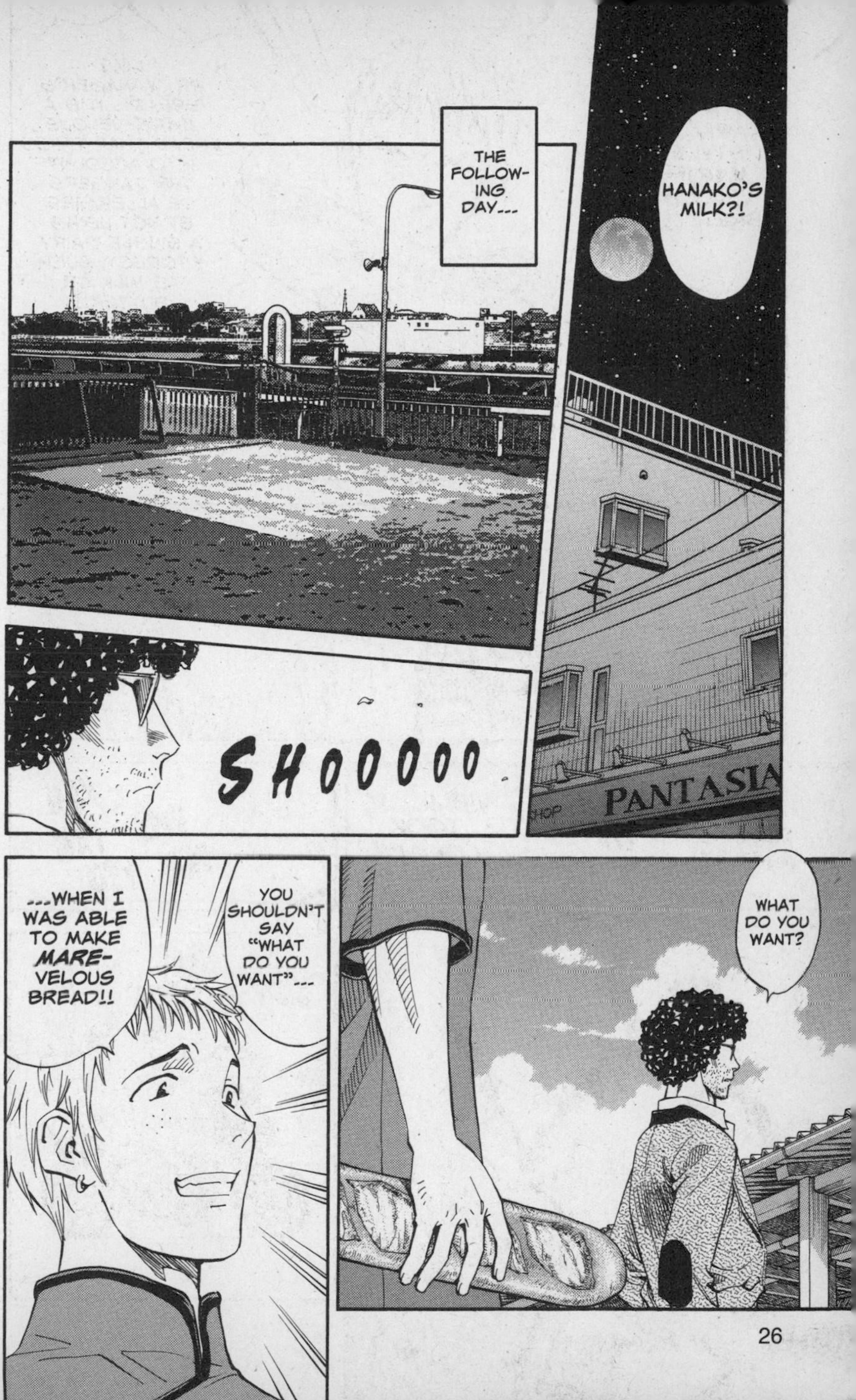
HANAKO'S MILK?!
THE FOLLOWING-ING DAY...
PANTASIA
SHOOOOO
WHAT DO YOU WANT?
YOU SHOULDN'T SAY "WHAT DO YOU WANT"...
...WHEN I WAS ABLE TO MAKE *MARE*-VELOUS BREAD!!

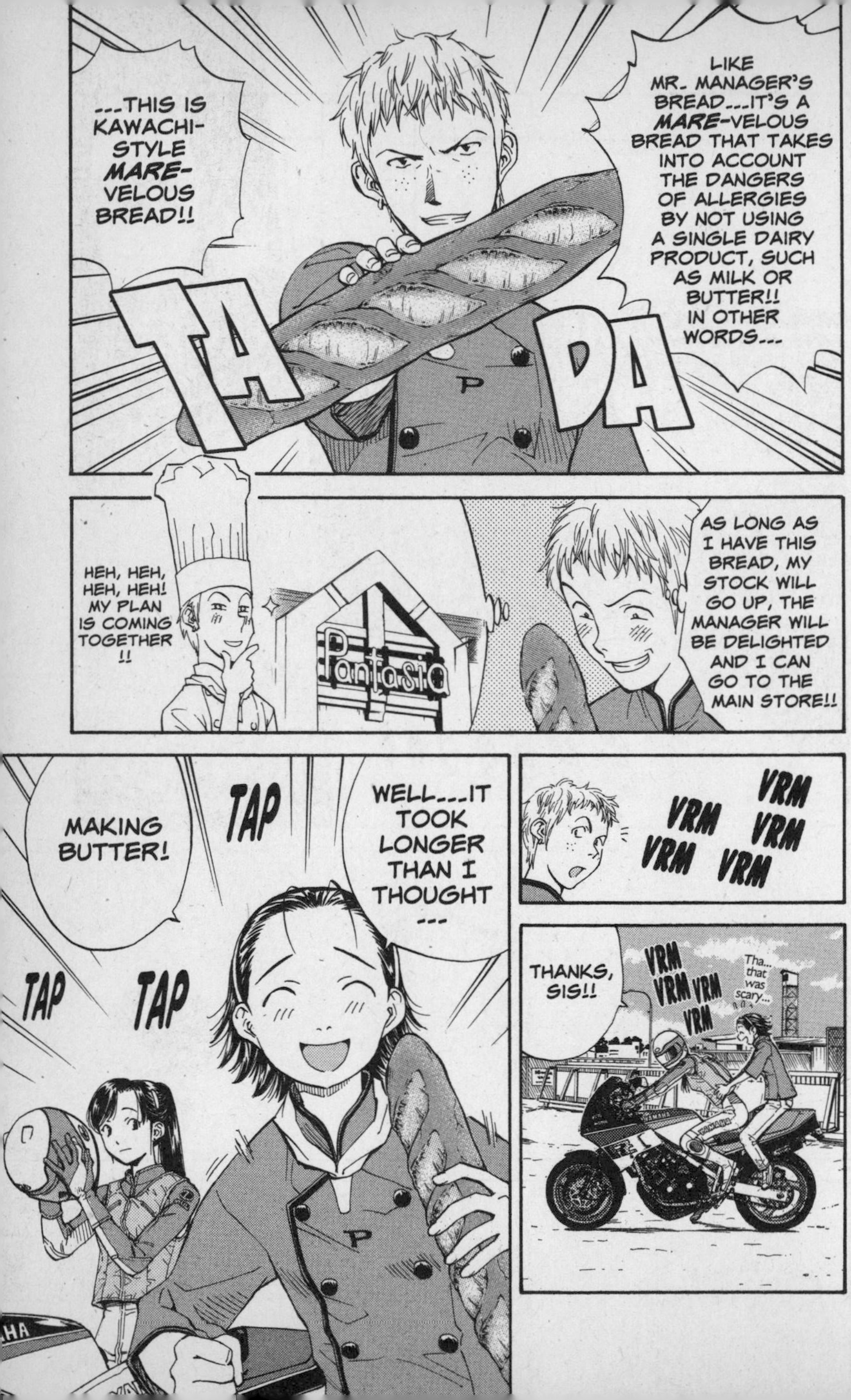
LIKE MR. MANAGER'S BREAD...IT'S A MARE-VELOUS BREAD THAT TAKES INTO ACCOUNT THE DANGERS OF ALLERGIES BY NOT USING A SINGLE DAIRY PRODUCT, SUCH AS MILK OR BUTTER!! IN OTHER WORDS...
...THIS IS KAWACHI-STYLE MARE-VELOUS BREAD!!
TA
DA
AS LONG AS I HAVE THIS BREAD, MY STOCK WILL GO UP, THE MANAGER WILL BE DELIGHTED AND I CAN GO TO THE MAIN STORE!!
Pantasia
HEH, HEH, HEH, HEH! MY PLAN IS COMING TOGETHER!!
VRM VRM VRM VRM VRM VRM
THANKS, SIS!!
VRM VRM VRM VRM
Tha... that was scary...
WELL...IT TOOK LONGER THAN I THOUGHT...
TAP
MAKING BUTTER!
TAP TAP

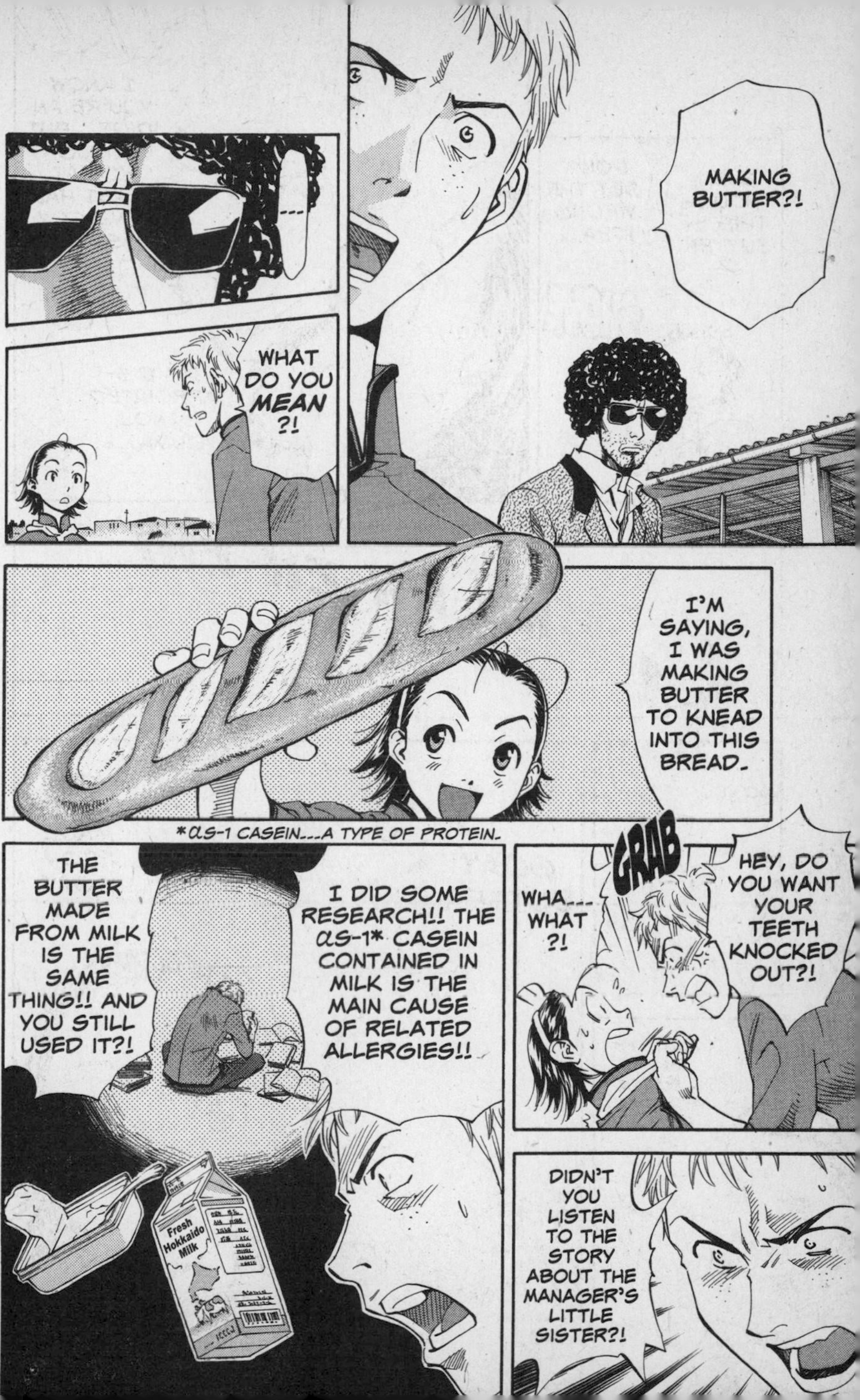
MAKING BUTTER?!

WHAT DO YOU MEAN?!
I'M SAYING, I WAS MAKING BUTTER TO KNEAD INTO THIS BREAD.
GRAB
HEY, DO YOU WANT YOUR TEETH KNOCKED OUT?!
WHA... WHAT?!
DIDN'T YOU LISTEN TO THE STORY ABOUT THE MANAGER'S LITTLE SISTER?!
I DID SOME RESEARCH!! THE αS-1* CASEIN CONTAINED IN MILK IS THE MAIN CAUSE OF RELATED ALLERGIES!!
THE BUTTER MADE FROM MILK IS THE SAME THING!! AND YOU STILL USED IT?!
Fresh Hokkaido Milk

*αS-1 CASEIN...A TYPE OF PROTEIN.

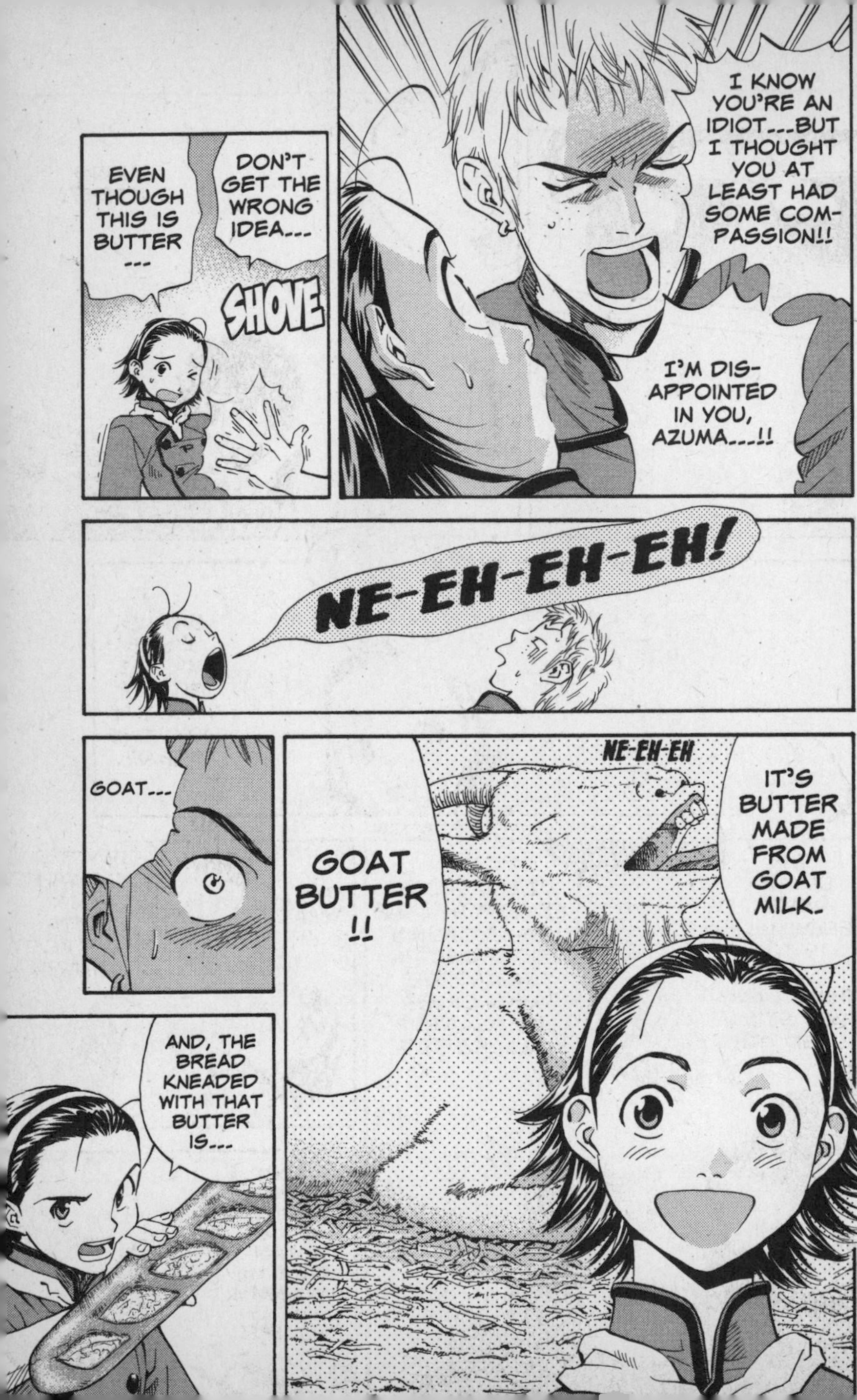
I KNOW YOU'RE AN IDIOT...BUT I THOUGHT YOU AT LEAST HAD SOME COM-PASSION!!
I'M DIS-APPOINTED IN YOU, AZUMA...!!
DON'T GET THE WRONG IDEA...
EVEN THOUGH THIS IS BUTTER ...
SHOVE
NE-EH-EH-EH!
IT'S BUTTER MADE FROM GOAT MILK.
NE-EH-EH
GOAT BUTTER !!
GOAT...
AND, THE BREAD KNEADED WITH THAT BUTTER IS...

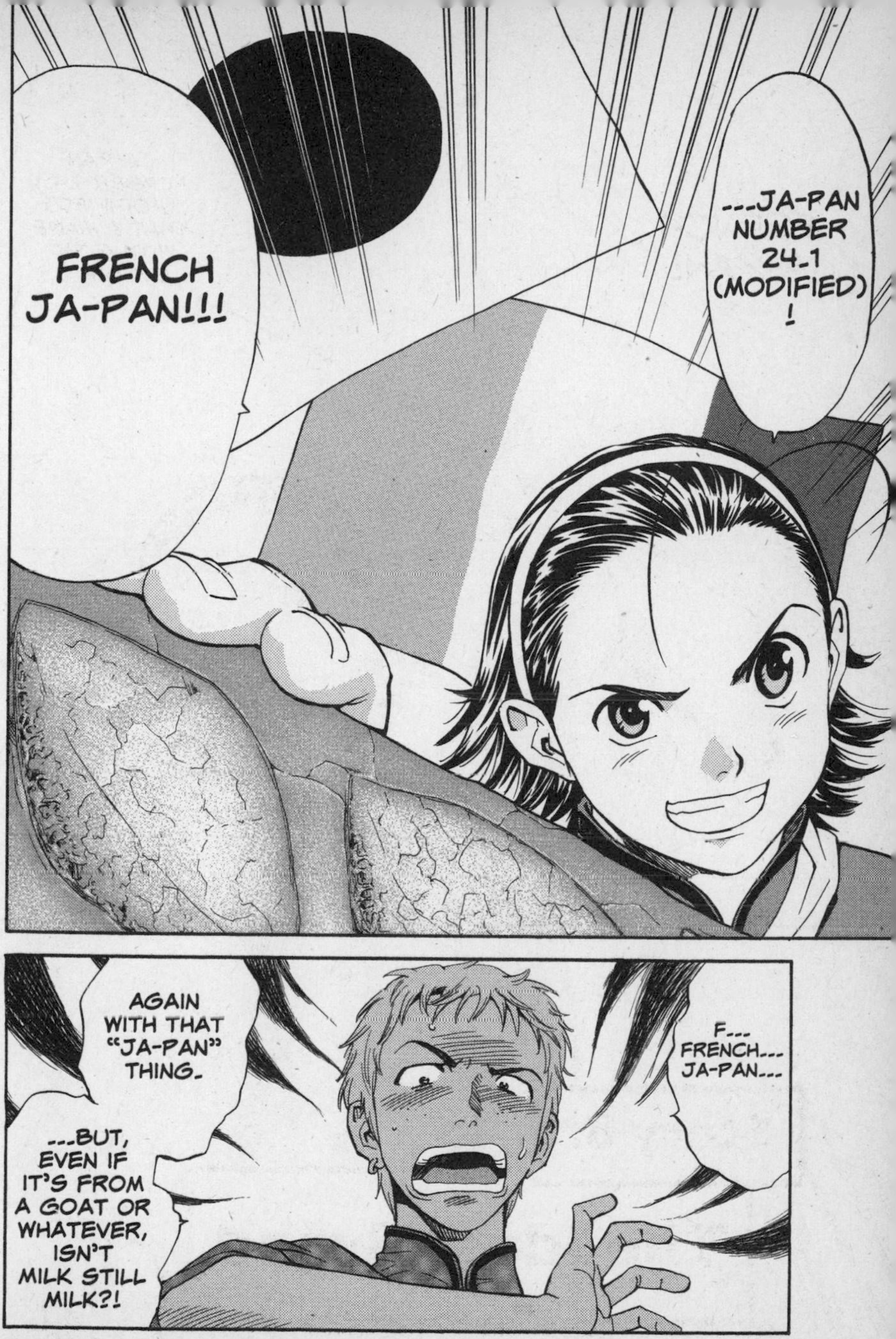
...JA-PAN NUMBER 24.1 (MODIFIED)!
FRENCH JA-PAN!!!
F... FRENCH... JA-PAN...
AGAIN WITH THAT "JA-PAN" THING.
...BUT, EVEN IF IT'S FROM A GOAT OR WHATEVER, ISN'T MILK STILL MILK?!

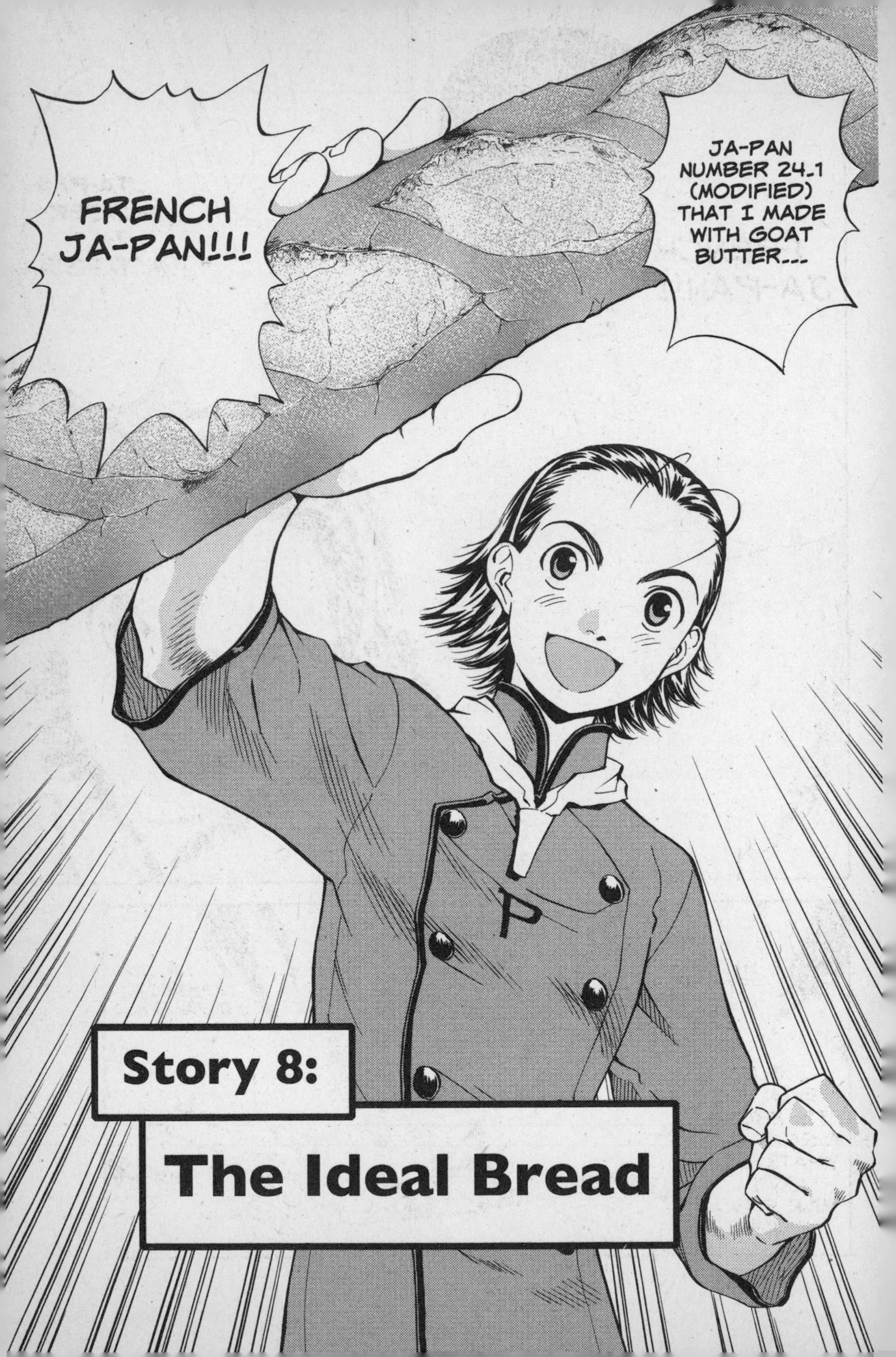
JA-PAN NUMBER 24.1 (MODIFIED) THAT I MADE WITH GOAT BUTTER...
FRENCH JA-PAN!!!
Story 8:
The Ideal Bread

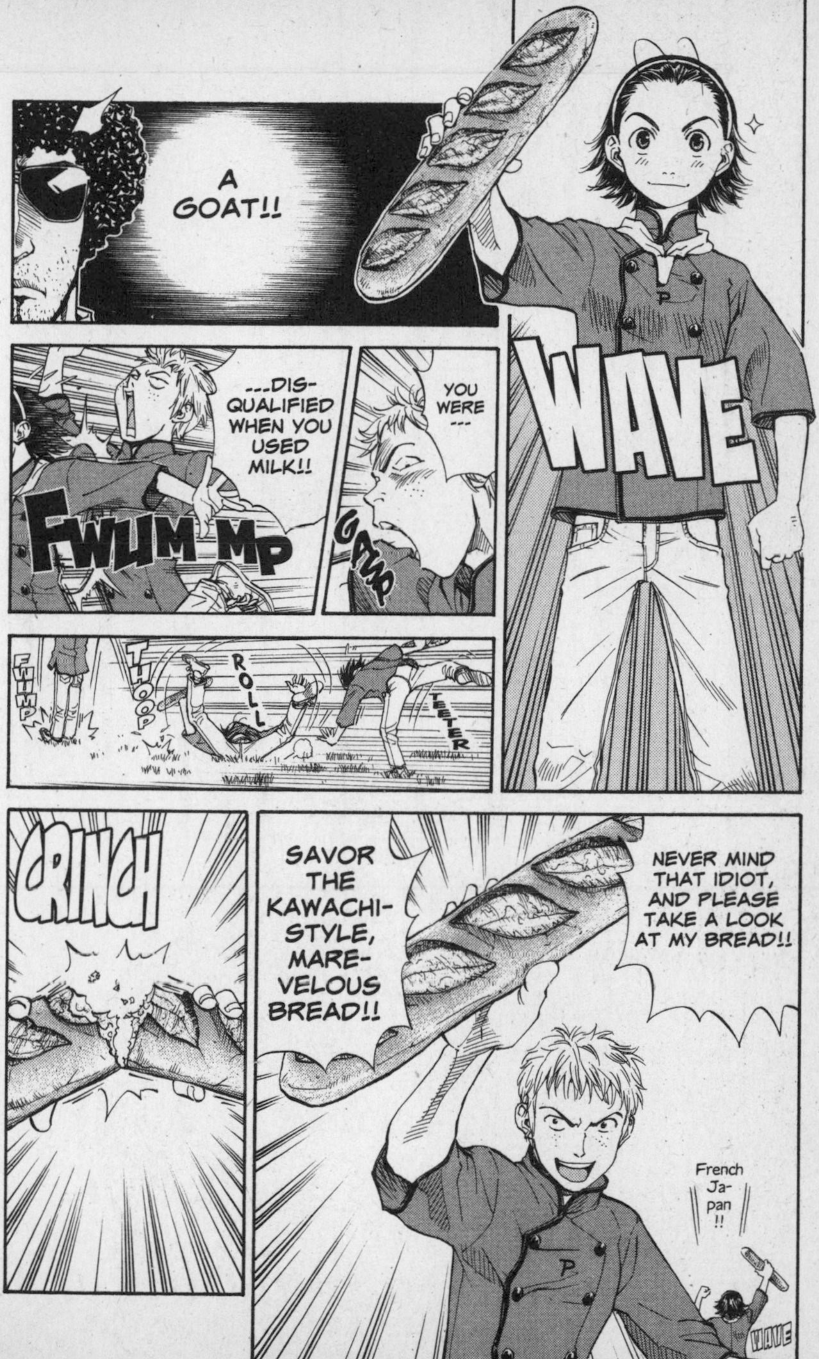
WAVE
A GOAT!!
YOU WERE ---
GAWP
---DIS-QUALIFIED WHEN YOU USED MILK!!
FWUM MP
TEETER
ROLL
THOOP
FWIMP
NEVER MIND THAT IDIOT, AND PLEASE TAKE A LOOK AT MY BREAD!!
SAVOR THE KAWACHI-STYLE, MARE-VELOUS BREAD!!
French Ja-pan !!
WAVE
CRINCH

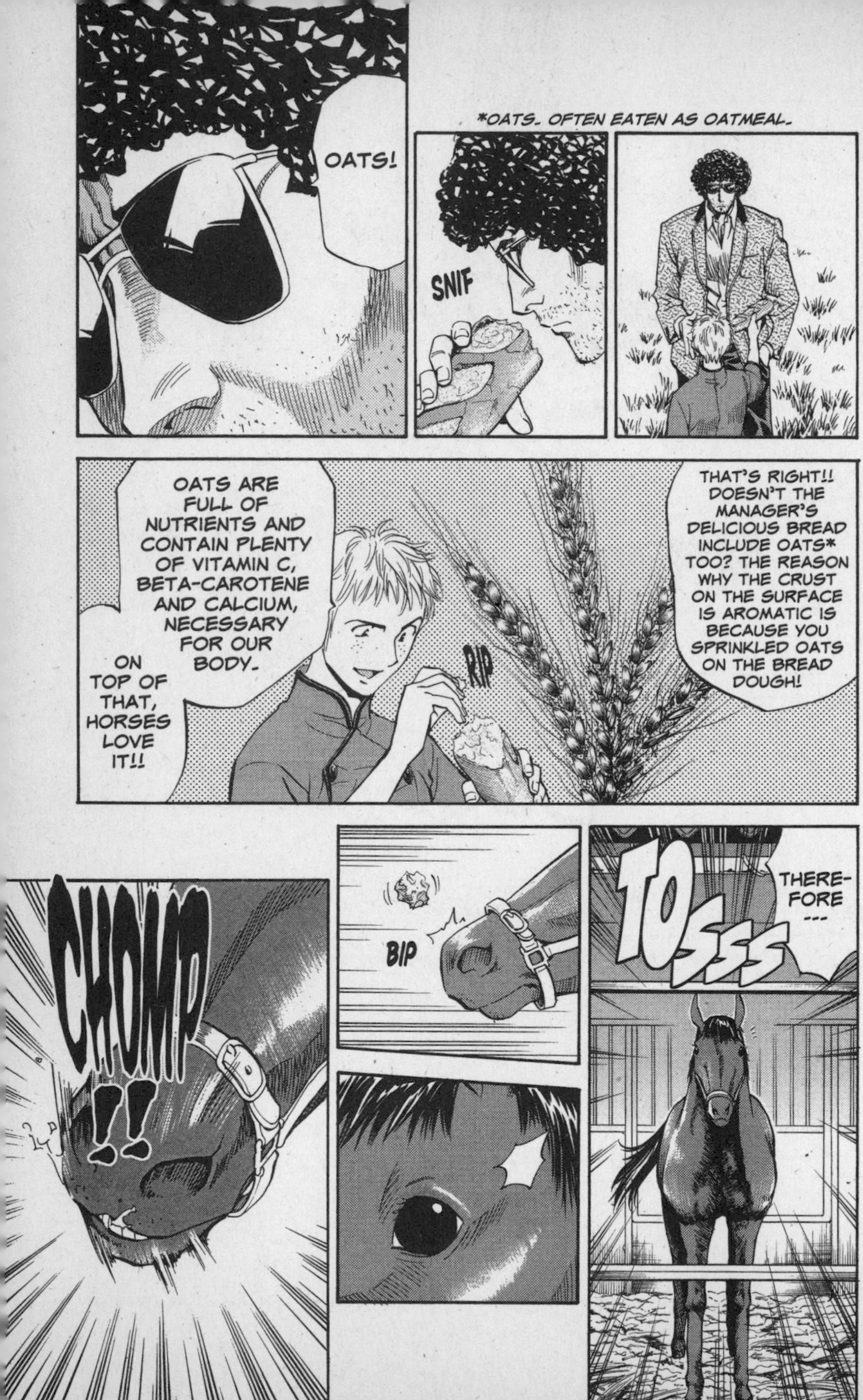
*OATS. OFTEN EATEN AS OATMEAL.
SNIF
OATS!
THAT'S RIGHT!! DOESN'T THE MANAGER'S DELICIOUS BREAD INCLUDE OATS* TOO? THE REASON WHY THE CRUST ON THE SURFACE IS AROMATIC IS BECAUSE YOU SPRINKLED OATS ON THE BREAD DOUGH!
RIP
OATS ARE FULL OF NUTRIENTS AND CONTAIN PLENTY OF VITAMIN C, BETA-CAROTENE AND CALCIUM, NECESSARY FOR OUR BODY.
ON TOP OF THAT, HORSES LOVE IT!!
THERE-FORE ---
TOSSS
BIP
CHOMP!!

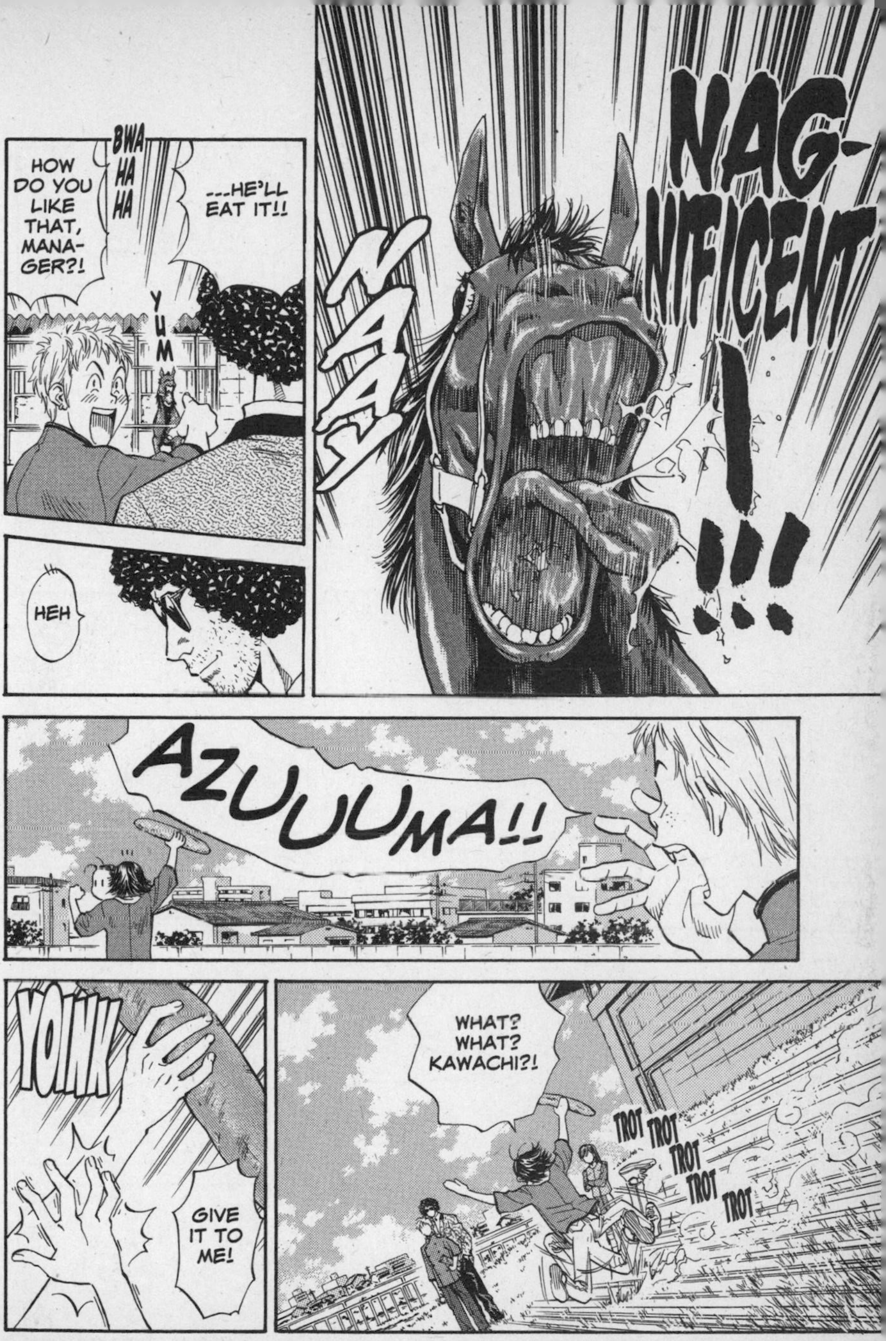
NAAAY
NAG-NIFICENT!!!!
HOW DO YOU LIKE THAT, MANAGER?!
BWA HA HA HA
---HE'LL EAT IT!!
YUM
HEH
AZUUUMA!!
WHAT? WHAT? KAWACHI?!
TROT TROT TROT TROT TROT
YOINK
GIVE IT TO ME!

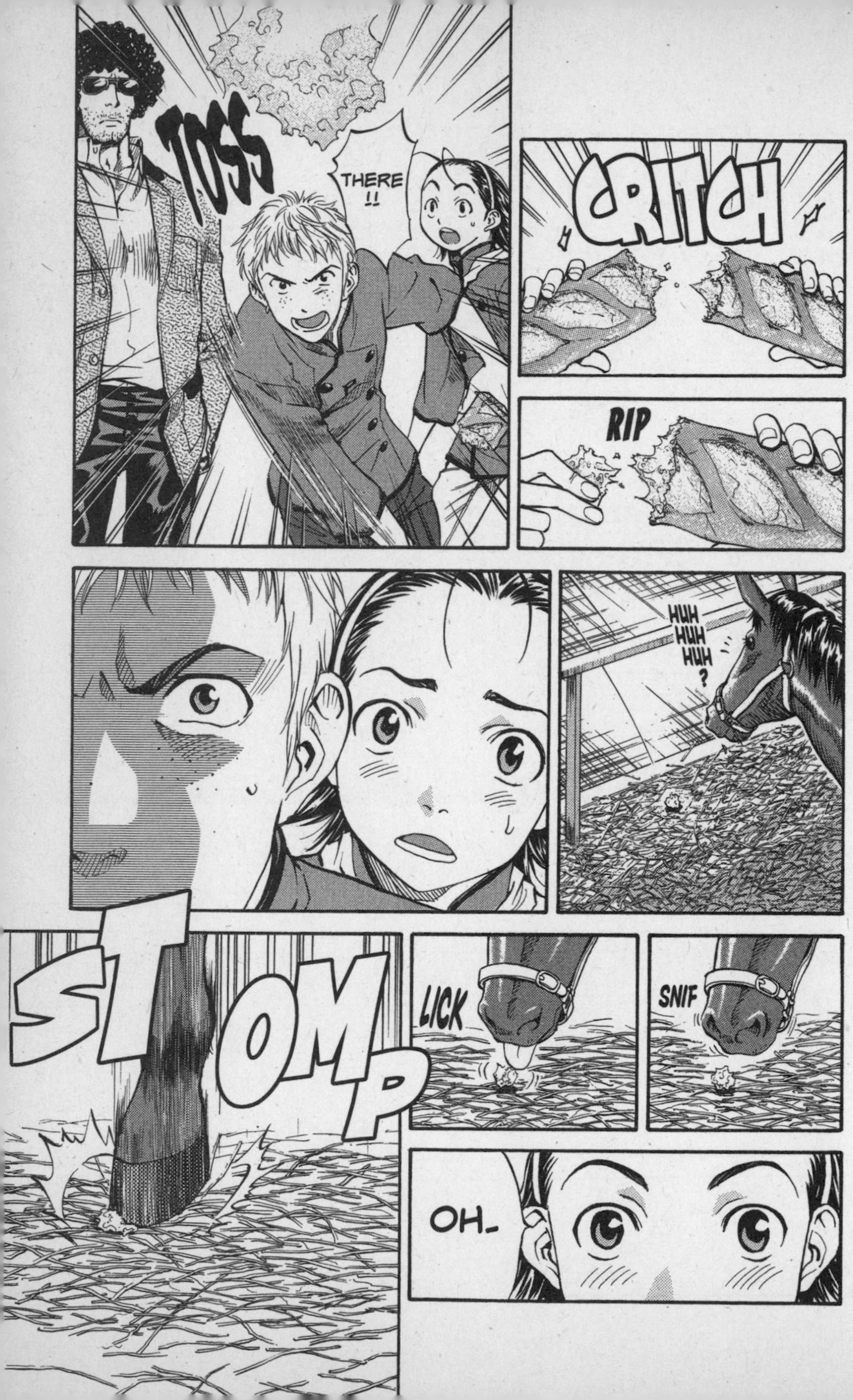
CRITCH
RIP
TOSS
THERE !!
HUH HUH HUH ?
SNIF
LICK
OH_
STOMP

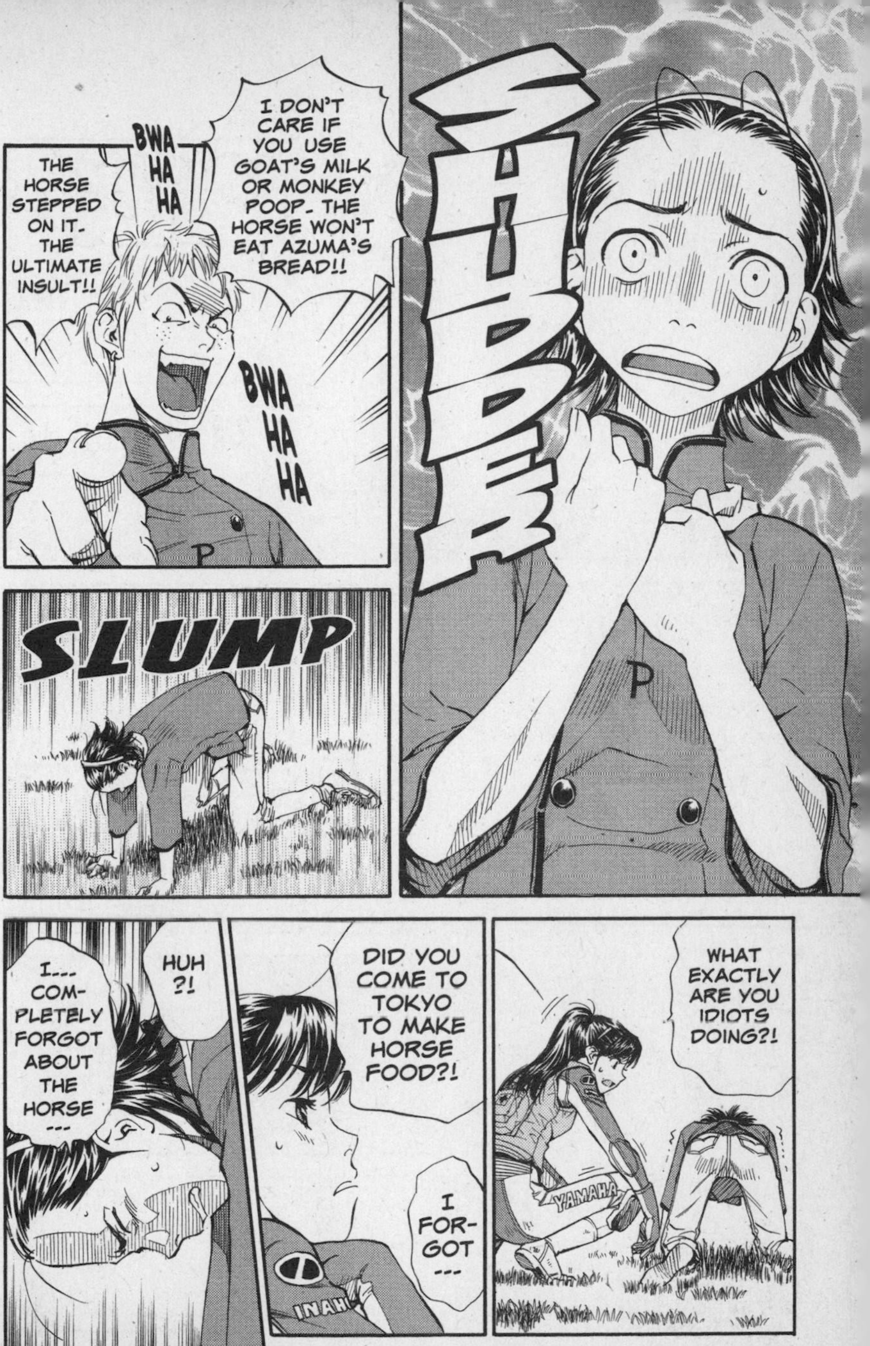
SHUDDER
I DON'T CARE IF YOU USE GOAT'S MILK OR MONKEY POOP. THE HORSE WON'T EAT AZUMA'S BREAD!!
BWA HA HA
THE HORSE STEPPED ON IT. THE ULTIMATE INSULT!!
BWA HA HA
SLUMP
WHAT EXACTLY ARE YOU IDIOTS DOING?!
DID YOU COME TO TOKYO TO MAKE HORSE FOOD?!
I FOR-GOT ---
HUH ?!
I--- COM-PLETELY FORGOT ABOUT THE HORSE ---

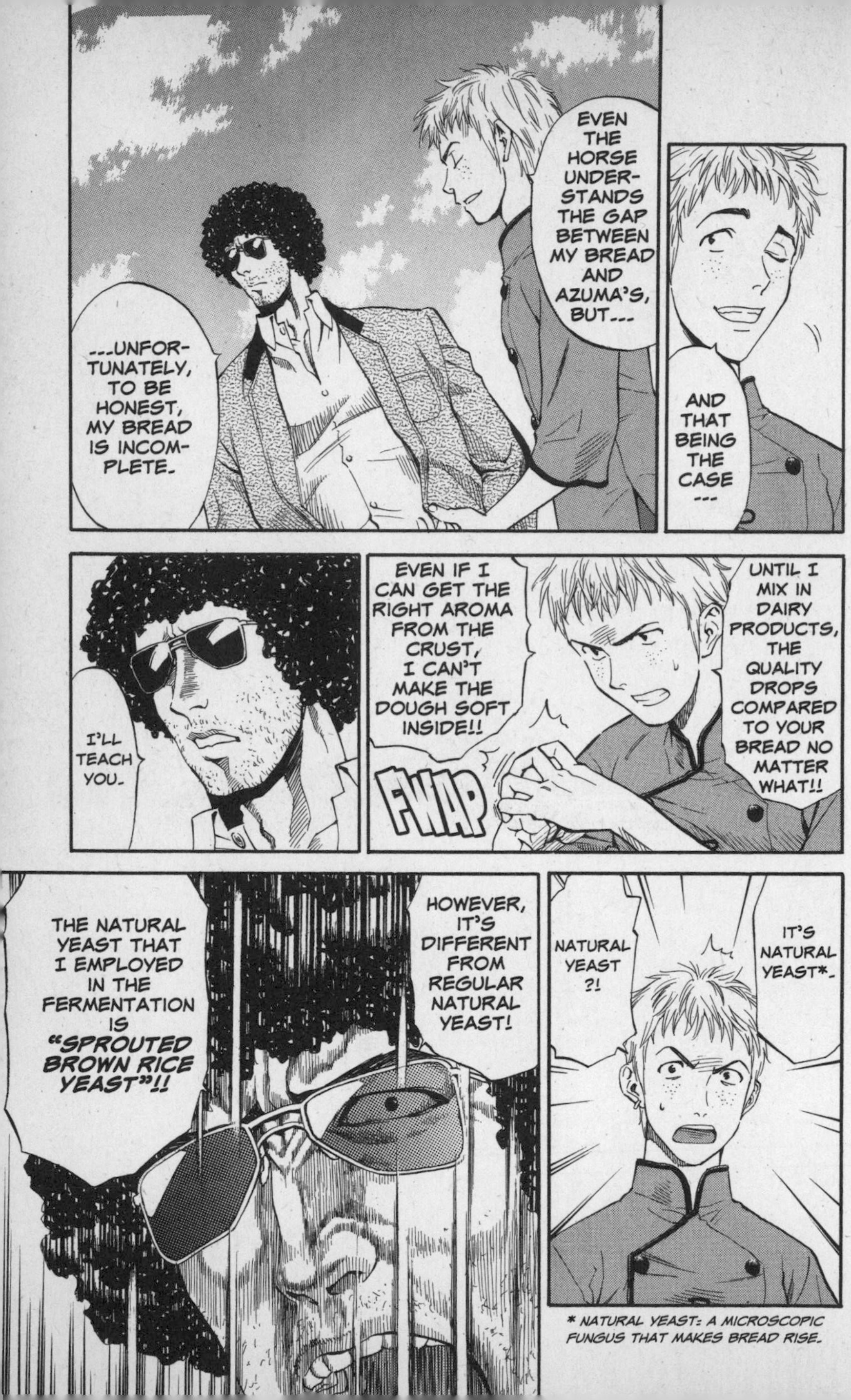
AND THAT BEING THE CASE...
EVEN THE HORSE UNDERSTANDS THE GAP BETWEEN MY BREAD AND AZUMA'S, BUT...
...UNFORTUNATELY, TO BE HONEST, MY BREAD IS INCOMPLETE.
UNTIL I MIX IN DAIRY PRODUCTS, THE QUALITY DROPS COMPARED TO YOUR BREAD NO MATTER WHAT!!
EVEN IF I CAN GET THE RIGHT AROMA FROM THE CRUST, I CAN'T MAKE THE DOUGH SOFT INSIDE!!
FWAP
I'LL TEACH YOU.
IT'S NATURAL YEAST*.
NATURAL YEAST?!
HOWEVER, IT'S DIFFERENT FROM REGULAR NATURAL YEAST!
THE NATURAL YEAST THAT I EMPLOYED IN THE FERMENTATION IS "SPROUTED BROWN RICE YEAST"!!

* NATURAL YEAST: A MICROSCOPIC FUNGUS THAT MAKES BREAD RISE.

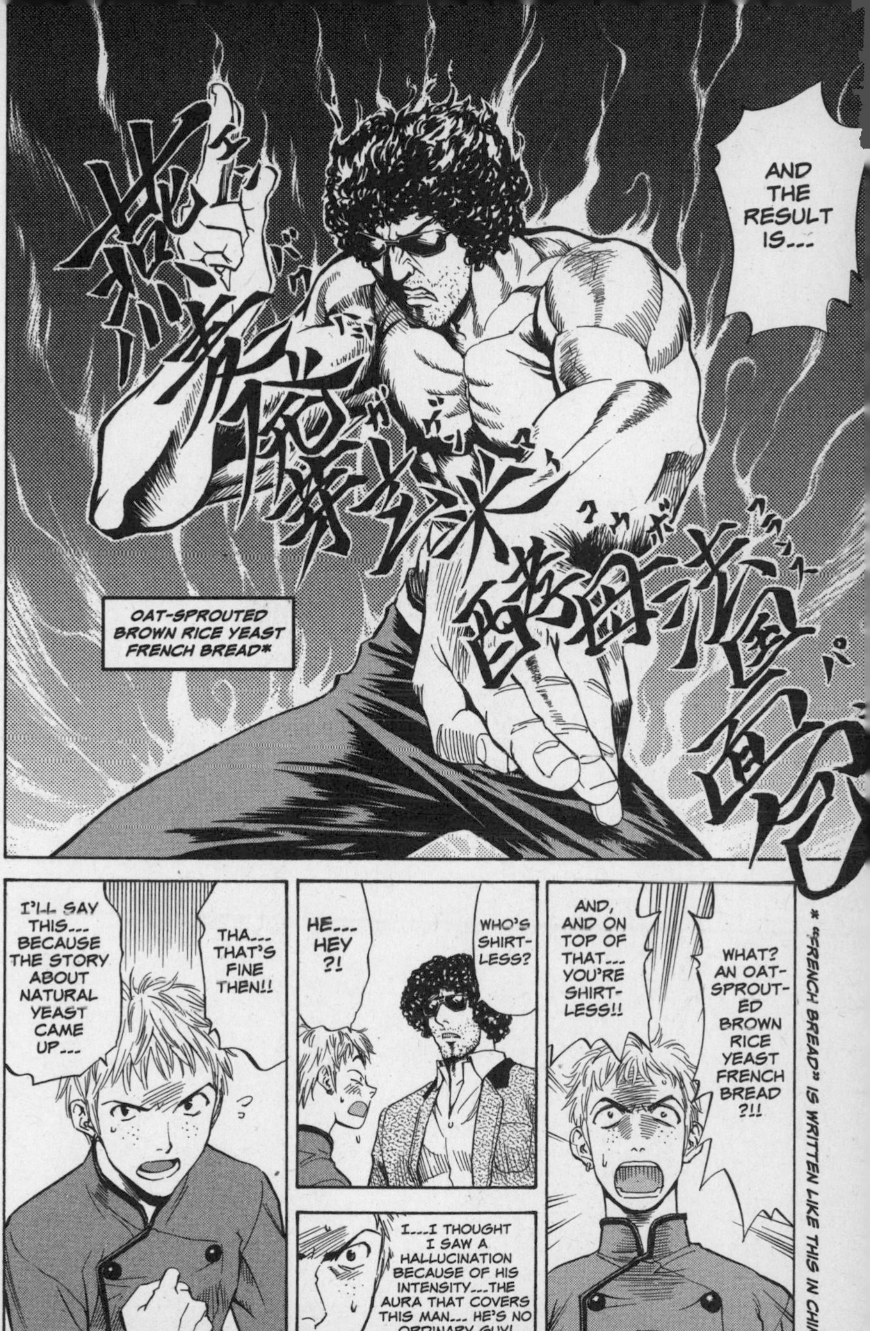
AND THE RESULT IS...
OAT-SPROUTED BROWN RICE YEAST FRENCH BREAD*
WHAT? AN OAT-SPROUTED BROWN RICE YEAST FRENCH BREAD ?!!
AND, AND ON TOP OF THAT... YOU'RE SHIRTLESS!!
WHO'S SHIRTLESS?
HE... HEY ?!
I... I THOUGHT I SAW A HALLUCINATION BECAUSE OF HIS INTENSITY... THE AURA THAT COVERS THIS MAN... HE'S NO ORDINARY GUY!
THA... THAT'S FINE THEN!!
I'LL SAY THIS... BECAUSE THE STORY ABOUT NATURAL YEAST CAME UP...

* "FRENCH BREAD" IS WRITTEN LIKE THIS IN CHINA.

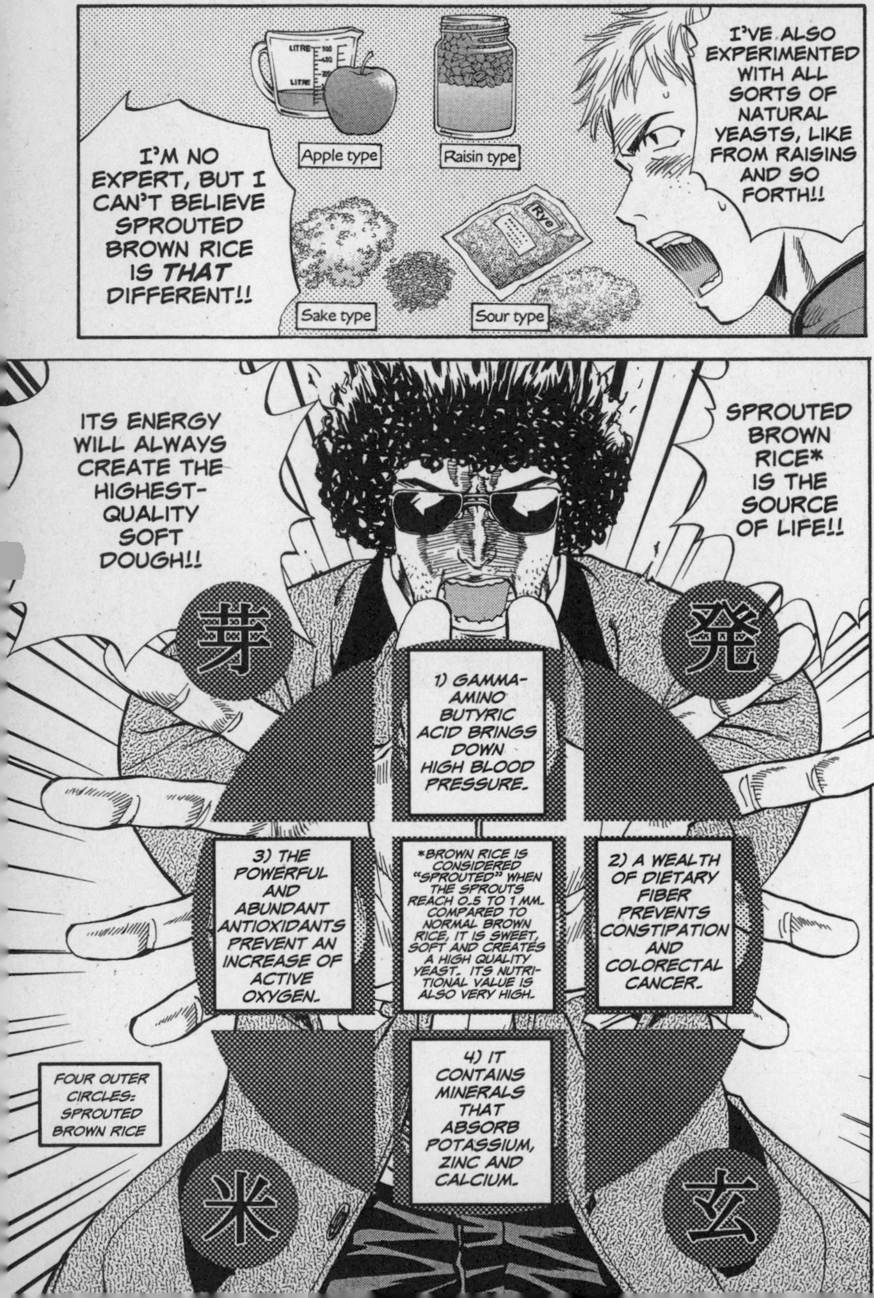
I'VE ALSO EXPERIMENTED WITH ALL SORTS OF NATURAL YEASTS, LIKE FROM RAISINS AND SO FORTH!!
Raisin type
Apple type
Sour type
Rye
Sake type
I'M NO EXPERT, BUT I CAN'T BELIEVE SPROUTED BROWN RICE IS *THAT* DIFFERENT!!
SPROUTED BROWN RICE* IS THE SOURCE OF LIFE!!
ITS ENERGY WILL ALWAYS CREATE THE HIGHEST-QUALITY SOFT DOUGH!!
発
芽
1) GAMMA-AMINO BUTYRIC ACID BRINGS DOWN HIGH BLOOD PRESSURE.
2) A WEALTH OF DIETARY FIBER PREVENTS CONSTIPATION AND COLORECTAL CANCER.
*BROWN RICE IS CONSIDERED "SPROUTED" WHEN THE SPROUTS REACH 0.5 TO 1 MM. COMPARED TO NORMAL BROWN RICE, IT IS SWEET, SOFT AND CREATES A HIGH QUALITY YEAST. ITS NUTRITIONAL VALUE IS ALSO VERY HIGH.
3) THE POWERFUL AND ABUNDANT ANTIOXIDANTS PREVENT AN INCREASE OF ACTIVE OXYGEN.
4) IT CONTAINS MINERALS THAT ABSORB POTASSIUM, ZINC AND CALCIUM.
玄
米
FOUR OUTER CIRCLES: SPROUTED BROWN RICE

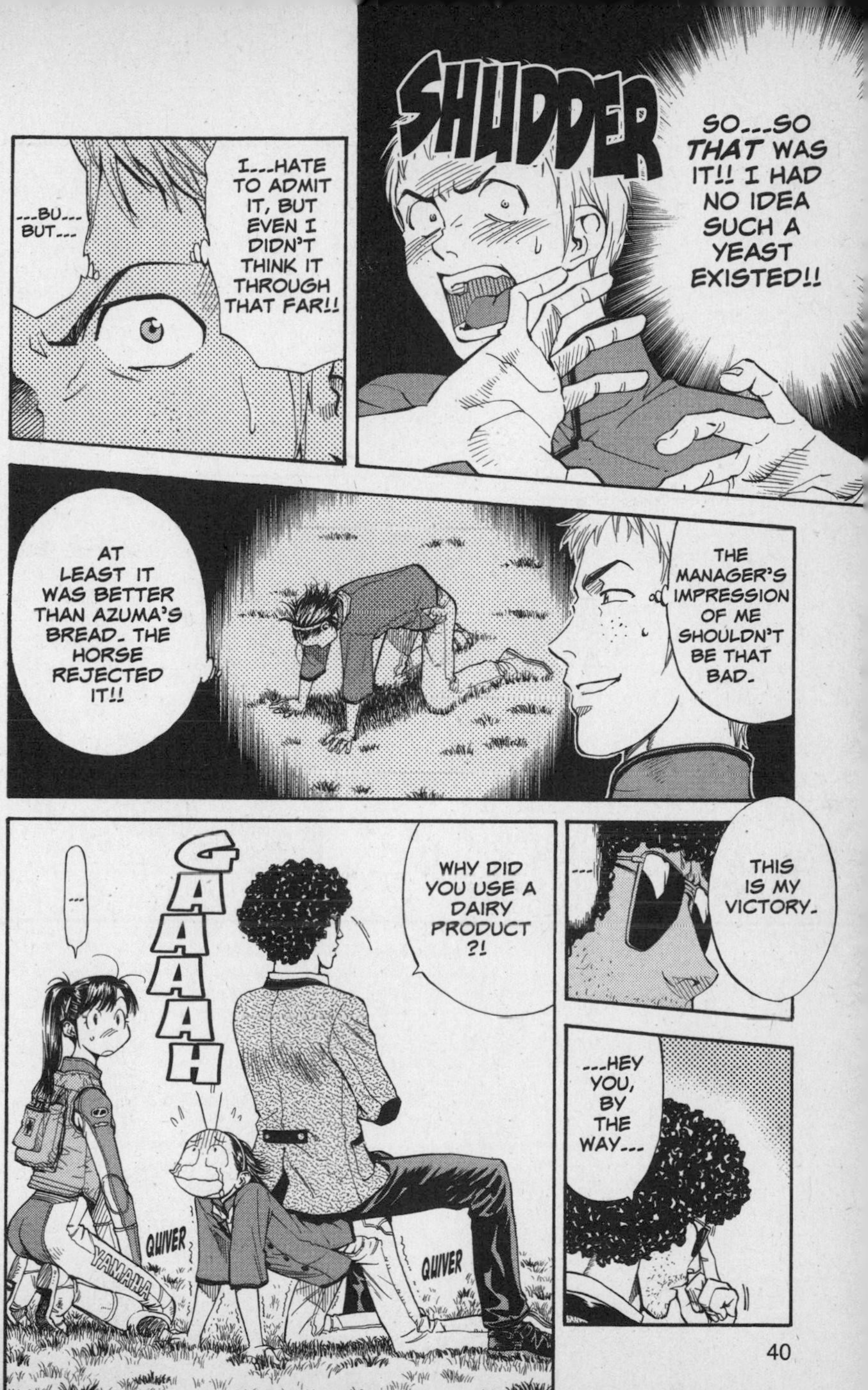
SHUDDER
SO...SO THAT WAS IT!! I HAD NO IDEA SUCH A YEAST EXISTED!!
I...HATE TO ADMIT IT, BUT EVEN I DIDN'T THINK IT THROUGH THAT FAR!!
...BU... BUT...
THE MANAGER'S IMPRESSION OF ME SHOULDN'T BE THAT BAD.
AT LEAST IT WAS BETTER THAN AZUMA'S BREAD. THE HORSE REJECTED IT!!
THIS IS MY VICTORY.
...
...HEY YOU, BY THE WAY...
WHY DID YOU USE A DAIRY PRODUCT?!
GAAAAAH
...
QUIVER
YAMAHA
QUIVER

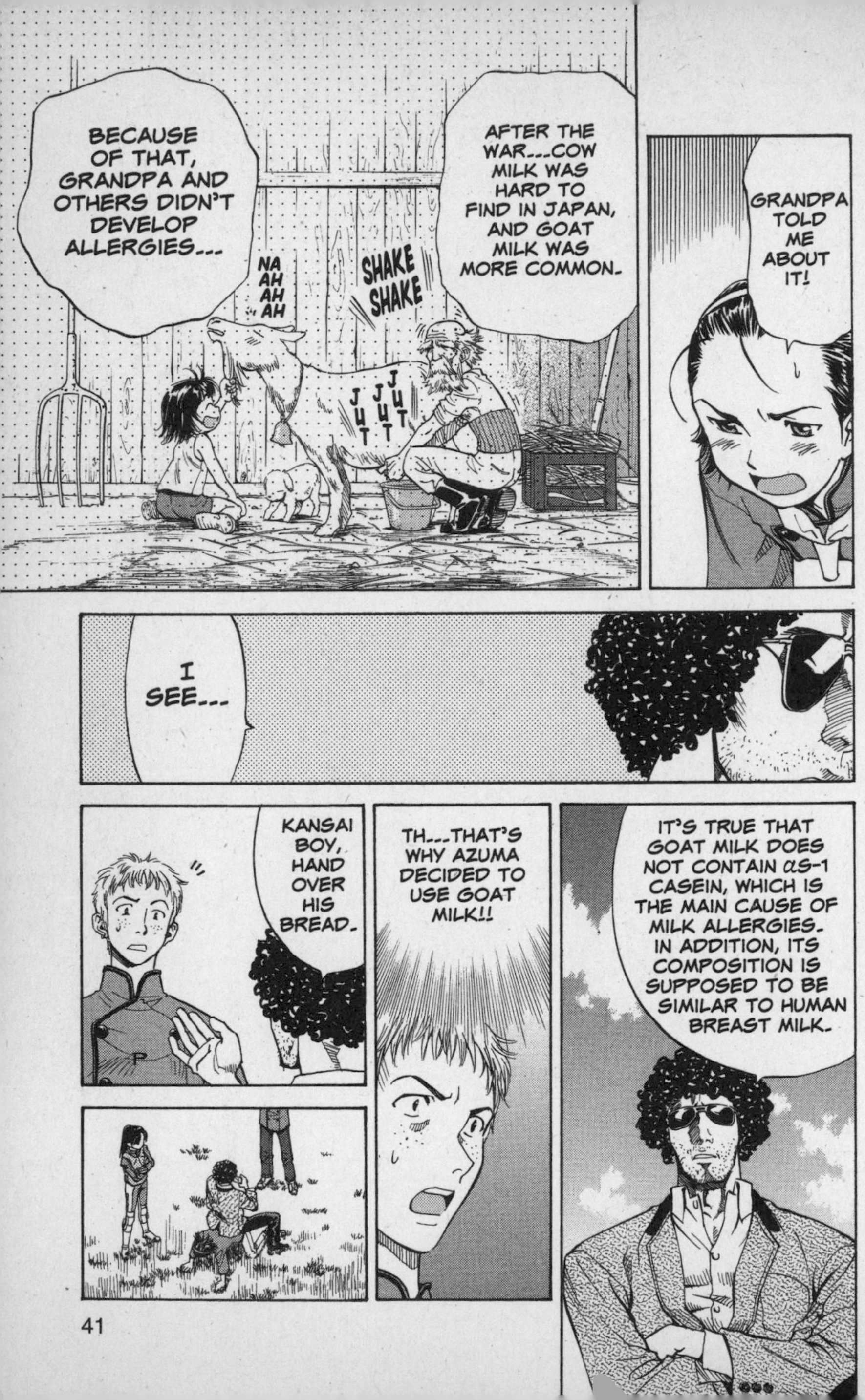
GRANDPA TOLD ME ABOUT IT!
AFTER THE WAR...COW MILK WAS HARD TO FIND IN JAPAN, AND GOAT MILK WAS MORE COMMON.
SHAKE SHAKE
JUT JUT JUT
NA AH AH AH
BECAUSE OF THAT, GRANDPA AND OTHERS DIDN'T DEVELOP ALLERGIES...
I SEE...
IT'S TRUE THAT GOAT MILK DOES NOT CONTAIN αS-1 CASEIN, WHICH IS THE MAIN CAUSE OF MILK ALLERGIES. IN ADDITION, ITS COMPOSITION IS SUPPOSED TO BE SIMILAR TO HUMAN BREAST MILK.
TH...THAT'S WHY AZUMA DECIDED TO USE GOAT MILK!!
KANSAI BOY, HAND OVER HIS BREAD.

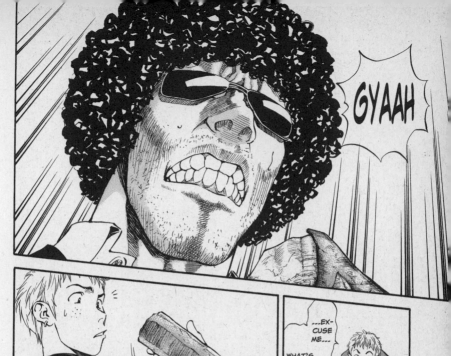

GYAAH

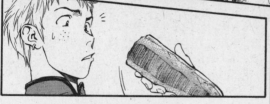

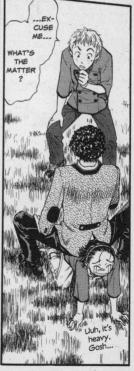

...EX-CUSE ME...

WHAT'S THE MATTER?

Uuh, it's heavy. Gosh...

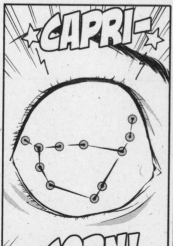

*CAPRI-

-CORN!

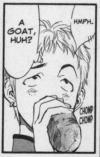

A GOAT, HUH?

HMPH.

CHOMP CHOMP

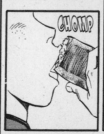

CHOMP

42

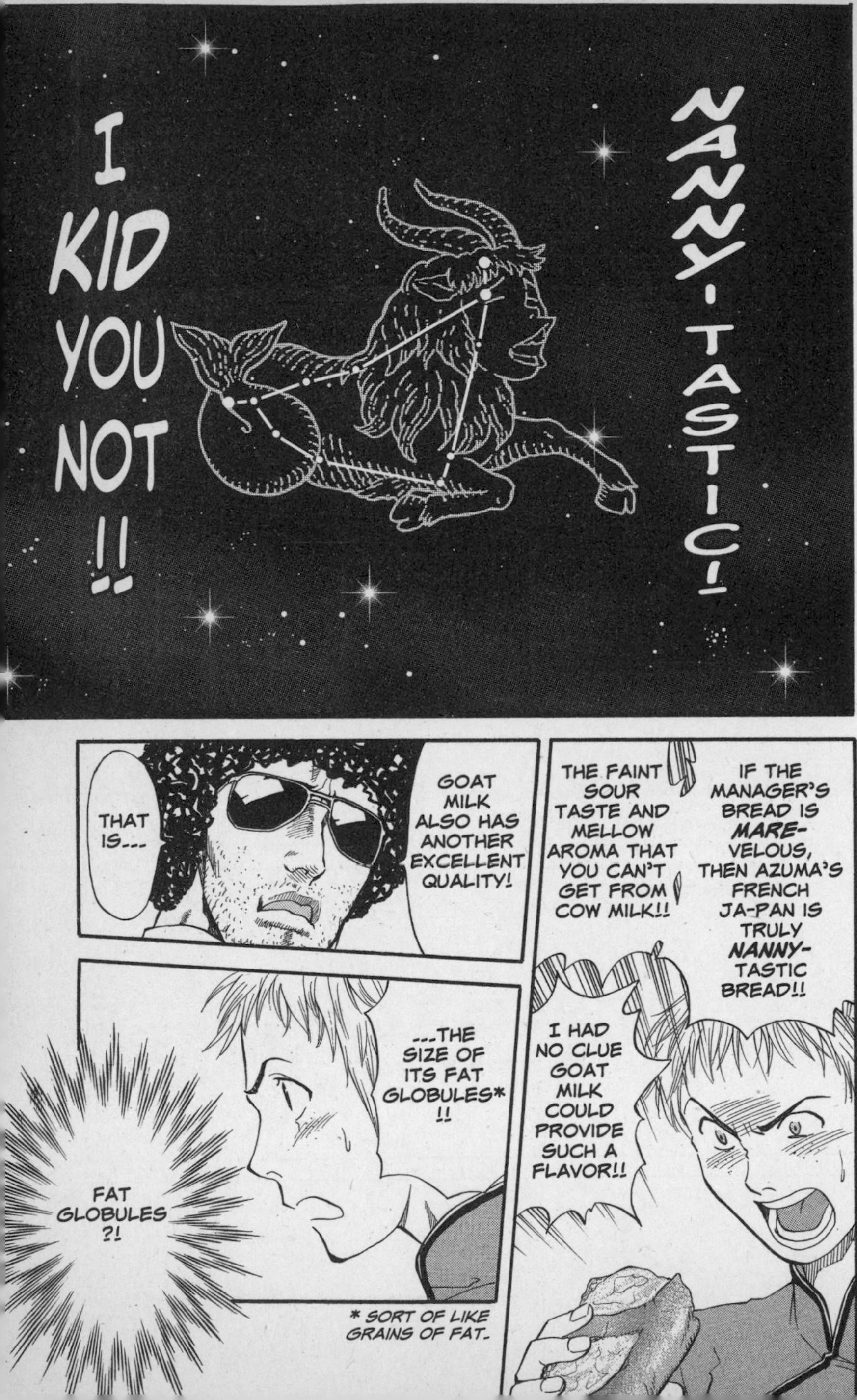
NANNY-TASTIC!
I KID YOU NOT!!
IF THE MANAGER'S BREAD IS MARE-VELOUS, THEN AZUMA'S FRENCH JA-PAN IS TRULY NANNY-TASTIC BREAD!!
THE FAINT SOUR TASTE AND MELLOW AROMA THAT YOU CAN'T GET FROM COW MILK!!
I HAD NO CLUE GOAT MILK COULD PROVIDE SUCH A FLAVOR!!
GOAT MILK ALSO HAS ANOTHER EXCELLENT QUALITY!
THAT IS...
...THE SIZE OF ITS FAT GLOBULES* !!
FAT GLOBULES ?!
* SORT OF LIKE GRAINS OF FAT.

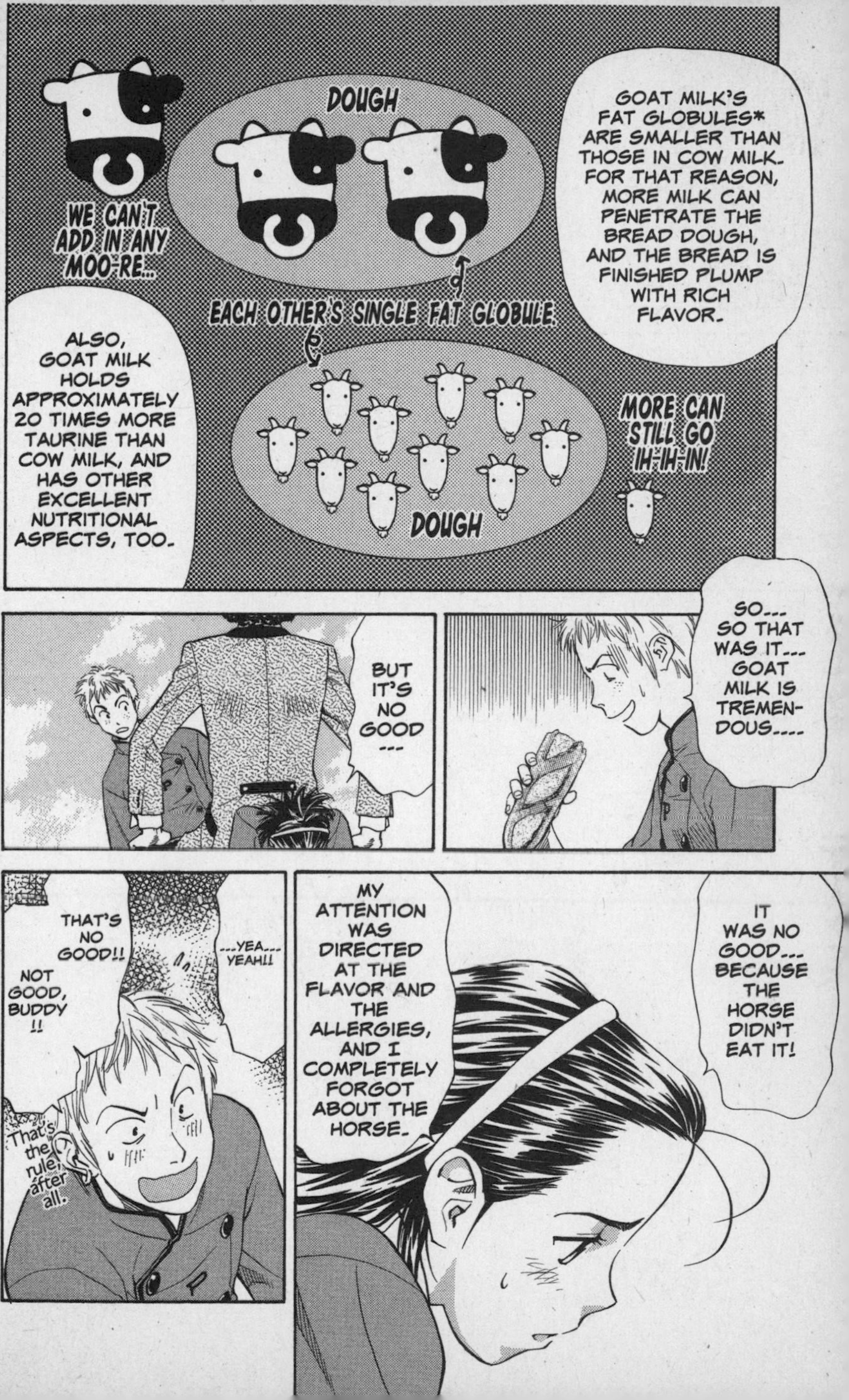
GOAT MILK'S FAT GLOBULES* ARE SMALLER THAN THOSE IN COW MILK. FOR THAT REASON, MORE MILK CAN PENETRATE THE BREAD DOUGH, AND THE BREAD IS FINISHED PLUMP WITH RICH FLAVOR.
DOUGH
WE CAN'T ADD IN ANY MOO-RE..
EACH OTHER'S SINGLE FAT GLOBULE.
MORE CAN STILL GO IH-IH-IN!
DOUGH
ALSO, GOAT MILK HOLDS APPROXIMATELY 20 TIMES MORE TAURINE THAN COW MILK, AND HAS OTHER EXCELLENT NUTRITIONAL ASPECTS, TOO.
SO... SO THAT WAS IT... GOAT MILK IS TREMEN-DOUS....
BUT IT'S NO GOOD...
IT WAS NO GOOD... BECAUSE THE HORSE DIDN'T EAT IT!
MY ATTENTION WAS DIRECTED AT THE FLAVOR AND THE ALLERGIES, AND I COMPLETELY FORGOT ABOUT THE HORSE.
...YEA... YEAH!!
THAT'S NO GOOD!!
NOT GOOD, BUDDY!!
That's the rule, after all.

* ACCORDING TO PROFESSOR KAWAHARA OF MIYAZAKI UNIVERSITY'S DEPARTMENT OF AGRICULTURE, A COW'S FAT GLOBULE IS 5 MICROMETERS WHILE A SHEEP'S IS 3.5 MICROMETERS. (A MICROMETER IS ONE-THOUSANDTH OF ONE MM). ALSO, THE ILLUSTRATION ON THE RIGHT IS STRICTLY METAPHORICAL, AND DOES NOT REFLECT ACTUAL ABSORPTION RATES.

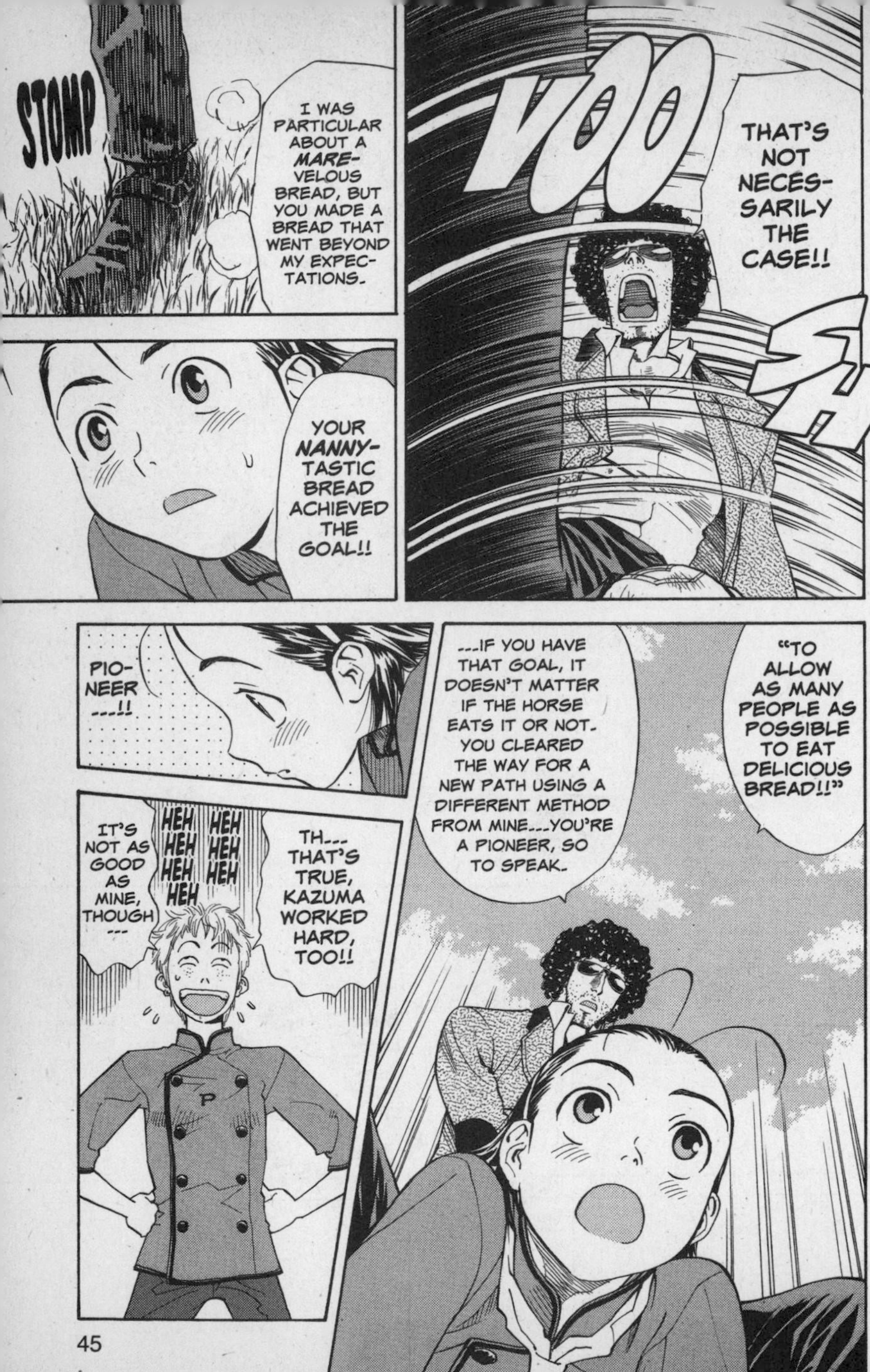
VOO
THAT'S NOT NECES-SARILY THE CASE!!
SH
STOMP
I WAS PARTICULAR ABOUT A MARE-VELOUS BREAD, BUT YOU MADE A BREAD THAT WENT BEYOND MY EXPEC-TATIONS.
YOUR NANNY-TASTIC BREAD ACHIEVED THE GOAL!!
"TO ALLOW AS MANY PEOPLE AS POSSIBLE TO EAT DELICIOUS BREAD!!"
...IF YOU HAVE THAT GOAL, IT DOESN'T MATTER IF THE HORSE EATS IT OR NOT. YOU CLEARED THE WAY FOR A NEW PATH USING A DIFFERENT METHOD FROM MINE...YOU'RE A PIONEER, SO TO SPEAK.
PIO-NEER ...!!
TH... THAT'S TRUE, KAZUMA WORKED HARD, TOO!!
HEH HEH HEH HEH HEH HEH HEH
IT'S NOT AS GOOD AS MINE, THOUGH ...

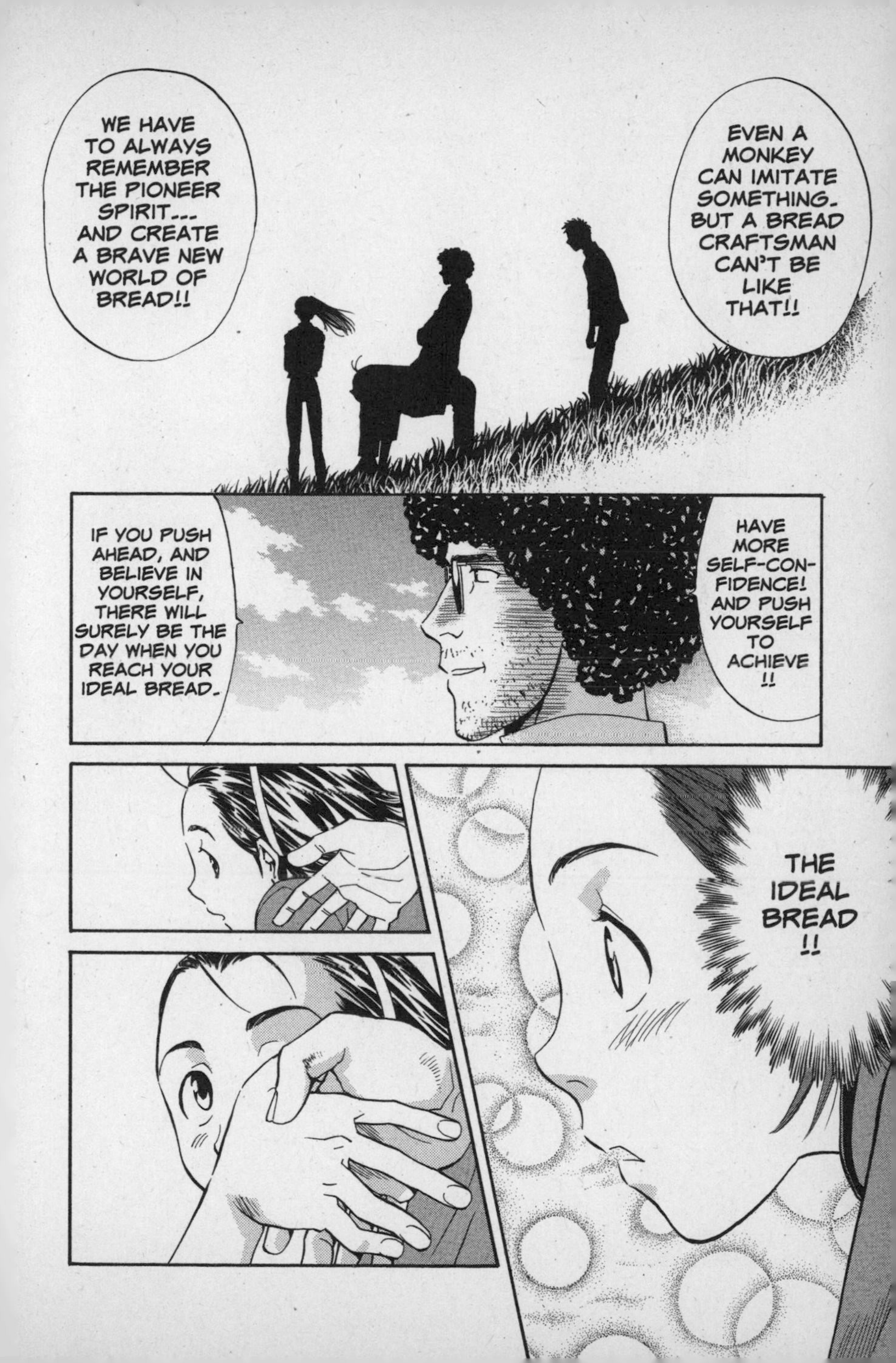
EVEN A MONKEY CAN IMITATE SOMETHING. BUT A BREAD CRAFTSMAN CAN'T BE LIKE THAT!!
WE HAVE TO ALWAYS REMEMBER THE PIONEER SPIRIT... AND CREATE A BRAVE NEW WORLD OF BREAD!!
HAVE MORE SELF-CONFIDENCE! AND PUSH YOURSELF TO ACHIEVE !!
IF YOU PUSH AHEAD, AND BELIEVE IN YOURSELF, THERE WILL SURELY BE THE DAY WHEN YOU REACH YOUR IDEAL BREAD.
THE IDEAL BREAD !!

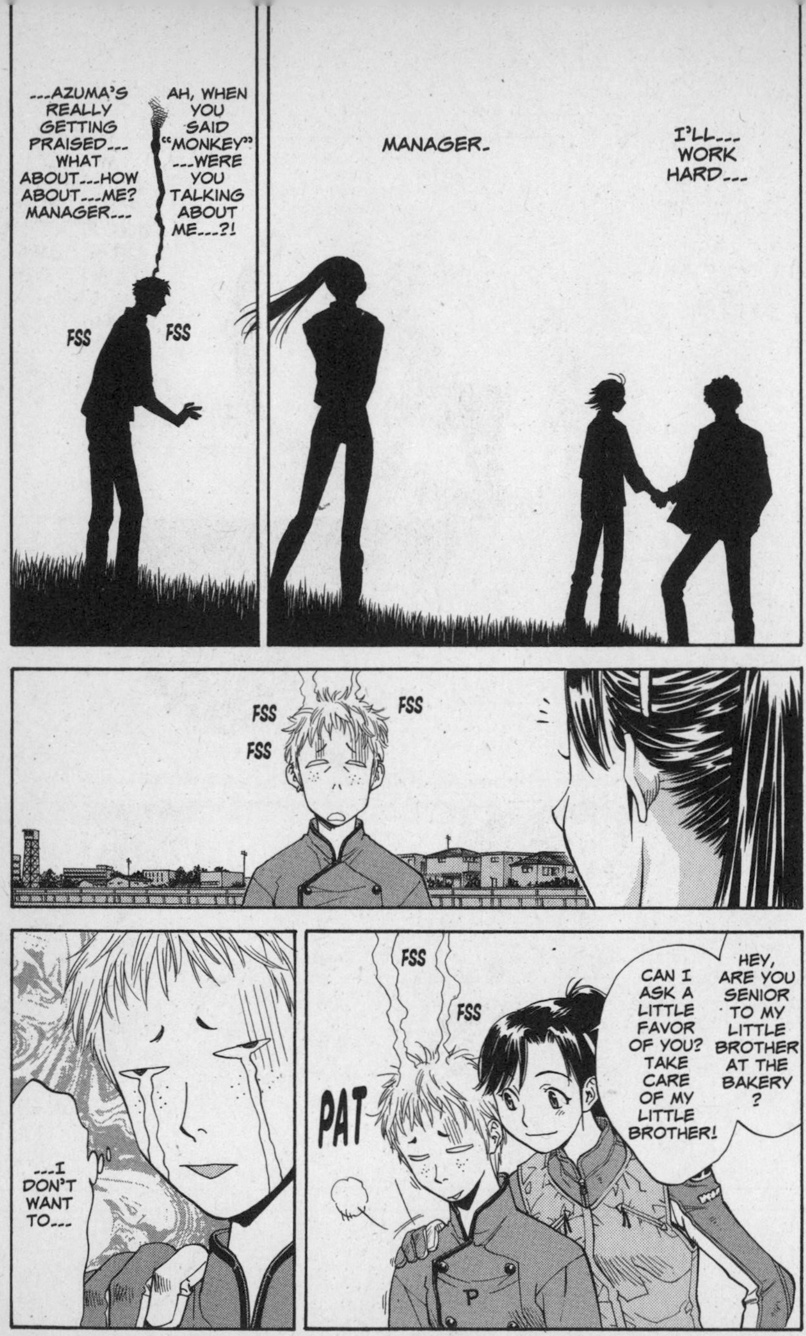

I'LL... WORK HARD...
MANAGER.
AH, WHEN YOU SAID "MONKEY" ...WERE YOU TALKING ABOUT ME...?!
...AZUMA'S REALLY GETTING PRAISED... WHAT ABOUT...HOW ABOUT...ME? MANAGER...
FSS
FSS
FSS
FSS
FSS
HEY, ARE YOU SENIOR TO MY LITTLE BROTHER AT THE BAKERY?
CAN I ASK A LITTLE FAVOR OF YOU? TAKE CARE OF MY LITTLE BROTHER!
FSS
FSS
PAT
...I DON'T WANT TO...

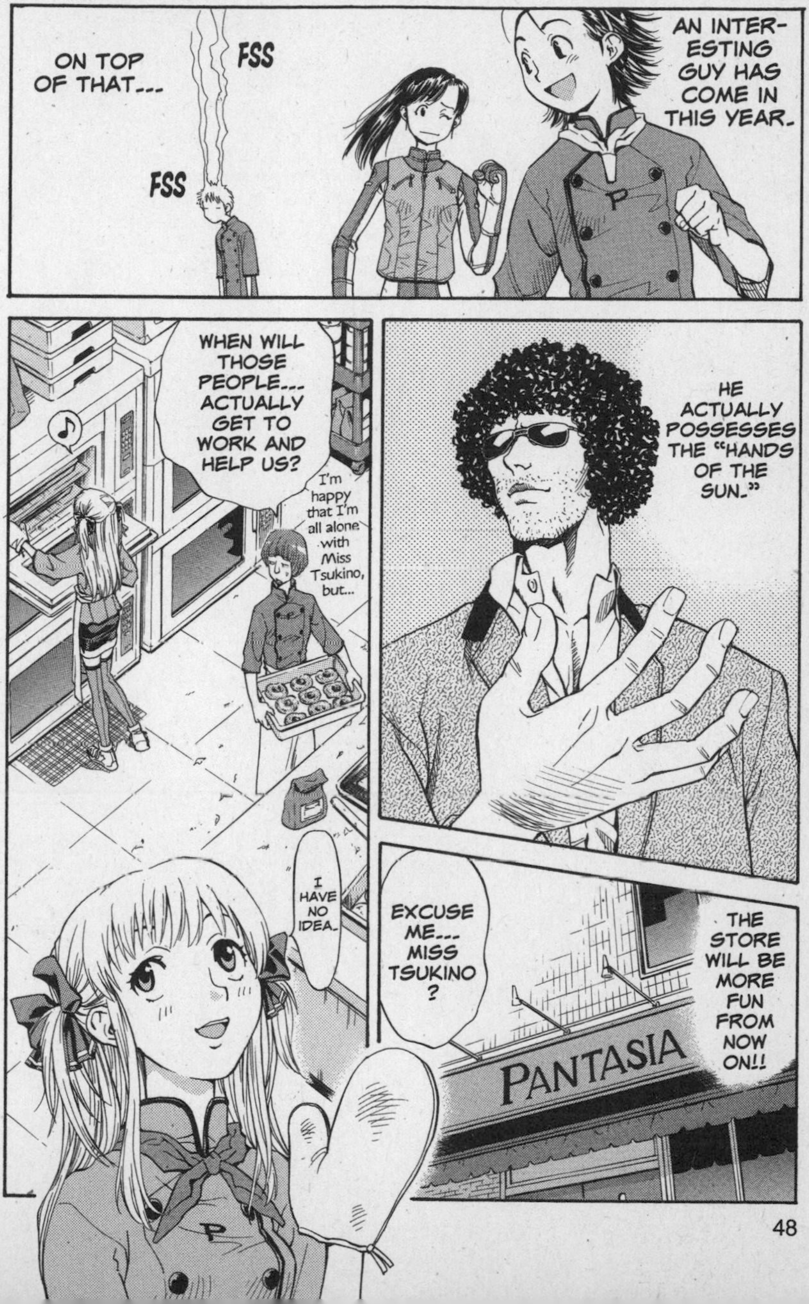
AN INTER-ESTING GUY HAS COME IN THIS YEAR.
FSS
ON TOP OF THAT...
FSS
HE ACTUALLY POSSESSES THE "HANDS OF THE SUN."
THE STORE WILL BE MORE FUN FROM NOW ON!!
PANTASIA
EXCUSE ME... MISS TSUKINO?
WHEN WILL THOSE PEOPLE... ACTUALLY GET TO WORK AND HELP US?
I'm happy that I'm all alone with Miss Tsukino, but...
I HAVE NO IDEA.

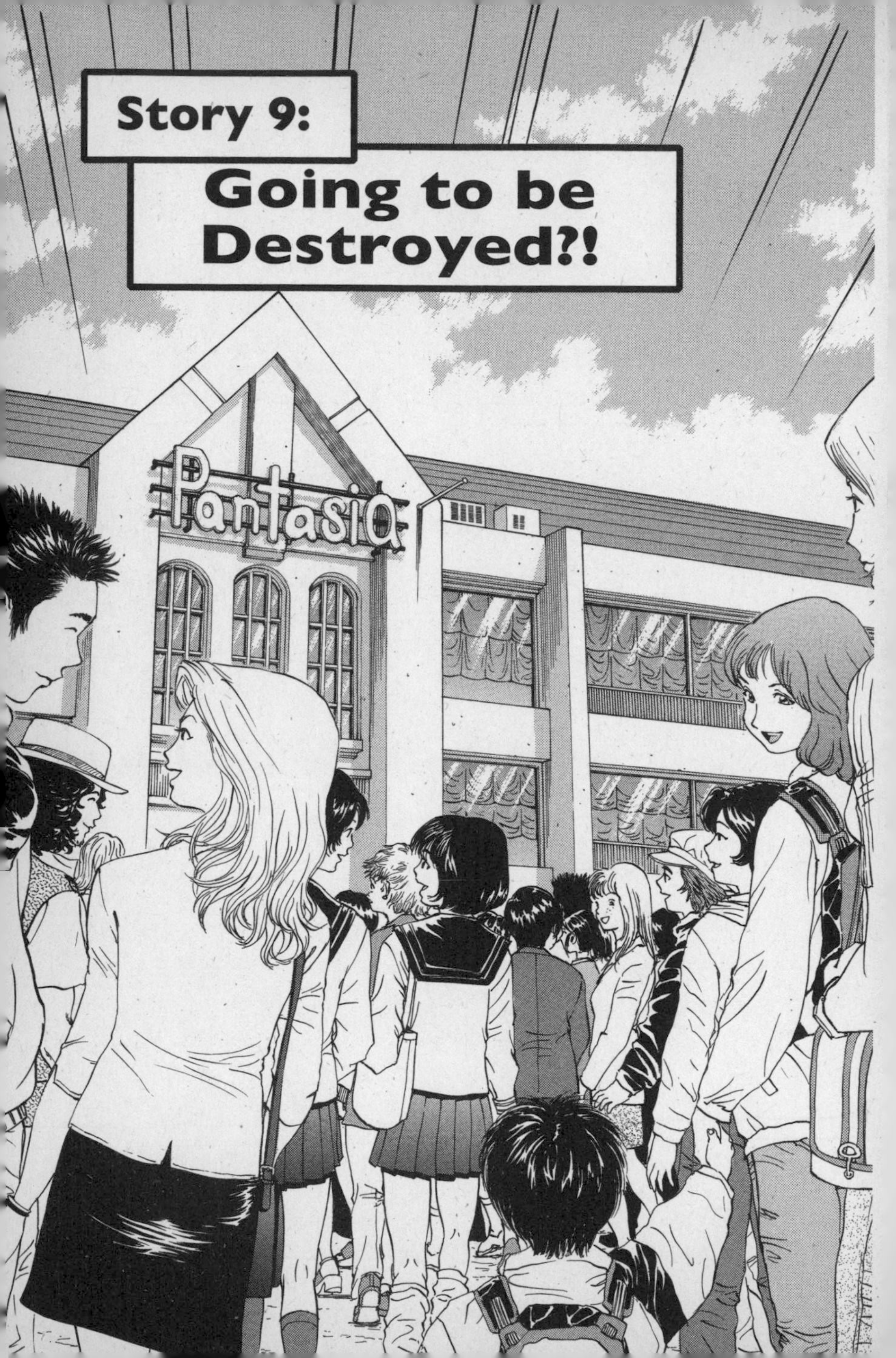
Story 9:
Going to be Destroyed?!
Pantasia

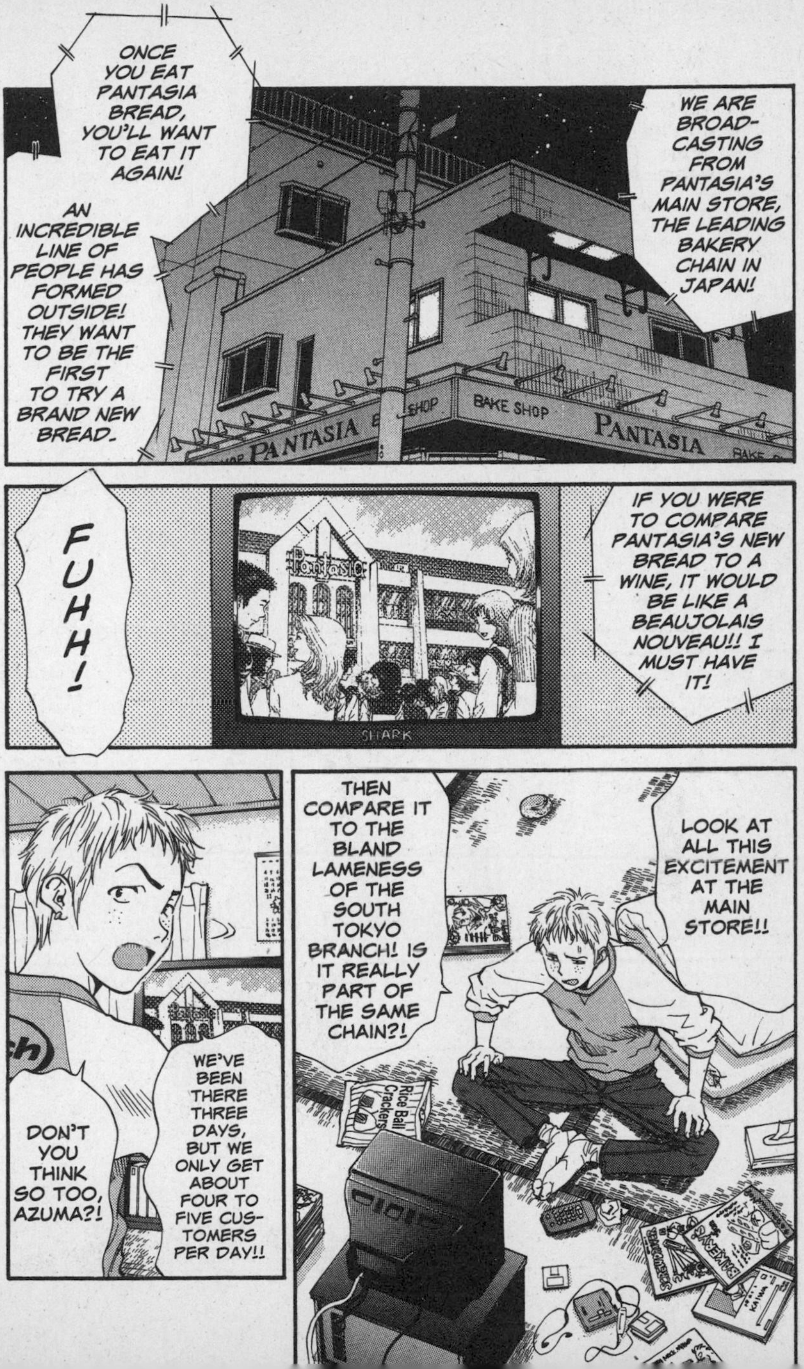
WE ARE BROAD-CASTING FROM PANTASIA'S MAIN STORE, THE LEADING BAKERY CHAIN IN JAPAN!
ONCE YOU EAT PANTASIA BREAD, YOU'LL WANT TO EAT IT AGAIN!
AN INCREDIBLE LINE OF PEOPLE HAS FORMED OUTSIDE! THEY WANT TO BE THE FIRST TO TRY A BRAND NEW BREAD.
BAKE SHOP PANTASIA
PANTASIA
IF YOU WERE TO COMPARE PANTASIA'S NEW BREAD TO A WINE, IT WOULD BE LIKE A BEAUJOLAIS NOUVEAU!! I MUST HAVE IT!
FUHH!
SHARK
LOOK AT ALL THIS EXCITEMENT AT THE MAIN STORE!!
THEN COMPARE IT TO THE BLAND LAMENESS OF THE SOUTH TOKYO BRANCH! IS IT REALLY PART OF THE SAME CHAIN?!
Rice Ball Crackers
WE'VE BEEN THERE THREE DAYS, BUT WE ONLY GET ABOUT FOUR TO FIVE CUS-TOMERS PER DAY!!
DON'T YOU THINK SO TOO, AZUMA?!

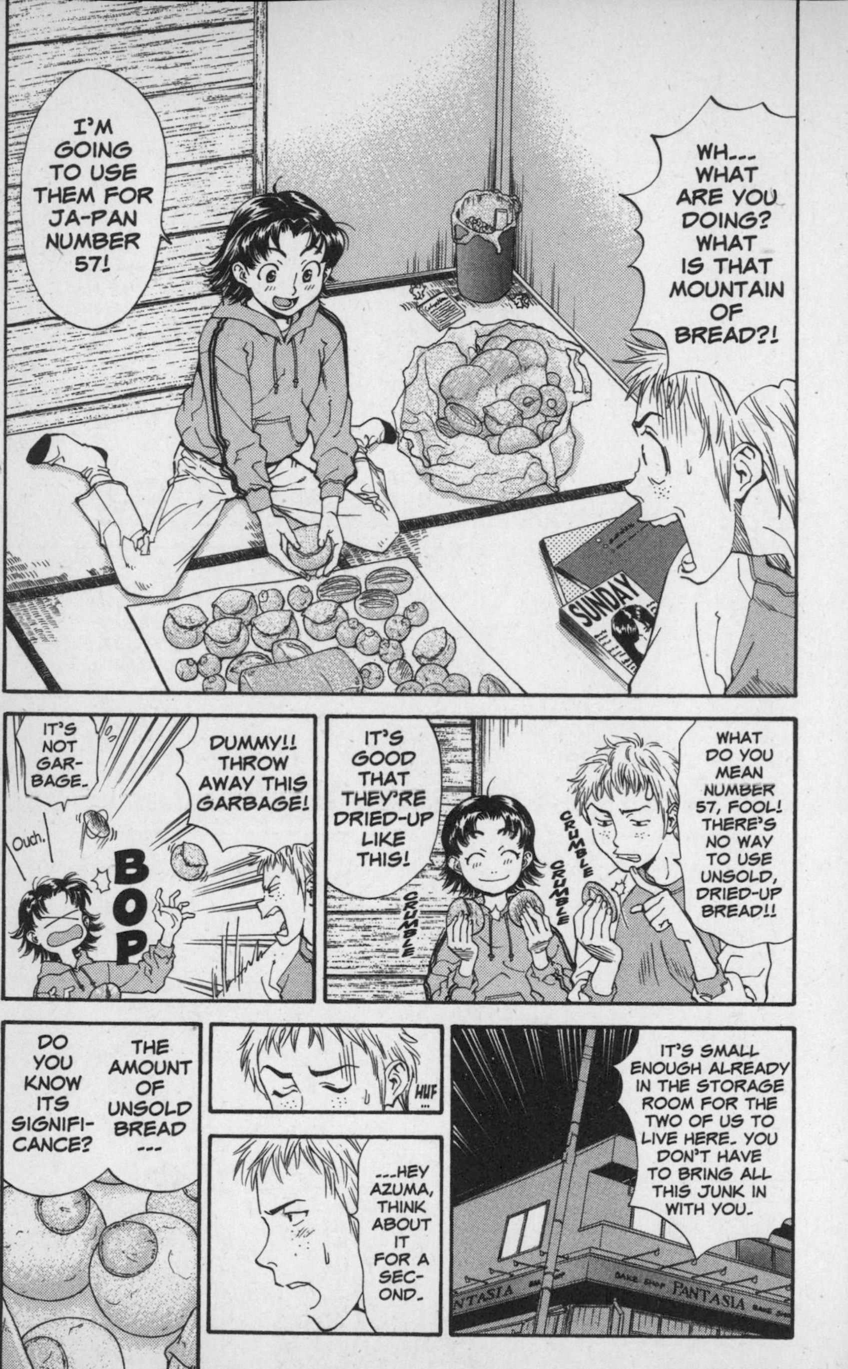
WH... WHAT ARE YOU DOING? WHAT IS THAT MOUNTAIN OF BREAD?!
I'M GOING TO USE THEM FOR JA-PAN NUMBER 57!
SUNDAY
WHAT DO YOU MEAN NUMBER 57, FOOL! THERE'S NO WAY TO USE UNSOLD, DRIED-UP BREAD!!
CRUMBLE
CRUMBLE
IT'S GOOD THAT THEY'RE DRIED-UP LIKE THIS!
CRUMBLE
DUMMY!! THROW AWAY THIS GARBAGE!
BOP
IT'S NOT GARBAGE.
Ouch.
IT'S SMALL ENOUGH ALREADY IN THE STORAGE ROOM FOR THE TWO OF US TO LIVE HERE. YOU DON'T HAVE TO BRING ALL THIS JUNK IN WITH YOU.
BAKE SHOP PANTASIA
HUF...
...HEY AZUMA, THINK ABOUT IT FOR A SECOND.
THE AMOUNT OF UNSOLD BREAD...
DO YOU KNOW ITS SIGNIFICANCE?

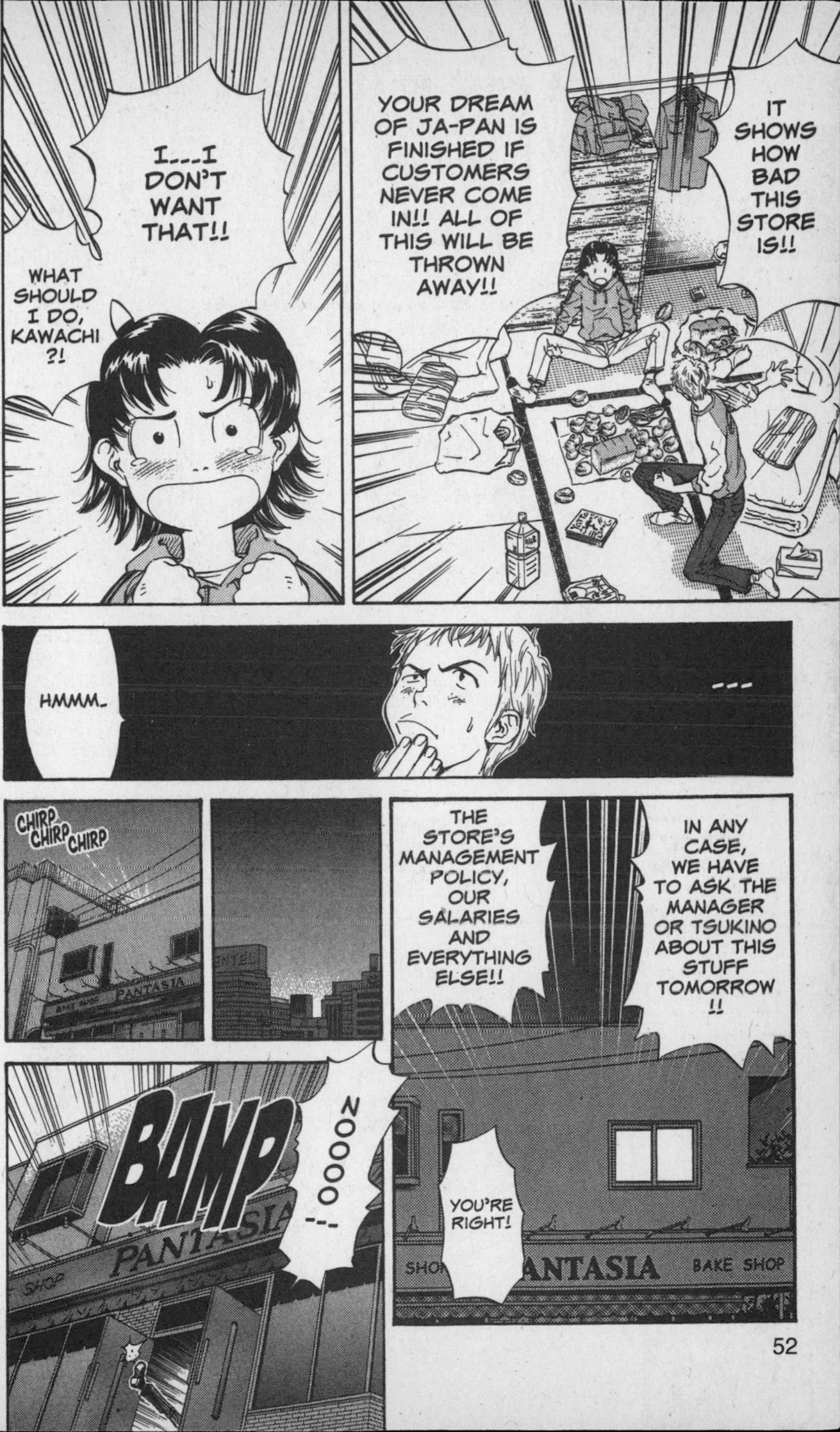
IT SHOWS HOW BAD THIS STORE IS!!
YOUR DREAM OF JA-PAN IS FINISHED IF CUSTOMERS NEVER COME IN!! ALL OF THIS WILL BE THROWN AWAY!!
I...I DON'T WANT THAT!!
WHAT SHOULD I DO, KAWACHI?!
...
HMMM.
IN ANY CASE, WE HAVE TO ASK THE MANAGER OR TSUKINO ABOUT THIS STUFF TOMORROW!!
THE STORE'S MANAGEMENT POLICY, OUR SALARIES AND EVERYTHING ELSE!!
CHIRP CHIRP CHIRP
PANTASIA
YOU'RE RIGHT!
PANTASIA BAKE SHOP
NOOOOO...
BAMP
PANTASIA

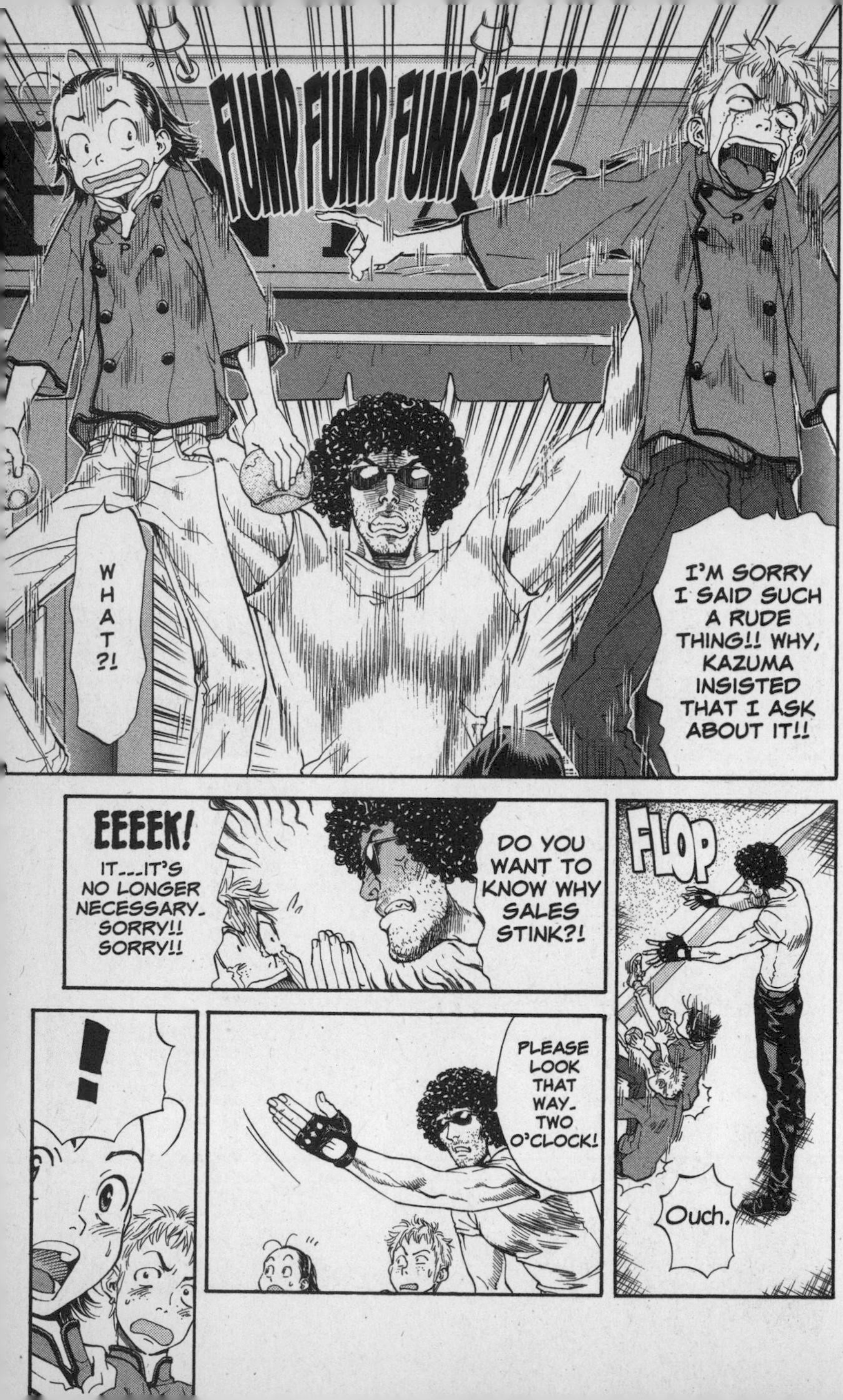
FUMP FUMP FUMP FUMP
I'M SORRY I SAID SUCH A RUDE THING!! WHY, KAZUMA INSISTED THAT I ASK ABOUT IT!!
WHAT?!
FLOP
Ouch.
DO YOU WANT TO KNOW WHY SALES STINK?!
EEEEK!
IT...IT'S NO LONGER NECESSARY. SORRY!! SORRY!!
PLEASE LOOK THAT WAY. TWO O'CLOCK!
!!

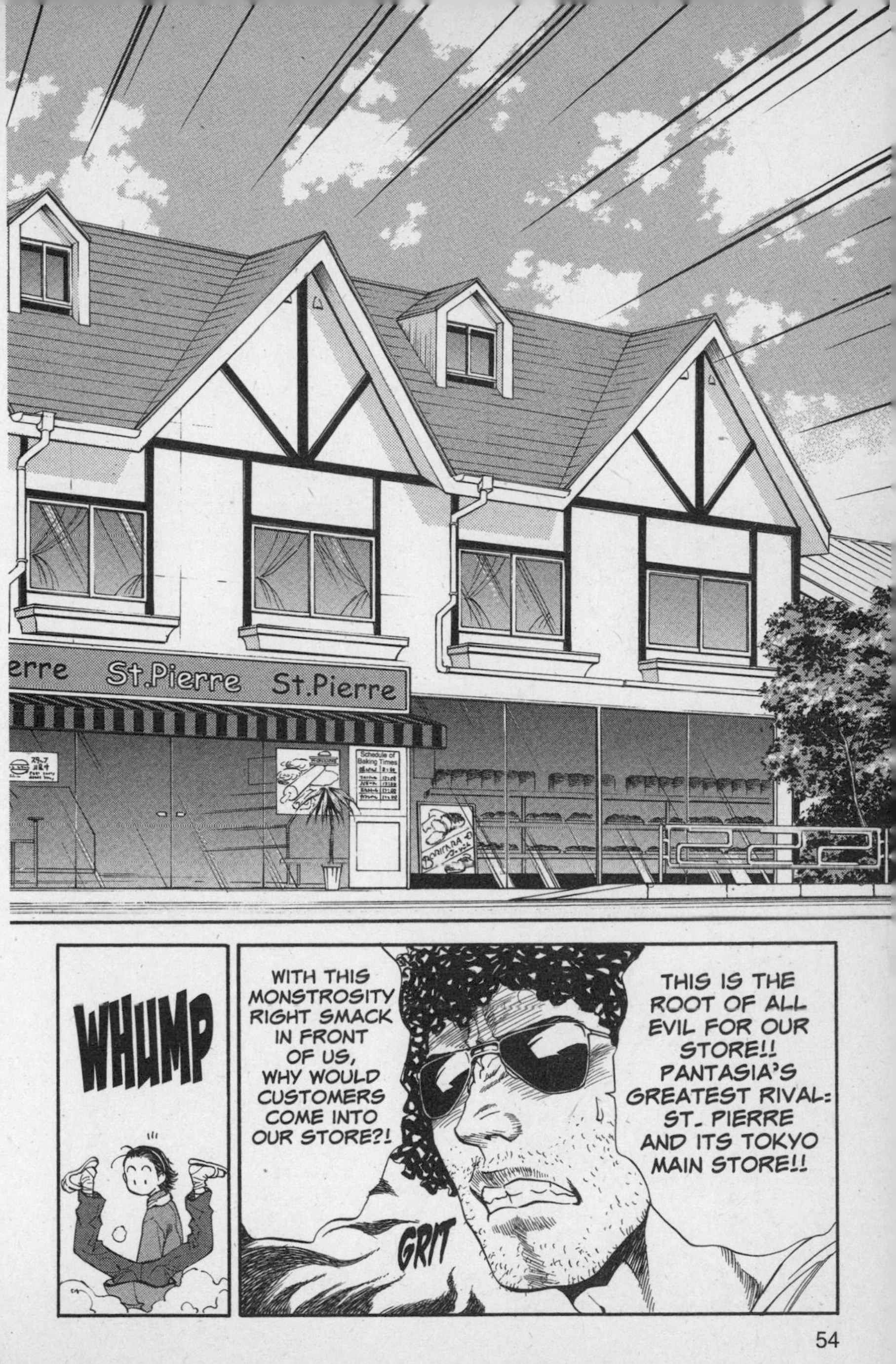
St.Pierre St.Pierre
Schedule of Baking Times
THIS IS THE ROOT OF ALL EVIL FOR OUR STORE!! PANTASIA'S GREATEST RIVAL: ST. PIERRE AND ITS TOKYO MAIN STORE!!
WITH THIS MONSTROSITY RIGHT SMACK IN FRONT OF US, WHY WOULD CUSTOMERS COME INTO OUR STORE?!
GRIT
WHUMP

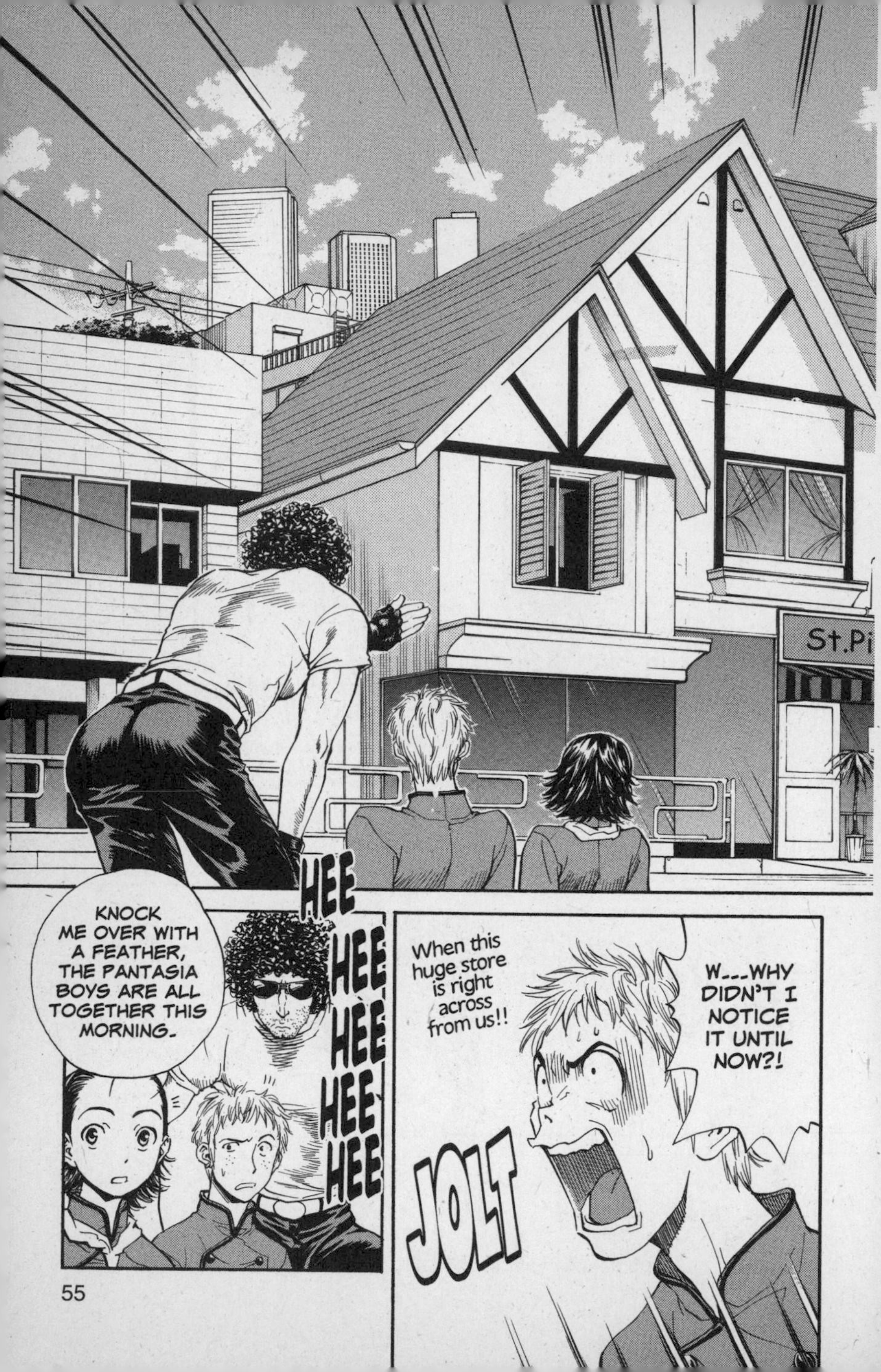
St.Pi
W---WHY DIDN'T I NOTICE IT UNTIL NOW?!
When this huge store is right across from us!!
JOLT
HEE HEE HEE HEE HEE
KNOCK ME OVER WITH A FEATHER, THE PANTASIA BOYS ARE ALL TOGETHER THIS MORNING.

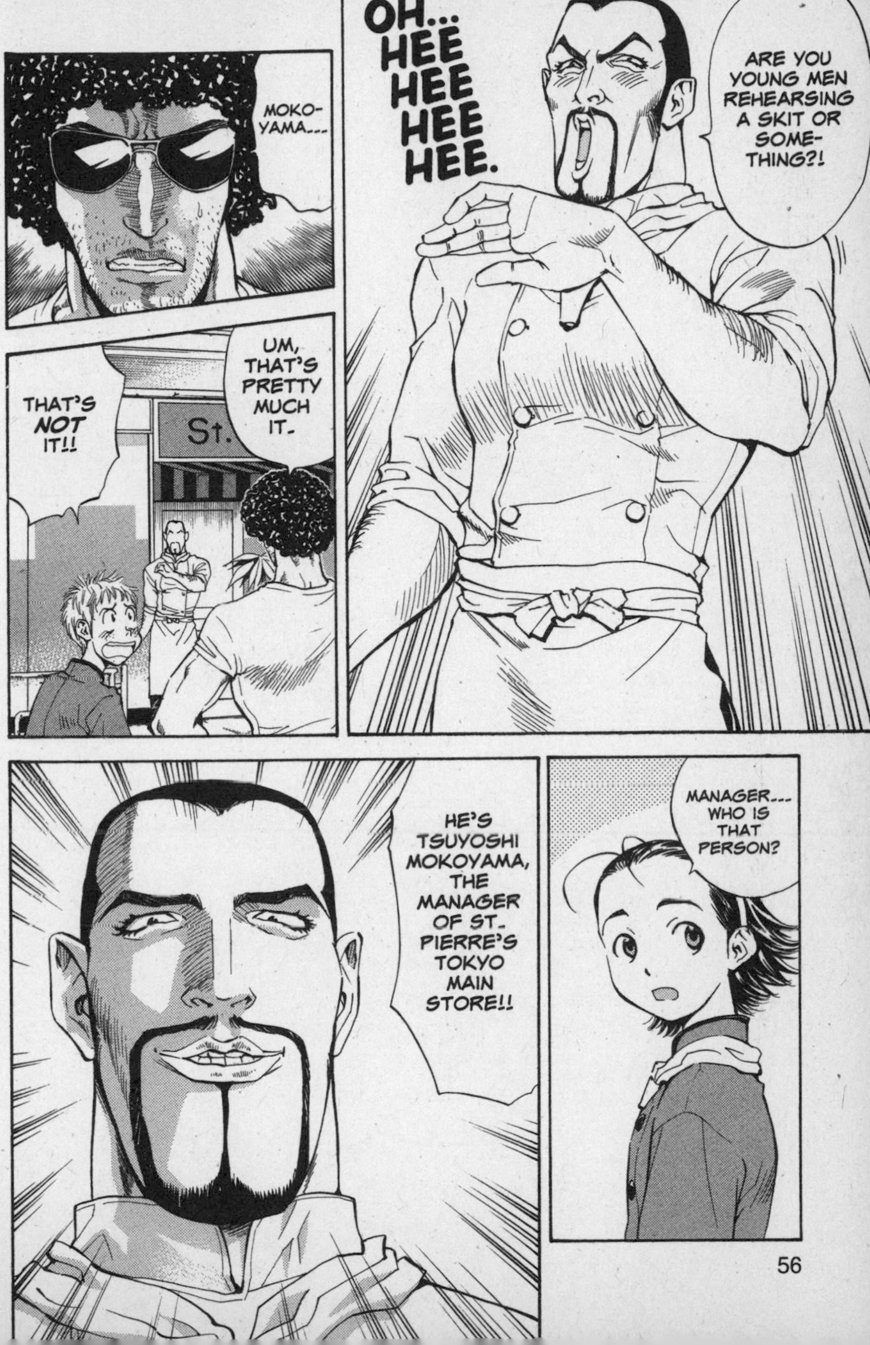

ARE YOU YOUNG MEN REHEARSING A SKIT OR SOME-THING?!
OH... HEE HEE HEE HEE.
MOKO-YAMA...
UM, THAT'S PRETTY MUCH IT.
THAT'S NOT IT!!
St.
MANAGER... WHO IS THAT PERSON?
HE'S TSUYOSHI MOKOYAMA, THE MANAGER OF ST. PIERRE'S TOKYO MAIN STORE!!

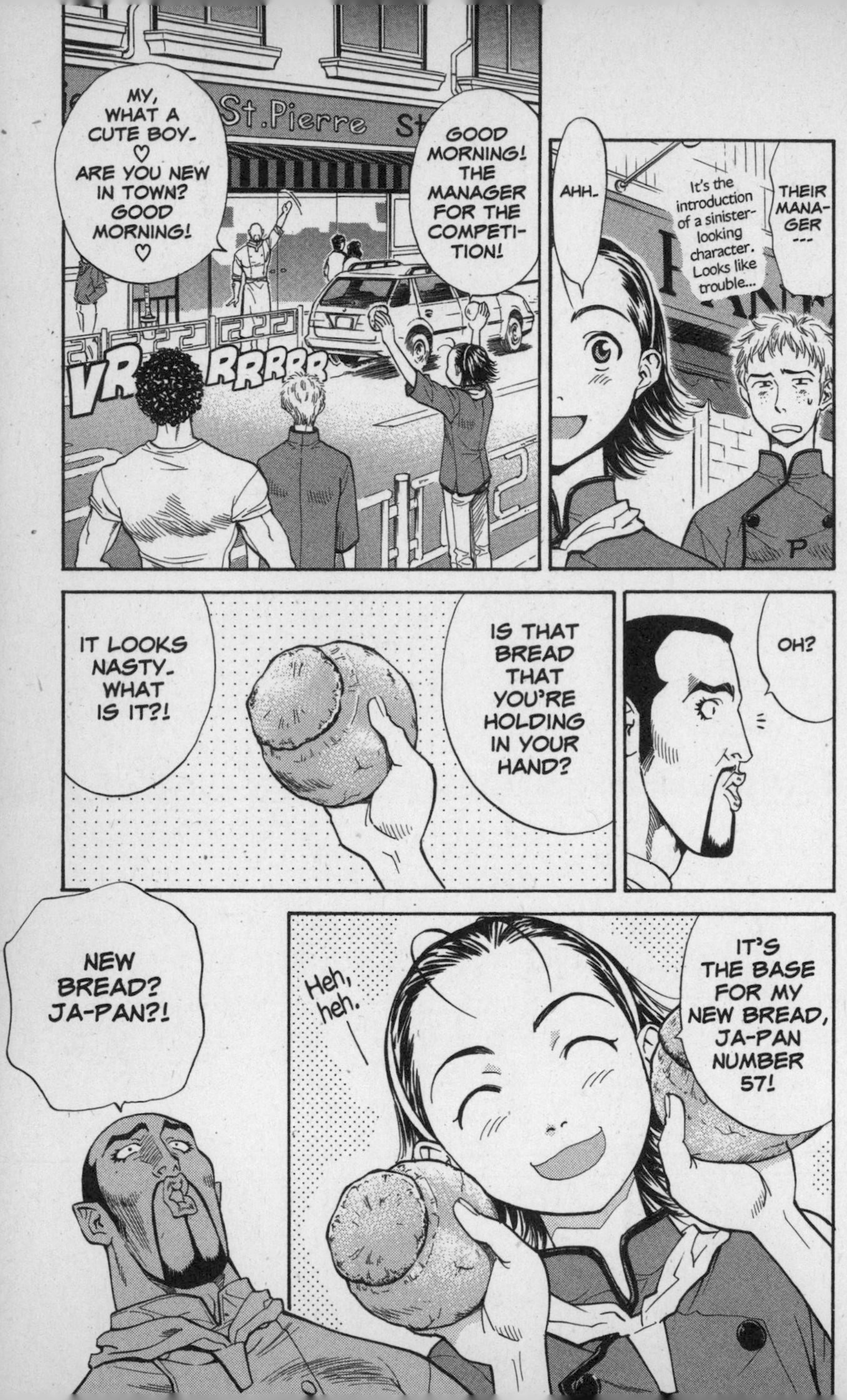
THEIR MANA-GER ---
It's the introduction of a sinister-looking character. Looks like trouble...
AHH.
GOOD MORNING! THE MANAGER FOR THE COMPETI-TION!
St.Pierre
MY, WHAT A CUTE BOY. ♡ ARE YOU NEW IN TOWN? GOOD MORNING! ♡
VR RRRRR
OH?
IS THAT BREAD THAT YOU'RE HOLDING IN YOUR HAND?
IT LOOKS NASTY. WHAT IS IT?!
IT'S THE BASE FOR MY NEW BREAD, JA-PAN NUMBER 57!
Heh, heh.
NEW BREAD? JA-PAN?!

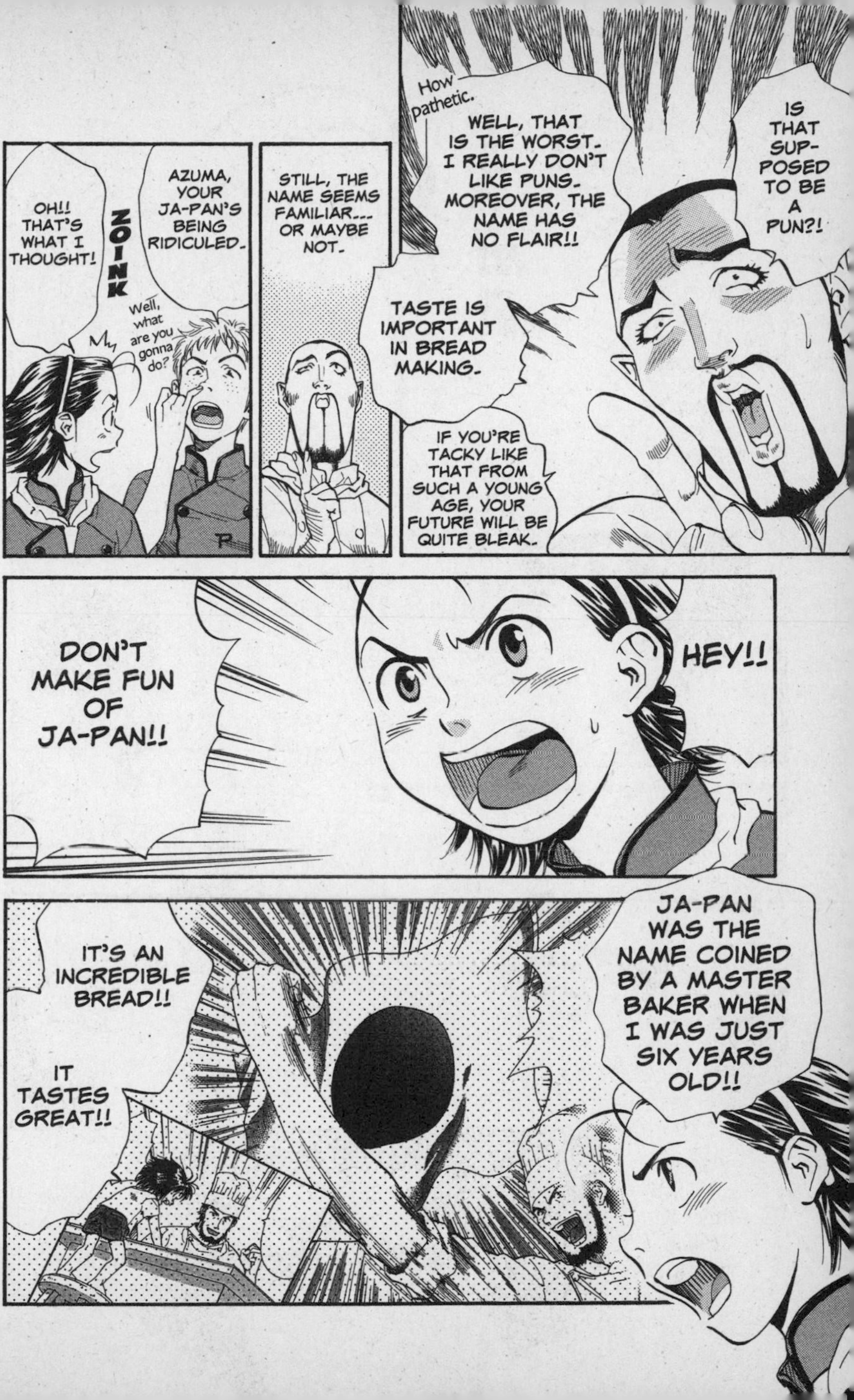

IS THAT SUP-POSED TO BE A PUN?!
How pathetic.
WELL, THAT IS THE WORST. I REALLY DON'T LIKE PUNS. MOREOVER, THE NAME HAS NO FLAIR!!
TASTE IS IMPORTANT IN BREAD MAKING.
IF YOU'RE TACKY LIKE THAT FROM SUCH A YOUNG AGE, YOUR FUTURE WILL BE QUITE BLEAK.
STILL, THE NAME SEEMS FAMILIAR... OR MAYBE NOT.
AZUMA, YOUR JA-PAN'S BEING RIDICULED.
ZOINK
Well, what are you gonna do?
OH!! THAT'S WHAT I THOUGHT!
HEY!!
DON'T MAKE FUN OF JA-PAN!!
JA-PAN WAS THE NAME COINED BY A MASTER BAKER WHEN I WAS JUST SIX YEARS OLD!!
IT'S AN INCREDIBLE BREAD!!
IT TASTES GREAT!!

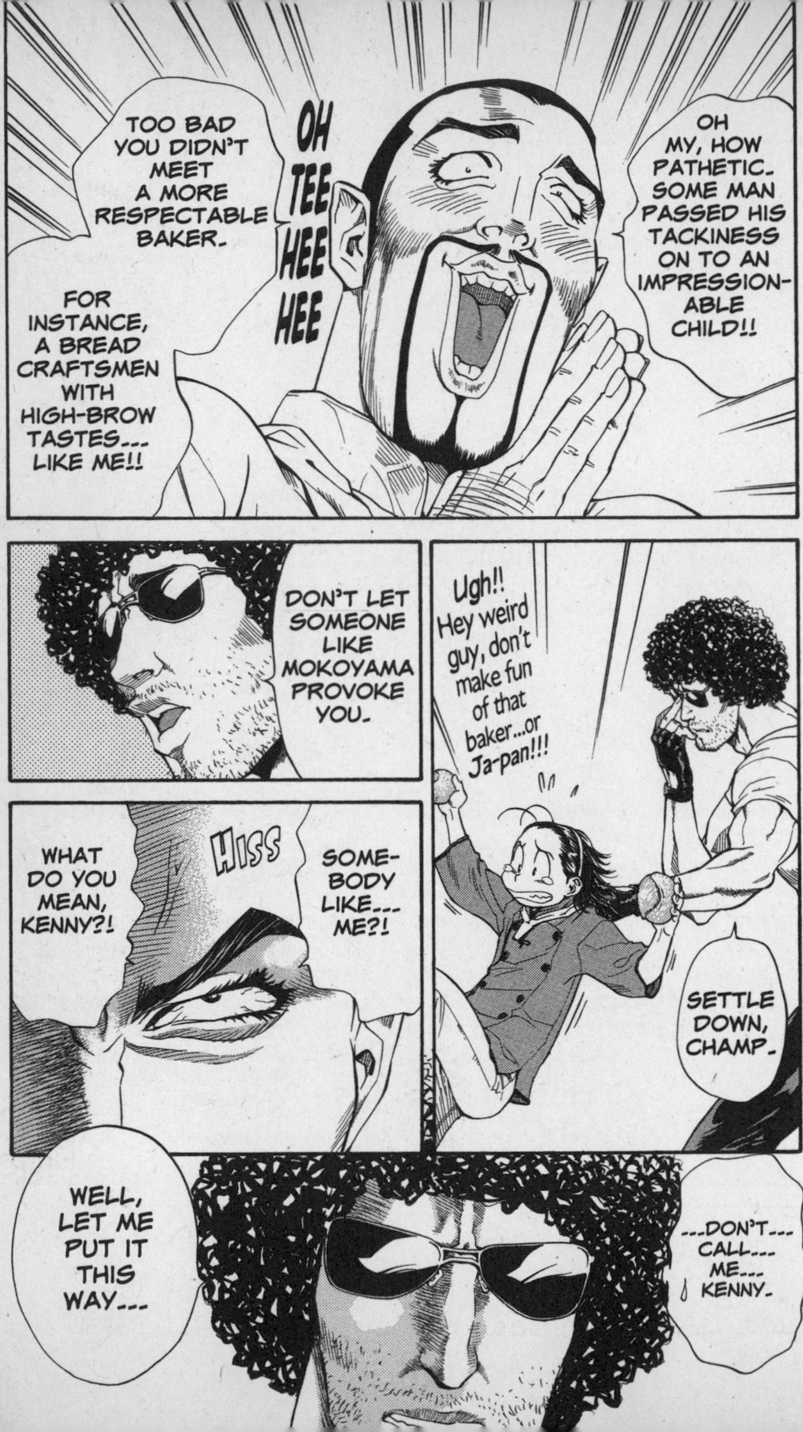
OH MY, HOW PATHETIC. SOME MAN PASSED HIS TACKINESS ON TO AN IMPRESSION-ABLE CHILD!!
OH TEE HEE HEE
TOO BAD YOU DIDN'T MEET A MORE RESPECTABLE BAKER.
FOR INSTANCE, A BREAD CRAFTSMEN WITH HIGH-BROW TASTES... LIKE ME!!
Ugh!! Hey weird guy, don't make fun of that baker...or Ja-pan!!!
SETTLE DOWN, CHAMP.
DON'T LET SOMEONE LIKE MOKOYAMA PROVOKE YOU.
SOME-BODY LIKE... ME?!
HISS
WHAT DO YOU MEAN, KENNY?!
...DON'T... CALL... ME... KENNY.
WELL, LET ME PUT IT THIS WAY...

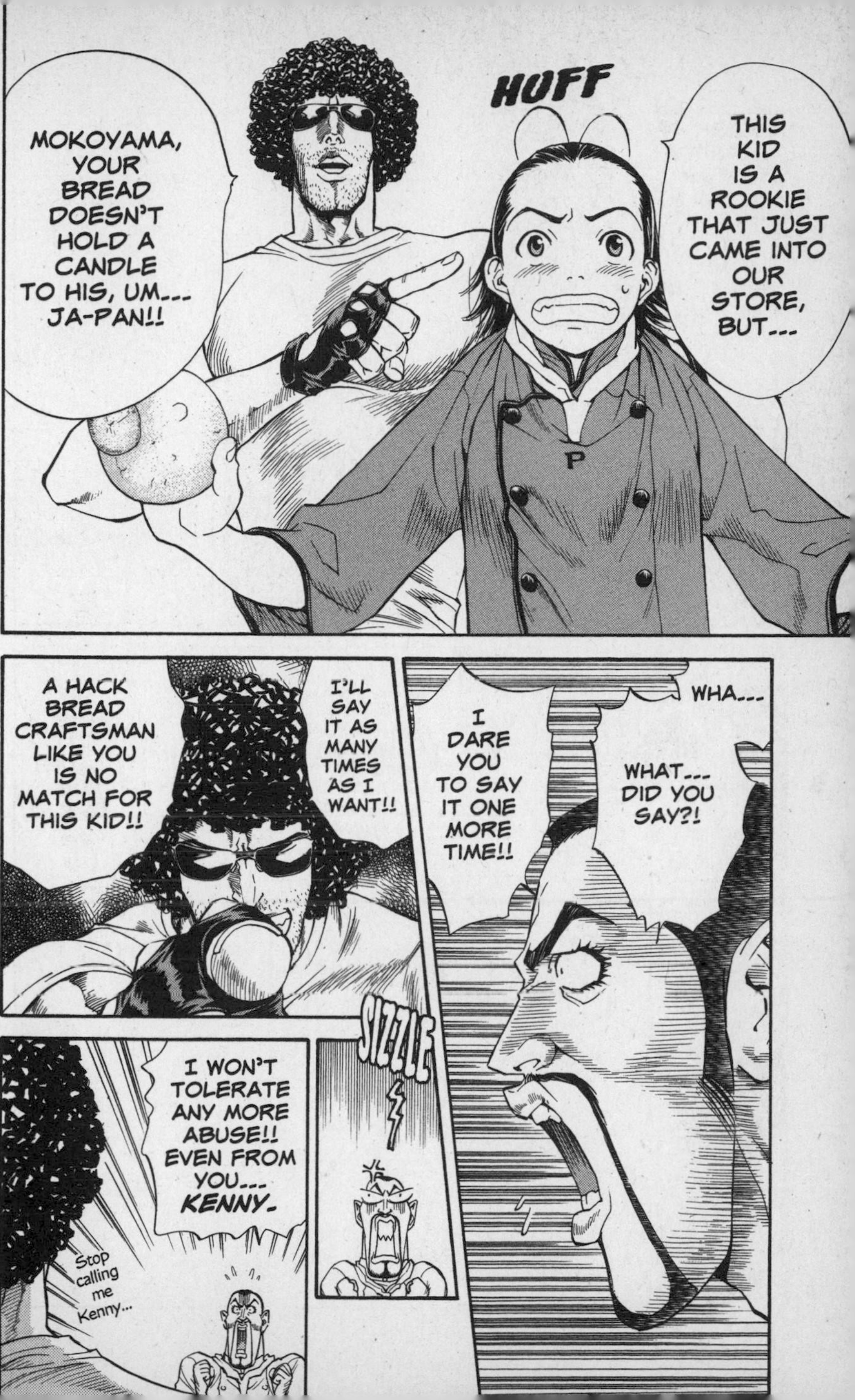
THIS KID IS A ROOKIE THAT JUST CAME INTO OUR STORE, BUT...
HUFF
MOKOYAMA, YOUR BREAD DOESN'T HOLD A CANDLE TO HIS, UM... JA-PAN!!
WHA...
WHAT... DID YOU SAY?!
I DARE YOU TO SAY IT ONE MORE TIME!!
I'LL SAY IT AS MANY TIMES AS I WANT!!
A HACK BREAD CRAFTSMAN LIKE YOU IS NO MATCH FOR THIS KID!!
SIZZLE
I WON'T TOLERATE ANY MORE ABUSE!! EVEN FROM YOU... *KENNY.*
Stop calling me Kenny...

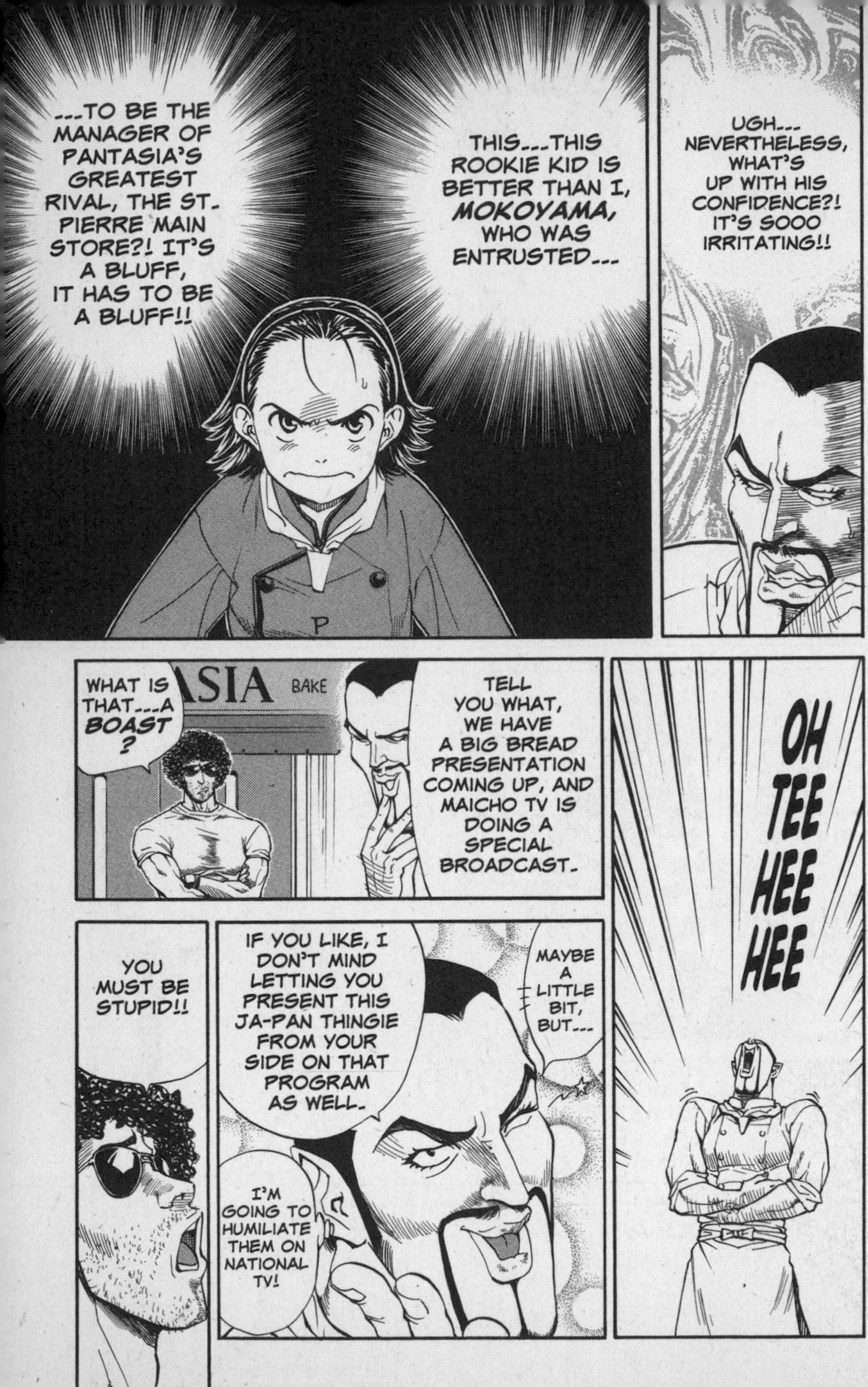
UGH... NEVERTHELESS, WHAT'S UP WITH HIS CONFIDENCE?! IT'S SOOO IRRITATING!!
THIS...THIS ROOKIE KID IS BETTER THAN I, *MOKOYAMA,* WHO WAS ENTRUSTED...
...TO BE THE MANAGER OF PANTASIA'S GREATEST RIVAL, THE ST. PIERRE MAIN STORE?! IT'S A BLUFF, IT HAS TO BE A BLUFF!!
OH TEE HEE HEE
TELL YOU WHAT, WE HAVE A BIG BREAD PRESENTATION COMING UP, AND MAICHO TV IS DOING A SPECIAL BROADCAST.
WHAT IS THAT...A *BOAST*?
MAYBE A LITTLE BIT, BUT...
IF YOU LIKE, I DON'T MIND LETTING YOU PRESENT THIS JA-PAN THINGIE FROM YOUR SIDE ON THAT PROGRAM AS WELL.
I'M GOING TO HUMILIATE THEM ON NATIONAL TV!
YOU MUST BE STUPID!!

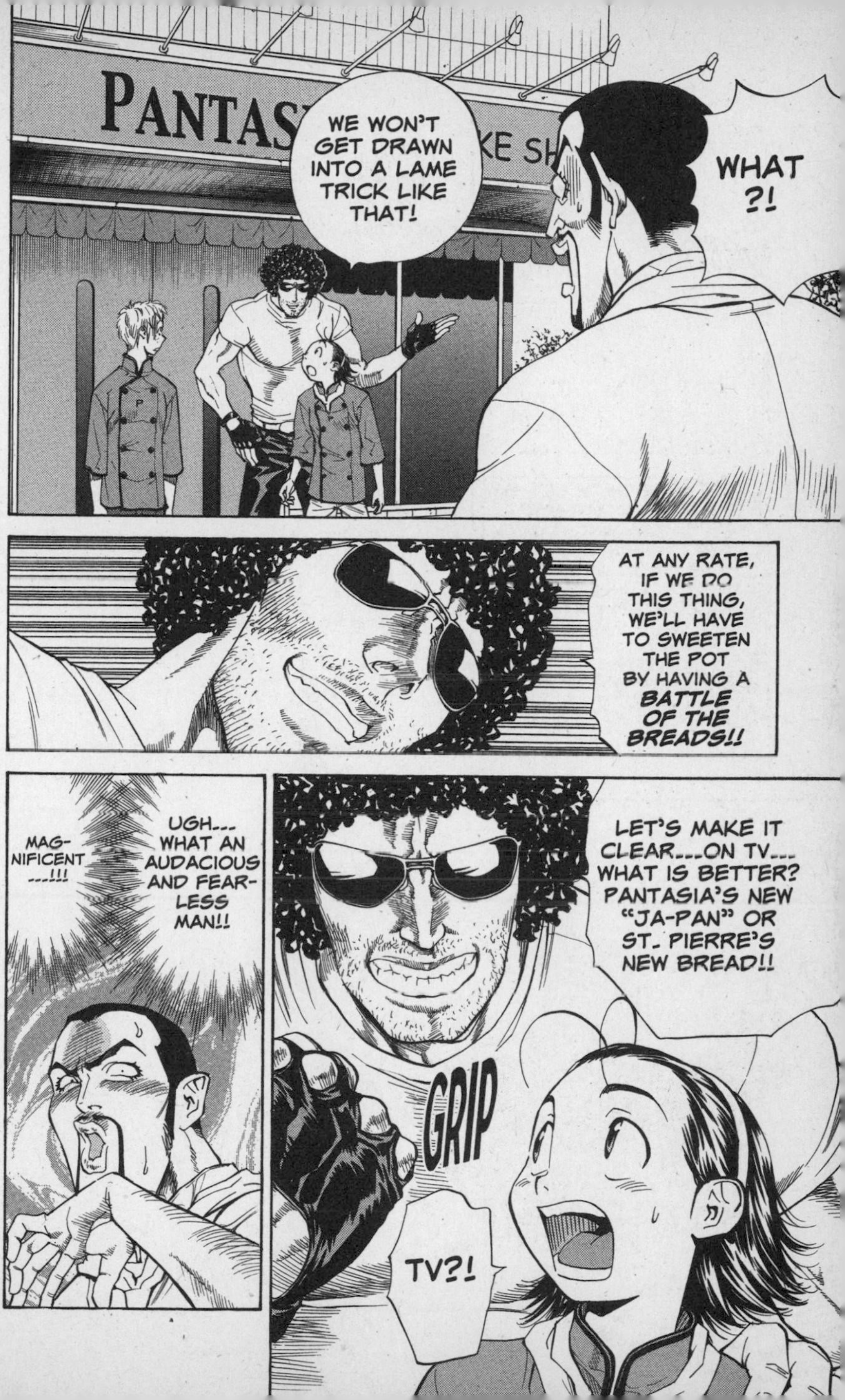

PANTAS
KE SH
WE WON'T GET DRAWN INTO A LAME TRICK LIKE THAT!
WHAT?!
AT ANY RATE, IF WE DO THIS THING, WE'LL HAVE TO SWEETEN THE POT BY HAVING A BATTLE OF THE BREADS!!
LET'S MAKE IT CLEAR...ON TV... WHAT IS BETTER? PANTASIA'S NEW "JA-PAN" OR ST. PIERRE'S NEW BREAD!!
GRIP
TV?!
UGH... WHAT AN AUDACIOUS AND FEAR-LESS MAN!!
MAG-NIFICENT...!!!

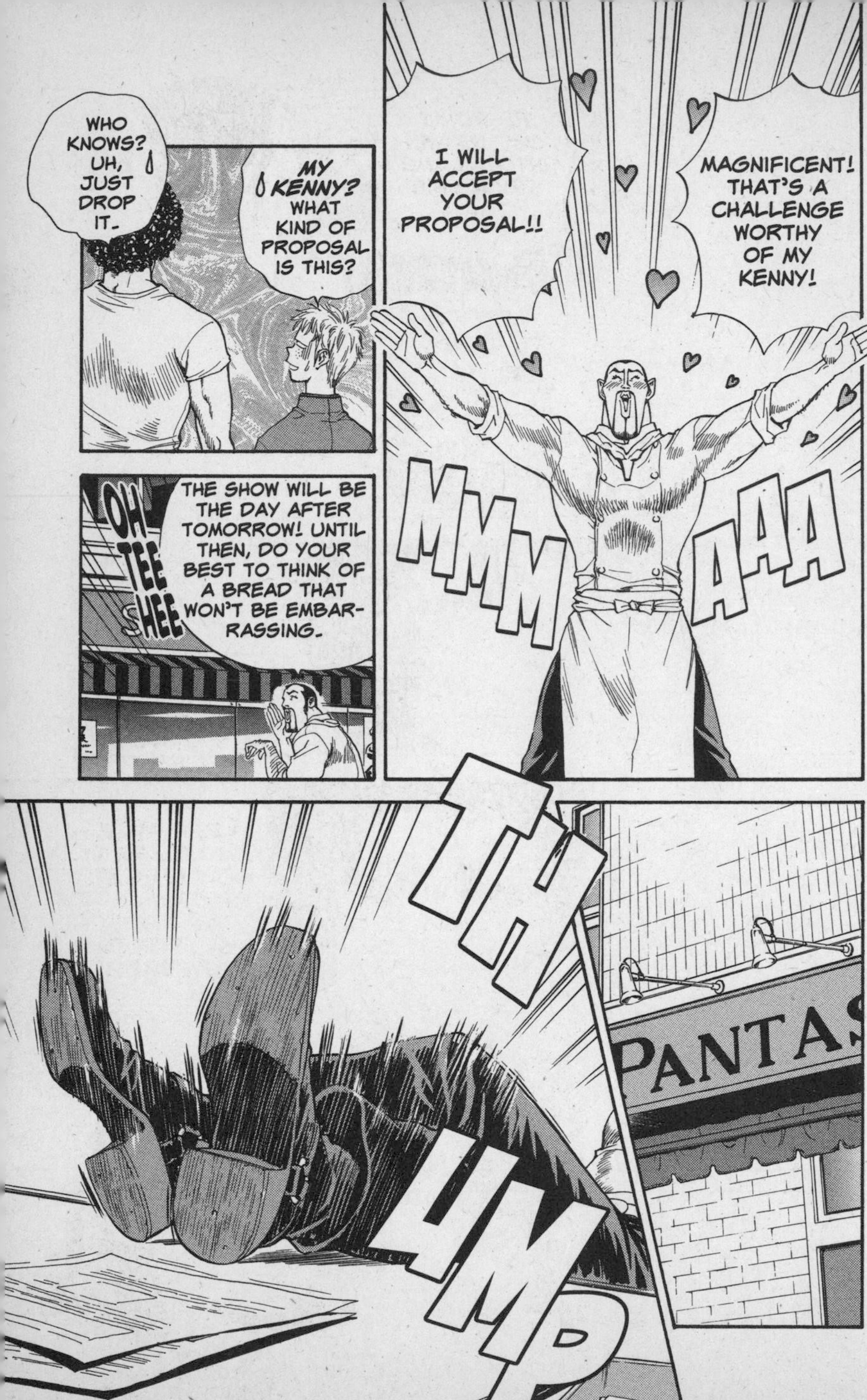
MAGNIFICENT! THAT'S A CHALLENGE WORTHY OF MY KENNY!
I WILL ACCEPT YOUR PROPOSAL!!
MMMAAA
MY KENNY? WHAT KIND OF PROPOSAL IS THIS?
WHO KNOWS? UH, JUST DROP IT.
THE SHOW WILL BE THE DAY AFTER TOMORROW! UNTIL THEN, DO YOUR BEST TO THINK OF A BREAD THAT WON'T BE EMBAR-RASSING.
OH TEE SHEE
THUMP
PANTAS

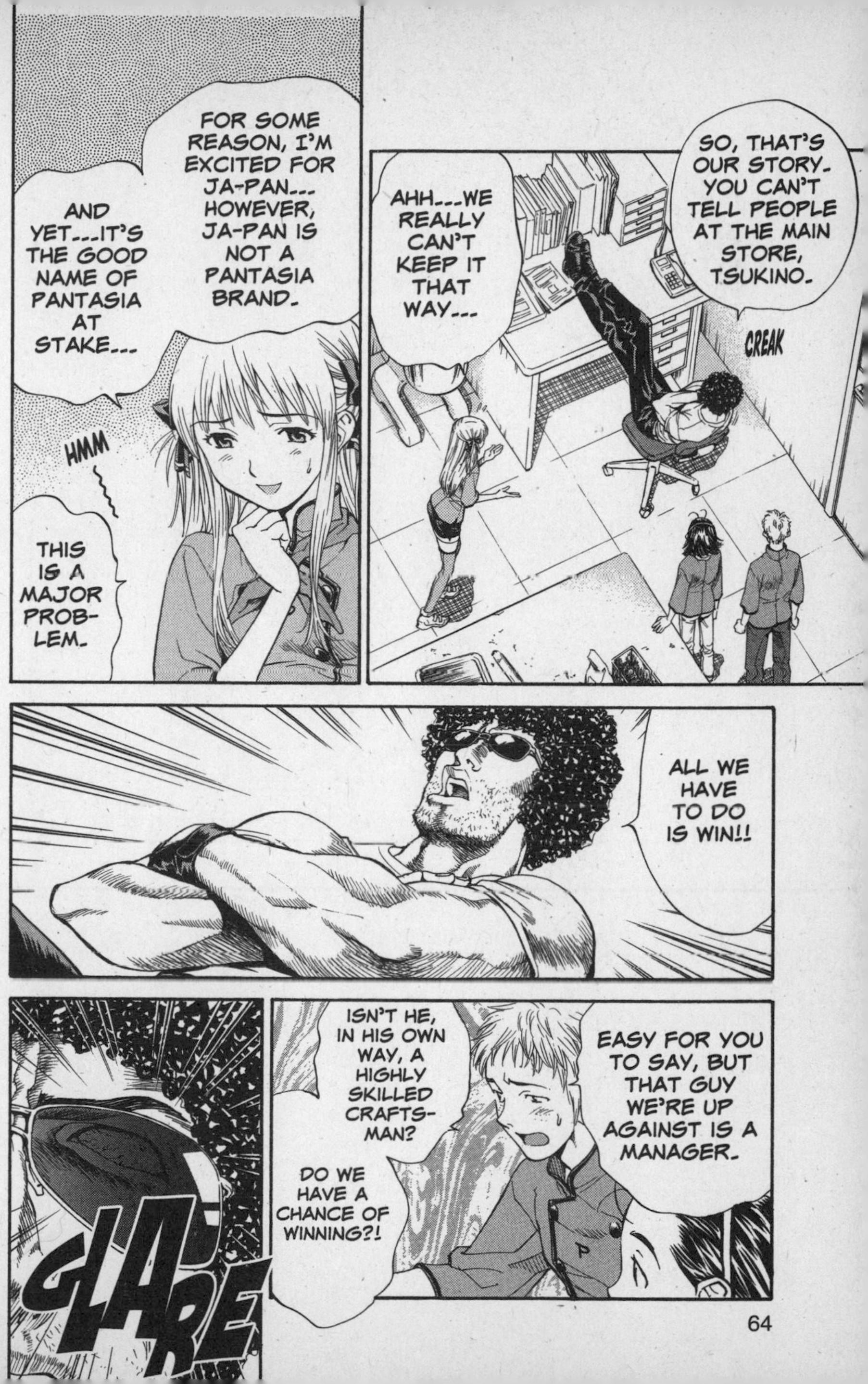
SO, THAT'S OUR STORY. YOU CAN'T TELL PEOPLE AT THE MAIN STORE, TSUKINO.
CREAK
AHH...WE REALLY CAN'T KEEP IT THAT WAY...
FOR SOME REASON, I'M EXCITED FOR JA-PAN... HOWEVER, JA-PAN IS NOT A PANTASIA BRAND.
AND YET...IT'S THE GOOD NAME OF PANTASIA AT STAKE...
HMM
THIS IS A MAJOR PROB-LEM.
ALL WE HAVE TO DO IS WIN!!
EASY FOR YOU TO SAY, BUT THAT GUY WE'RE UP AGAINST IS A MANAGER.
ISN'T HE, IN HIS OWN WAY, A HIGHLY SKILLED CRAFTS-MAN?
DO WE HAVE A CHANCE OF WINNING?!
GLARE

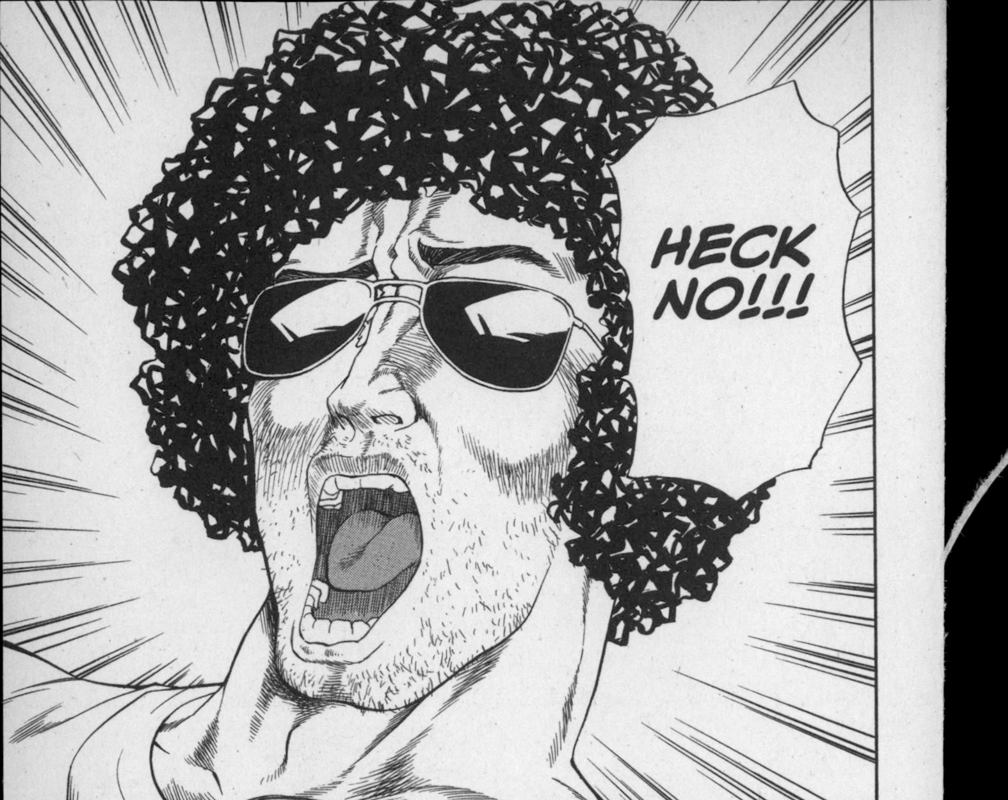
HECK NO!!!

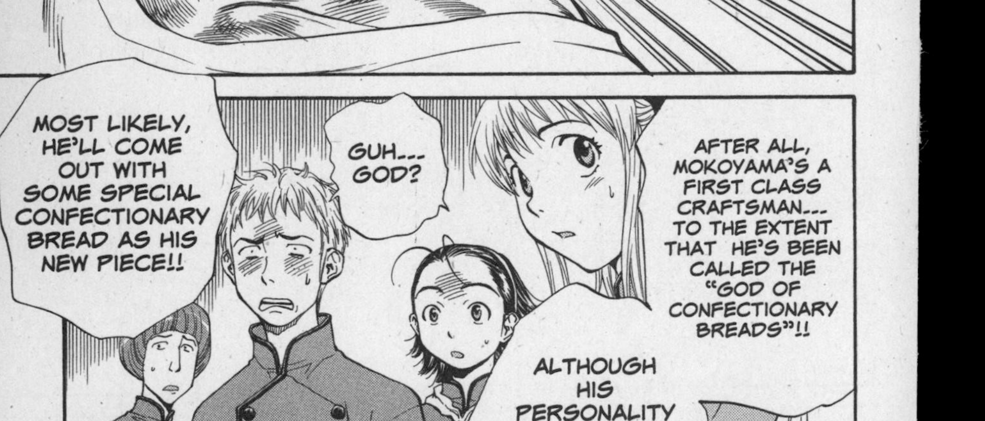
AFTER ALL, MOKOYAMA'S A FIRST CLASS CRAFTSMAN... TO THE EXTENT THAT HE'S BEEN CALLED THE "GOD OF CONFECTIONARY BREADS"!!
GUH... GOD?
MOST LIKELY, HE'LL COME OUT WITH SOME SPECIAL CONFECTIONARY BREAD AS HIS NEW PIECE!!
ALTHOUGH HIS PERSONALITY IS... SPECIAL, HIS SKILLS ARE FOR REAL!!

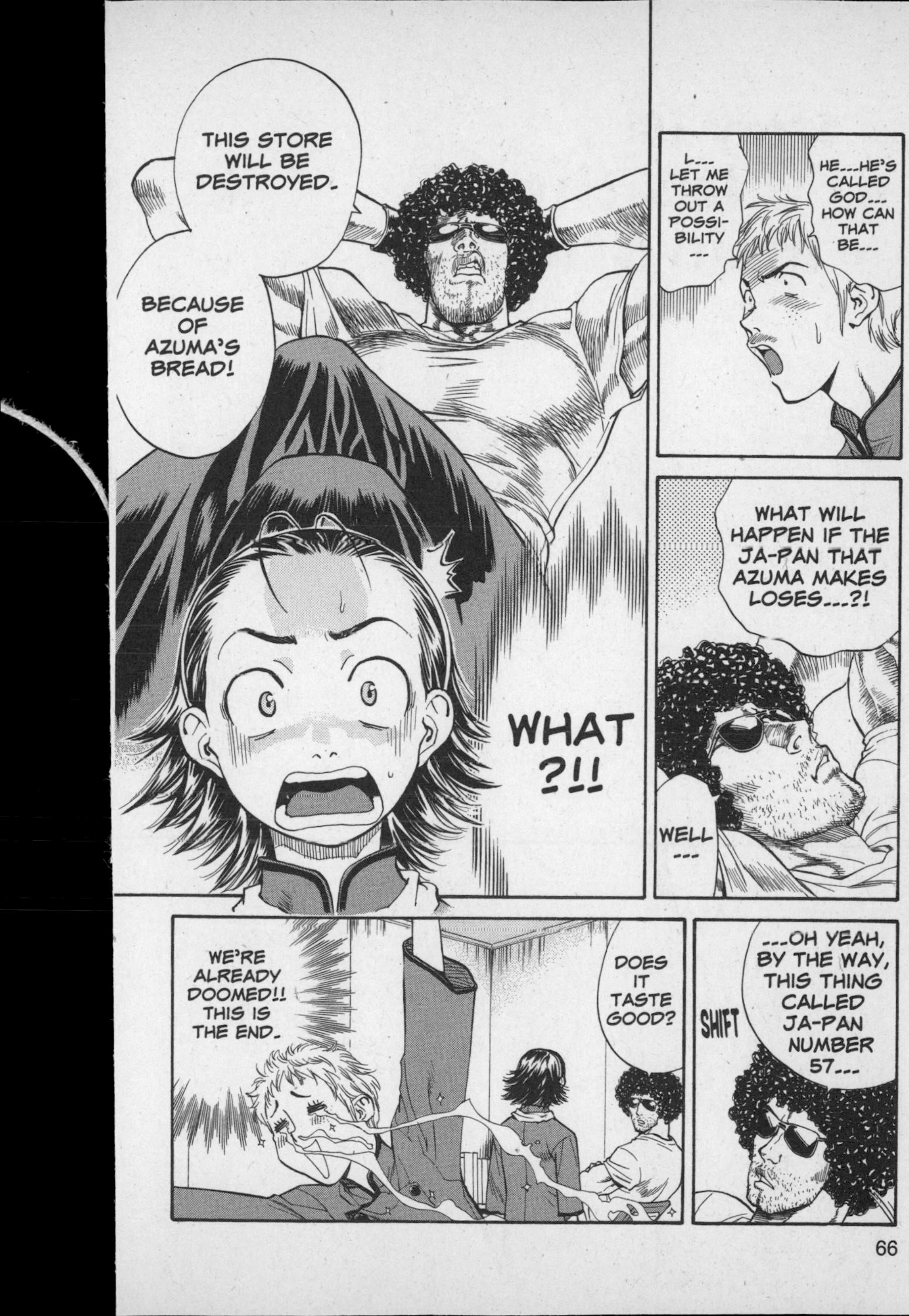

HE...HE'S CALLED GOD... HOW CAN THAT BE...
L... LET ME THROW OUT A POSSIBILITY...
WHAT WILL HAPPEN IF THE JA-PAN THAT AZUMA MAKES LOSES...?!
WELL...
THIS STORE WILL BE DESTROYED.
BECAUSE OF AZUMA'S BREAD!
WHAT ?!!
...OH YEAH, BY THE WAY, THIS THING CALLED JA-PAN NUMBER 57...
SHIFT
DOES IT TASTE GOOD?
WE'RE ALREADY DOOMED!! THIS IS THE END.

Story 10: It's the Main Store!!

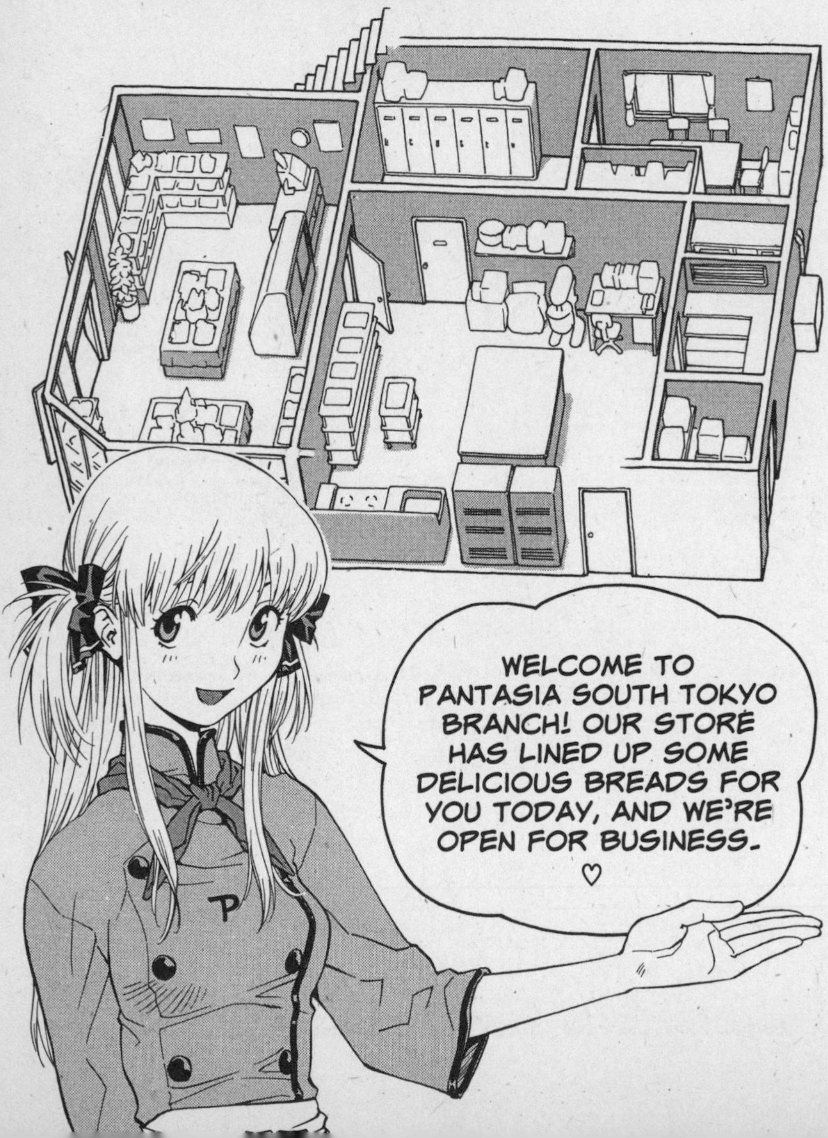
WELCOME TO PANTASIA SOUTH TOKYO BRANCH! OUR STORE HAS LINED UP SOME DELICIOUS BREADS FOR YOU TODAY, AND WE'RE OPEN FOR BUSINESS. ♡
P

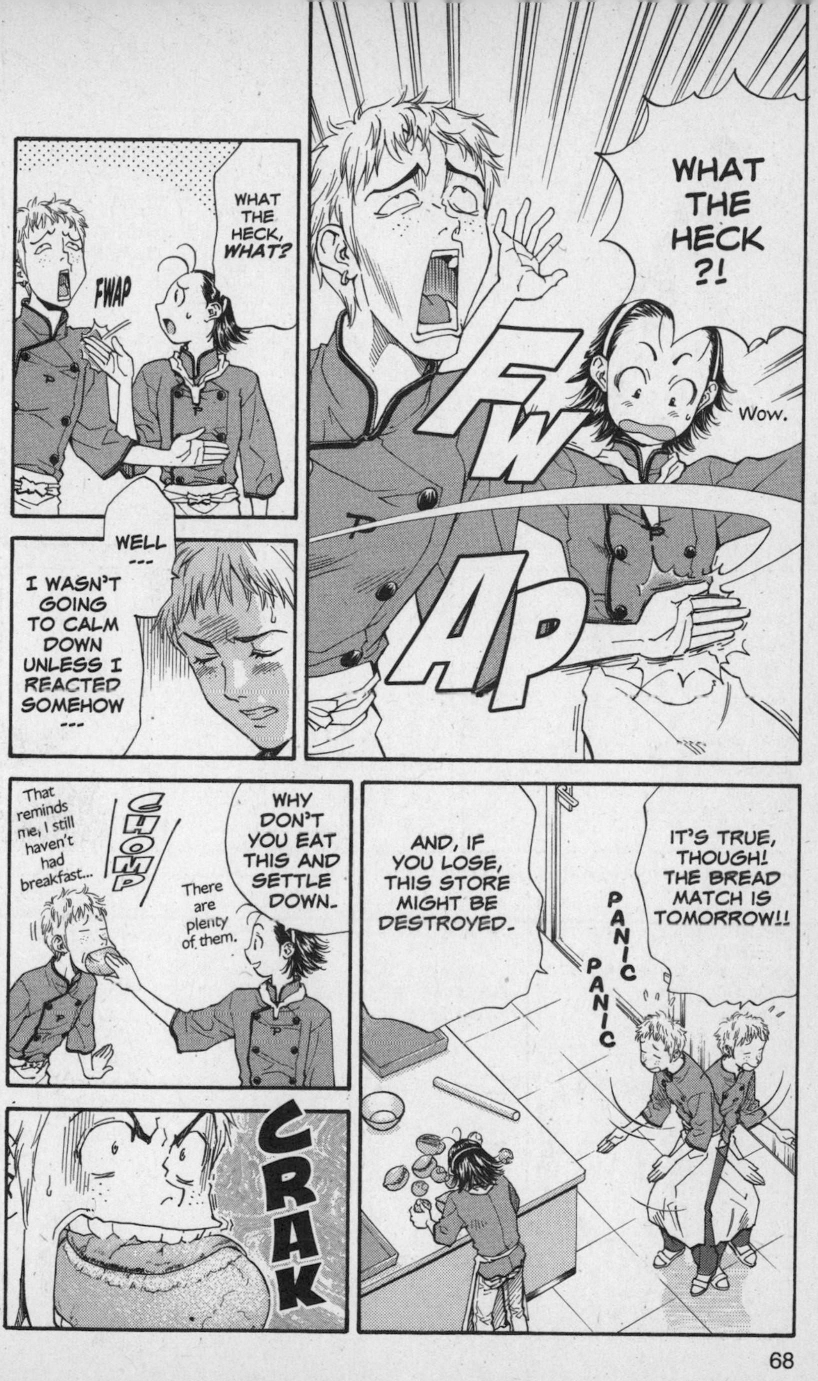
WHAT THE HECK ?!
Wow.
FWAP
WHAT THE HECK, WHAT?
FWAP
WELL ---
I WASN'T GOING TO CALM DOWN UNLESS I REACTED SOMEHOW ---
IT'S TRUE, THOUGH! THE BREAD MATCH IS TOMORROW!!
PANIC PANIC
AND, IF YOU LOSE, THIS STORE MIGHT BE DESTROYED.
WHY DON'T YOU EAT THIS AND SETTLE DOWN.
There are plenty of them.
CHOMP
That reminds me, I still haven't had breakfast...
CRAK

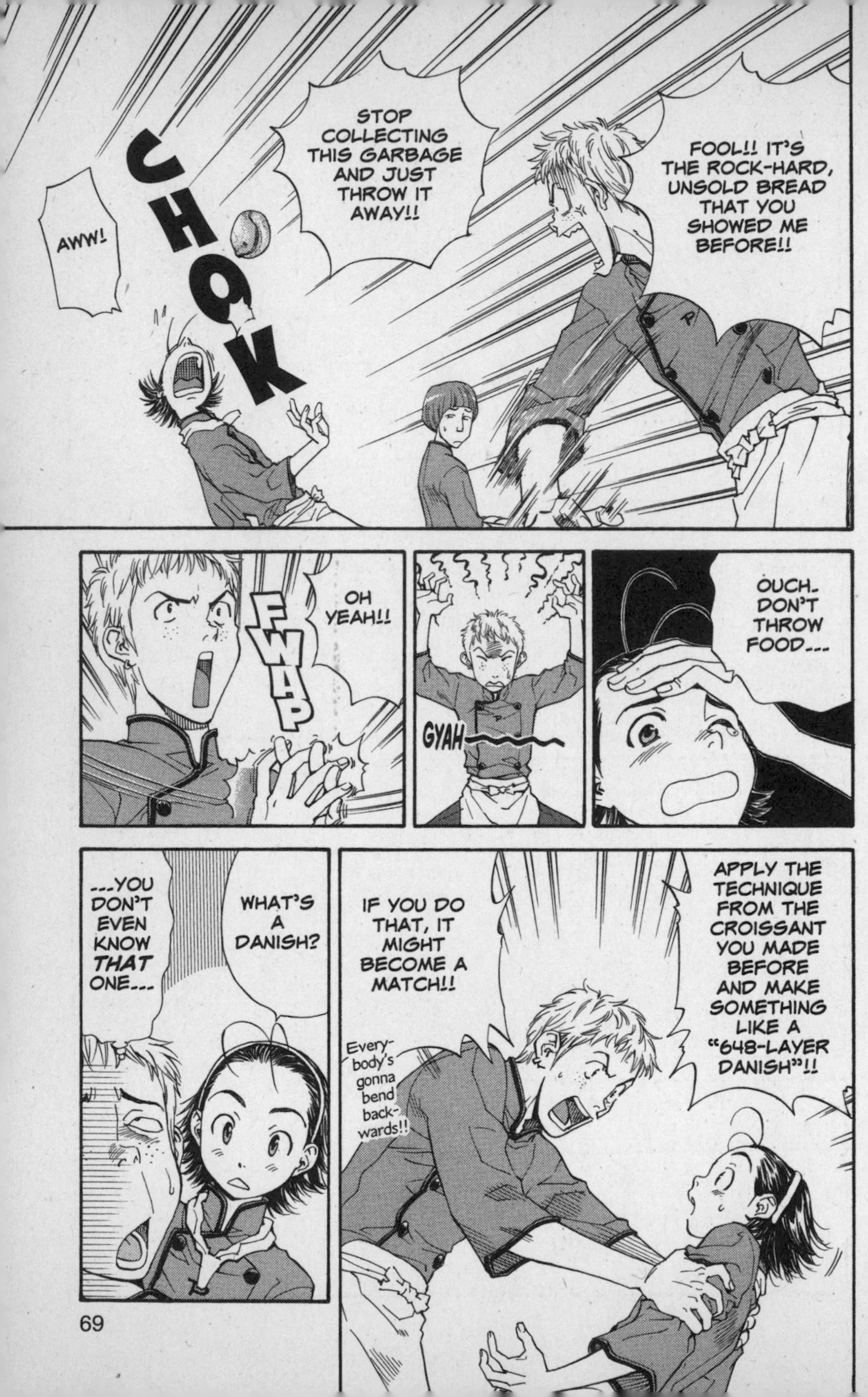
FOOL!! IT'S THE ROCK-HARD, UNSOLD BREAD THAT YOU SHOWED ME BEFORE!!
STOP COLLECTING THIS GARBAGE AND JUST THROW IT AWAY!!
CHOK
AWW!
OUCH. DON'T THROW FOOD...
GYAH
OH YEAH!!
FWAP
APPLY THE TECHNIQUE FROM THE CROISSANT YOU MADE BEFORE AND MAKE SOMETHING LIKE A "648-LAYER DANISH"!!
IF YOU DO THAT, IT MIGHT BECOME A MATCH!!
Everybody's gonna bend backwards!!
WHAT'S A DANISH?
...YOU DON'T EVEN KNOW *THAT* ONE...

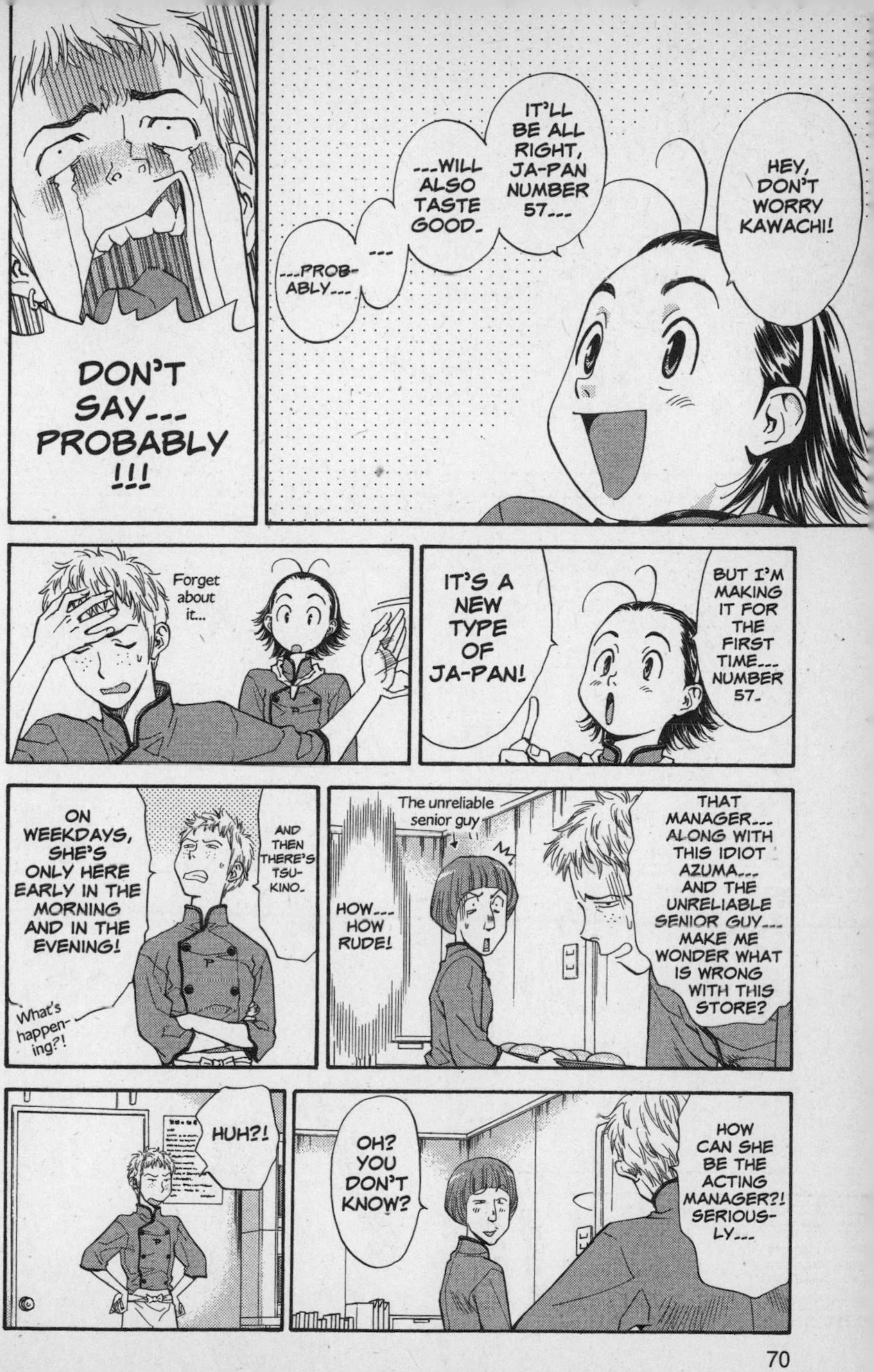
HEY, DON'T WORRY KAWACHI!
IT'LL BE ALL RIGHT, JA-PAN NUMBER 57...
...WILL ALSO TASTE GOOD.
...
...PROB-ABLY...
DON'T SAY... PROBABLY!!!
BUT I'M MAKING IT FOR THE FIRST TIME... NUMBER 57.
IT'S A NEW TYPE OF JA-PAN!
Forget about it...
THAT MANAGER... ALONG WITH THIS IDIOT AZUMA... AND THE UNRELIABLE SENIOR GUY... MAKE ME WONDER WHAT IS WRONG WITH THIS STORE?
The unreliable senior guy
HOW... HOW RUDE!
AND THEN THERE'S TSU-KINO.
ON WEEKDAYS, SHE'S ONLY HERE EARLY IN THE MORNING AND IN THE EVENING!
What's happen-ing?!
HOW CAN SHE BE THE ACTING MANAGER?! SERIOUS-LY...
OH? YOU DON'T KNOW?
HUH?!

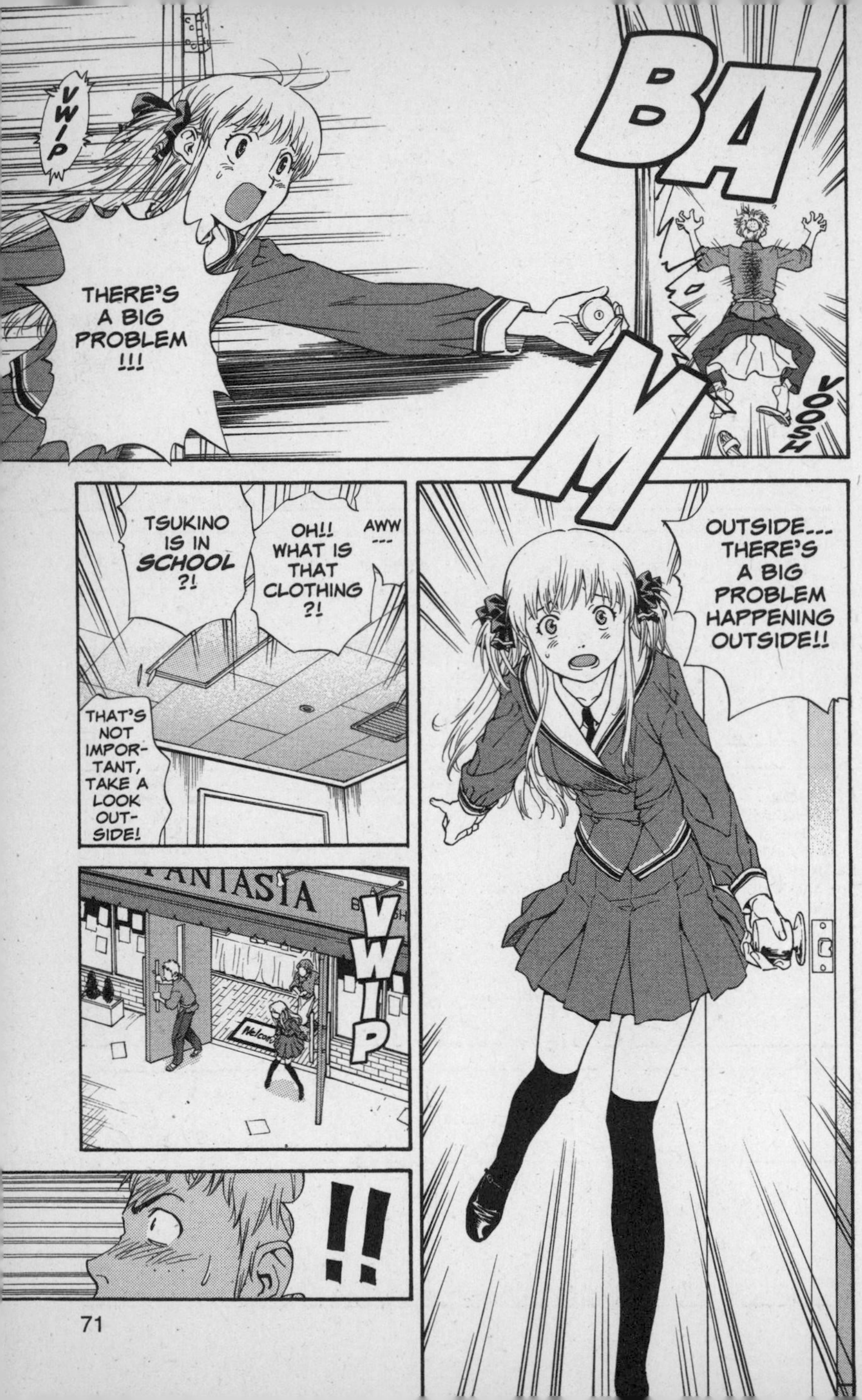
BAM
VOOSH
VWIP
THERE'S A BIG PROBLEM !!!
OUTSIDE... THERE'S A BIG PROBLEM HAPPENING OUTSIDE!!
AWW ---
OH!! WHAT IS THAT CLOTHING ?!
TSUKINO IS IN SCHOOL ?!
THAT'S NOT IMPORTANT, TAKE A LOOK OUTSIDE!
FANTASIA
VWIP
!!

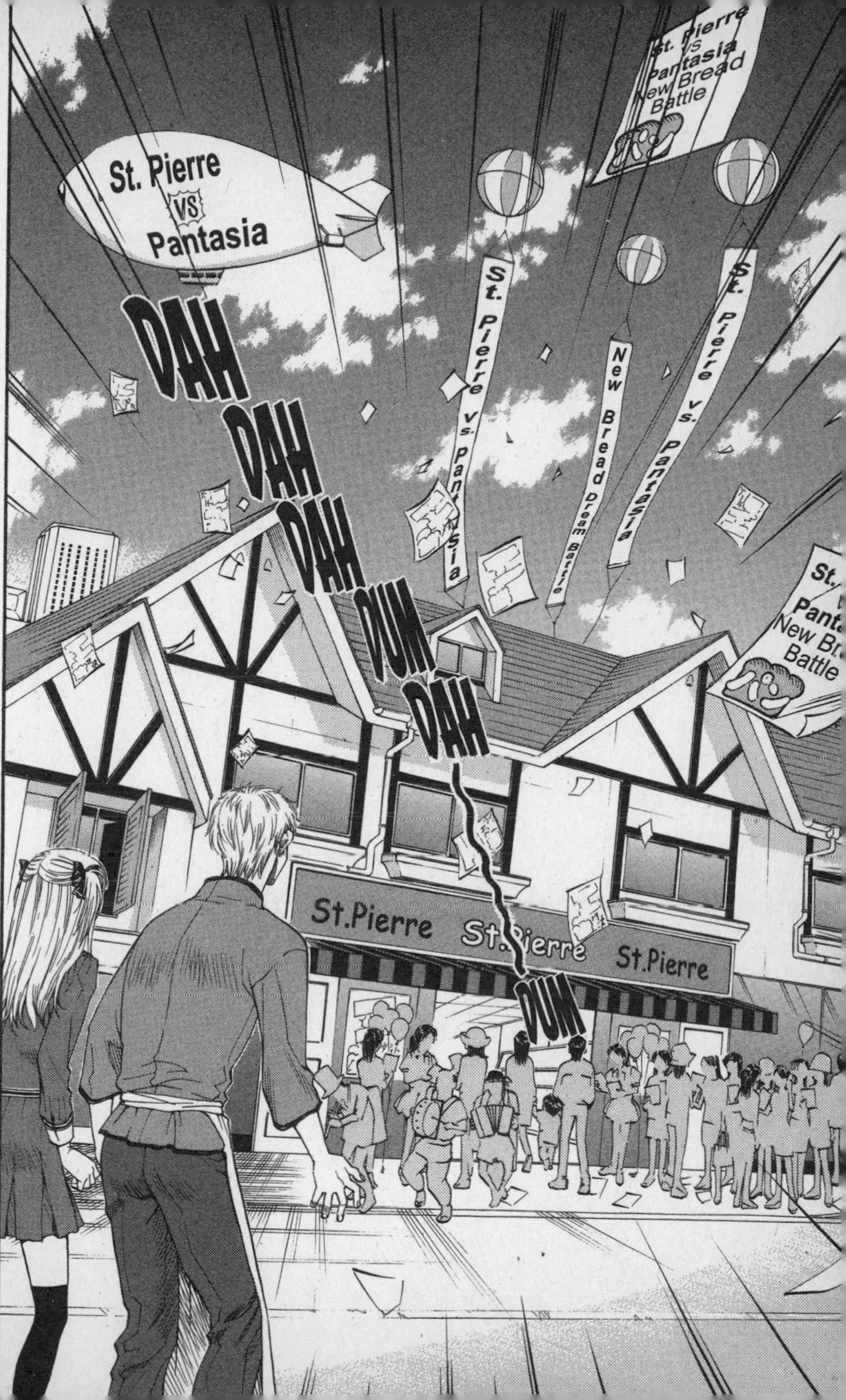
St. Pierre VS Pantasia New Bread Battle
St. Pierre VS Pantasia
St. Pierre vs. Pantasia
New Bread Dream Battle
St. Pierre vs. Pantasia
DAH DAH DAH DUM DAH DUM
St.Pierre
St.Pierre
St.Pierre

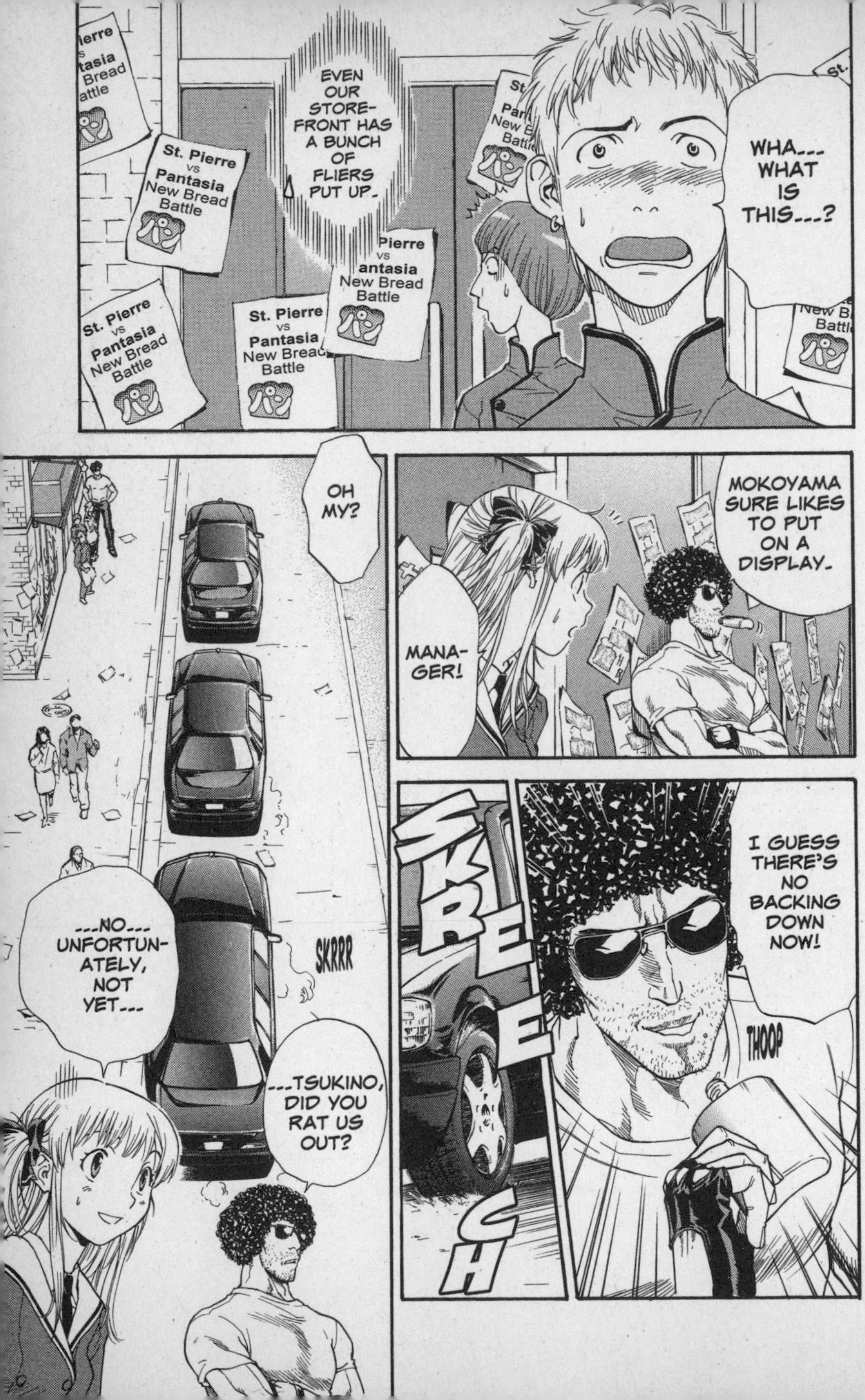
WHA... WHAT IS THIS...?
EVEN OUR STOREFRONT HAS A BUNCH OF FLIERS PUT UP.
St. Pierre vs Pantasia New Bread Battle
MOKOYAMA SURE LIKES TO PUT ON A DISPLAY.
MANAGER!
I GUESS THERE'S NO BACKING DOWN NOW!
THOOP
SKREEECH
OH MY?
...TSUKINO, DID YOU RAT US OUT?
...NO... UNFORTUNATELY, NOT YET...
SKRRR

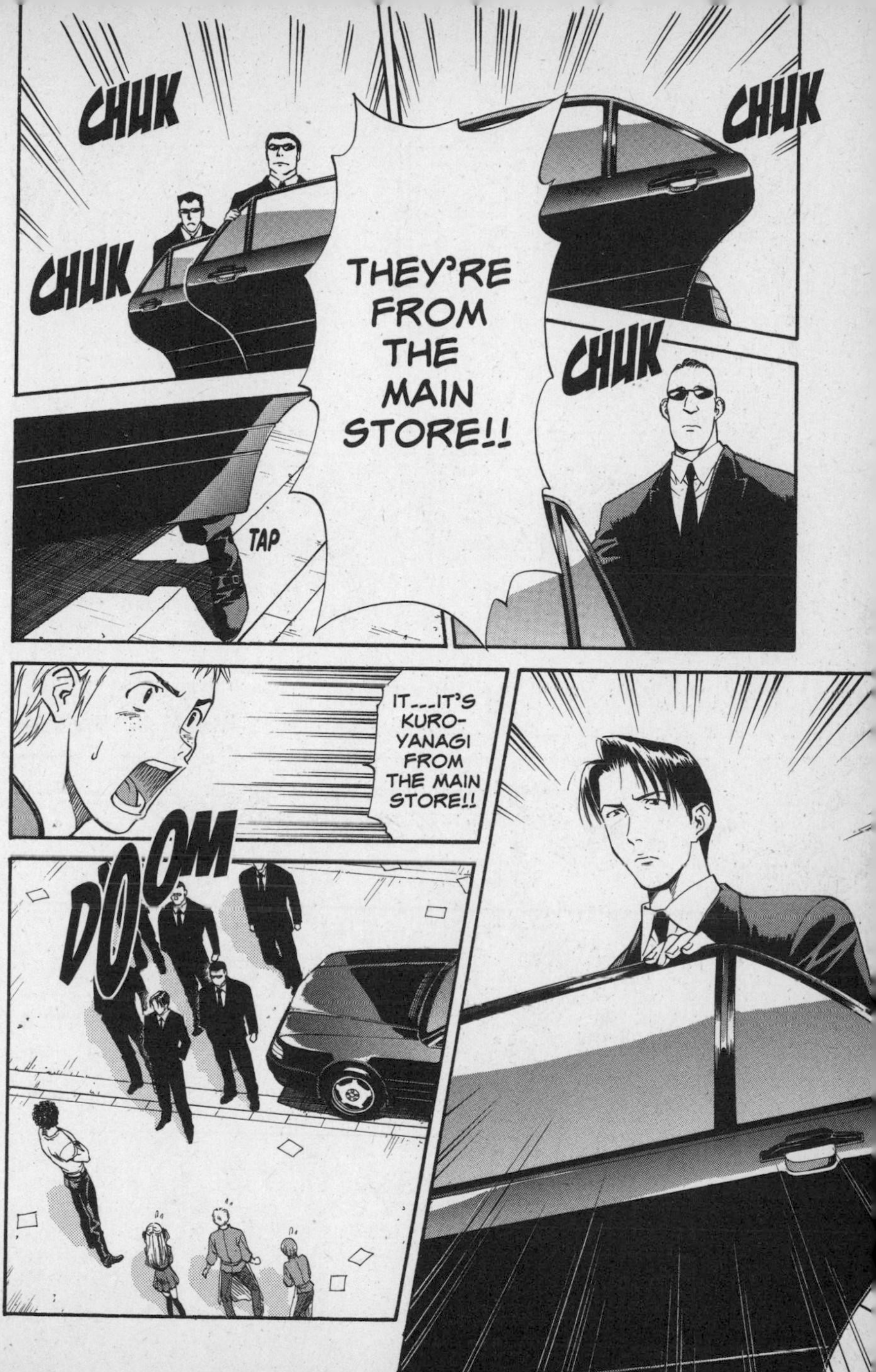
CHUK
CHUK
CHUK
THEY'RE FROM THE MAIN STORE!!
CHUK
TAP
IT---IT'S KURO-YANAGI FROM THE MAIN STORE!!
DOOM

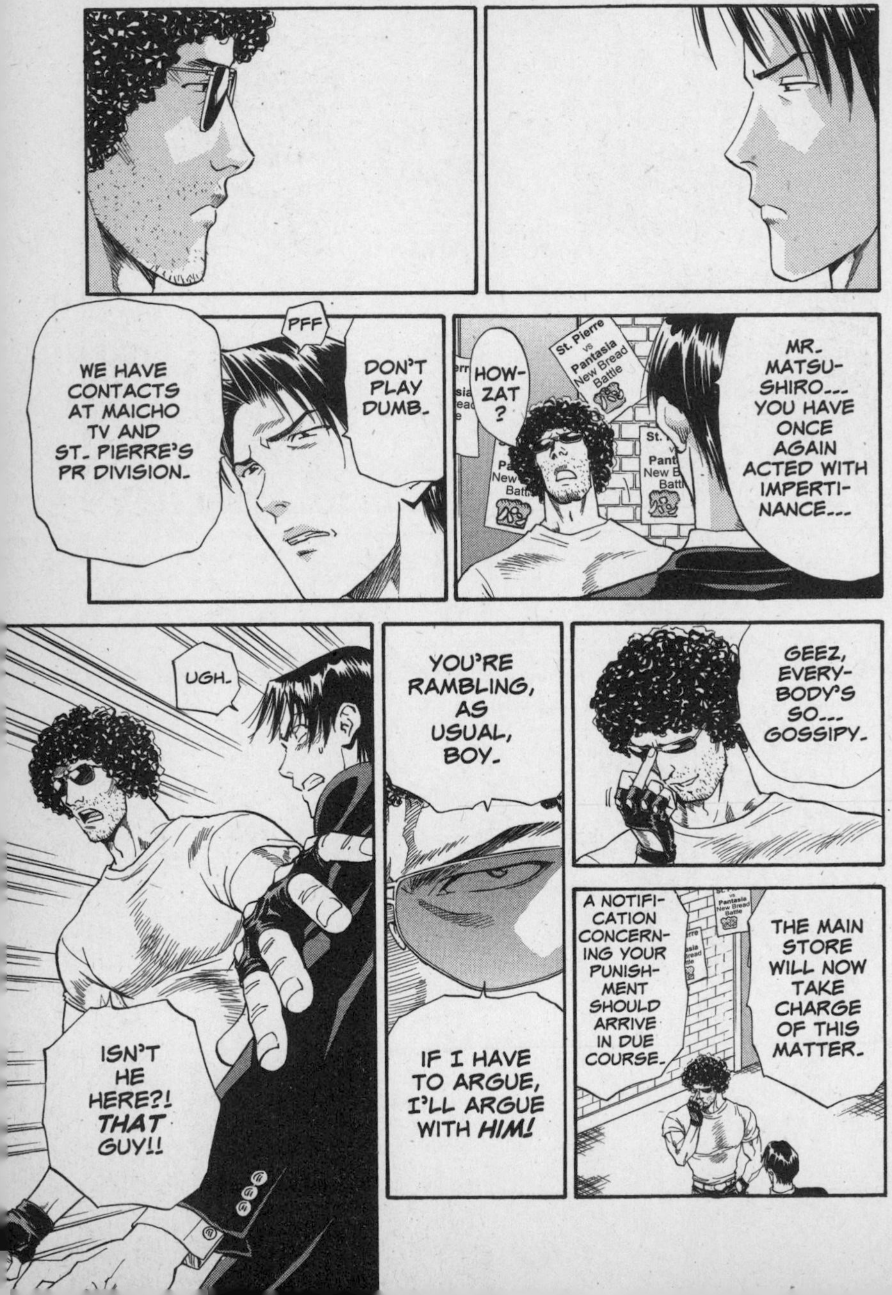
MR. MATSUSHIRO... YOU HAVE ONCE AGAIN ACTED WITH IMPERTINANCE...
HOW-ZAT?
St. Pierre vs Pantasia New Bread Battle
DON'T PLAY DUMB.
PFF
WE HAVE CONTACTS AT MAICHO TV AND ST. PIERRE'S PR DIVISION.
GEEZ, EVERYBODY'S SO... GOSSIPY.
THE MAIN STORE WILL NOW TAKE CHARGE OF THIS MATTER.
A NOTIFICATION CONCERNING YOUR PUNISHMENT SHOULD ARRIVE IN DUE COURSE.
YOU'RE RAMBLING, AS USUAL, BOY.
IF I HAVE TO ARGUE, I'LL ARGUE WITH *HIM!*
UGH.
ISN'T HE HERE?! *THAT* GUY!!

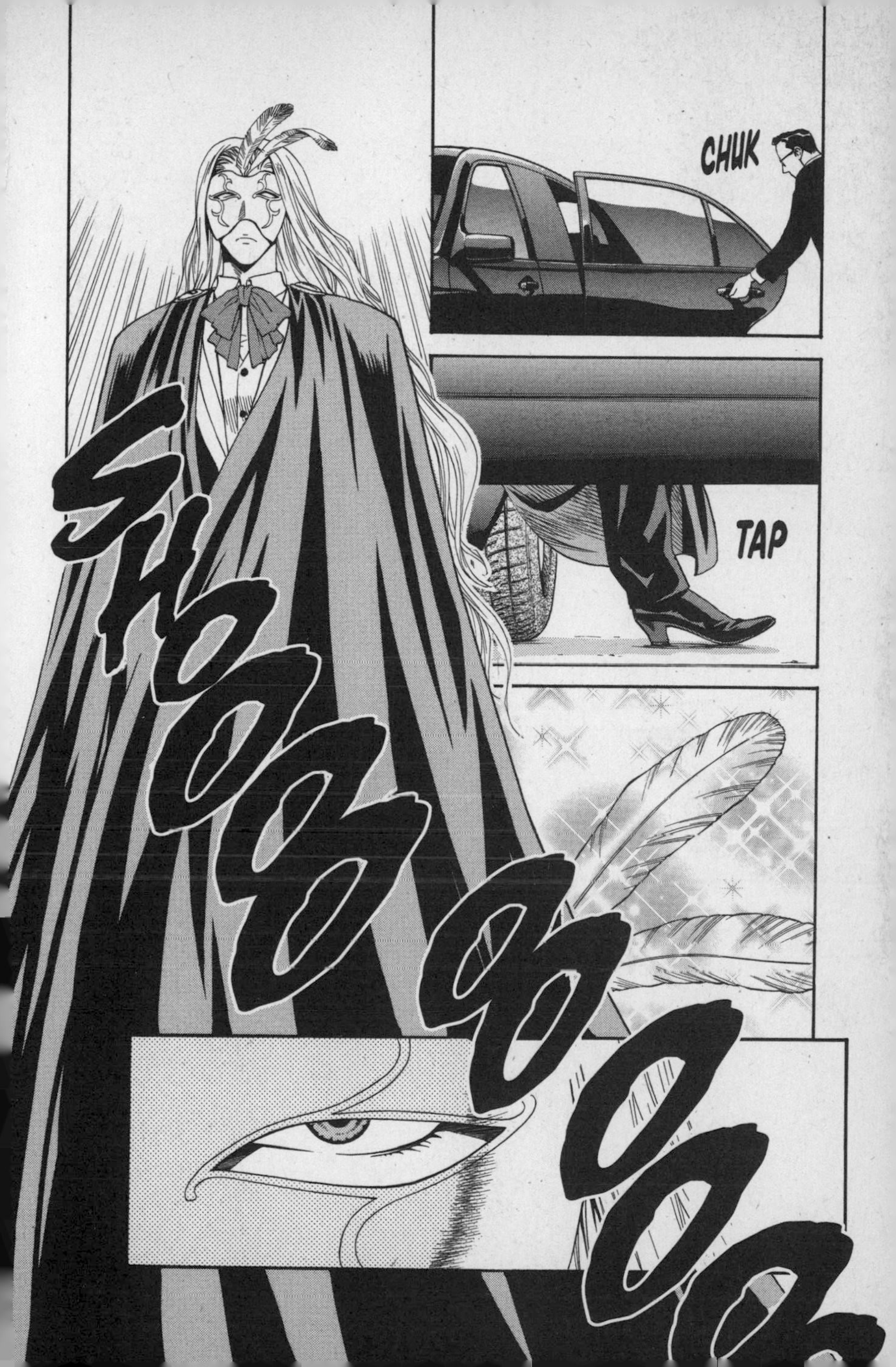
CHUK
TAP
SHOOOOOOOOOOO

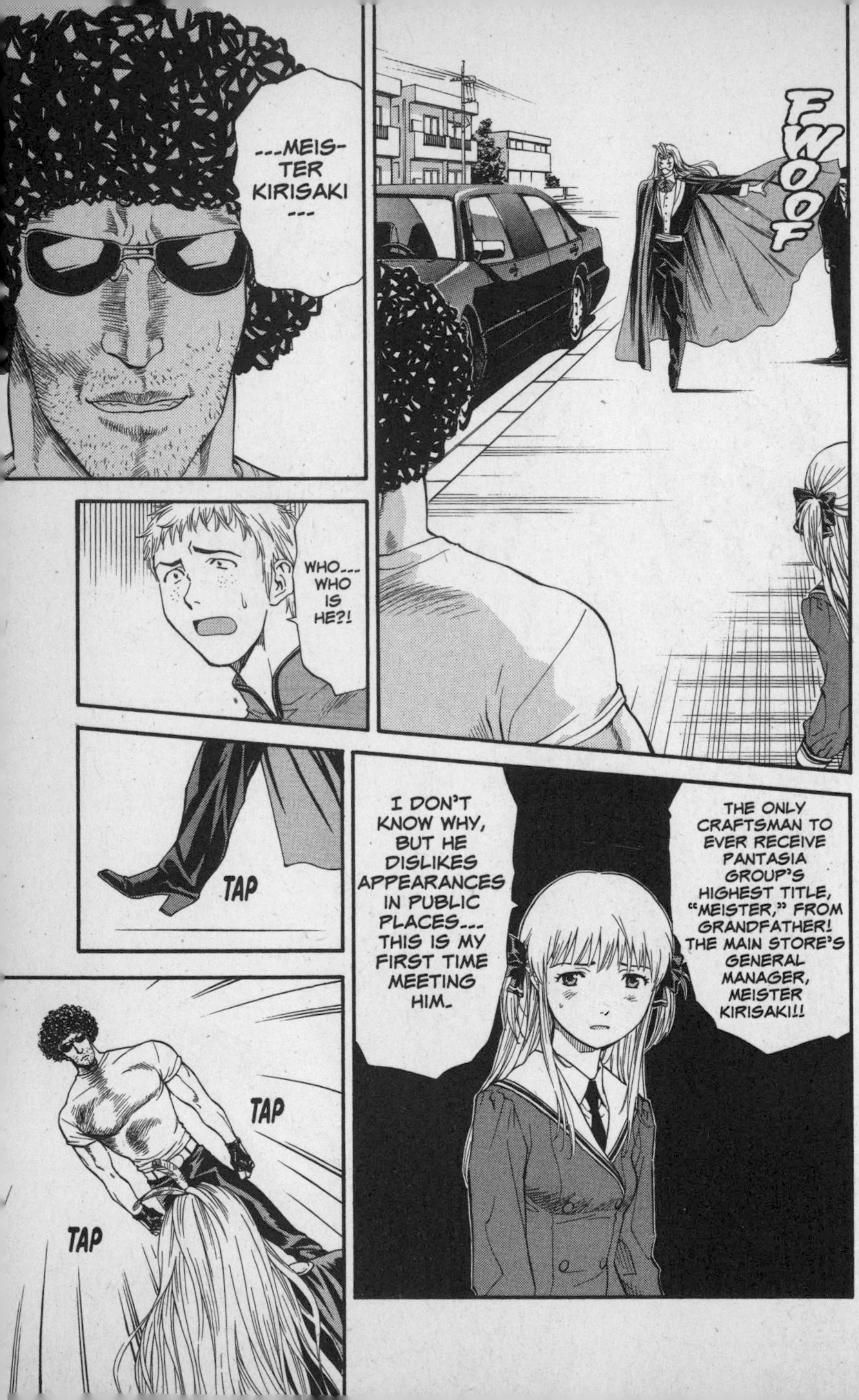
FWOOF
---MEISTER KIRISAKI ---
WHO... WHO IS HE?!
THE ONLY CRAFTSMAN TO EVER RECEIVE PANTASIA GROUP'S HIGHEST TITLE, "MEISTER," FROM GRANDFATHER! THE MAIN STORE'S GENERAL MANAGER, MEISTER KIRISAKI!!
I DON'T KNOW WHY, BUT HE DISLIKES APPEARANCES IN PUBLIC PLACES... THIS IS MY FIRST TIME MEETING HIM.
TAP
TAP
TAP

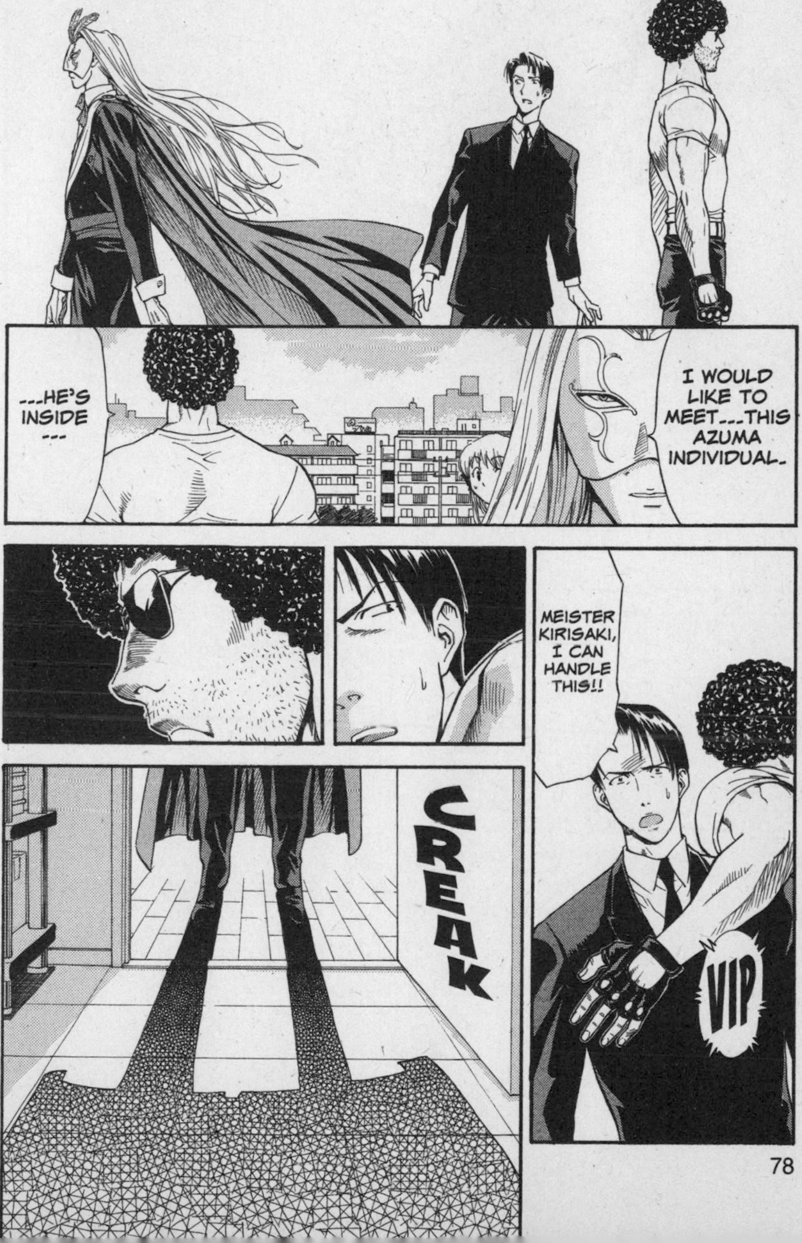
I WOULD LIKE TO MEET... THIS AZUMA INDIVIDUAL.
...HE'S INSIDE...
MEISTER KIRISAKI, I CAN HANDLE THIS!!
VIP
CREAK

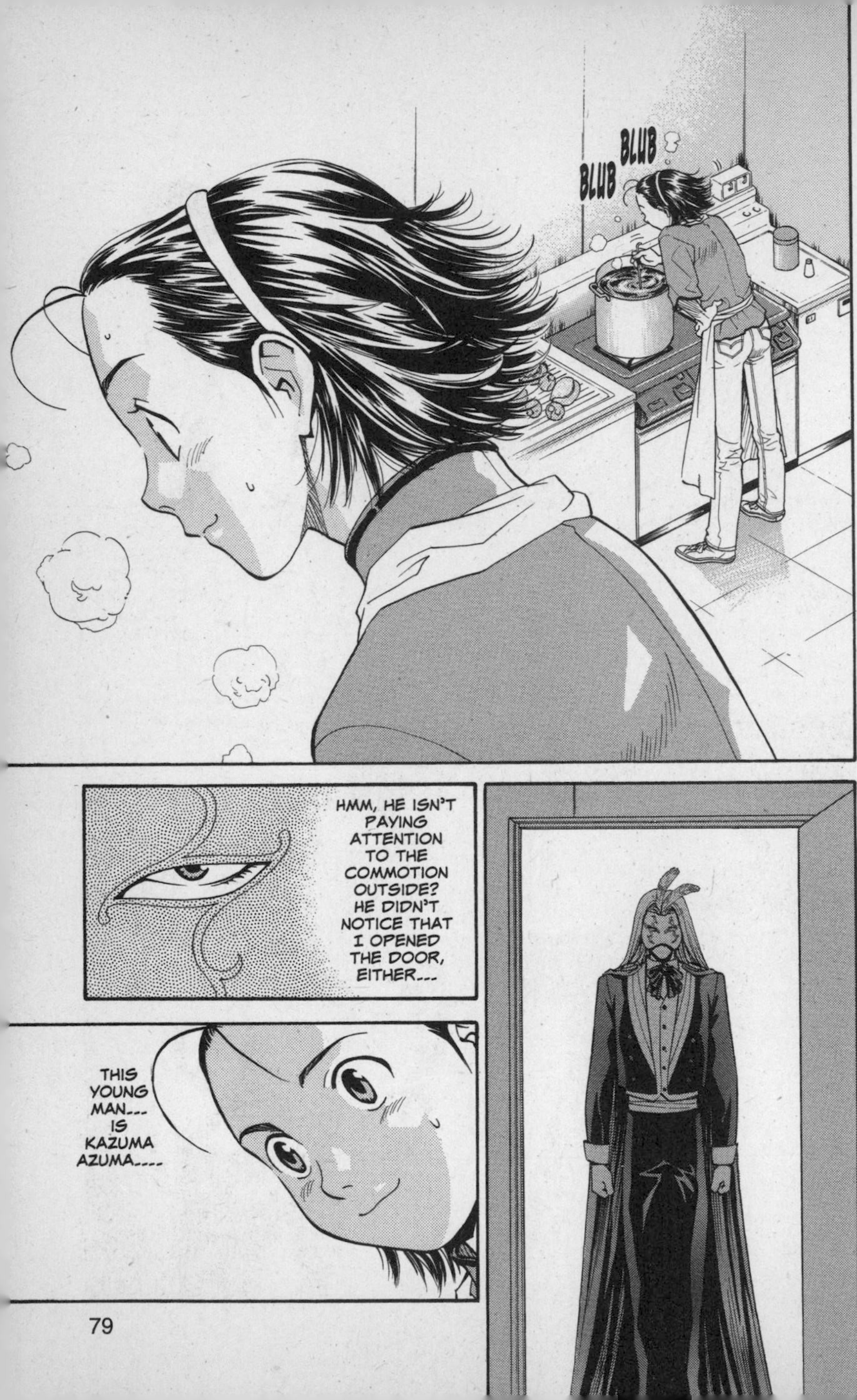
BLUB
BLUB
HMM, HE ISN'T PAYING ATTENTION TO THE COMMOTION OUTSIDE? HE DIDN'T NOTICE THAT I OPENED THE DOOR, EITHER...
THIS YOUNG MAN... IS KAZUMA AZUMA....

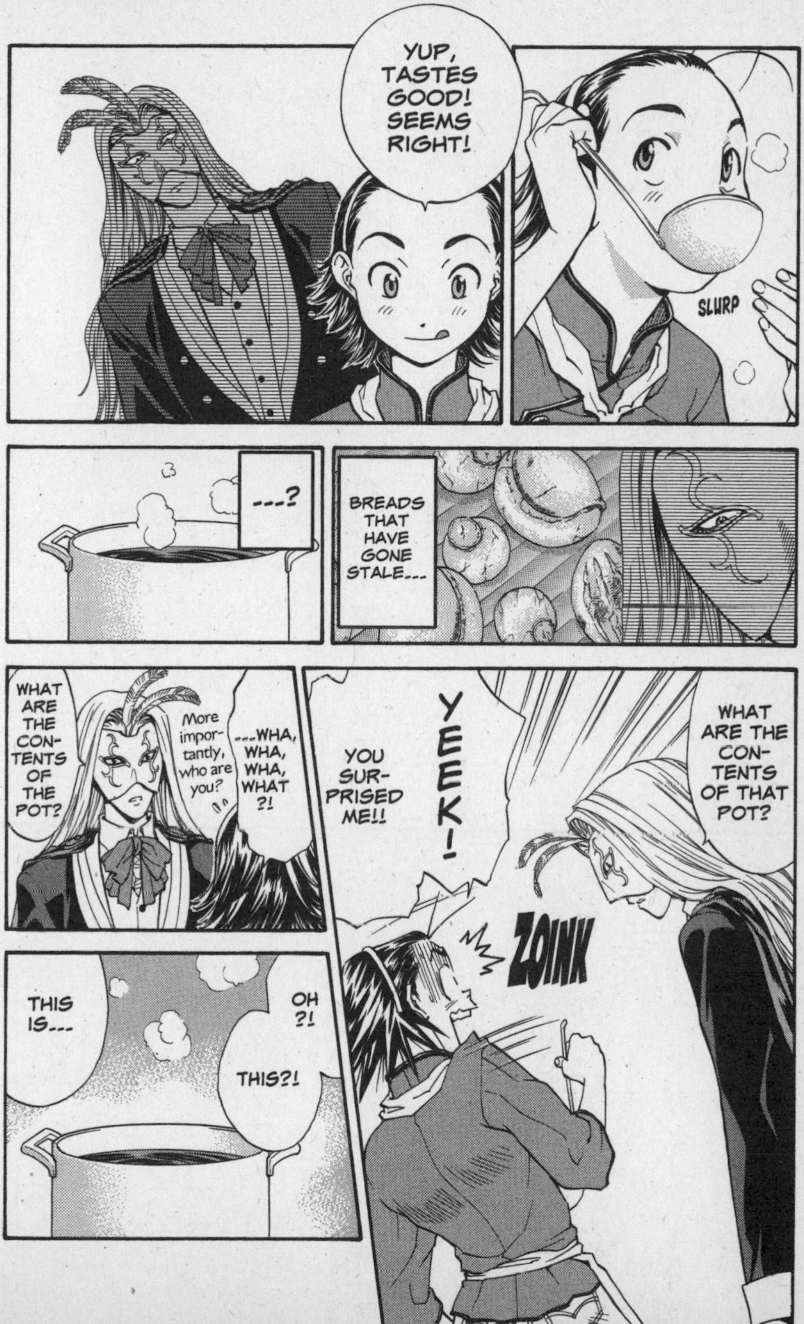
SLURP
YUP, TASTES GOOD! SEEMS RIGHT!
BREADS THAT HAVE GONE STALE...
...?
WHAT ARE THE CONTENTS OF THAT POT?
YEEK!
YOU SURPRISED ME!!
ZOINK
...WHA, WHA, WHA, WHAT ?!
More importantly, who are you?
WHAT ARE THE CONTENTS OF THE POT?
OH?!
THIS?!
THIS IS...

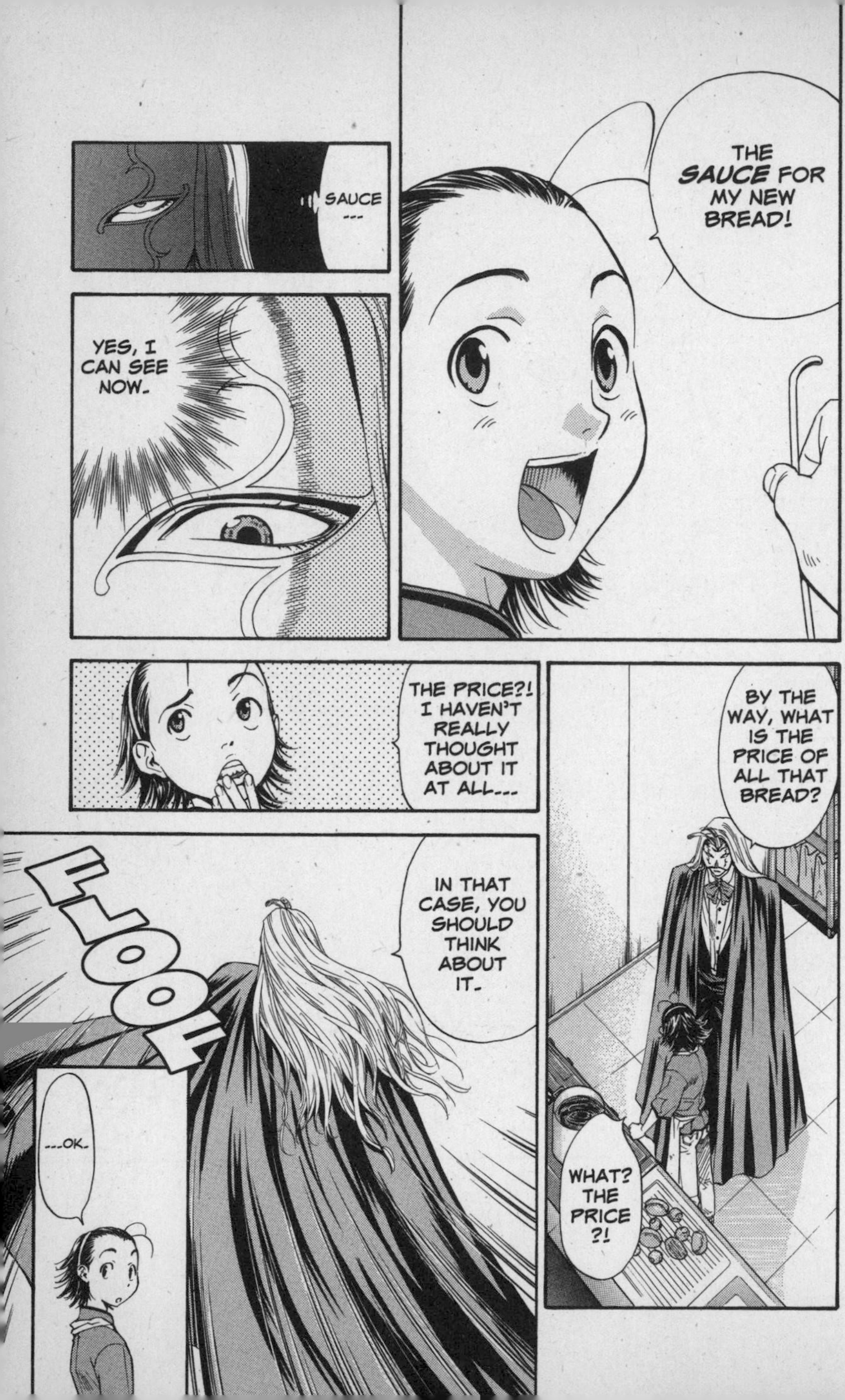
THE SAUCE FOR MY NEW BREAD!
SAUCE ---
YES, I CAN SEE NOW.
BY THE WAY, WHAT IS THE PRICE OF ALL THAT BREAD?
WHAT? THE PRICE?!
THE PRICE?! I HAVEN'T REALLY THOUGHT ABOUT IT AT ALL...
IN THAT CASE, YOU SHOULD THINK ABOUT IT.
FLOOF
...OK.

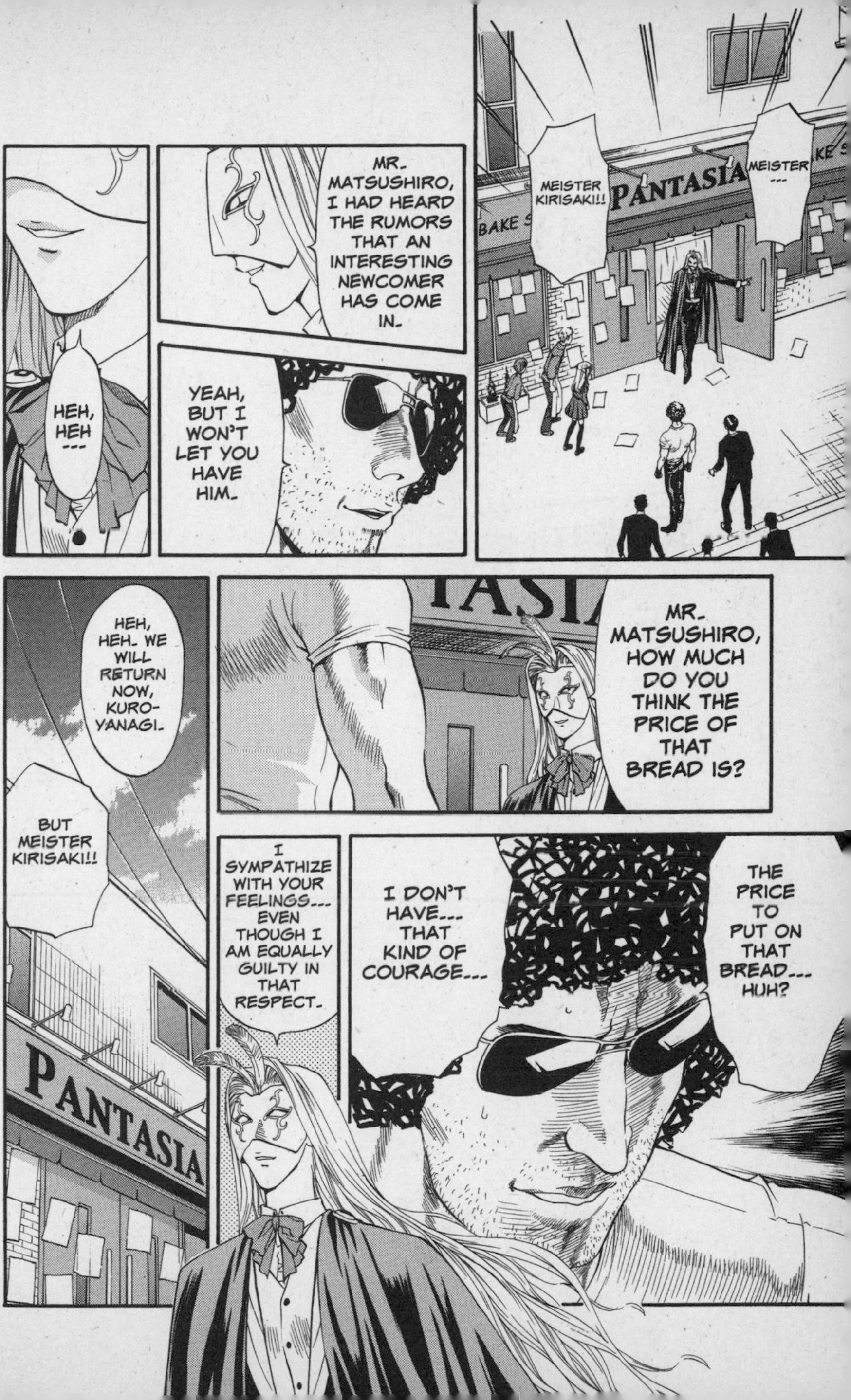
MEISTER ---
MEISTER KIRISAKI!!
PANTASIA
MR. MATSUSHIRO, I HAD HEARD THE RUMORS THAT AN INTERESTING NEWCOMER HAS COME IN.
YEAH, BUT I WON'T LET YOU HAVE HIM.
HEH, HEH ---
MR. MATSUSHIRO, HOW MUCH DO YOU THINK THE PRICE OF THAT BREAD IS?
THE PRICE TO PUT ON THAT BREAD... HUH?
I DON'T HAVE... THAT KIND OF COURAGE...
I SYMPATHIZE WITH YOUR FEELINGS... EVEN THOUGH I AM EQUALLY GUILTY IN THAT RESPECT.
HEH, HEH. WE WILL RETURN NOW, KURO-YANAGI.
BUT MEISTER KIRISAKI!!
PANTASIA

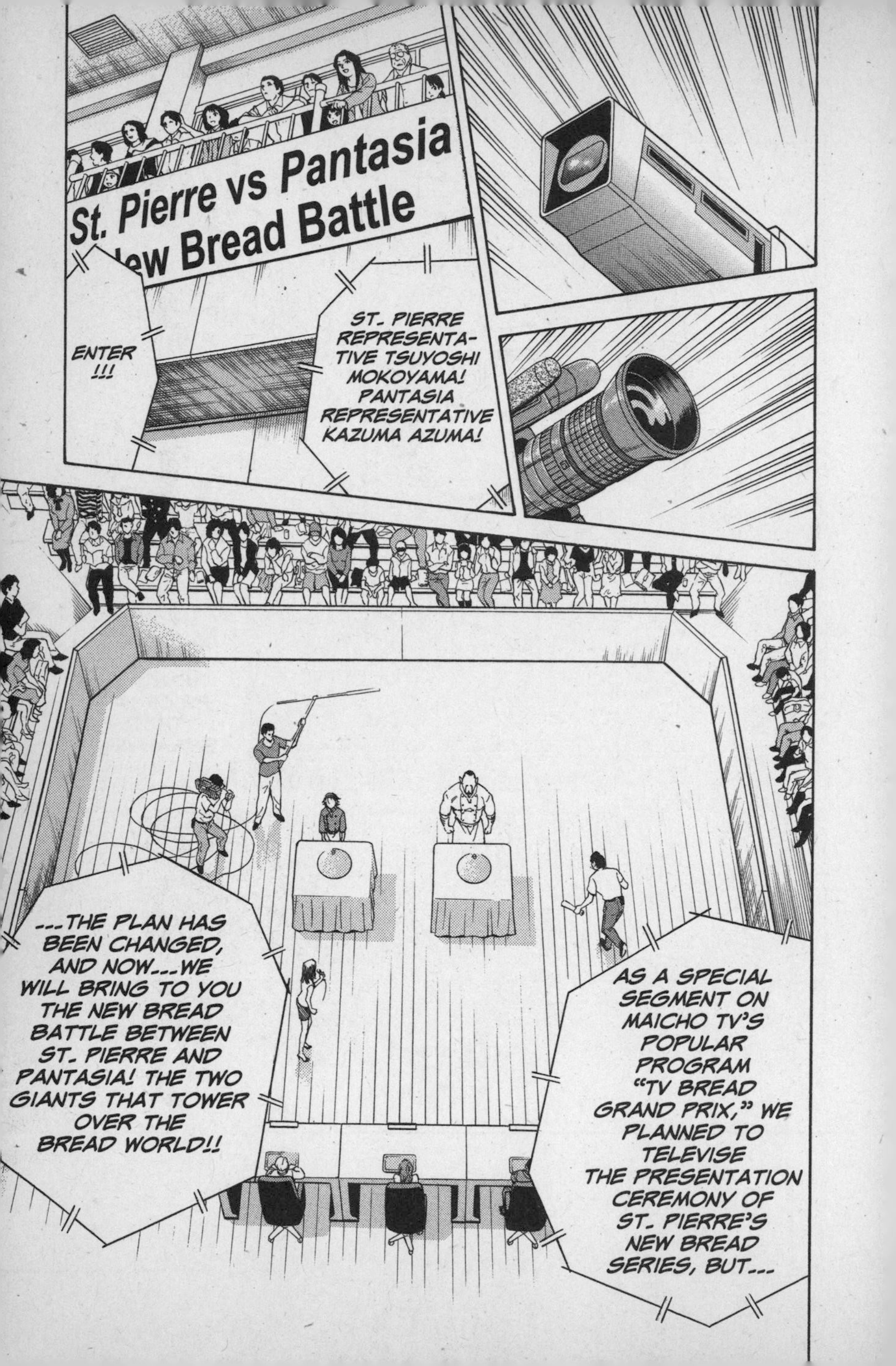
St. Pierre vs Pantasia
Bread Battle
ST. PIERRE REPRESENTATIVE TSUYOSHI MOKOYAMA! PANTASIA REPRESENTATIVE KAZUMA AZUMA!
ENTER!!!
AS A SPECIAL SEGMENT ON MAICHO TV'S POPULAR PROGRAM "TV BREAD GRAND PRIX," WE PLANNED TO TELEVISE THE PRESENTATION CEREMONY OF ST. PIERRE'S NEW BREAD SERIES, BUT...
...THE PLAN HAS BEEN CHANGED, AND NOW...WE WILL BRING TO YOU THE NEW BREAD BATTLE BETWEEN ST. PIERRE AND PANTASIA! THE TWO GIANTS THAT TOWER OVER THE BREAD WORLD!!

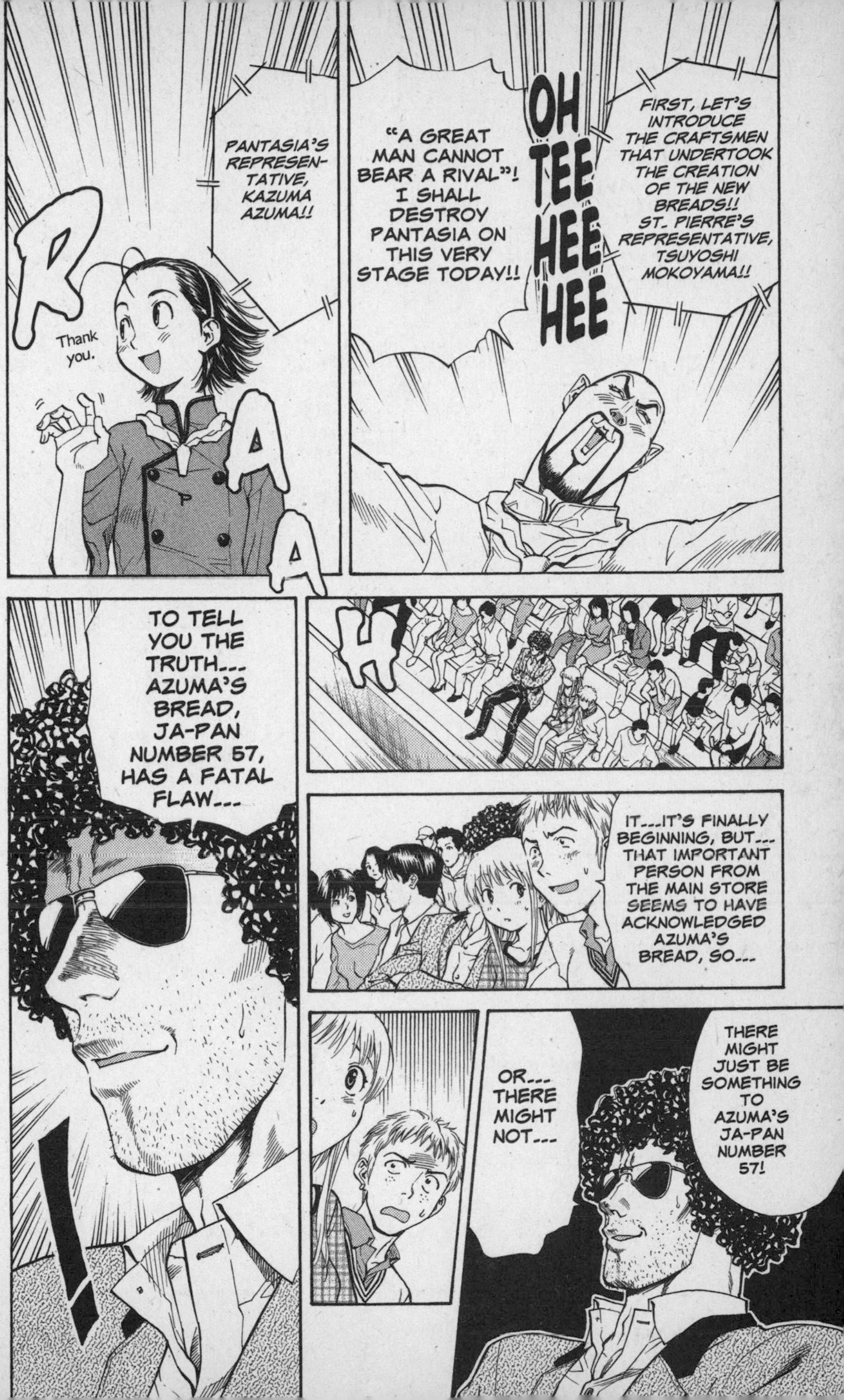
FIRST, LET'S INTRODUCE THE CRAFTSMEN THAT UNDERTOOK THE CREATION OF THE NEW BREADS!! ST. PIERRE'S REPRESENTATIVE, TSUYOSHI MOKOYAMA!!
OH TEE HEE HEE HEE
"A GREAT MAN CANNOT BEAR A RIVAL"! I SHALL DESTROY PANTASIA ON THIS VERY STAGE TODAY!!
PANTASIA'S REPRESEN-TATIVE, KAZUMA AZUMA!!
RAA
Thank you.
H
IT...IT'S FINALLY BEGINNING, BUT... THAT IMPORTANT PERSON FROM THE MAIN STORE SEEMS TO HAVE ACKNOWLEDGED AZUMA'S BREAD, SO...
THERE MIGHT JUST BE SOMETHING TO AZUMA'S JA-PAN NUMBER 57!
OR... THERE MIGHT NOT...
TO TELL YOU THE TRUTH... AZUMA'S BREAD, JA-PAN NUMBER 57, HAS A FATAL FLAW...
!

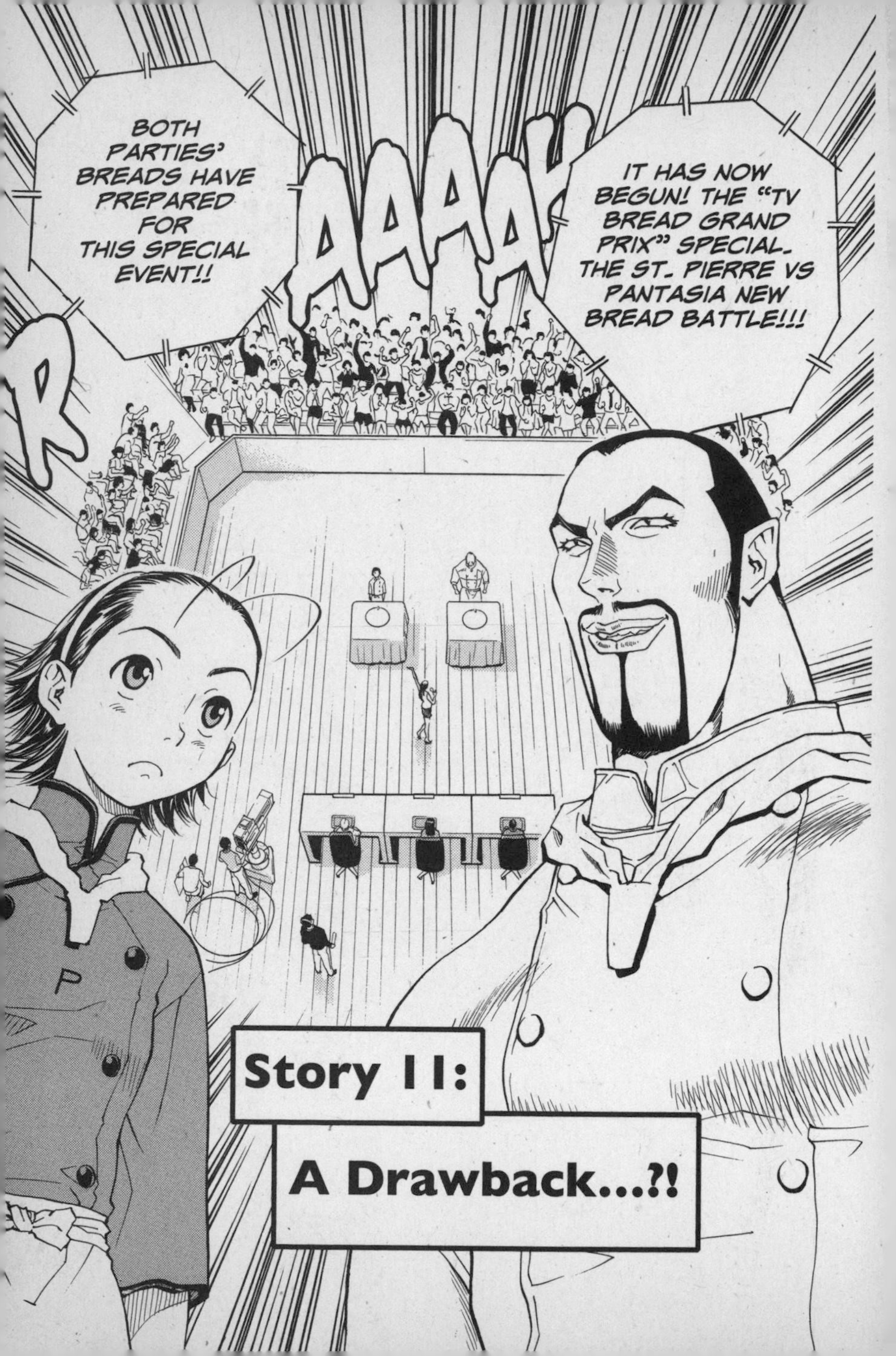
IT HAS NOW BEGUN! THE "TV BREAD GRAND PRIX" SPECIAL. THE ST. PIERRE VS PANTASIA NEW BREAD BATTLE!!!
AAAA
R
BOTH PARTIES' BREADS HAVE PREPARED FOR THIS SPECIAL EVENT!!

Story 11: A Drawback...?!

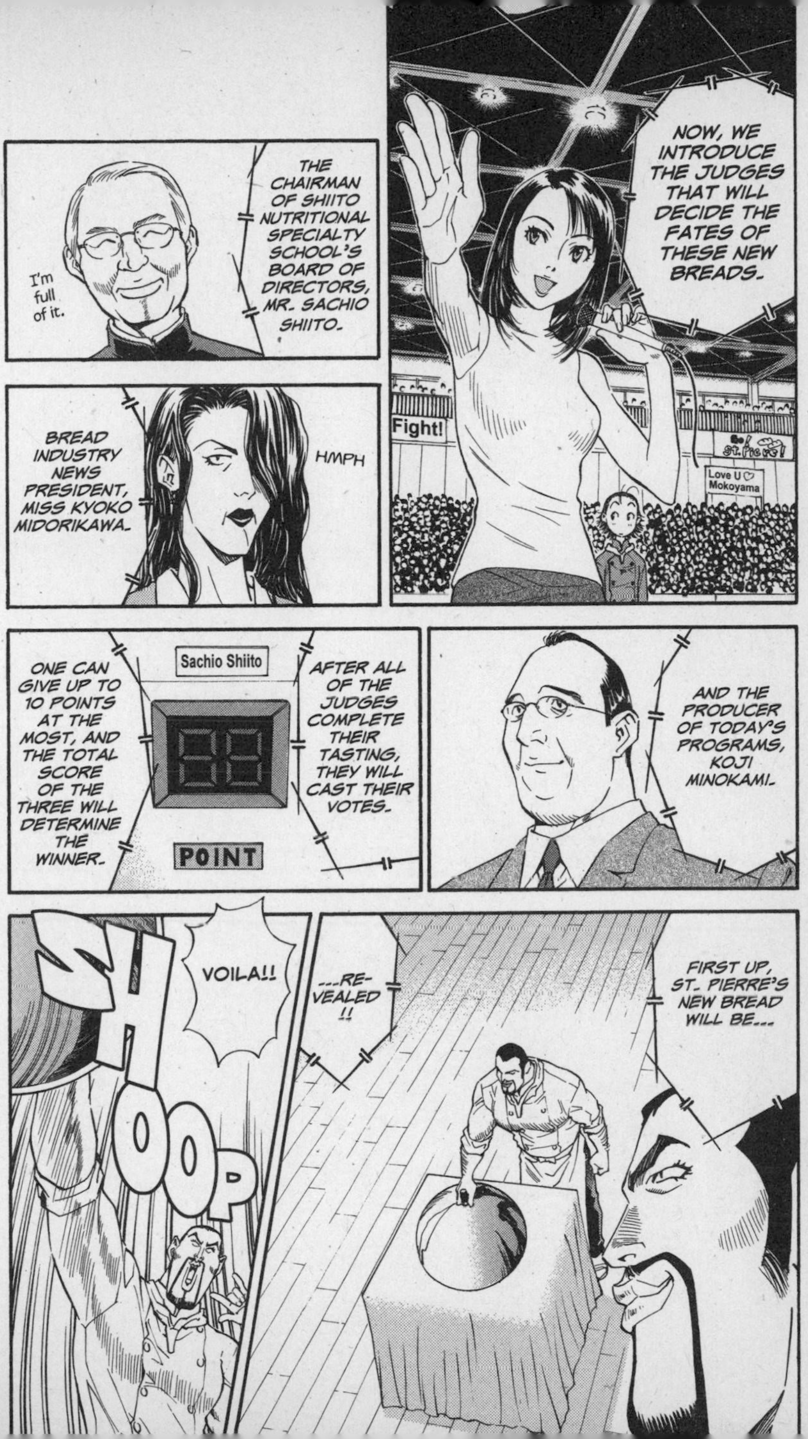
NOW, WE INTRODUCE THE JUDGES THAT WILL DECIDE THE FATES OF THESE NEW BREADS.
Fight!
Love U ♡ Mokoyama
THE CHAIRMAN OF SHIITO NUTRITIONAL SPECIALTY SCHOOL'S BOARD OF DIRECTORS, MR. SACHIO SHIITO.
I'm full of it.
BREAD INDUSTRY NEWS PRESIDENT, MISS KYOKO MIDORIKAWA.
HMPH
AND THE PRODUCER OF TODAY'S PROGRAMS, KOJI MINOKAMI.
AFTER ALL OF THE JUDGES COMPLETE THEIR TASTING, THEY WILL CAST THEIR VOTES.
Sachio Shiito
POINT
ONE CAN GIVE UP TO 10 POINTS AT THE MOST, AND THE TOTAL SCORE OF THE THREE WILL DETERMINE THE WINNER.
FIRST UP, ST. PIERRE'S NEW BREAD WILL BE...
...RE-VEALED!!
VOILA!!
SHOOOP

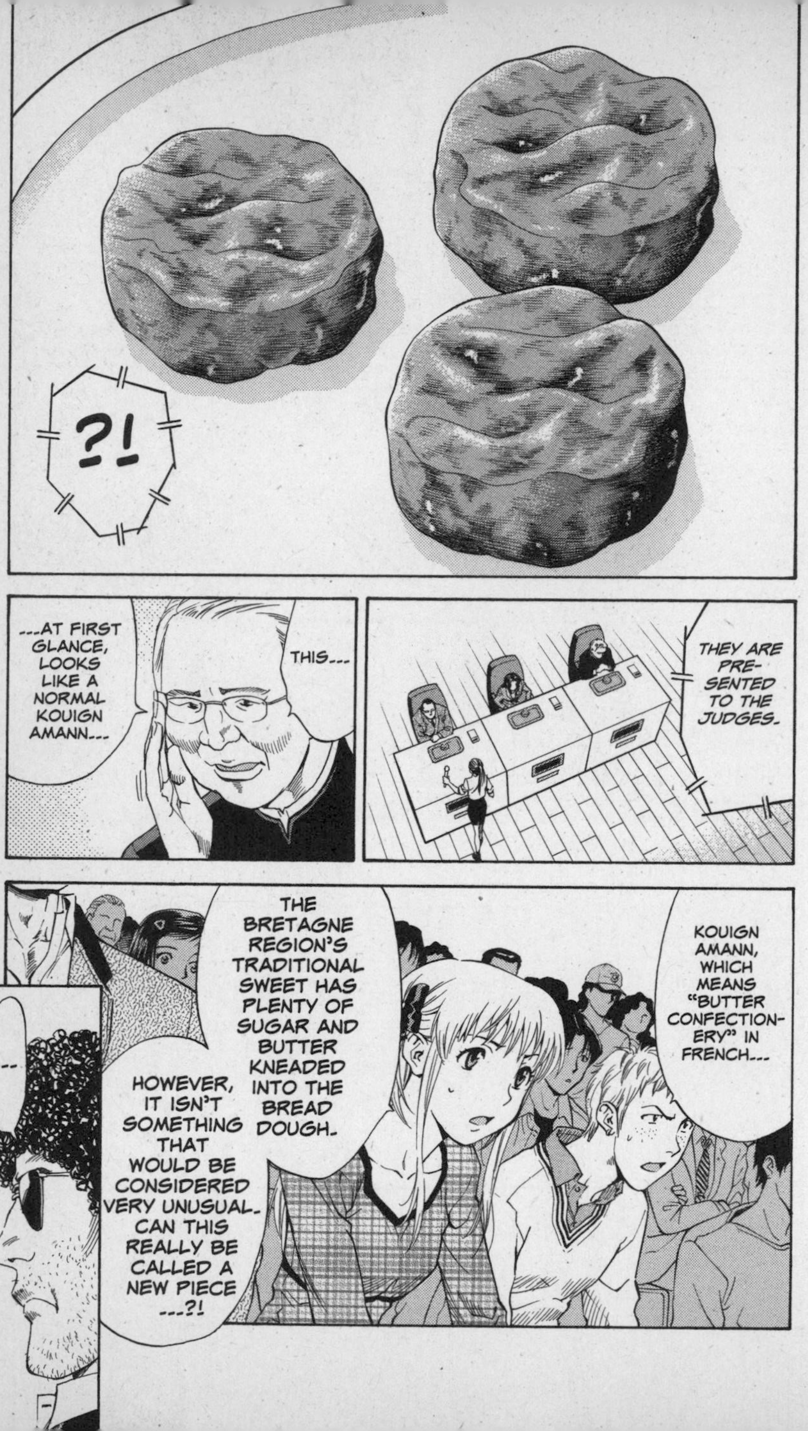
?!
THEY ARE PRESENTED TO THE JUDGES.
THIS...
...AT FIRST GLANCE, LOOKS LIKE A NORMAL KOUIGN AMANN...
KOUIGN AMANN, WHICH MEANS "BUTTER CONFECTIONERY" IN FRENCH...
THE BRETAGNE REGION'S TRADITIONAL SWEET HAS PLENTY OF SUGAR AND BUTTER KNEADED INTO THE BREAD DOUGH.
HOWEVER, IT ISN'T SOMETHING THAT WOULD BE CONSIDERED VERY UNUSUAL. CAN THIS REALLY BE CALLED A NEW PIECE...?!
...

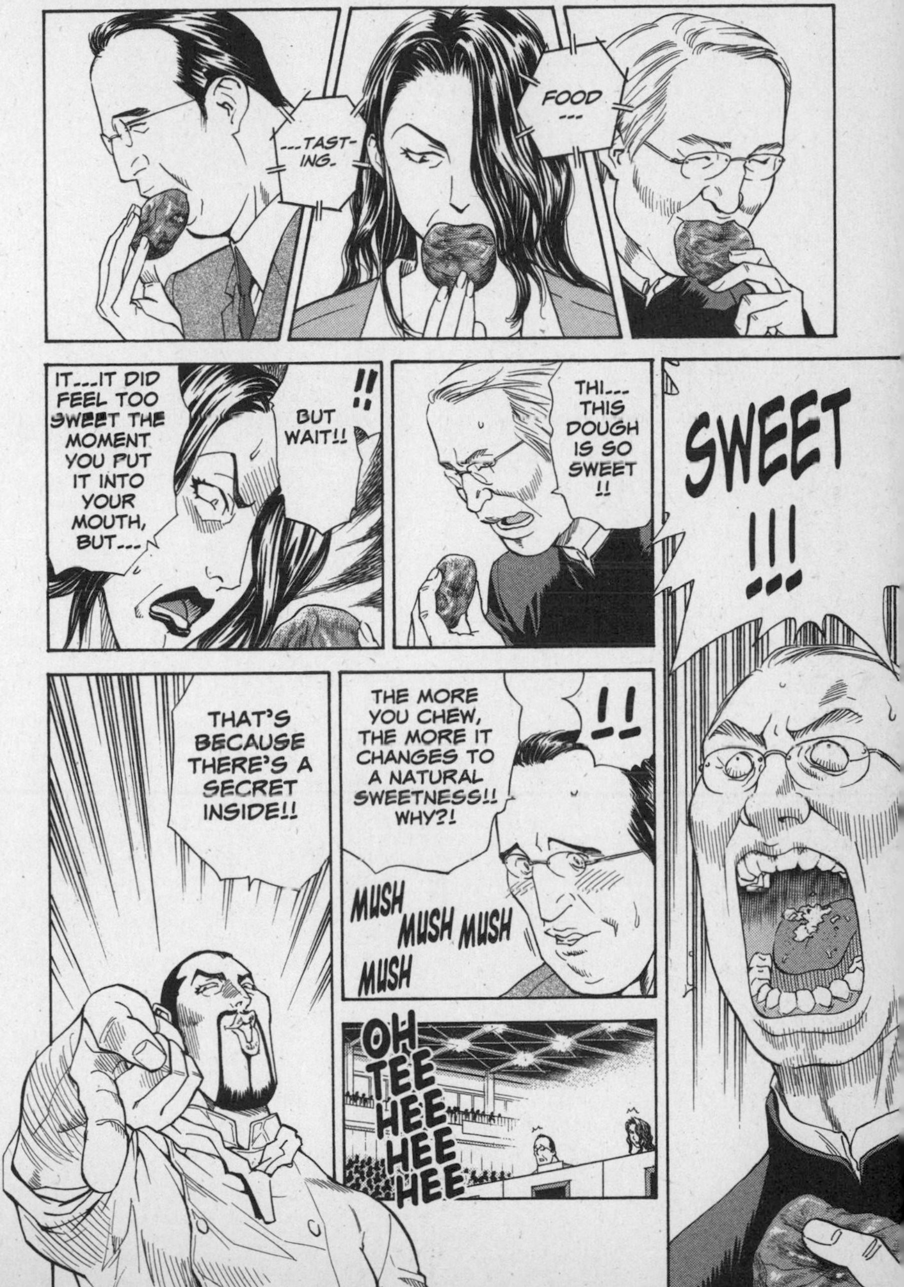
FOOD ---
---TASTING.
SWEET !!!
THI--- THIS DOUGH IS SO SWEET !!
!!
BUT WAIT!!
IT---IT DID FEEL TOO SWEET THE MOMENT YOU PUT IT INTO YOUR MOUTH, BUT---
!!
THE MORE YOU CHEW, THE MORE IT CHANGES TO A NATURAL SWEETNESS!! WHY?!
MUSH MUSH MUSH MUSH
OH TEE HEE HEE HEE
THAT'S BECAUSE THERE'S A SECRET INSIDE!!

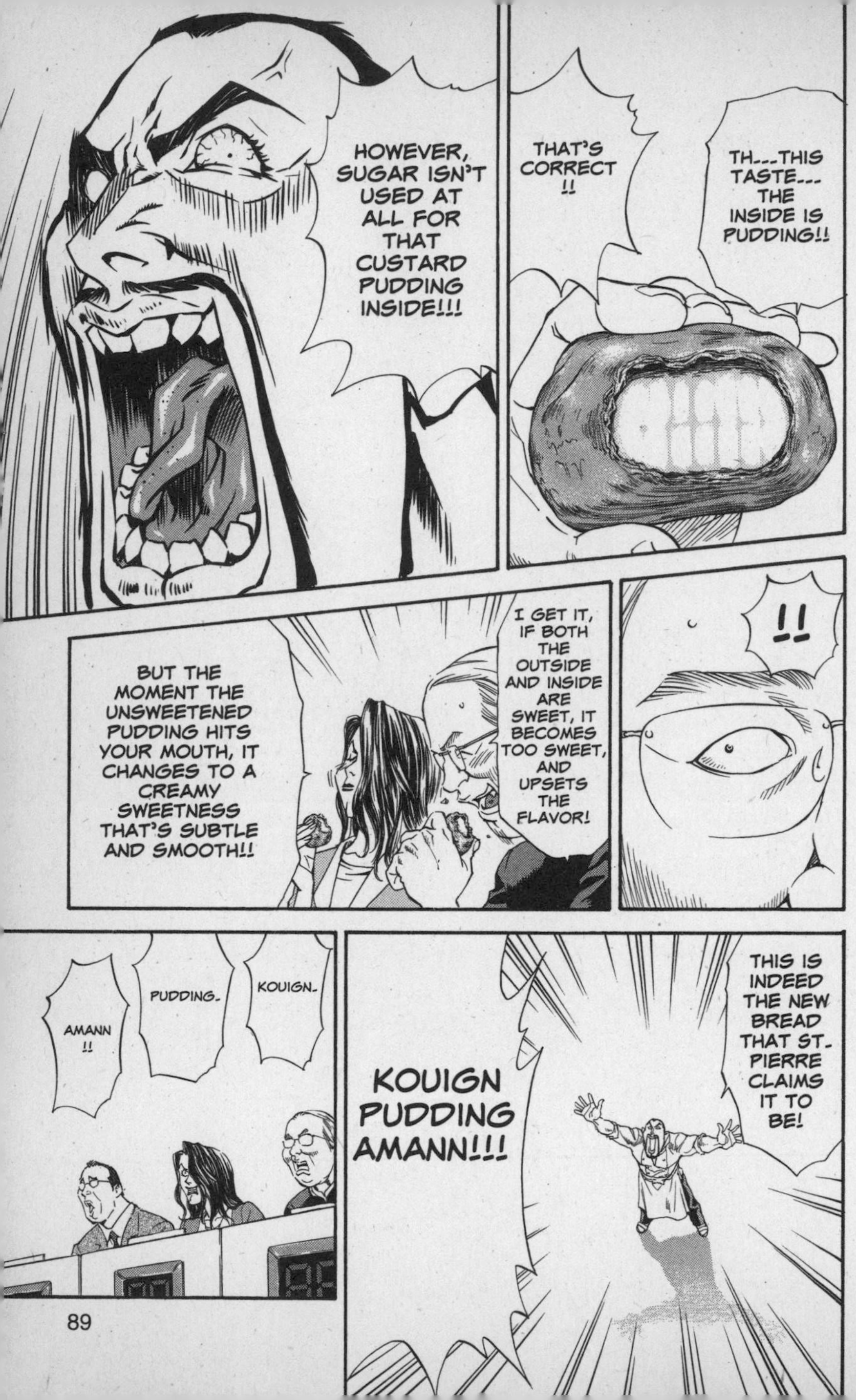
TH...THIS TASTE... THE INSIDE IS PUDDING!!
THAT'S CORRECT!!
HOWEVER, SUGAR ISN'T USED AT ALL FOR THAT CUSTARD PUDDING INSIDE!!!
!!
I GET IT, IF BOTH THE OUTSIDE AND INSIDE ARE SWEET, IT BECOMES TOO SWEET, AND UPSETS THE FLAVOR!
BUT THE MOMENT THE UNSWEETENED PUDDING HITS YOUR MOUTH, IT CHANGES TO A CREAMY SWEETNESS THAT'S SUBTLE AND SMOOTH!!
THIS IS INDEED THE NEW BREAD THAT ST. PIERRE CLAIMS IT TO BE!
KOUIGN PUDDING AMANN!!!
KOUIGN-
PUDDING-
AMANN!!

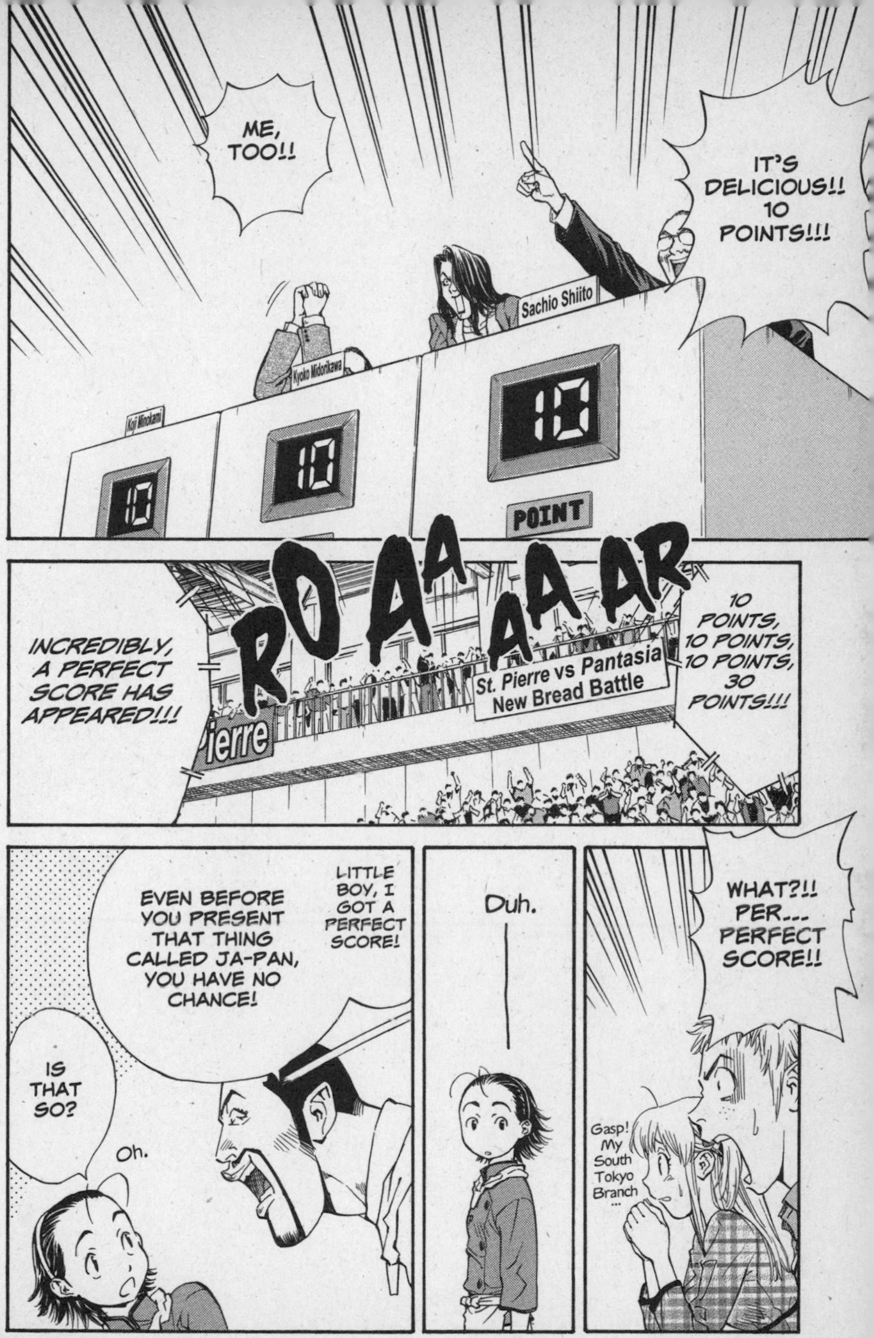
IT'S DELICIOUS!! 10 POINTS!!!
ME, TOO!!
Sachio Shiito
Kyoko Midorikawa
Koji Minokami
10
10
10
POINT
10 POINTS, 10 POINTS, 10 POINTS, 30 POINTS!!!
ROAAAAAR
St. Pierre vs Pantasia New Bread Battle
Pierre
INCREDIBLY, A PERFECT SCORE HAS APPEARED!!!
WHAT?!! PER... PERFECT SCORE!!
Gasp! My South Tokyo Branch ...
Duh.
LITTLE BOY, I GOT A PERFECT SCORE!
EVEN BEFORE YOU PRESENT THAT THING CALLED JA-PAN, YOU HAVE NO CHANCE!
IS THAT SO?
Oh.

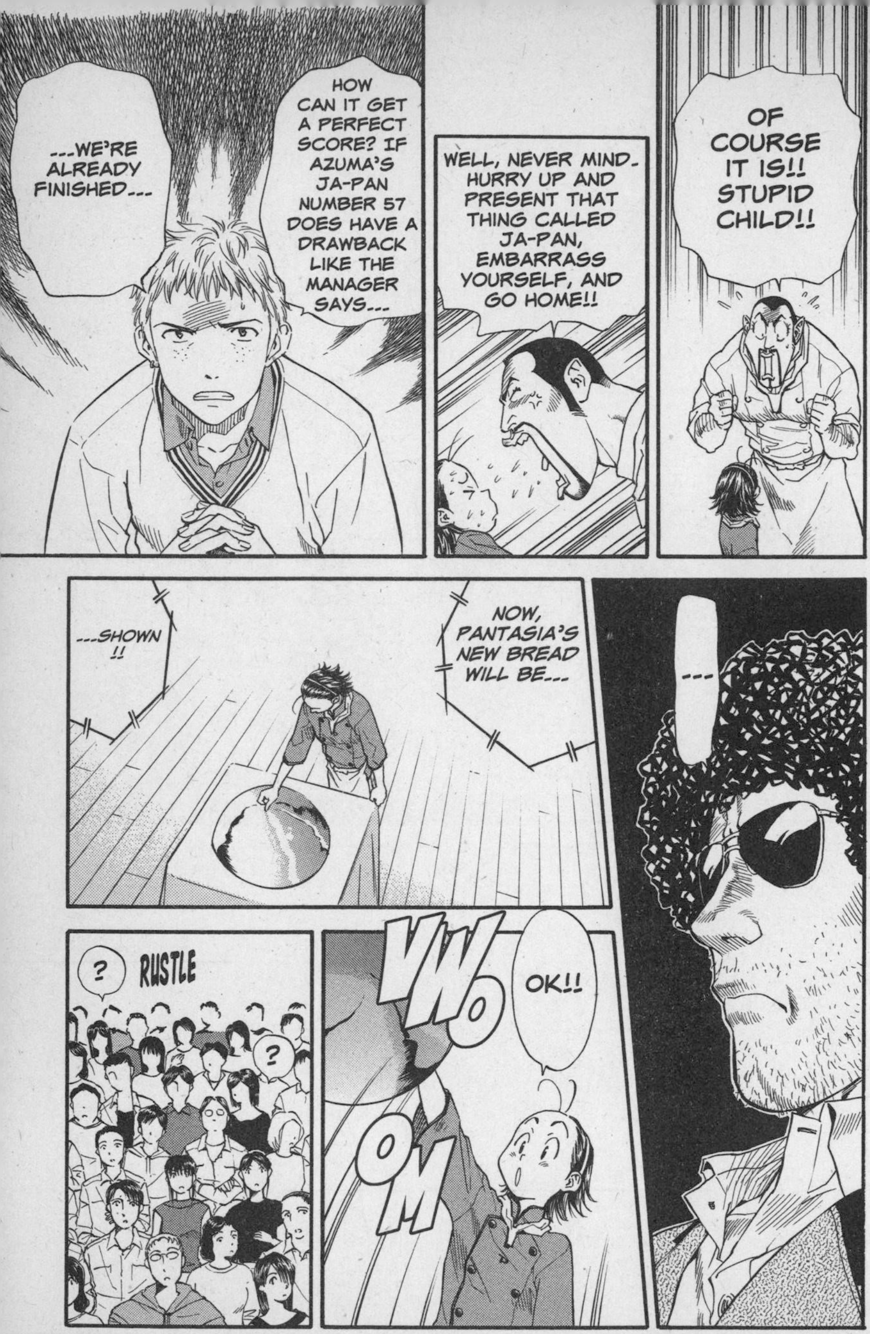
OF COURSE IT IS!! STUPID CHILD!!
WELL, NEVER MIND. HURRY UP AND PRESENT THAT THING CALLED JA-PAN, EMBARRASS YOURSELF, AND GO HOME!!
HOW CAN IT GET A PERFECT SCORE? IF AZUMA'S JA-PAN NUMBER 57 DOES HAVE A DRAWBACK LIKE THE MANAGER SAYS...
...WE'RE ALREADY FINISHED...
...
NOW, PANTASIA'S NEW BREAD WILL BE...
...SHOWN !!
VWOOM
OK!!
?
RUSTLE
?

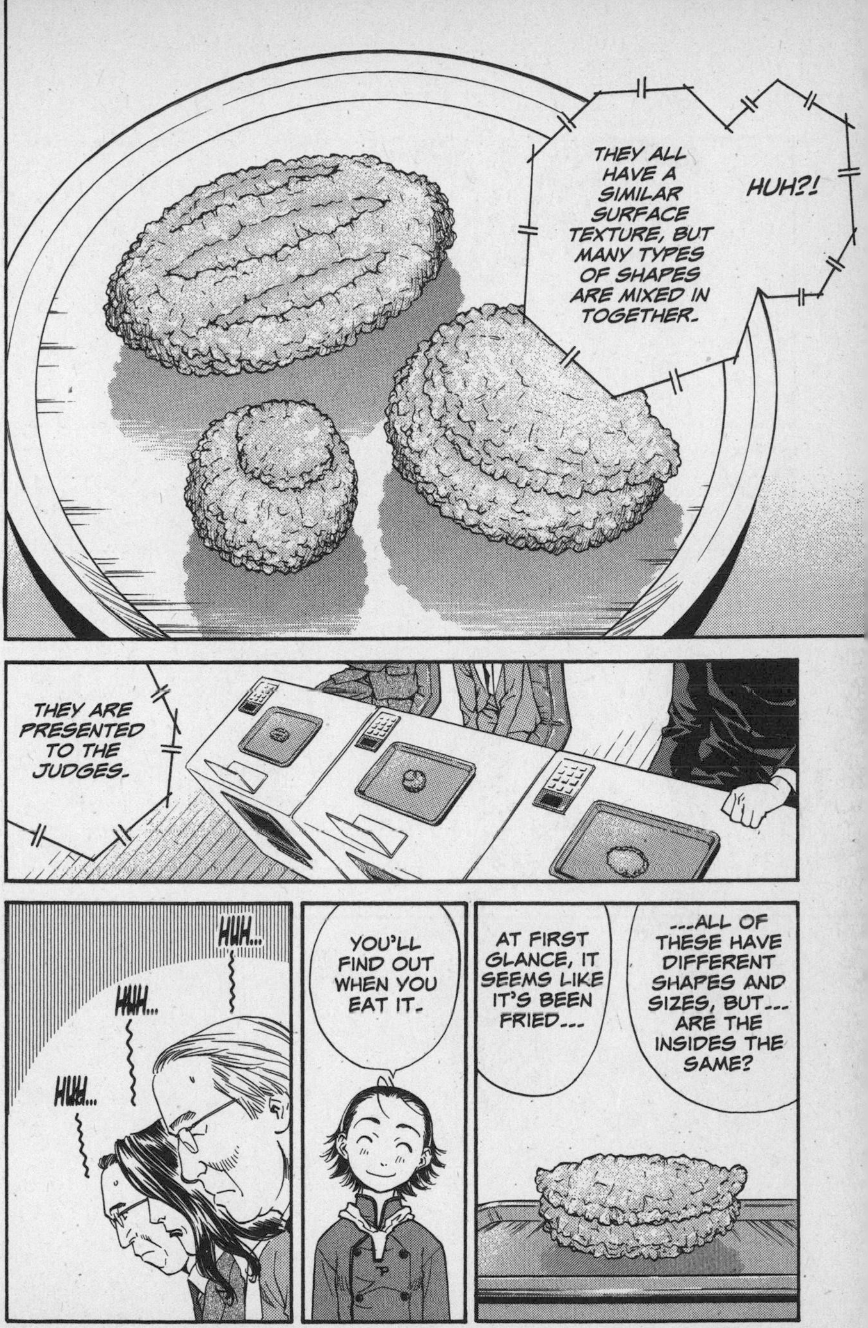
HUH?!
THEY ALL HAVE A SIMILAR SURFACE TEXTURE, BUT MANY TYPES OF SHAPES ARE MIXED IN TOGETHER.
THEY ARE PRESENTED TO THE JUDGES.
AT FIRST GLANCE, IT SEEMS LIKE IT'S BEEN FRIED...
...ALL OF THESE HAVE DIFFERENT SHAPES AND SIZES, BUT... ARE THE INSIDES THE SAME?
YOU'LL FIND OUT WHEN YOU EAT IT.
HUH...
HUH...
HUH...

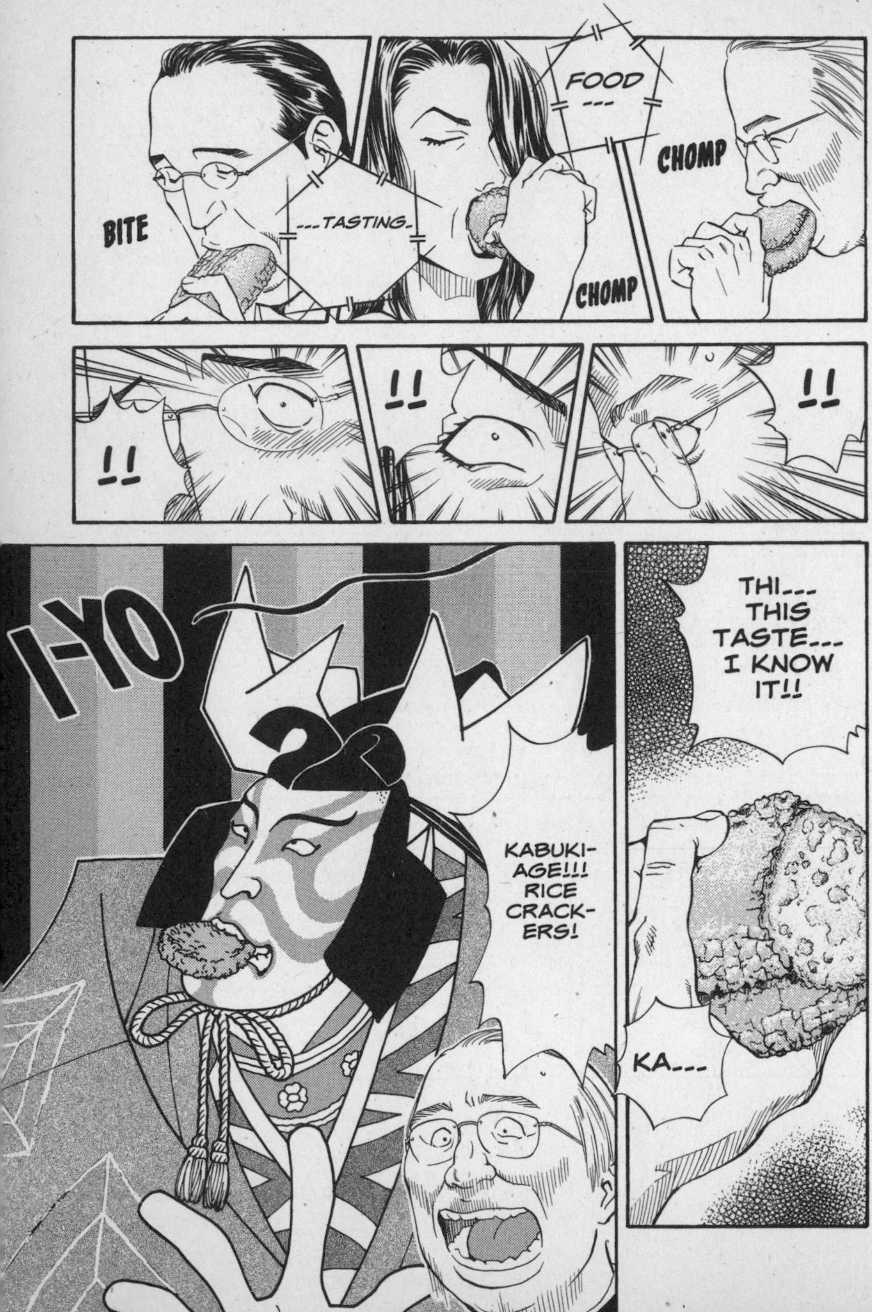
CHOMP
FOOD ---
CHOMP
BITE
---TASTING---
!!
!!
!!
THI--- THIS TASTE--- I KNOW IT!!
KA---
I-YO
KABUKI-AGE!!! RICE CRACK-ERS!

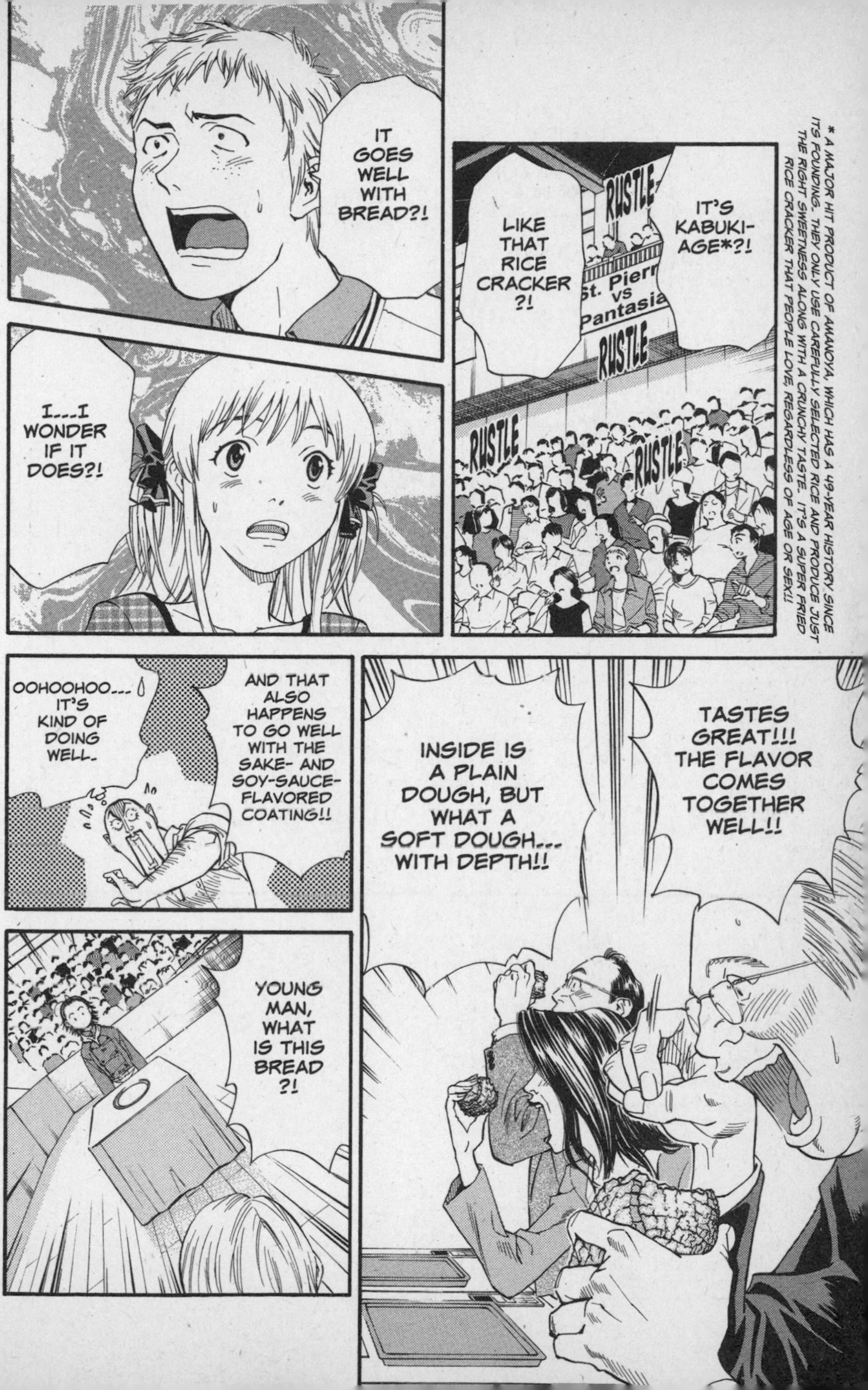
IT'S KABUKI-AGE*?!
LIKE THAT RICE CRACKER?!
RUSTLE
St. Pierre vs Pantasia
RUSTLE
RUSTLE
RUSTLE
IT GOES WELL WITH BREAD?!
I...I WONDER IF IT DOES?!
TASTES GREAT!!! THE FLAVOR COMES TOGETHER WELL!!
INSIDE IS A PLAIN DOUGH, BUT WHAT A SOFT DOUGH... WITH DEPTH!!
AND THAT ALSO HAPPENS TO GO WELL WITH THE SAKE- AND SOY-SAUCE-FLAVORED COATING!!
OOHOOHOO... IT'S KIND OF DOING WELL.
YOUNG MAN, WHAT IS THIS BREAD?!

* A MAJOR HIT PRODUCT OF AMANOYA, WHICH HAS A 49-YEAR HISTORY SINCE ITS FOUNDING. THEY ONLY USE CAREFULLY SELECTED RICE AND PRODUCE JUST THE RIGHT SWEETNESS ALONG WITH A CRUNCHY TASTE. IT'S A SUPER FRIED RICE CRACKER THAT PEOPLE LOVE, REGARDLESS OF AGE OR SEX!!

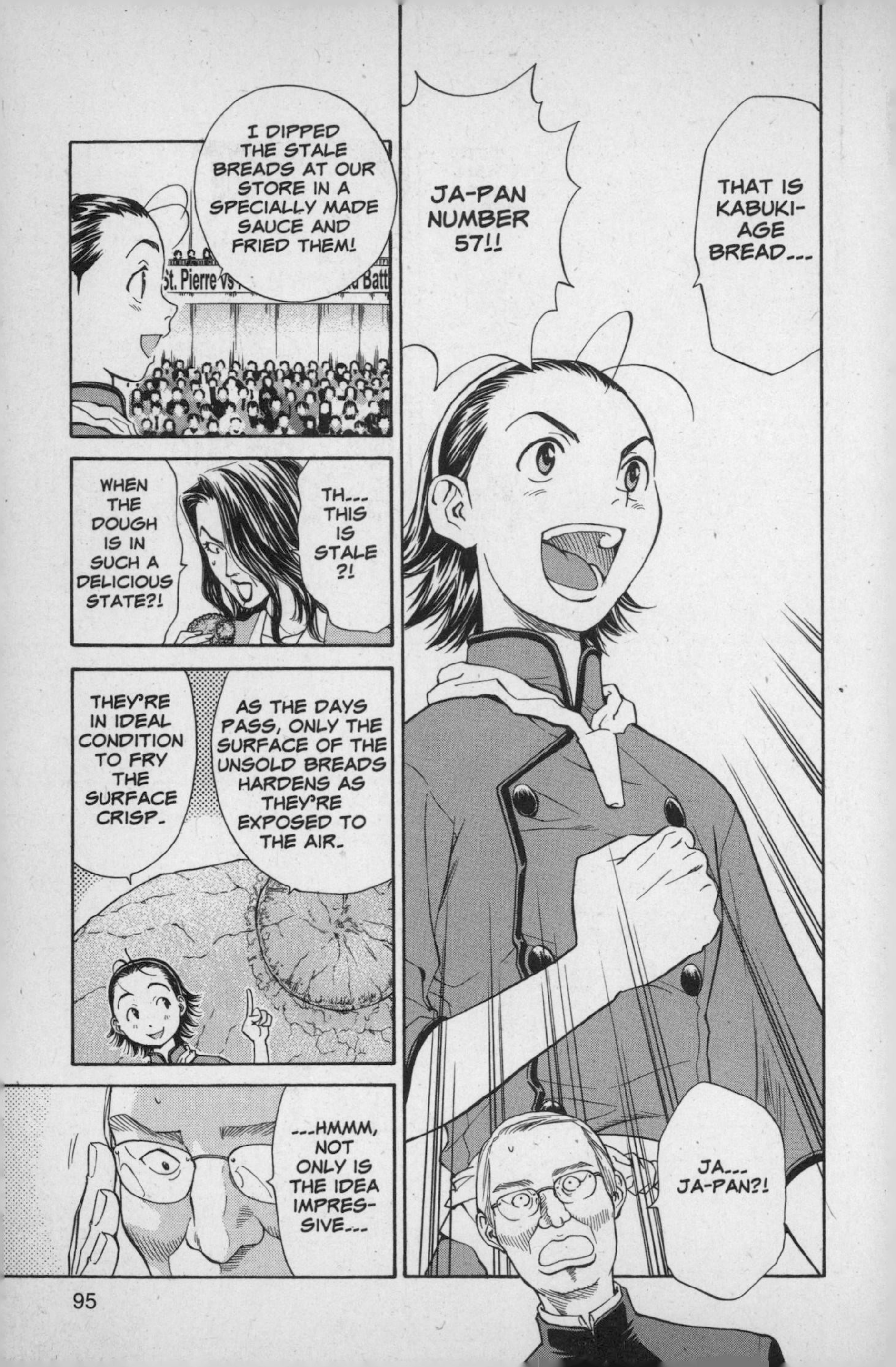
THAT IS KABUKI-AGE BREAD...
JA-PAN NUMBER 57!!
JA... JA-PAN?!
I DIPPED THE STALE BREADS AT OUR STORE IN A SPECIALLY MADE SAUCE AND FRIED THEM!
St. Pierre vs
TH... THIS IS STALE?!
WHEN THE DOUGH IS IN SUCH A DELICIOUS STATE?!
AS THE DAYS PASS, ONLY THE SURFACE OF THE UNSOLD BREADS HARDENS AS THEY'RE EXPOSED TO THE AIR.
THEY'RE IN IDEAL CONDITION TO FRY THE SURFACE CRISP.
...HMMM, NOT ONLY IS THE IDEA IMPRESSIVE...

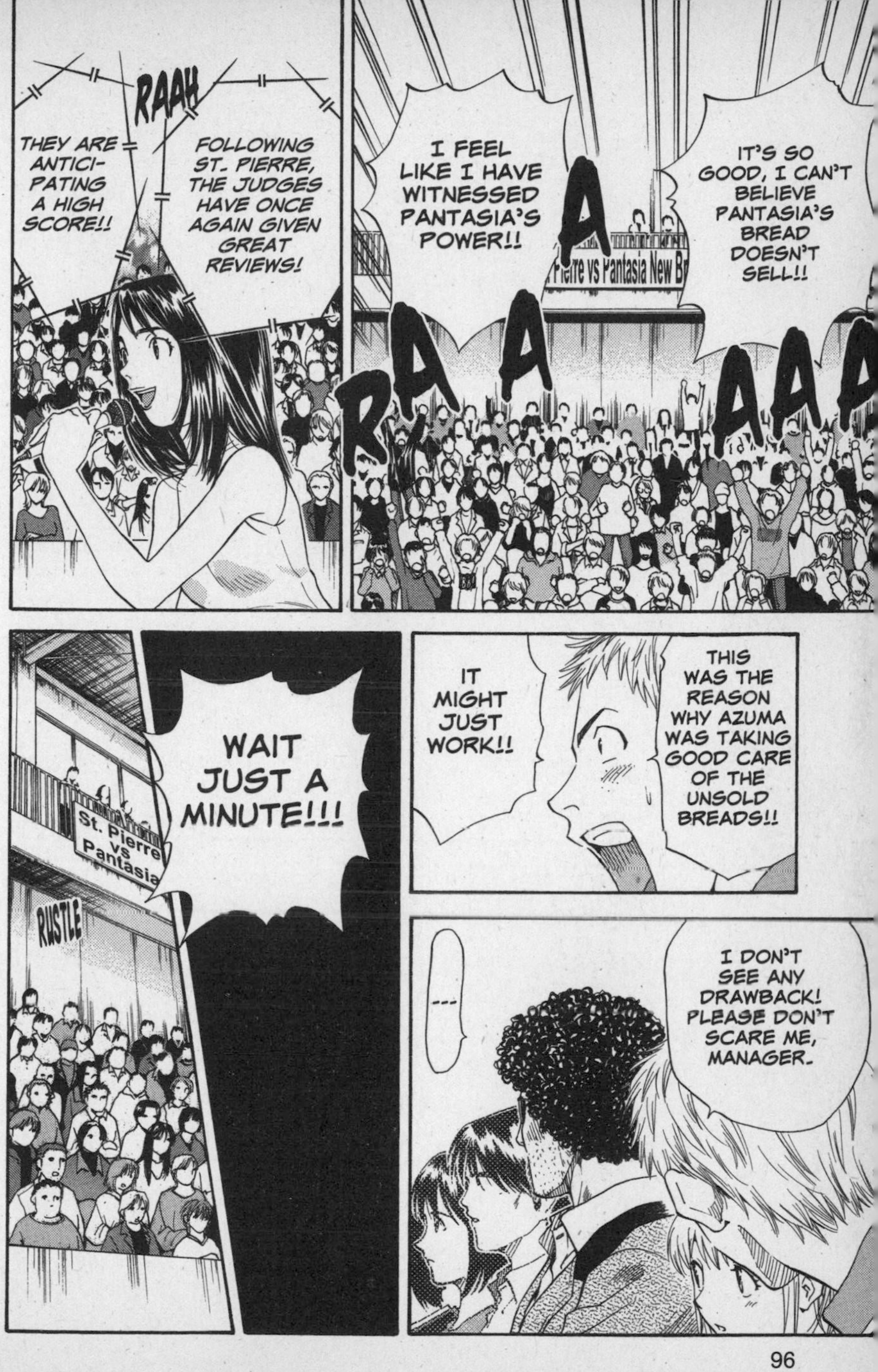
IT'S SO GOOD, I CAN'T BELIEVE PANTASIA'S BREAD DOESN'T SELL!!
I FEEL LIKE I HAVE WITNESSED PANTASIA'S POWER!!
Pierre vs Pantasia New B
RAAAAA
FOLLOWING ST. PIERRE, THE JUDGES HAVE ONCE AGAIN GIVEN GREAT REVIEWS!
THEY ARE ANTICI-PATING A HIGH SCORE!!
RAAH
THIS WAS THE REASON WHY AZUMA WAS TAKING GOOD CARE OF THE UNSOLD BREADS!!
IT MIGHT JUST WORK!!
I DON'T SEE ANY DRAWBACK! PLEASE DON'T SCARE ME, MANAGER.
...
WAIT JUST A MINUTE!!!
St. Pierre vs Pantasia
RUSTLE

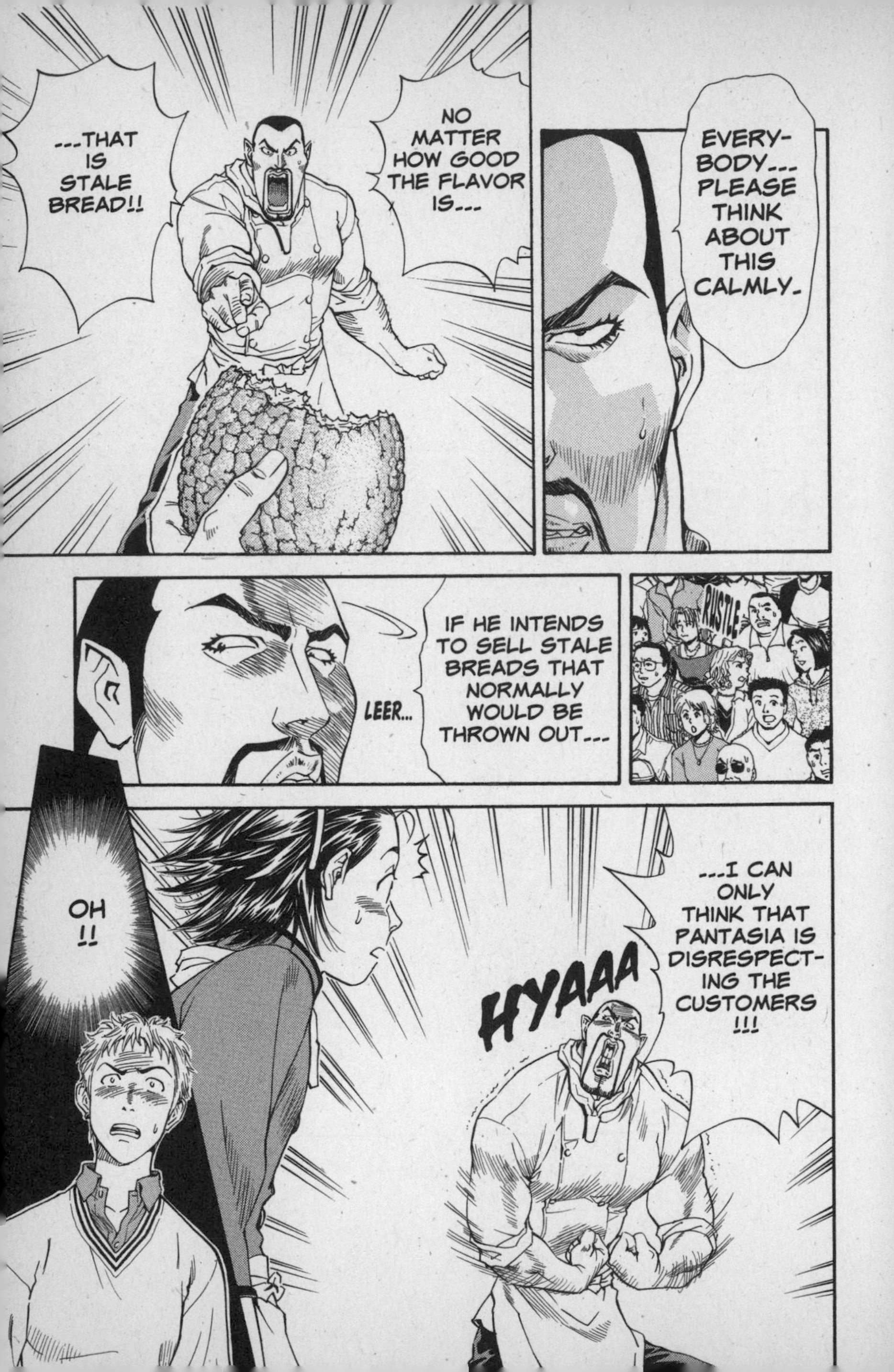
EVERY-BODY... PLEASE THINK ABOUT THIS CALMLY.
NO MATTER HOW GOOD THE FLAVOR IS...
...THAT IS STALE BREAD!!
RUSTLE
IF HE INTENDS TO SELL STALE BREADS THAT NORMALLY WOULD BE THROWN OUT...
LEER...
...I CAN ONLY THINK THAT PANTASIA IS DISRESPECT-ING THE CUSTOMERS!!!
HYAAA
OH!!

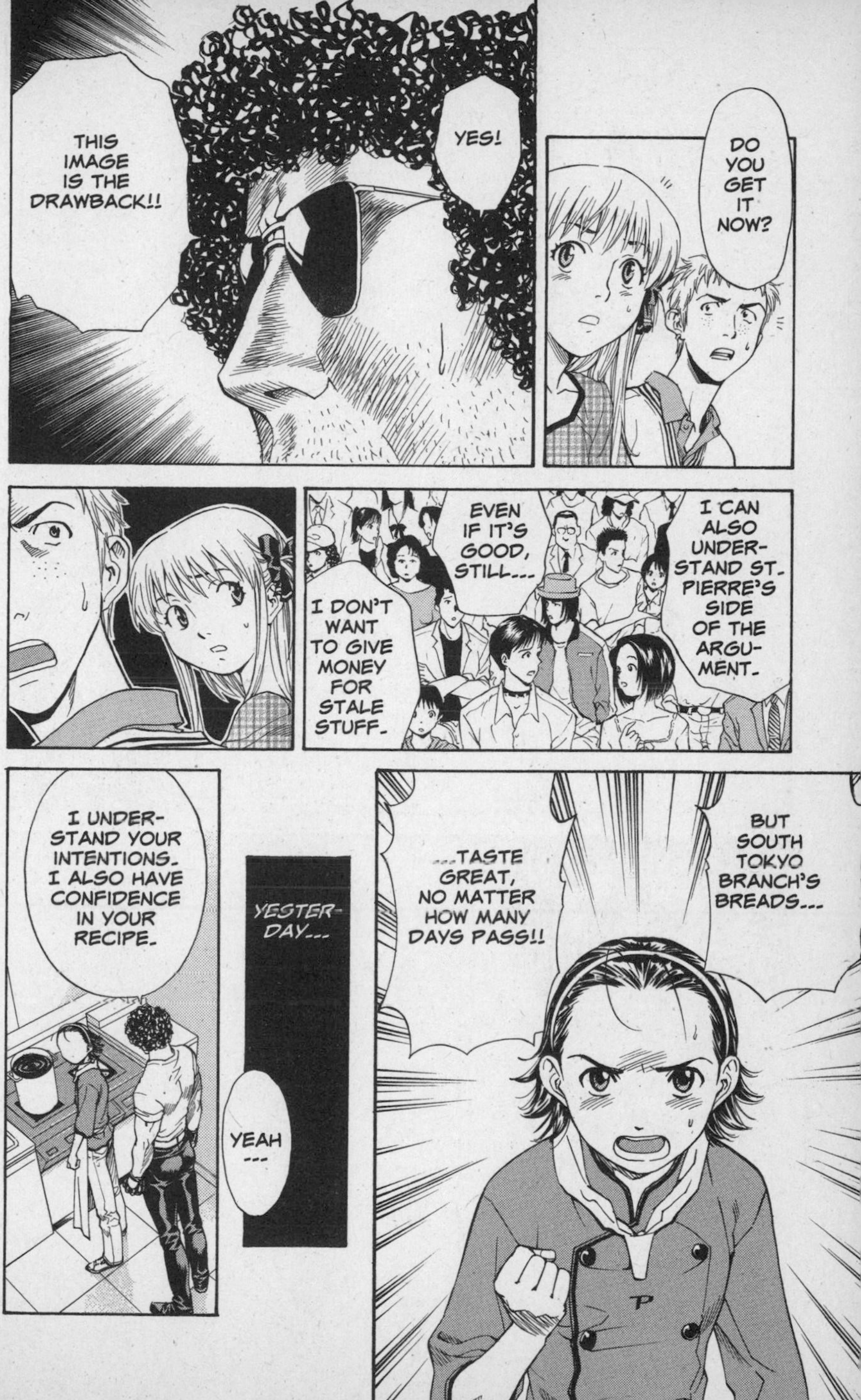
DO YOU GET IT NOW?
YES!
THIS IMAGE IS THE DRAWBACK!!
I CAN ALSO UNDERSTAND ST. PIERRE'S SIDE OF THE ARGUMENT.
EVEN IF IT'S GOOD, STILL...
I DON'T WANT TO GIVE MONEY FOR STALE STUFF.
BUT SOUTH TOKYO BRANCH'S BREADS...
...TASTE GREAT, NO MATTER HOW MANY DAYS PASS!!
YESTERDAY...
I UNDERSTAND YOUR INTENTIONS. I ALSO HAVE CONFIDENCE IN YOUR RECIPE.
YEAH...

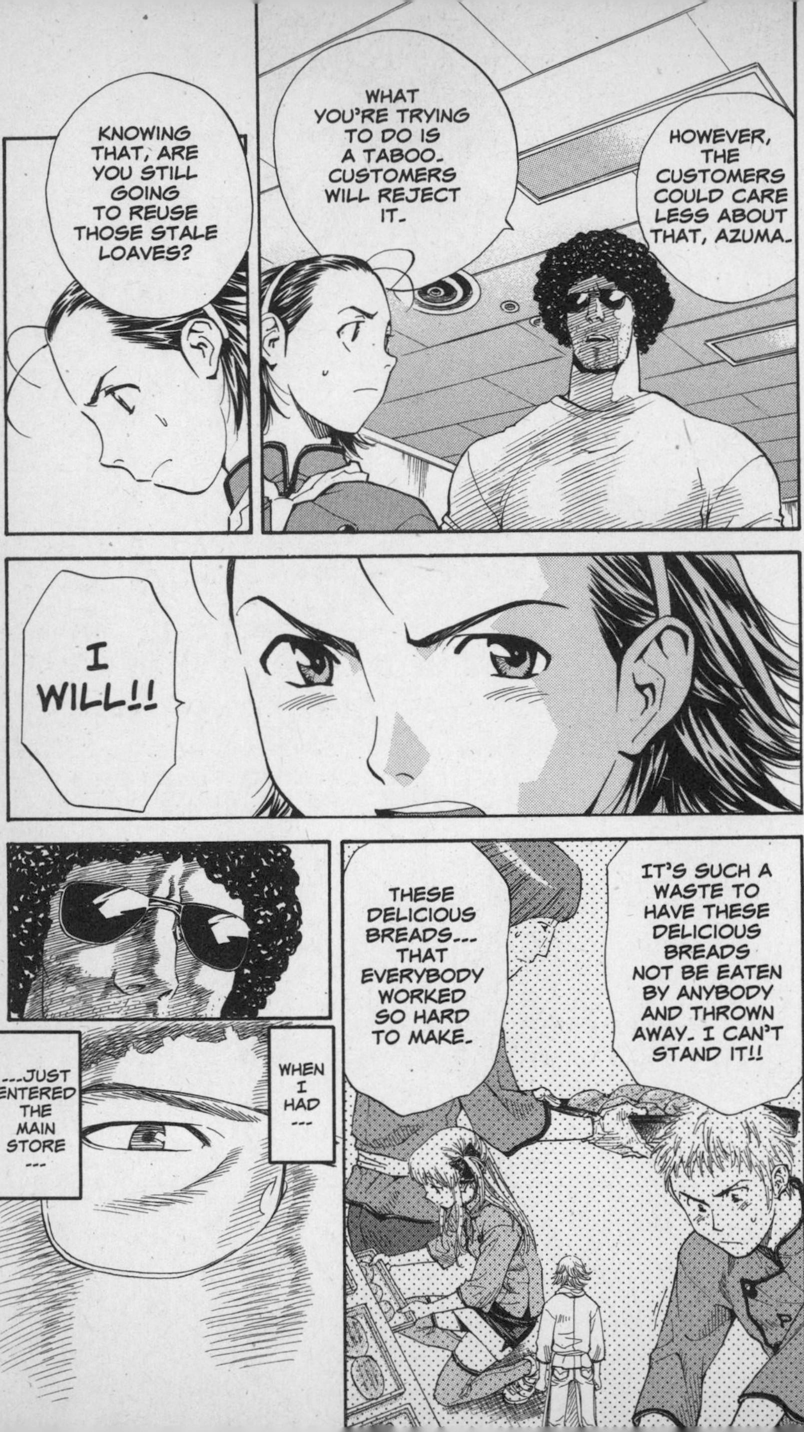
HOWEVER, THE CUSTOMERS COULD CARE LESS ABOUT THAT, AZUMA.
WHAT YOU'RE TRYING TO DO IS A TABOO. CUSTOMERS WILL REJECT IT.
KNOWING THAT, ARE YOU STILL GOING TO REUSE THOSE STALE LOAVES?
I WILL!!
IT'S SUCH A WASTE TO HAVE THESE DELICIOUS BREADS NOT BE EATEN BY ANYBODY AND THROWN AWAY. I CAN'T STAND IT!!
THESE DELICIOUS BREADS... THAT EVERYBODY WORKED SO HARD TO MAKE.
WHEN I HAD ...
...JUST ENTERED THE MAIN STORE ...

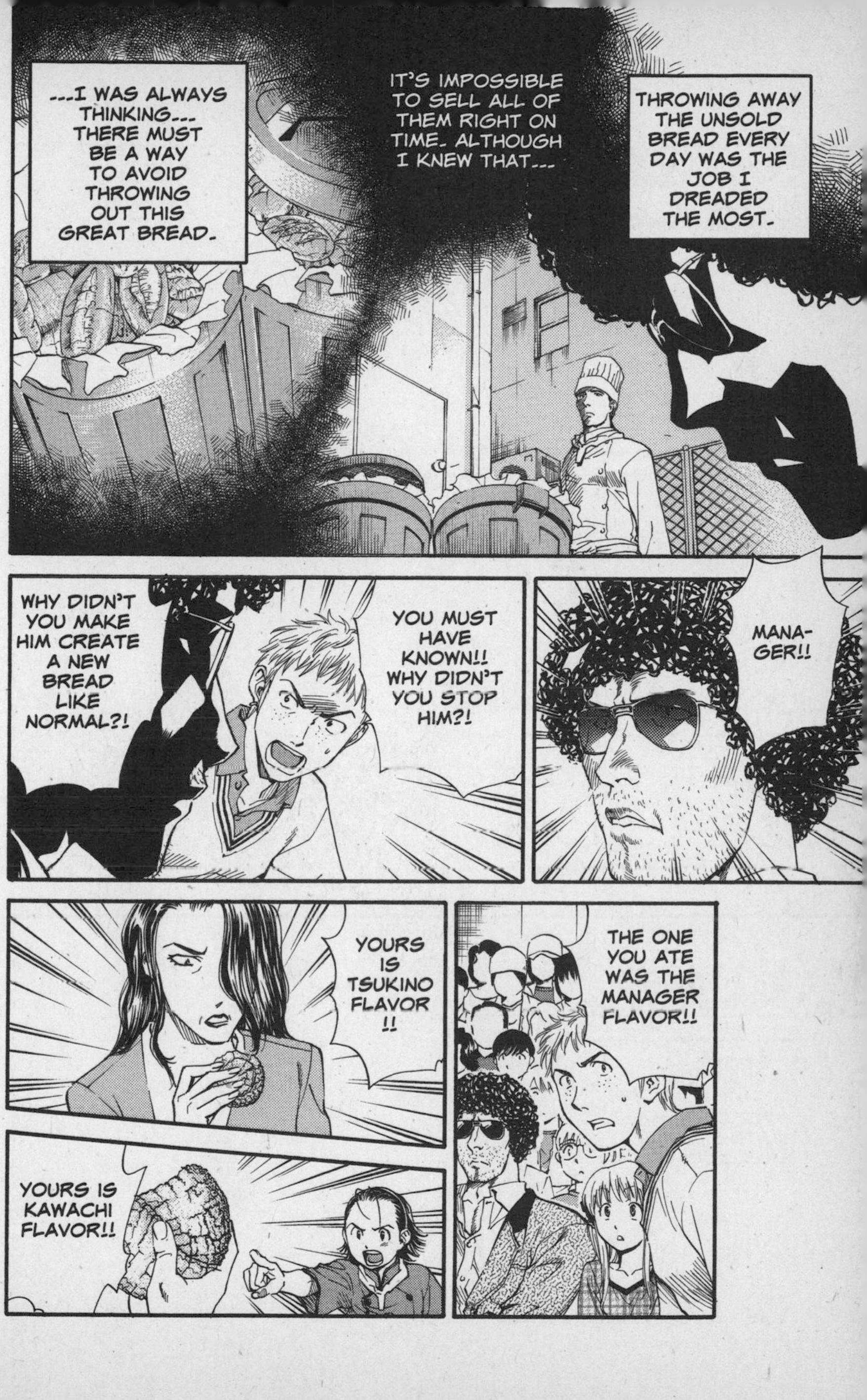
THROWING AWAY THE UNSOLD BREAD EVERY DAY WAS THE JOB I DREADED THE MOST.
IT'S IMPOSSIBLE TO SELL ALL OF THEM RIGHT ON TIME. ALTHOUGH I KNEW THAT...
...I WAS ALWAYS THINKING... THERE MUST BE A WAY TO AVOID THROWING OUT THIS GREAT BREAD.
MANA-GER!!
YOU MUST HAVE KNOWN!! WHY DIDN'T YOU STOP HIM?!
WHY DIDN'T YOU MAKE HIM CREATE A NEW BREAD LIKE NORMAL?!
THE ONE YOU ATE WAS THE MANAGER FLAVOR!!
YOURS IS TSUKINO FLAVOR!!
YOURS IS KAWACHI FLAVOR!!

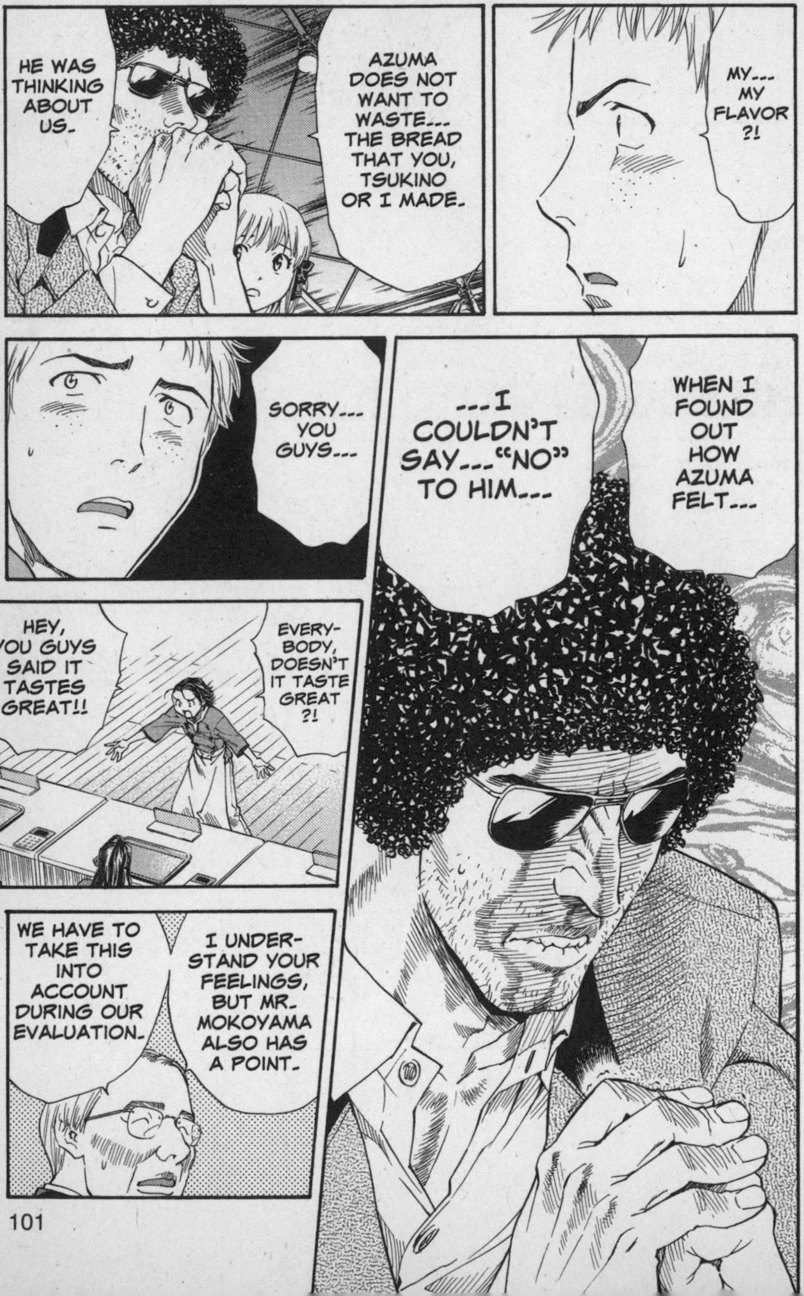
MY... MY FLAVOR ?!
AZUMA DOES NOT WANT TO WASTE... THE BREAD THAT YOU, TSUKINO OR I MADE.
HE WAS THINKING ABOUT US.
WHEN I FOUND OUT HOW AZUMA FELT...
...I COULDN'T SAY... "NO" TO HIM...
SORRY... YOU GUYS...
EVERY-BODY, DOESN'T IT TASTE GREAT ?!
HEY, YOU GUYS SAID IT TASTES GREAT!!
I UNDER-STAND YOUR FEELINGS, BUT MR. MOKOYAMA ALSO HAS A POINT.
WE HAVE TO TAKE THIS INTO ACCOUNT DURING OUR EVALUATION.

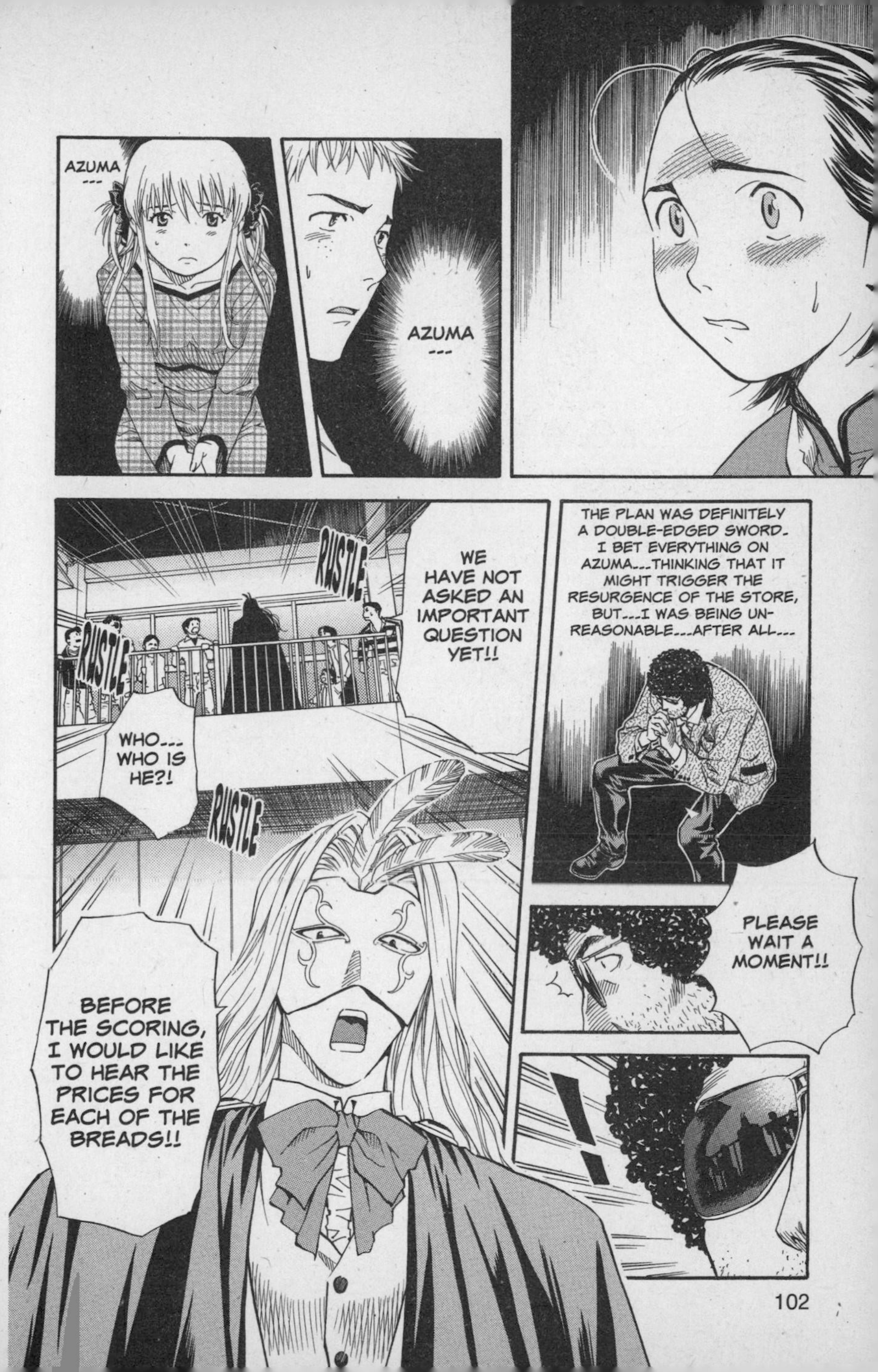
AZUMA---
AZUMA---
THE PLAN WAS DEFINITELY A DOUBLE-EDGED SWORD. I BET EVERYTHING ON AZUMA...THINKING THAT IT MIGHT TRIGGER THE RESURGENCE OF THE STORE, BUT...I WAS BEING UNREASONABLE...AFTER ALL...
PLEASE WAIT A MOMENT!!
WE HAVE NOT ASKED AN IMPORTANT QUESTION YET!!
RUSTLE
RUSTLE
WHO... WHO IS HE?!
RUSTLE
BEFORE THE SCORING, I WOULD LIKE TO HEAR THE PRICES FOR EACH OF THE BREADS!!

Story 12: Meister's Secret Plan

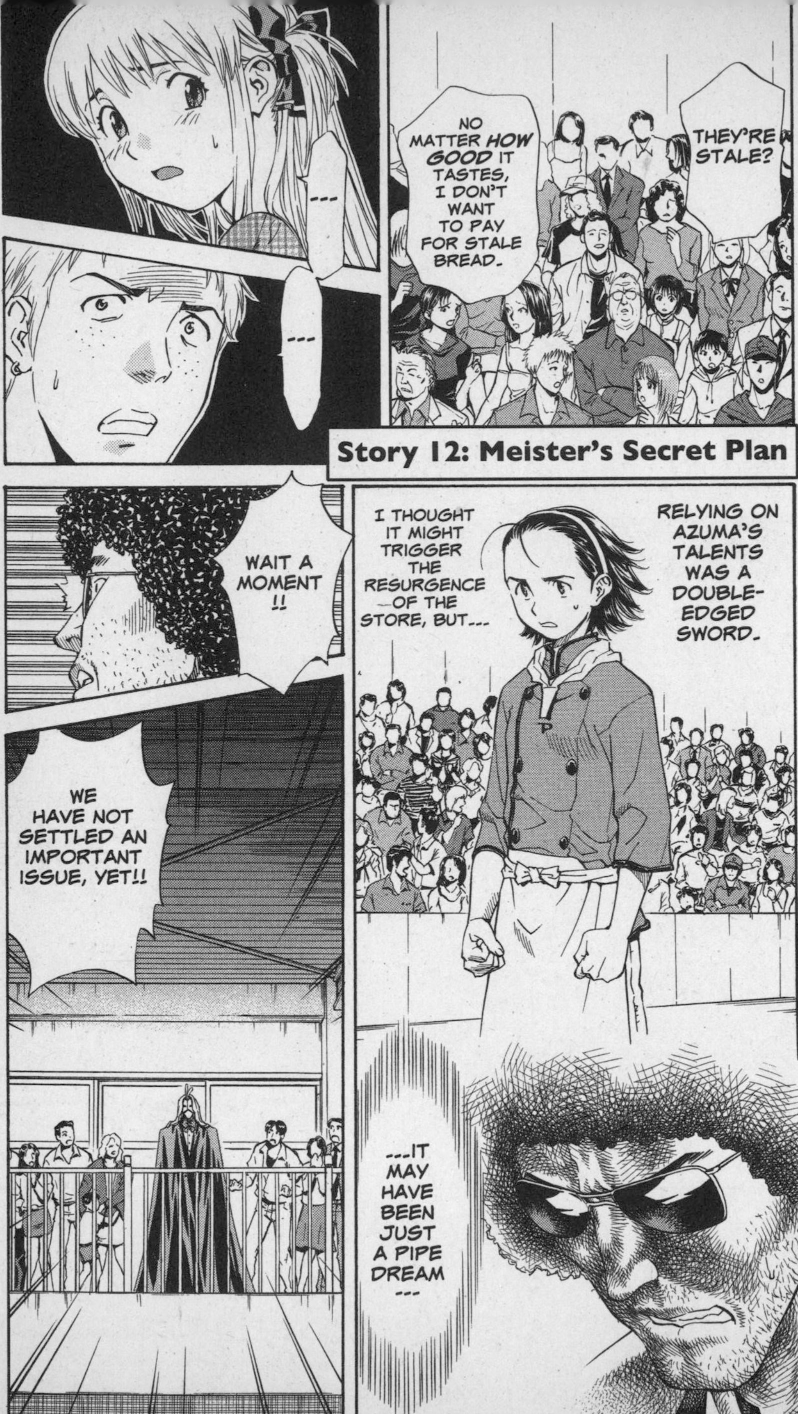
THEY'RE STALE?
NO MATTER HOW GOOD IT TASTES, I DON'T WANT TO PAY FOR STALE BREAD.

RELYING ON AZUMA'S TALENTS WAS A DOUBLE-EDGED SWORD.
I THOUGHT IT MIGHT TRIGGER THE RESURGENCE OF THE STORE, BUT...
...IT MAY HAVE BEEN JUST A PIPE DREAM...
WAIT A MOMENT!!
WE HAVE NOT SETTLED AN IMPORTANT ISSUE, YET!!

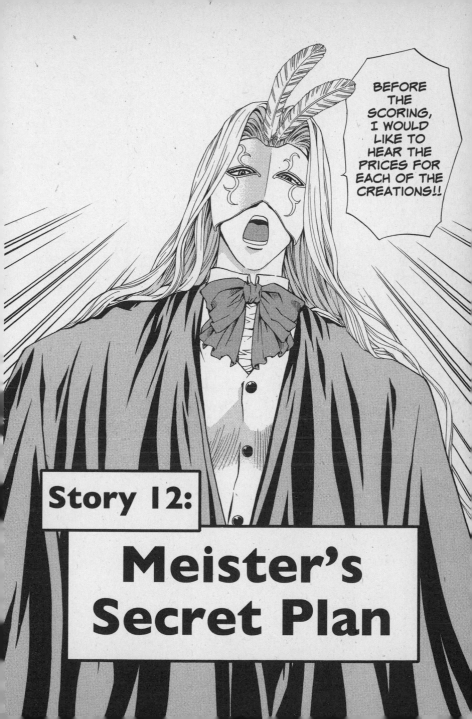

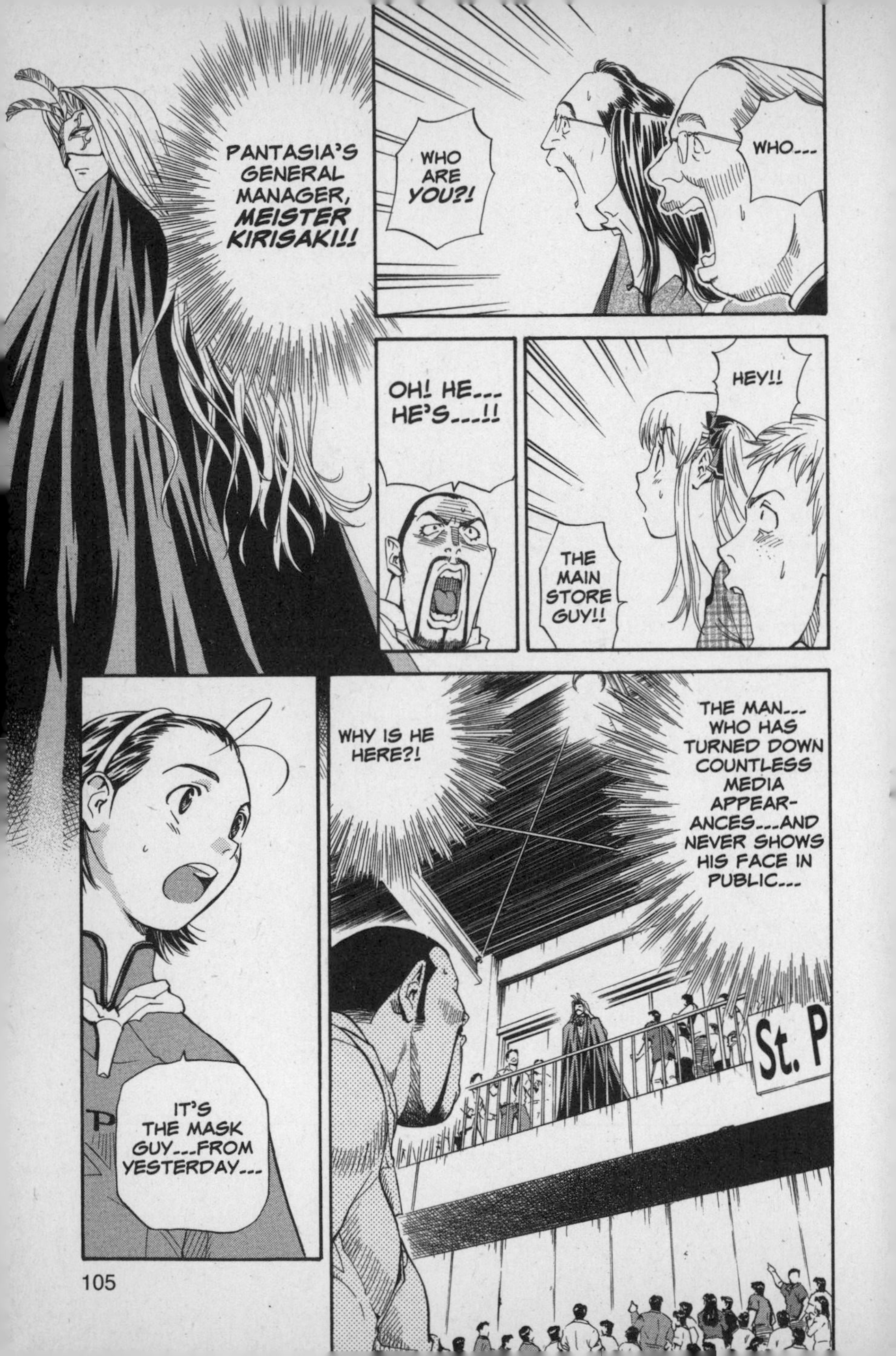
WHO...
WHO ARE YOU?!
HEY!!
THE MAIN STORE GUY!!
OH! HE... HE'S...!!
PANTASIA'S GENERAL MANAGER, MEISTER KIRISAKI!!
THE MAN... WHO HAS TURNED DOWN COUNTLESS MEDIA APPEAR-ANCES...AND NEVER SHOWS HIS FACE IN PUBLIC...
WHY IS HE HERE?!
St. P
IT'S THE MASK GUY...FROM YESTERDAY...

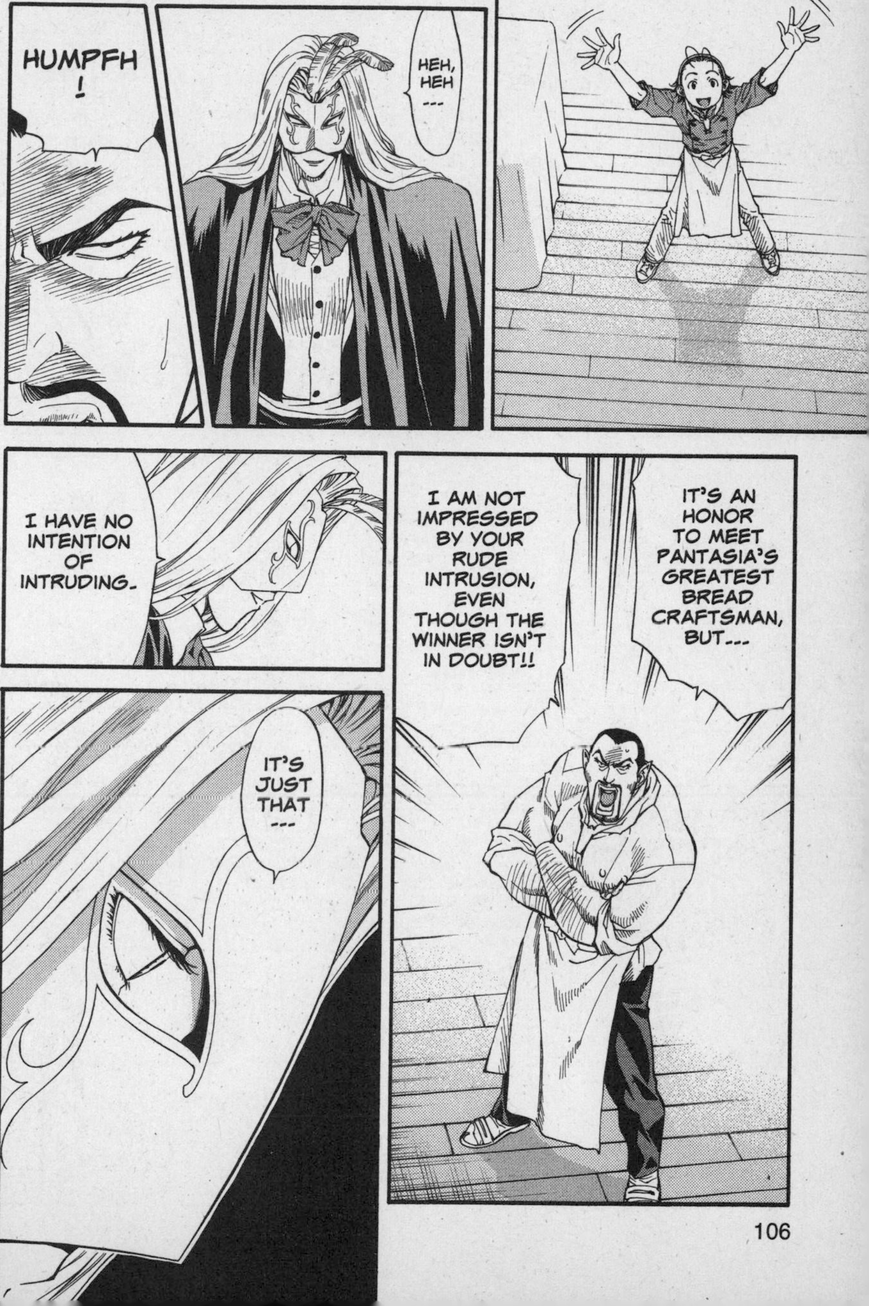
HEH, HEH ---
HUMPFH !
IT'S AN HONOR TO MEET PANTASIA'S GREATEST BREAD CRAFTSMAN, BUT...
I AM NOT IMPRESSED BY YOUR RUDE INTRUSION, EVEN THOUGH THE WINNER ISN'T IN DOUBT!!
I HAVE NO INTENTION OF INTRUDING.
IT'S JUST THAT ---

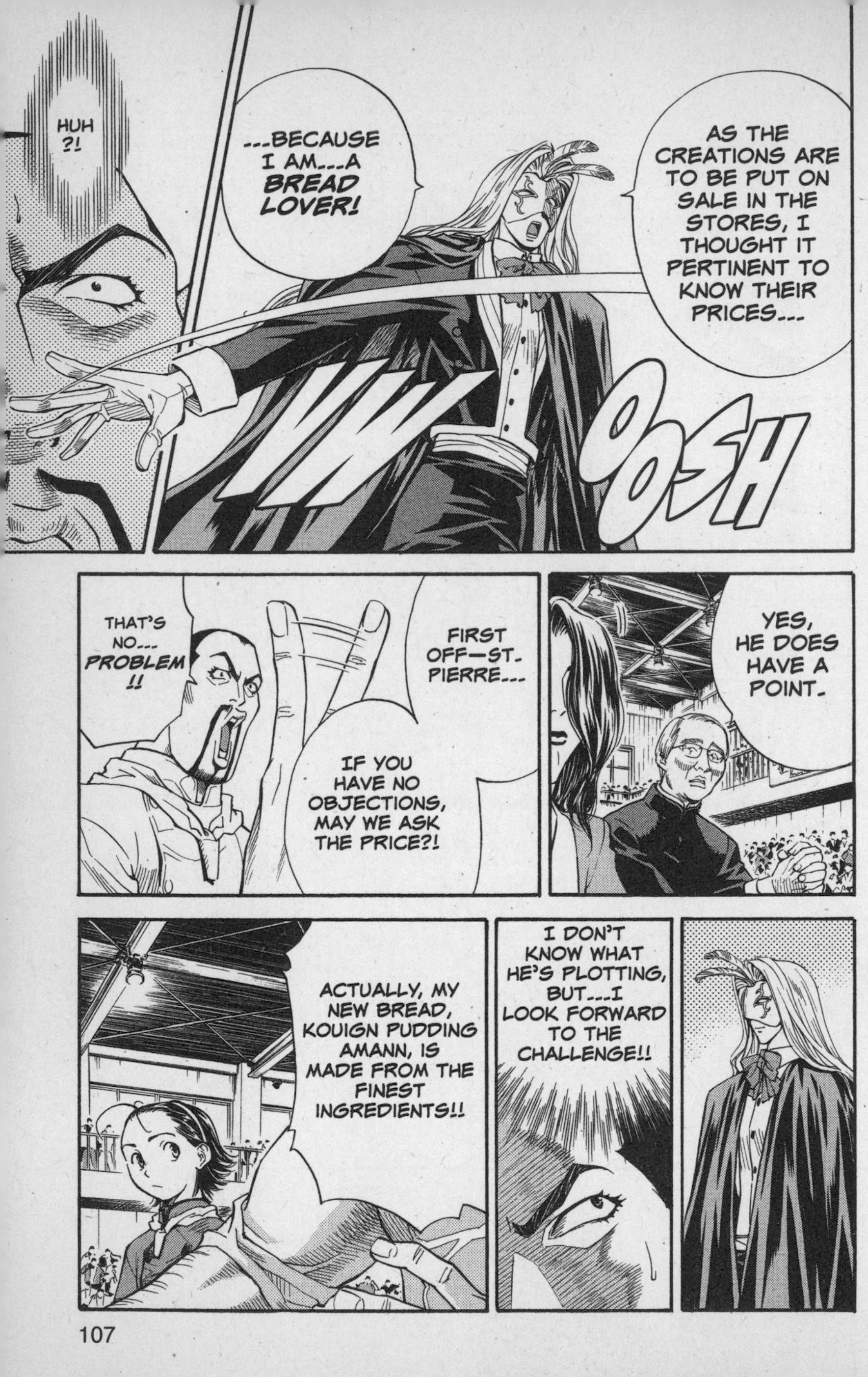
AS THE CREATIONS ARE TO BE PUT ON SALE IN THE STORES, I THOUGHT IT PERTINENT TO KNOW THEIR PRICES...
...BECAUSE I AM...A BREAD LOVER!
HUH ?!
WHOOSH
YES, HE DOES HAVE A POINT.
FIRST OFF—ST. PIERRE...
IF YOU HAVE NO OBJECTIONS, MAY WE ASK THE PRICE?!
THAT'S NO... PROBLEM !!
I DON'T KNOW WHAT HE'S PLOTTING, BUT...I LOOK FORWARD TO THE CHALLENGE!!
ACTUALLY, MY NEW BREAD, KOUIGN PUDDING AMANN, IS MADE FROM THE FINEST INGREDIENTS!!

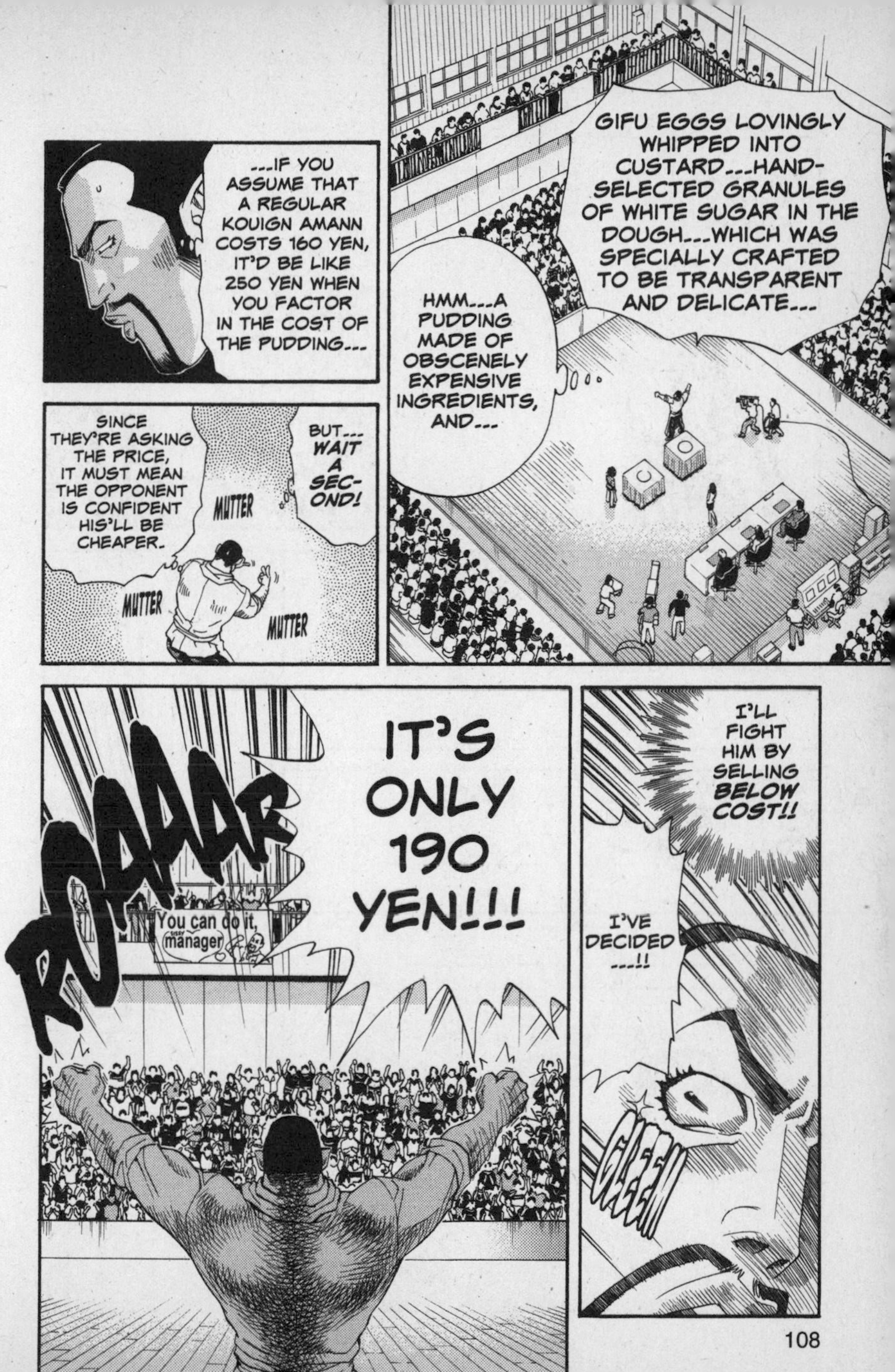

GIFU EGGS LOVINGLY WHIPPED INTO CUSTARD...HAND-SELECTED GRANULES OF WHITE SUGAR IN THE DOUGH...WHICH WAS SPECIALLY CRAFTED TO BE TRANSPARENT AND DELICATE...
HMM...A PUDDING MADE OF OBSCENELY EXPENSIVE INGREDIENTS, AND...
...IF YOU ASSUME THAT A REGULAR KOUIGN AMANN COSTS 160 YEN, IT'D BE LIKE 250 YEN WHEN YOU FACTOR IN THE COST OF THE PUDDING...
BUT... WAIT A SECOND!
SINCE THEY'RE ASKING THE PRICE, IT MUST MEAN THE OPPONENT IS CONFIDENT HIS'LL BE CHEAPER.
MUTTER
MUTTER
MUTTER
I'LL FIGHT HIM BY SELLING BELOW COST!!
I'VE DECIDED ...!!
IT'S ONLY 190 YEN!!!
ROAAAR
You can do it, manager

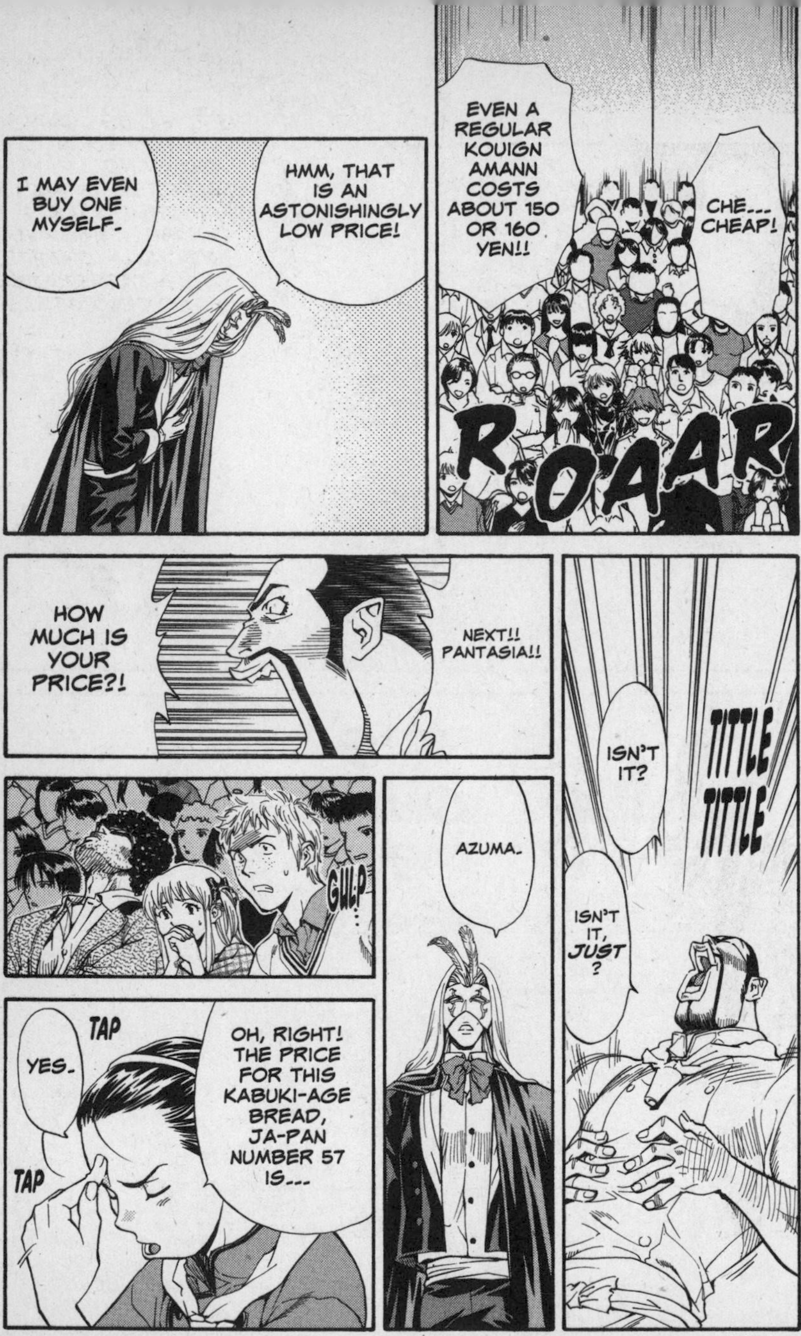
CHE... CHEAP!
EVEN A REGULAR KOUIGN AMANN COSTS ABOUT 150 OR 160 YEN!!
ROAAR
HMM, THAT IS AN ASTONISHINGLY LOW PRICE!
I MAY EVEN BUY ONE MYSELF.
TITTLE TITTLE
ISN'T IT?
ISN'T IT, JUST?
NEXT!! PANTASIA!!
HOW MUCH IS YOUR PRICE?!
AZUMA.
GULP
OH, RIGHT! THE PRICE FOR THIS KABUKI-AGE BREAD, JA-PAN NUMBER 57 IS...
TAP
YES.
TAP

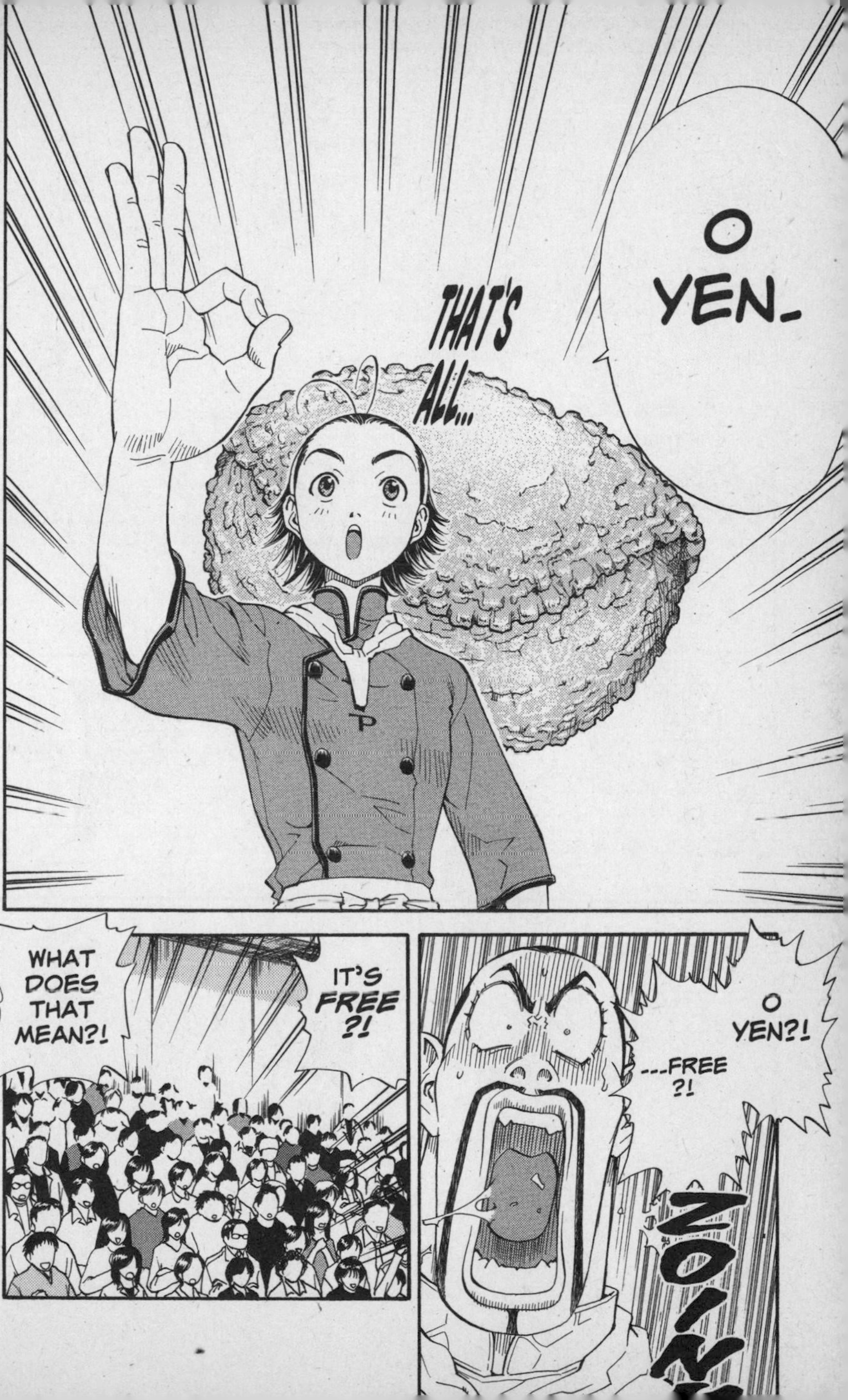
0 YEN_
THAT'S ALL...
0 YEN?!
---FREE ?!
ZOIN
IT'S FREE ?!
WHAT DOES THAT MEAN?!

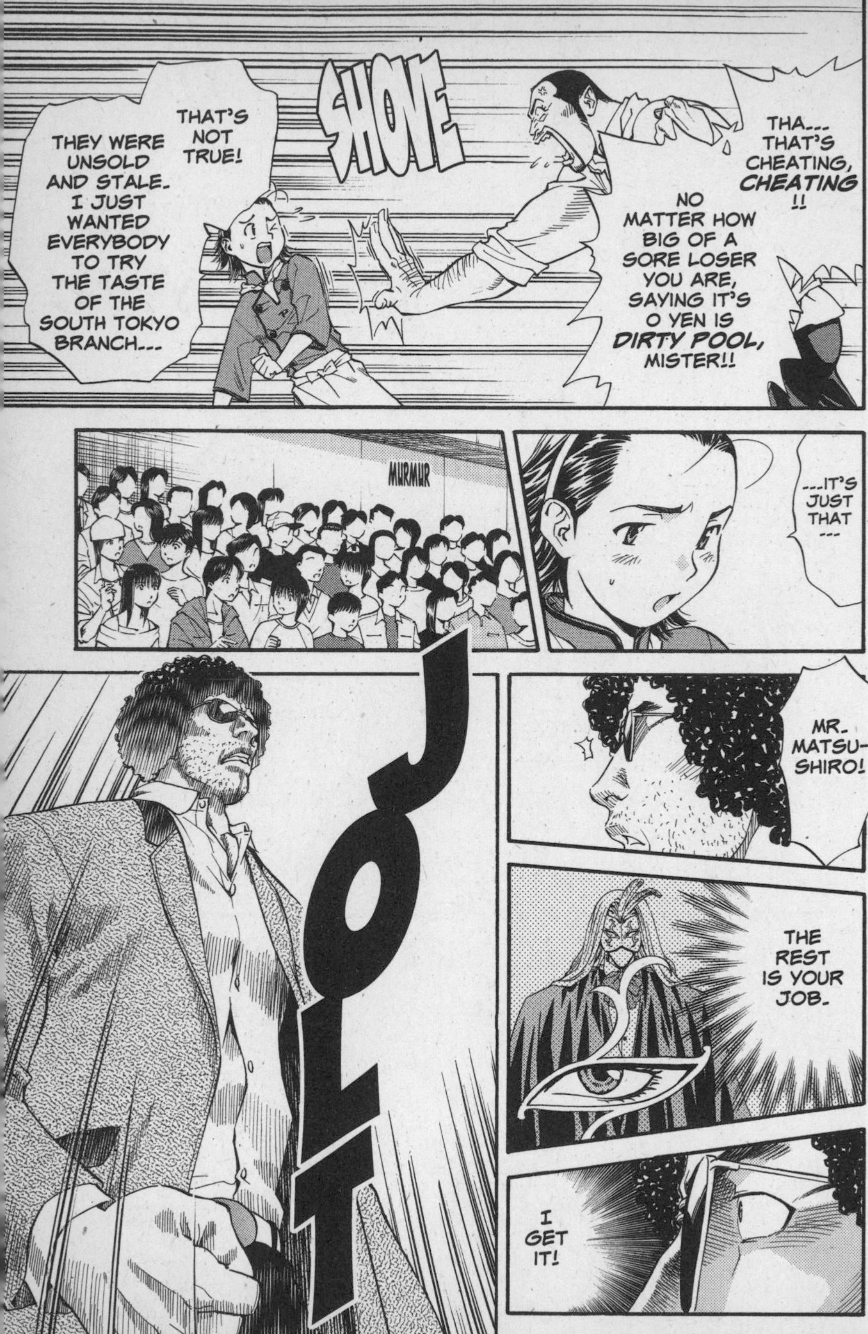
THA... THAT'S CHEATING, CHEATING!!
NO MATTER HOW BIG OF A SORE LOSER YOU ARE, SAYING IT'S 0 YEN IS DIRTY POOL, MISTER!!
SHOVE
THAT'S NOT TRUE!
THEY WERE UNSOLD AND STALE. I JUST WANTED EVERYBODY TO TRY THE TASTE OF THE SOUTH TOKYO BRANCH...
...IT'S JUST THAT ...
MURMUR
MR. MATSUSHIRO!
THE REST IS YOUR JOB.
I GET IT!
JOLT

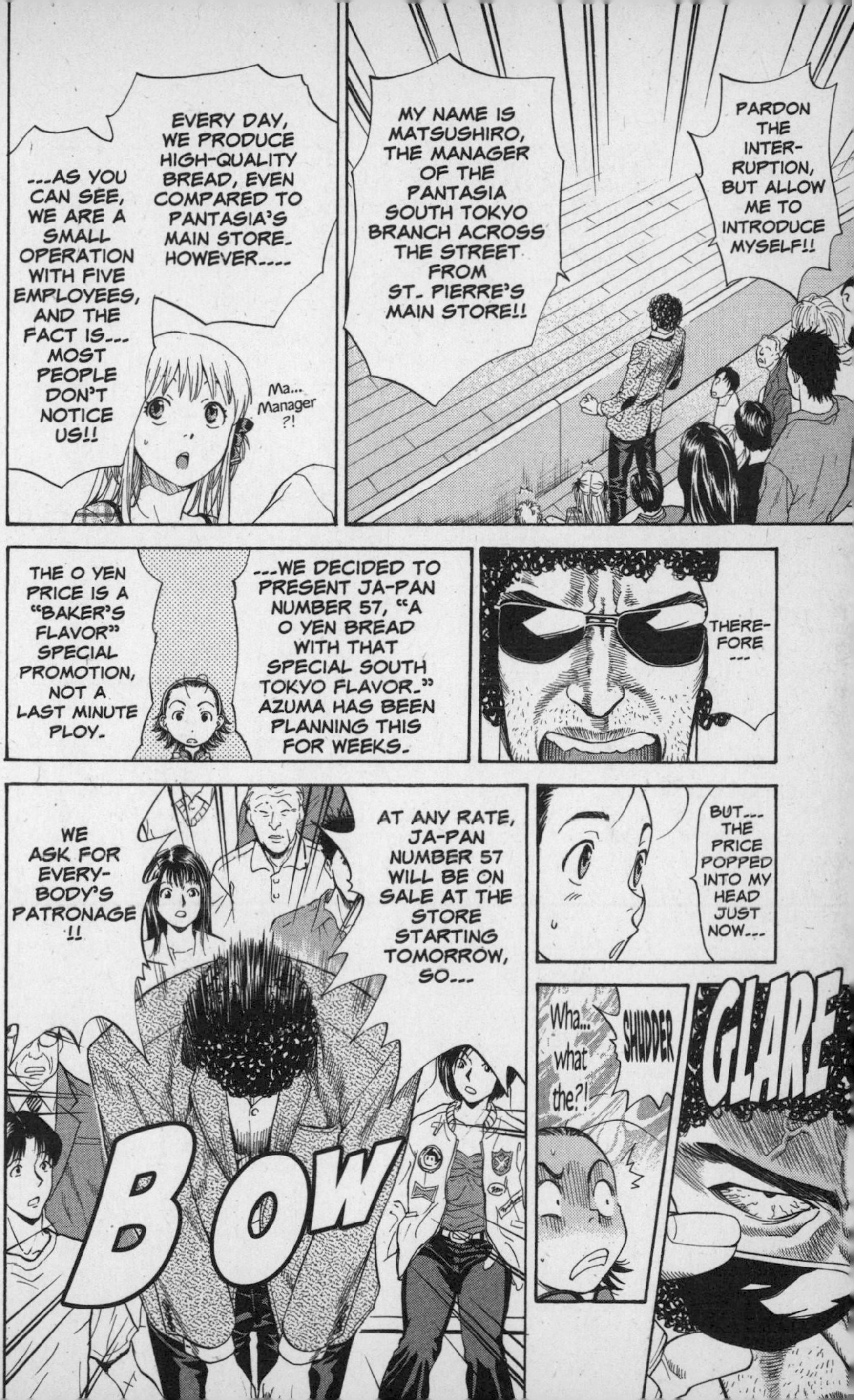
PARDON THE INTER-RUPTION, BUT ALLOW ME TO INTRODUCE MYSELF!!
MY NAME IS MATSUSHIRO, THE MANAGER OF THE PANTASIA SOUTH TOKYO BRANCH ACROSS THE STREET FROM ST. PIERRE'S MAIN STORE!!
...AS YOU CAN SEE, WE ARE A SMALL OPERATION WITH FIVE EMPLOYEES, AND THE FACT IS... MOST PEOPLE DON'T NOTICE US!!
EVERY DAY, WE PRODUCE HIGH-QUALITY BREAD, EVEN COMPARED TO PANTASIA'S MAIN STORE. HOWEVER....
Ma... Manager?!
THERE-FORE ...
...WE DECIDED TO PRESENT JA-PAN NUMBER 57, "A 0 YEN BREAD WITH THAT SPECIAL SOUTH TOKYO FLAVOR." AZUMA HAS BEEN PLANNING THIS FOR WEEKS.
THE 0 YEN PRICE IS A "BAKER'S FLAVOR" SPECIAL PROMOTION, NOT A LAST MINUTE PLOY.
BUT... THE PRICE POPPED INTO MY HEAD JUST NOW...
GLARE
SHUDDER
Wha... what the?!
AT ANY RATE, JA-PAN NUMBER 57 WILL BE ON SALE AT THE STORE STARTING TOMORROW, SO...
WE ASK FOR EVERY-BODY'S PATRONAGE !!
BOW

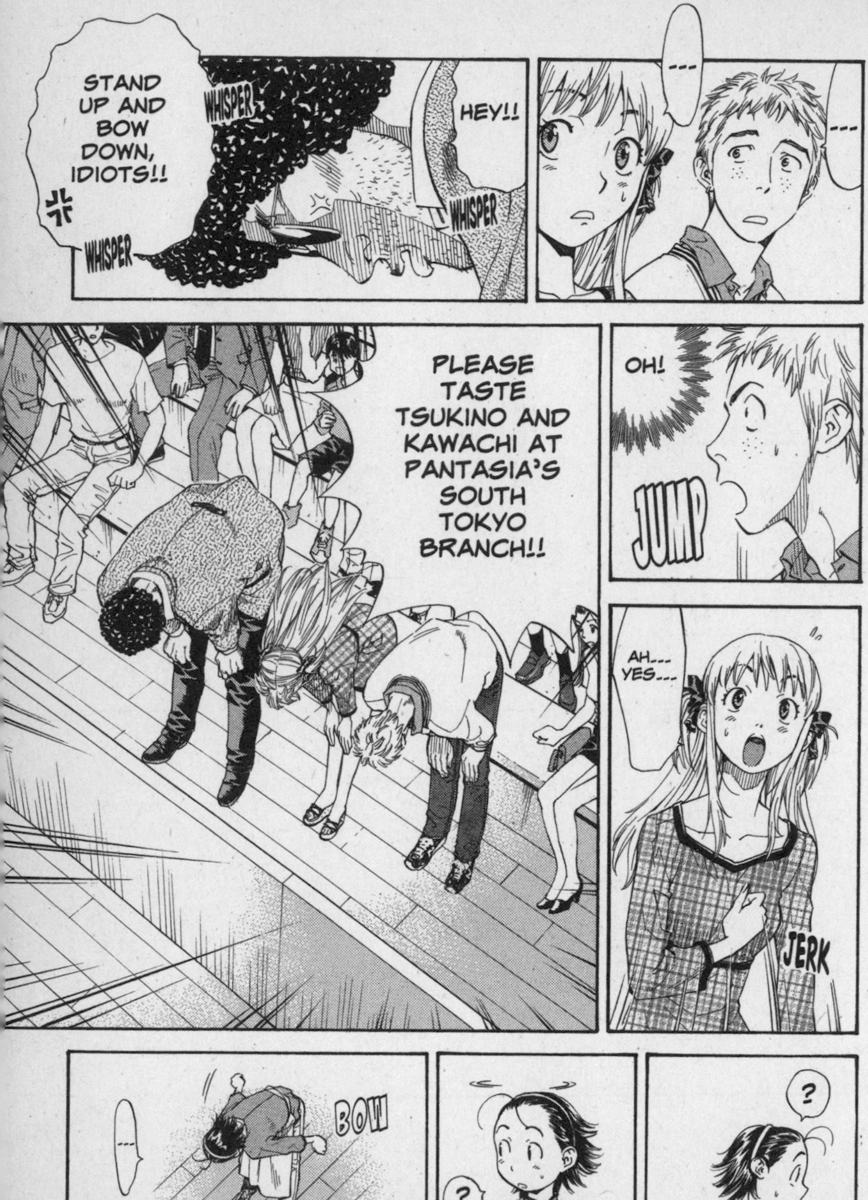
...
...
HEY!!
WHISPER
WHISPER
STAND UP AND BOW DOWN, IDIOTS!!
WHISPER
OH!
JUMP
AH... YES...
JERK
PLEASE TASTE TSUKINO AND KAWACHI AT PANTASIA'S SOUTH TOKYO BRANCH!!
?
?
BOW
...

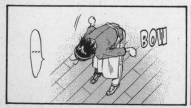

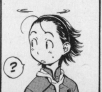

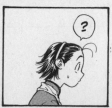

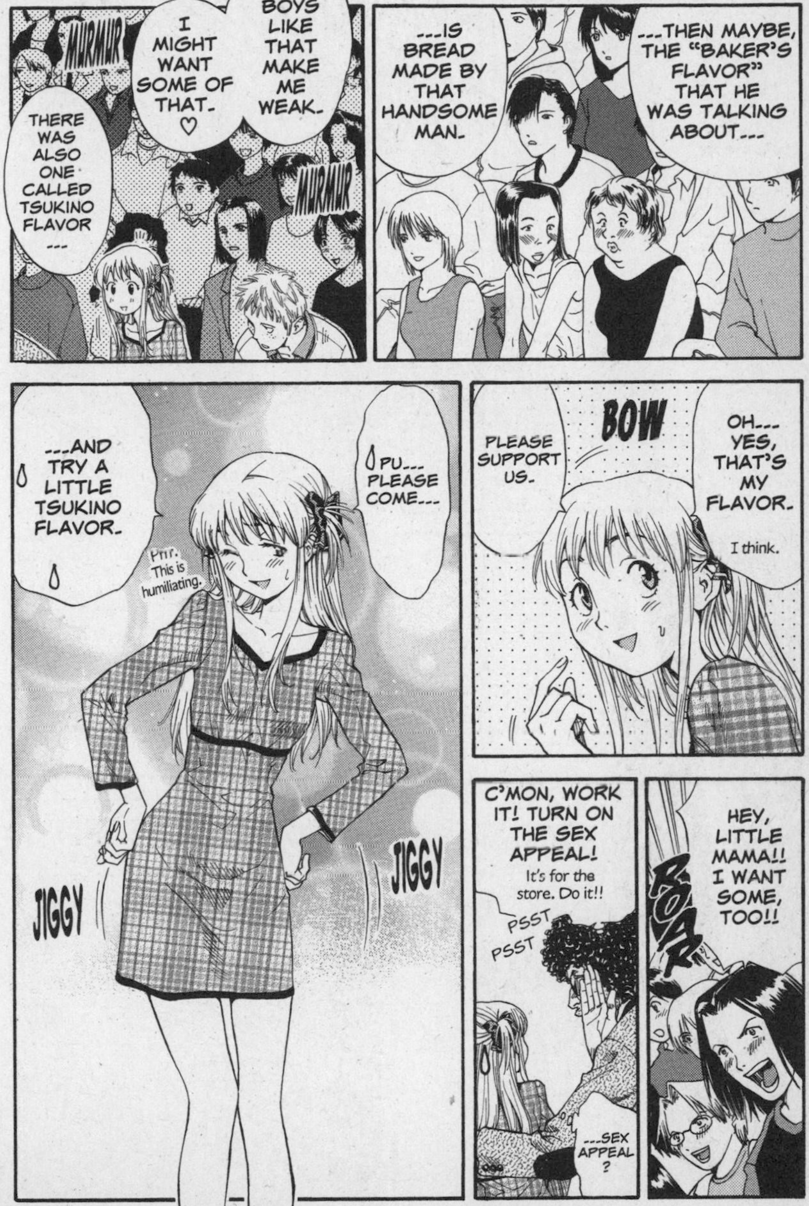

...THEN MAYBE, THE "BAKER'S FLAVOR" THAT HE WAS TALKING ABOUT...
...IS BREAD MADE BY THAT HANDSOME MAN.
BAD BOYS LIKE THAT MAKE ME WEAK.
I MIGHT WANT SOME OF THAT. ♡
MURMUR
THERE WAS ALSO ONE CALLED TSUKINO FLAVOR ...
MURMUR
OH... YES, THAT'S MY FLAVOR.
I think.
BOW
PLEASE SUPPORT US.
HEY, LITTLE MAMA!! I WANT SOME, TOO!!
C'MON, WORK IT! TURN ON THE SEX APPEAL!
It's for the store. Do it!!
PSST
PSST
...SEX APPEAL?
PU... PLEASE COME...
This is humiliating.
...AND TRY A LITTLE TSUKINO FLAVOR.
JIGGY
JIGGY

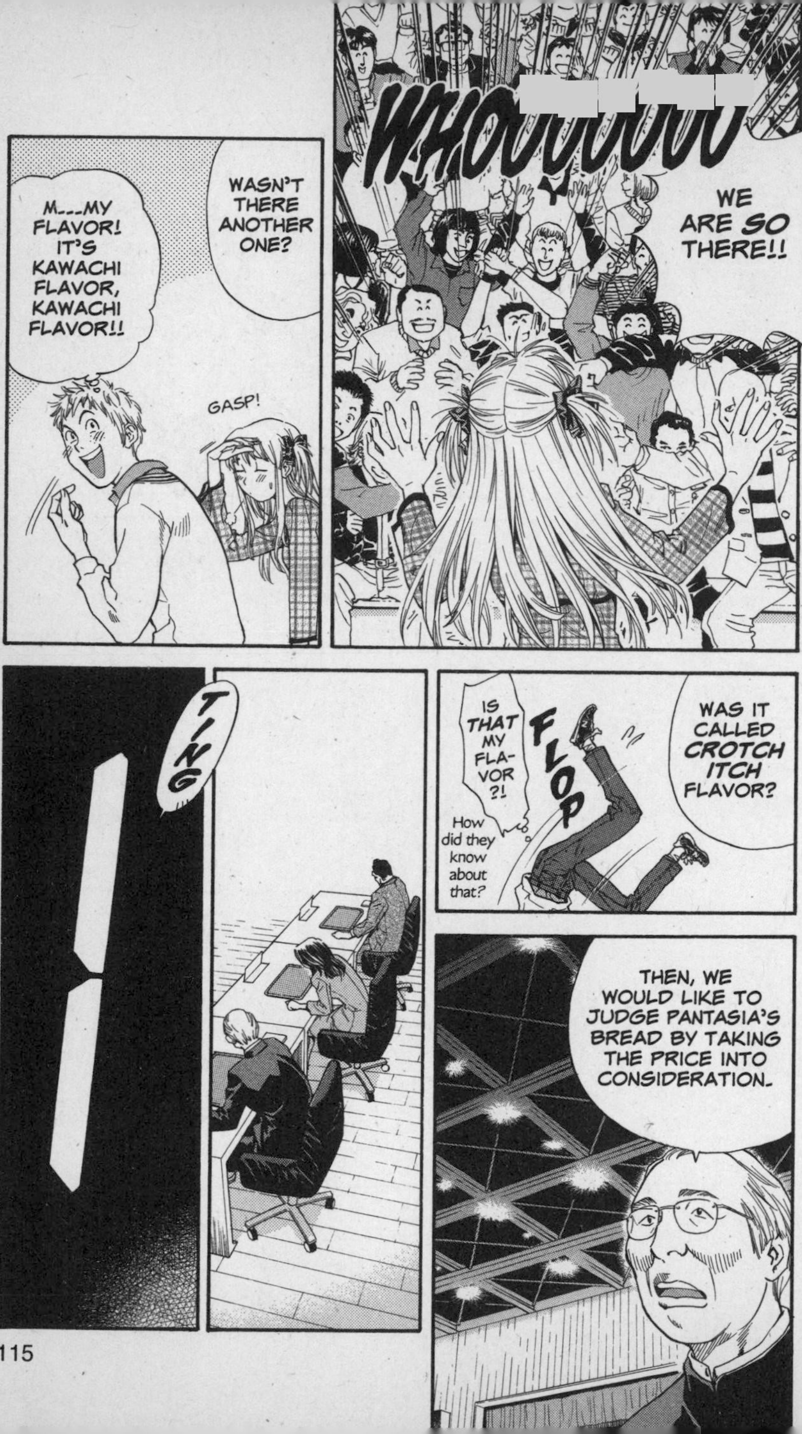
WHOOOOOO
WE ARE SO THERE!!
WASN'T THERE ANOTHER ONE?
M...MY FLAVOR! IT'S KAWACHI FLAVOR, KAWACHI FLAVOR!!
GASP!
WAS IT CALLED CROTCH ITCH FLAVOR?
FLOP
IS THAT MY FLAVOR?!
How did they know about that?
THEN, WE WOULD LIKE TO JUDGE PANTASIA'S BREAD BY TAKING THE PRICE INTO CONSIDERATION.
TING

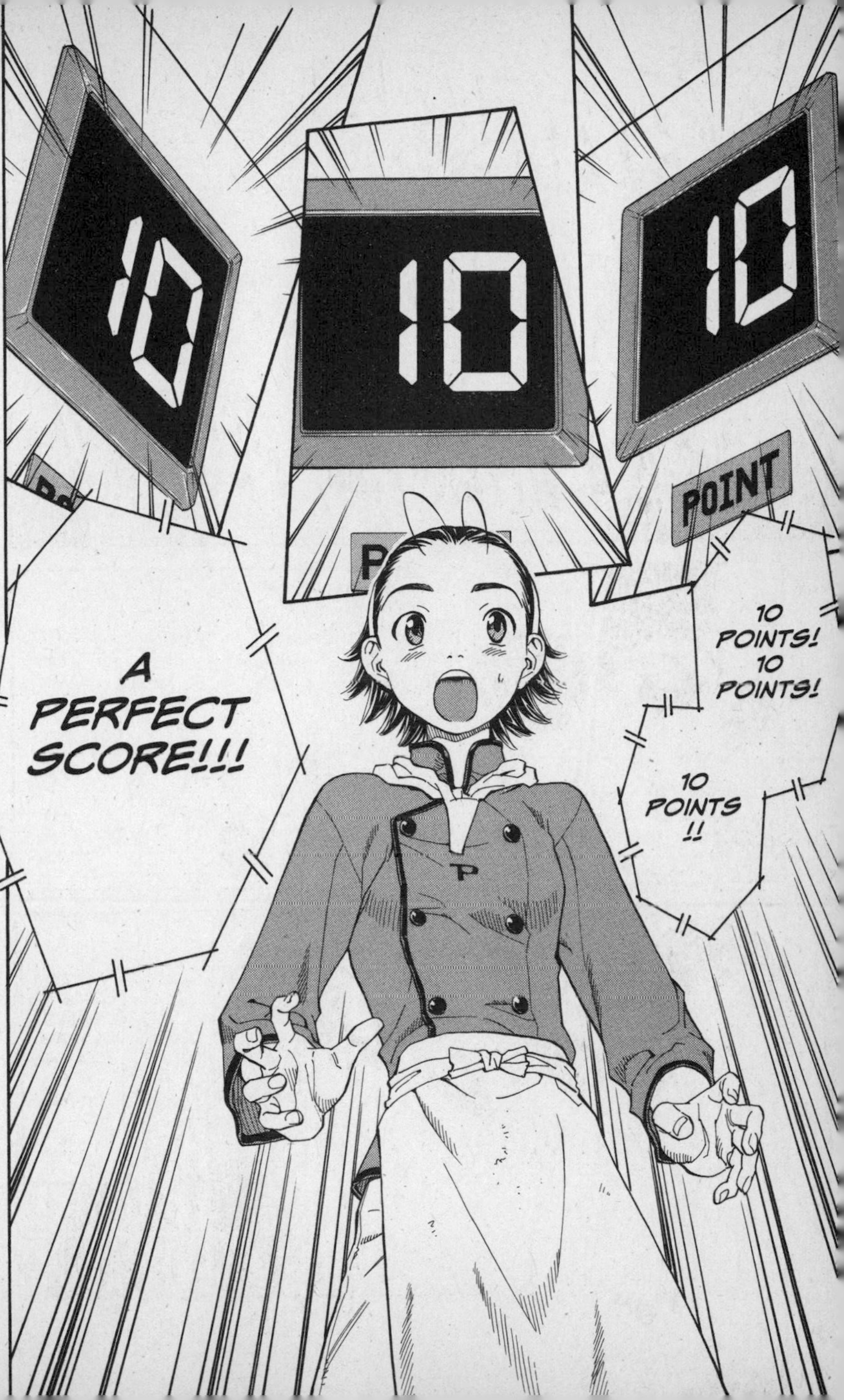
10
10
10
POINT
10 POINTS! 10 POINTS!
10 POINTS !!
A PERFECT SCORE!!!

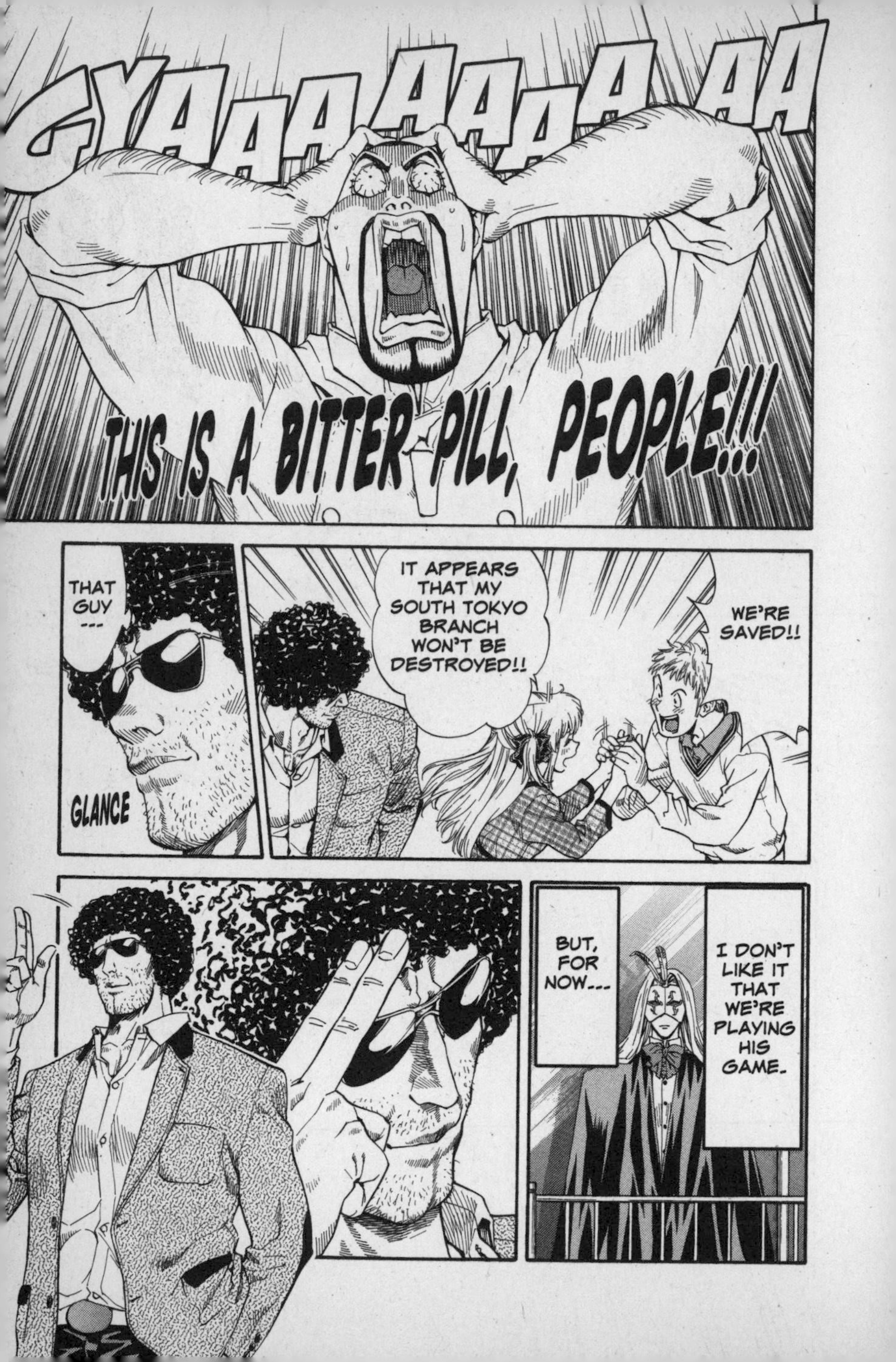
CYAAAAAAAAA
THIS IS A BITTER PILL, PEOPLE!!!
IT APPEARS THAT MY SOUTH TOKYO BRANCH WON'T BE DESTROYED!!
WE'RE SAVED!!
THAT GUY ---
GLANCE
I DON'T LIKE IT THAT WE'RE PLAYING HIS GAME.
BUT, FOR NOW...

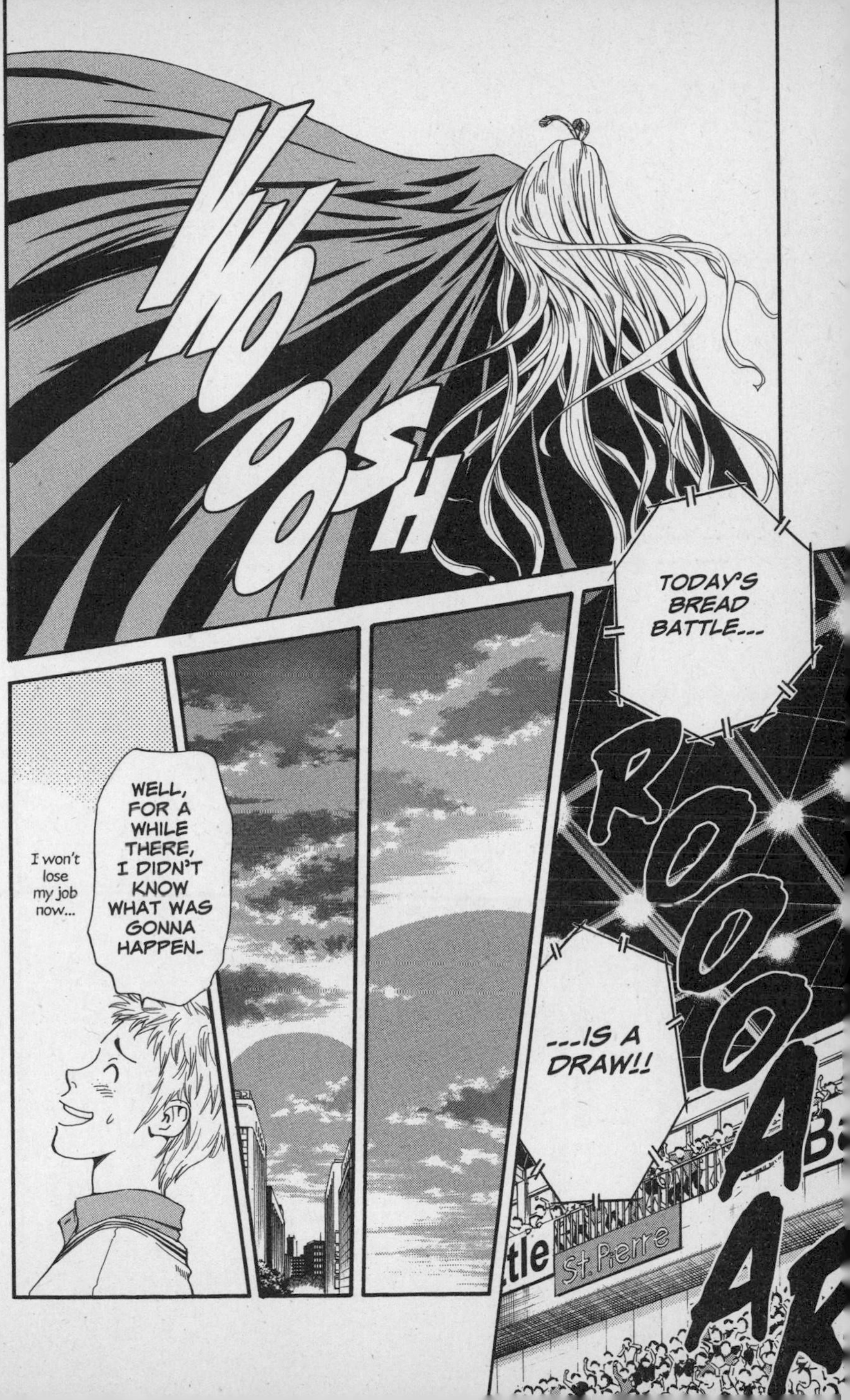
WHOOOOSH
TODAY'S BREAD BATTLE...
ROOOOAAAR
...IS A DRAW!!
St.Pierre
WELL, FOR A WHILE THERE, I DIDN'T KNOW WHAT WAS GONNA HAPPEN.
I won't lose my job now...

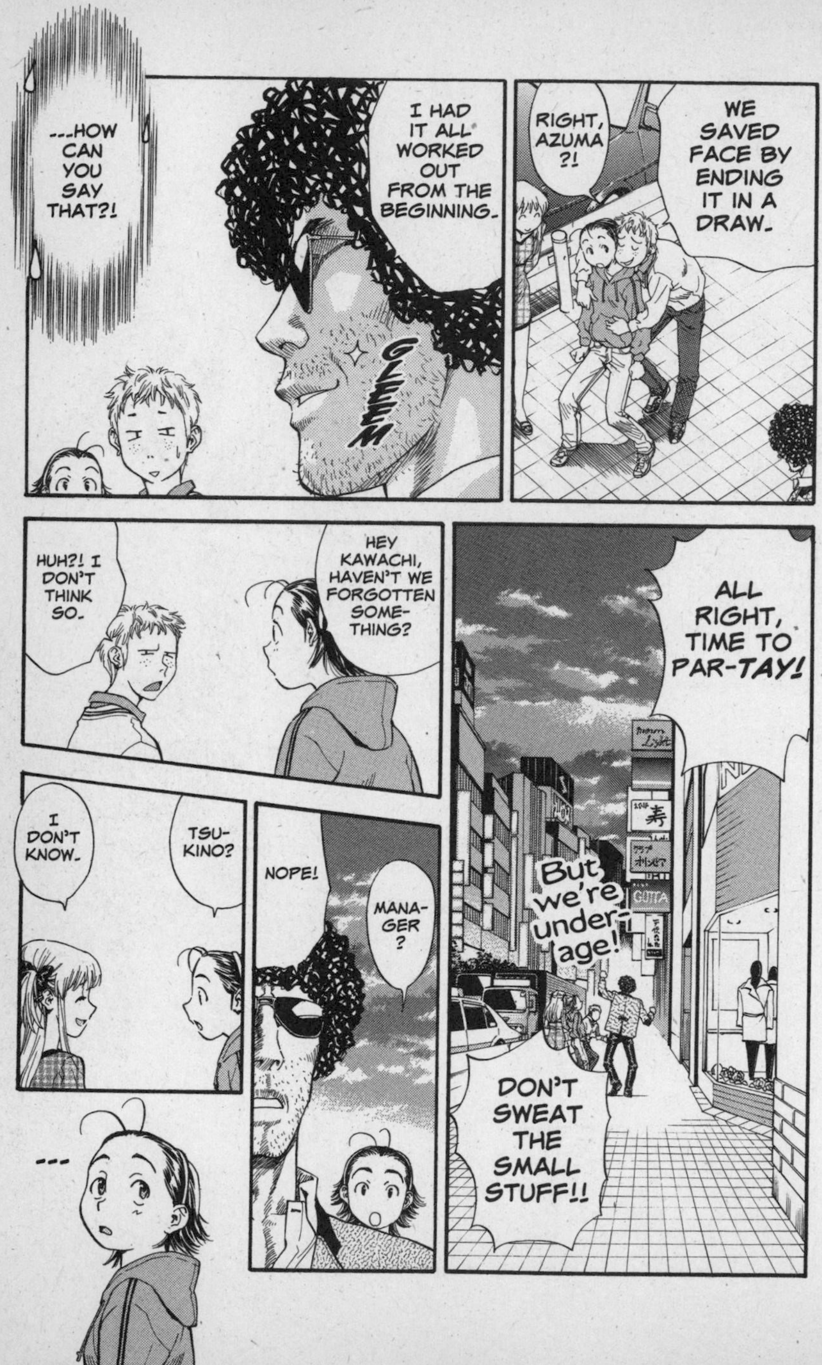
WE SAVED FACE BY ENDING IT IN A DRAW.
RIGHT, AZUMA?!
I HAD IT ALL WORKED OUT FROM THE BEGINNING.
GLEEEM
...HOW CAN YOU SAY THAT?!
ALL RIGHT, TIME TO PAR-TAY!
But we're under-age!
DON'T SWEAT THE SMALL STUFF!!
HEY KAWACHI, HAVEN'T WE FORGOTTEN SOME-THING?
HUH?! I DON'T THINK SO.
MANA-GER?
NOPE!
TSU-KINO?
I DON'T KNOW.
...

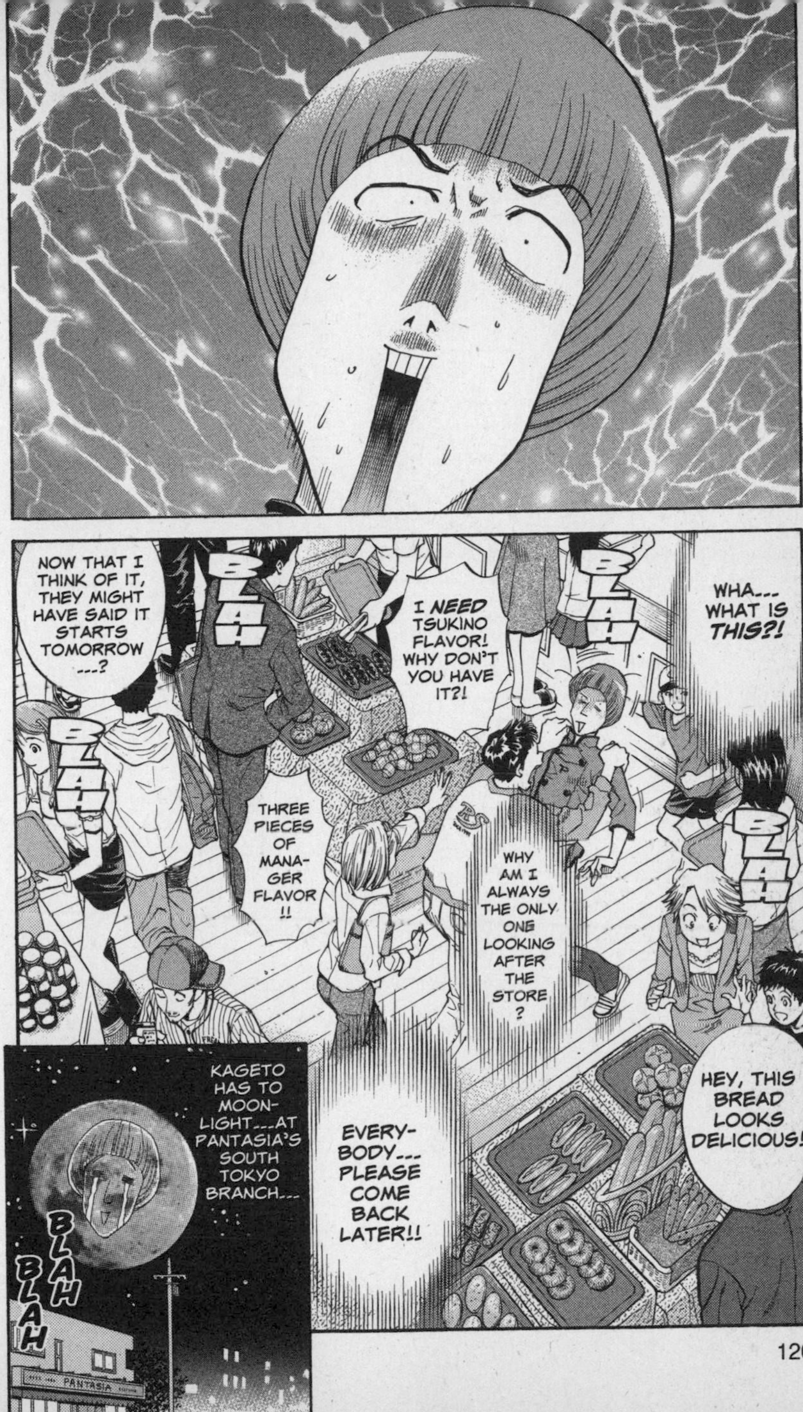
WHA... WHAT IS *THIS?!*
BLAH
I *NEED* TSUKINO FLAVOR! WHY DON'T YOU HAVE IT?!
BLAH
NOW THAT I THINK OF IT, THEY MIGHT HAVE SAID IT STARTS TOMORROW ...?
BLAH
BLAH
WHY AM I ALWAYS THE ONLY ONE LOOKING AFTER THE STORE ?
THREE PIECES OF MANAGER FLAVOR !!
HEY, THIS BREAD LOOKS DELICIOUS!
EVERYBODY... PLEASE COME BACK LATER!!
KAGETO HAS TO MOONLIGHT...AT PANTASIA'S SOUTH TOKYO BRANCH...
BLAH
BLAH
PANTASIA

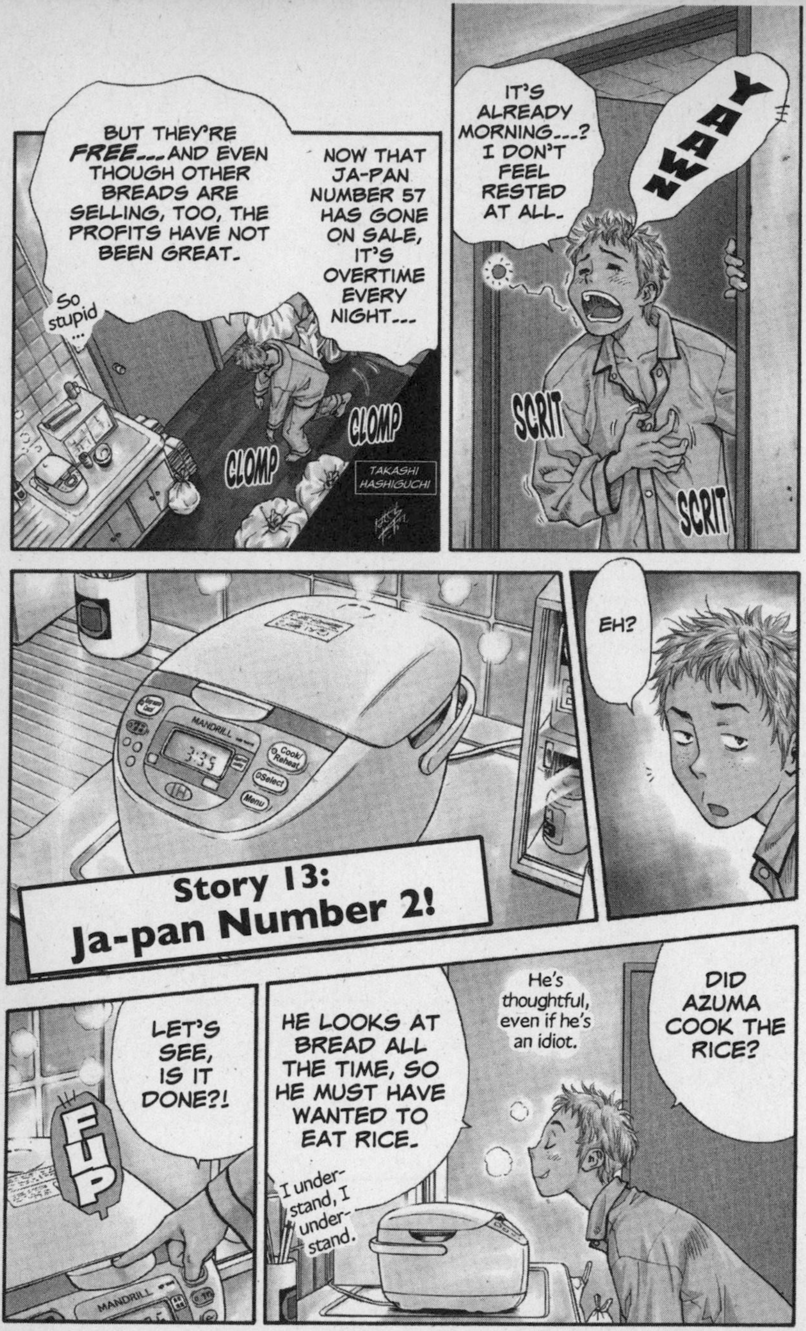
YAAWN
IT'S ALREADY MORNING...? I DON'T FEEL RESTED AT ALL.
SCRIT
SCRIT
NOW THAT JA-PAN NUMBER 57 HAS GONE ON SALE, IT'S OVERTIME EVERY NIGHT...
BUT THEY'RE *FREE*... AND EVEN THOUGH OTHER BREADS ARE SELLING, TOO, THE PROFITS HAVE NOT BEEN GREAT.
So stupid...
CLOMP
CLOMP
TAKASHI HASHIGUCHI
EH?
Story 13: Ja-pan Number 2!
DID AZUMA COOK THE RICE?
He's thoughtful, even if he's an idiot.
HE LOOKS AT BREAD ALL THE TIME, SO HE MUST HAVE WANTED TO EAT RICE.
I under-stand, I under-stand.
LET'S SEE, IS IT DONE?!
FUP

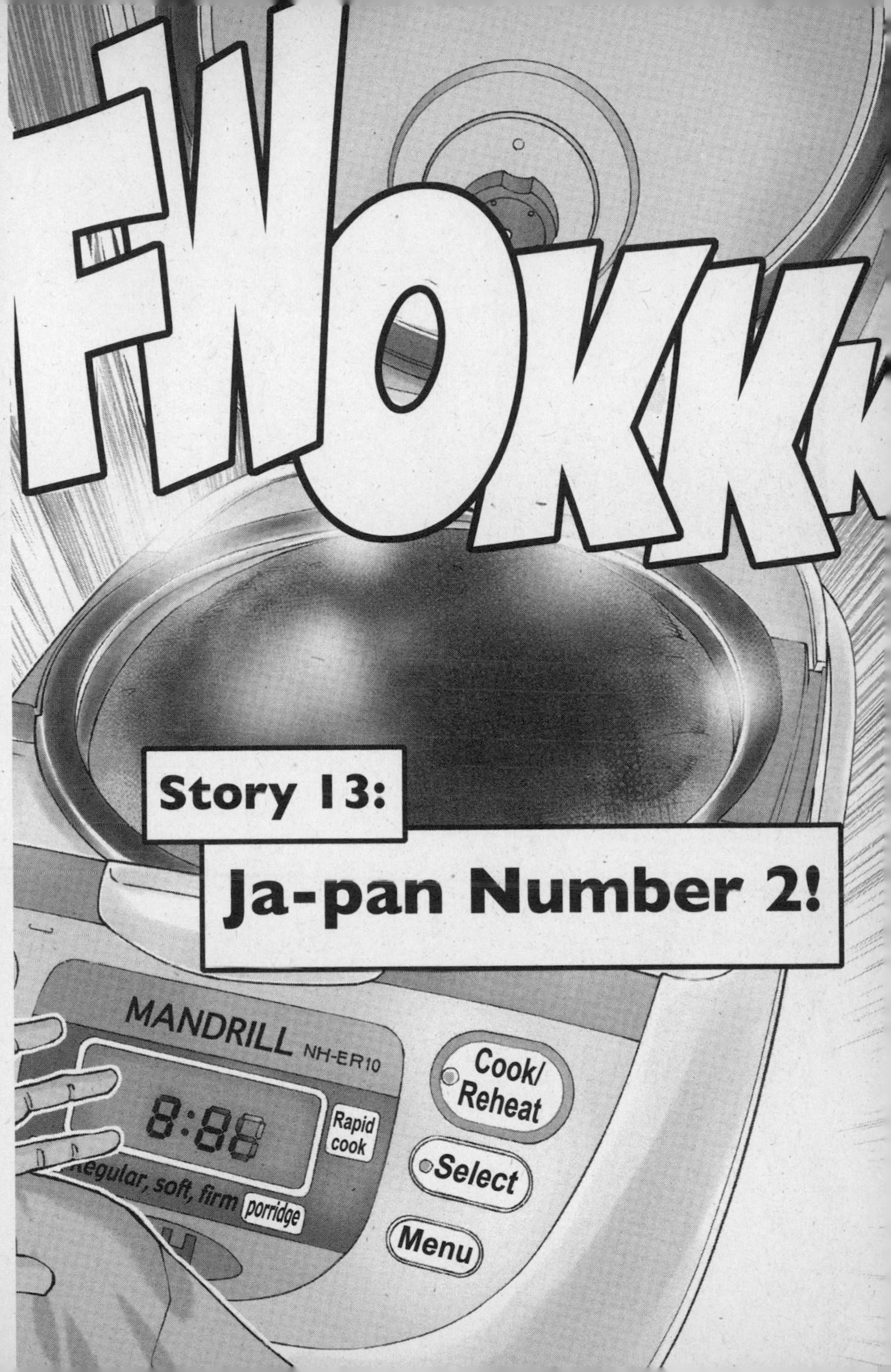
FWOKK
Story 13:
Ja-pan Number 2!
MANDRILL NH-ER10
8:88
Rapid cook
Regular, soft, firm
porridge
Cook/ Reheat
Select
Menu

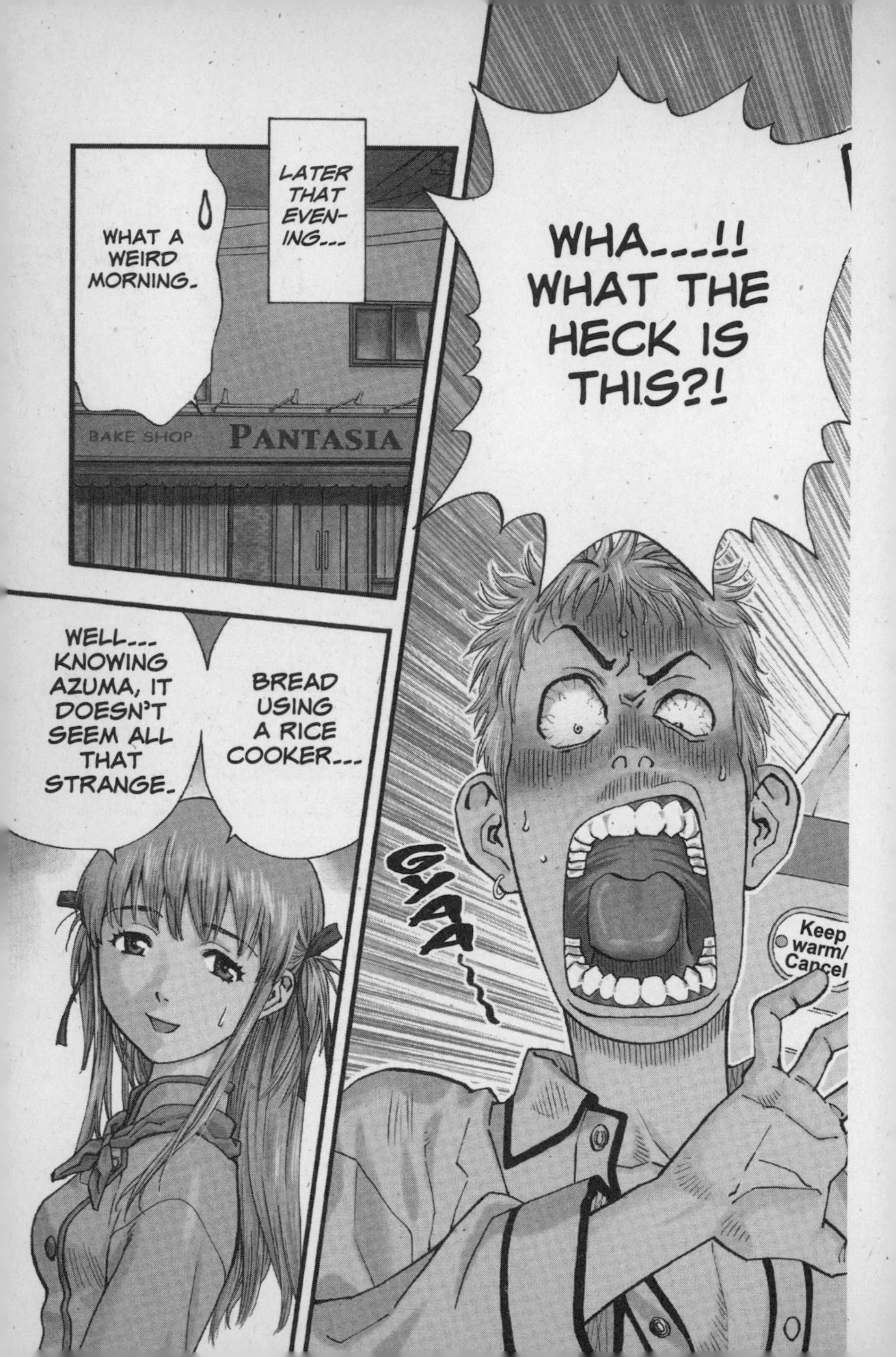
WHA...!! WHAT THE HECK IS THIS?!
GYAA...
Keep warm/ Cancel
LATER THAT EVEN-ING...
WHAT A WEIRD MORNING.
BAKE SHOP
PANTASIA
BREAD USING A RICE COOKER...
WELL... KNOWING AZUMA, IT DOESN'T SEEM ALL THAT STRANGE.

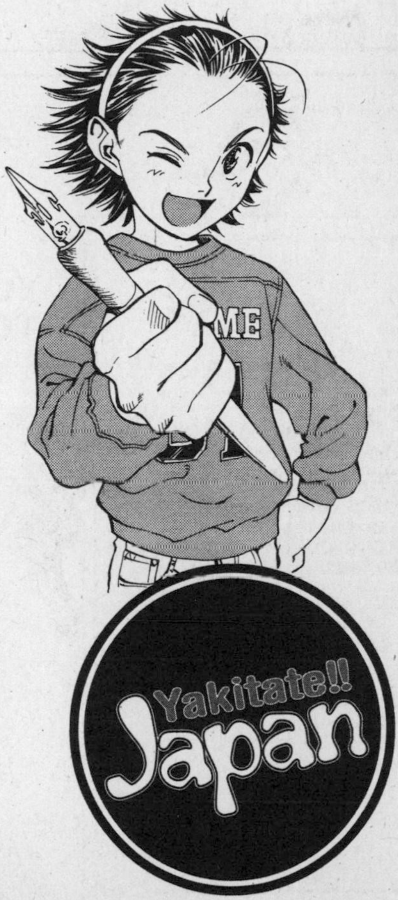
Yakitate!!
Japan

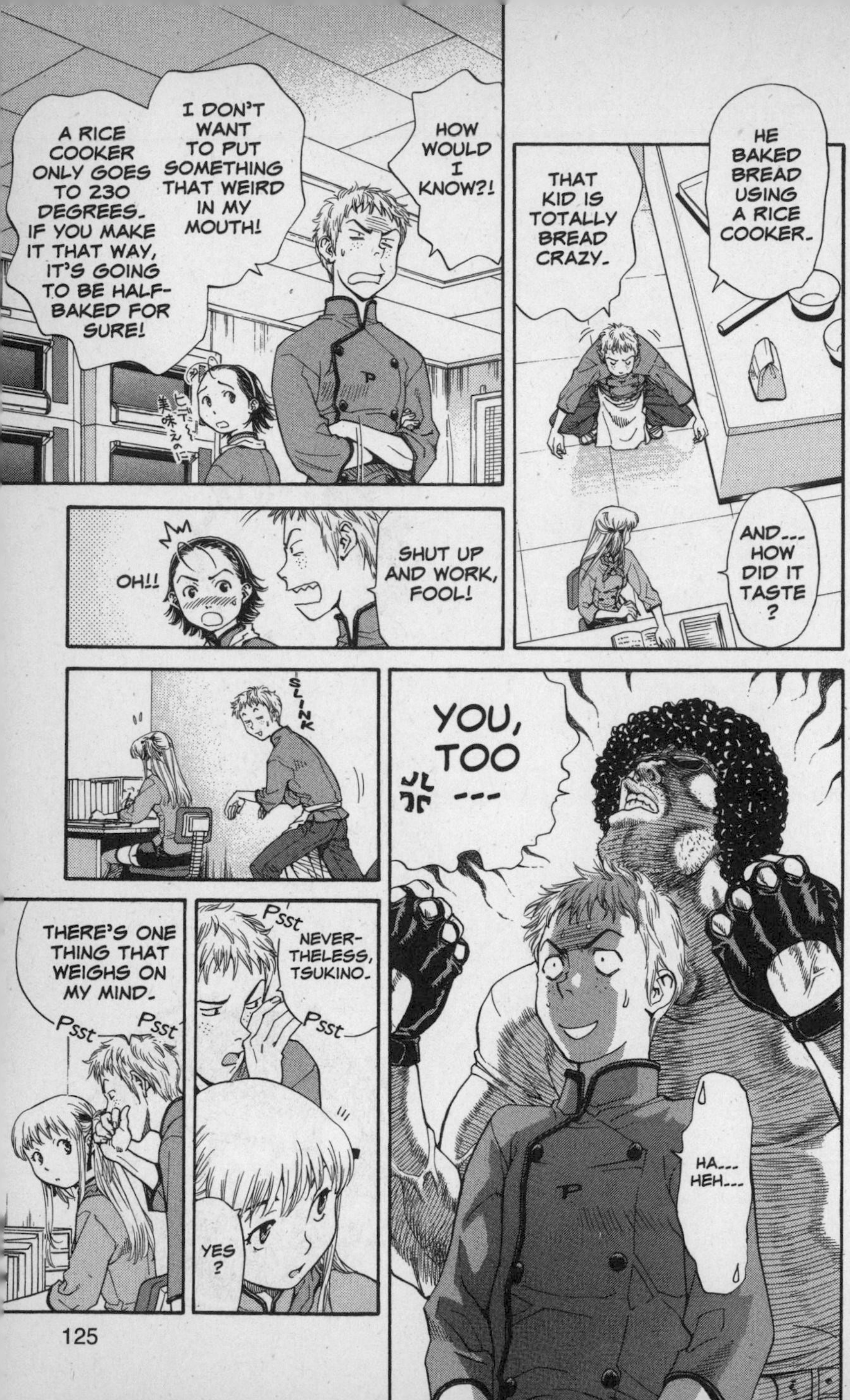
HE BAKED BREAD USING A RICE COOKER.
THAT KID IS TOTALLY BREAD CRAZY.
AND... HOW DID IT TASTE?
HOW WOULD I KNOW?!
I DON'T WANT TO PUT SOMETHING THAT WEIRD IN MY MOUTH!
A RICE COOKER ONLY GOES TO 230 DEGREES. IF YOU MAKE IT THAT WAY, IT'S GOING TO BE HALF-BAKED FOR SURE!
SHUT UP AND WORK, FOOL!
OH!!
YOU, TOO ---
HA... HEH...
SLINK
Psst
NEVERTHELESS, TSUKINO.
Psst
YES?
THERE'S ONE THING THAT WEIGHS ON MY MIND.
Psst
Psst

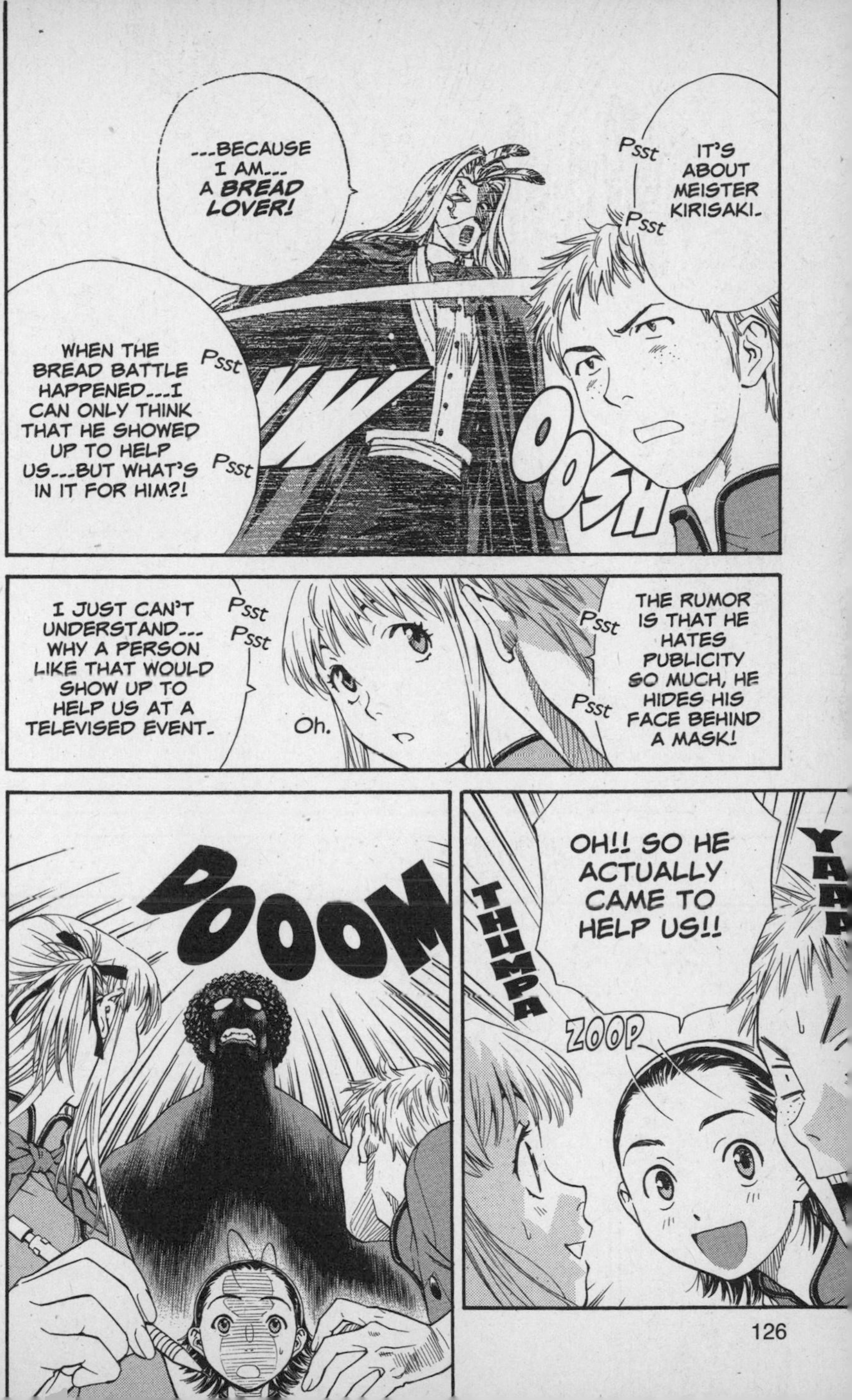
Psst
IT'S ABOUT MEISTER KIRISAKI...
Psst
...BECAUSE I AM... A BREAD LOVER!
WHOOSH
WHEN THE BREAD BATTLE HAPPENED... I CAN ONLY THINK THAT HE SHOWED UP TO HELP US... BUT WHAT'S IN IT FOR HIM?!
Psst
Psst
Psst
THE RUMOR IS THAT HE HATES PUBLICITY SO MUCH, HE HIDES HIS FACE BEHIND A MASK!
Psst
Oh.
Psst
Psst
I JUST CAN'T UNDERSTAND... WHY A PERSON LIKE THAT WOULD SHOW UP TO HELP US AT A TELEVISED EVENT...
OH!! SO HE ACTUALLY CAME TO HELP US!!
THUMPA
ZOOP
DOOOM

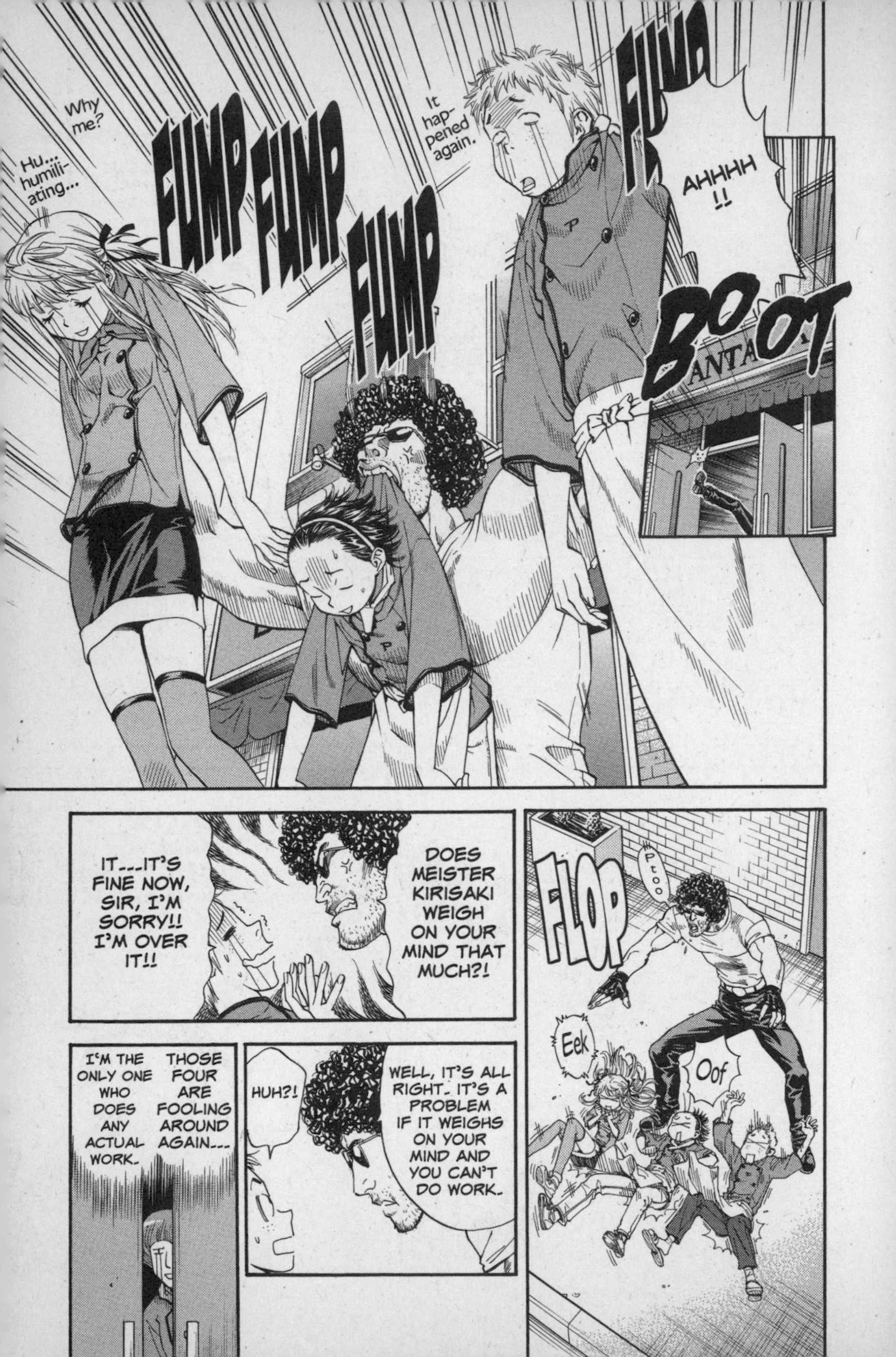
AHHHH !!
BOOT
It hap-pened again.
FUMP FUMP FUMP
Why me?
Hu... humili-ating...
FLOP
Ptoo
Eek
Oof
DOES MEISTER KIRISAKI WEIGH ON YOUR MIND THAT MUCH?!
IT...IT'S FINE NOW, SIR, I'M SORRY!! I'M OVER IT!!
WELL, IT'S ALL RIGHT. IT'S A PROBLEM IF IT WEIGHS ON YOUR MIND AND YOU CAN'T DO WORK.
HUH?!
THOSE FOUR ARE FOOLING AROUND AGAIN...
I'M THE ONLY ONE WHO DOES ANY ACTUAL WORK.

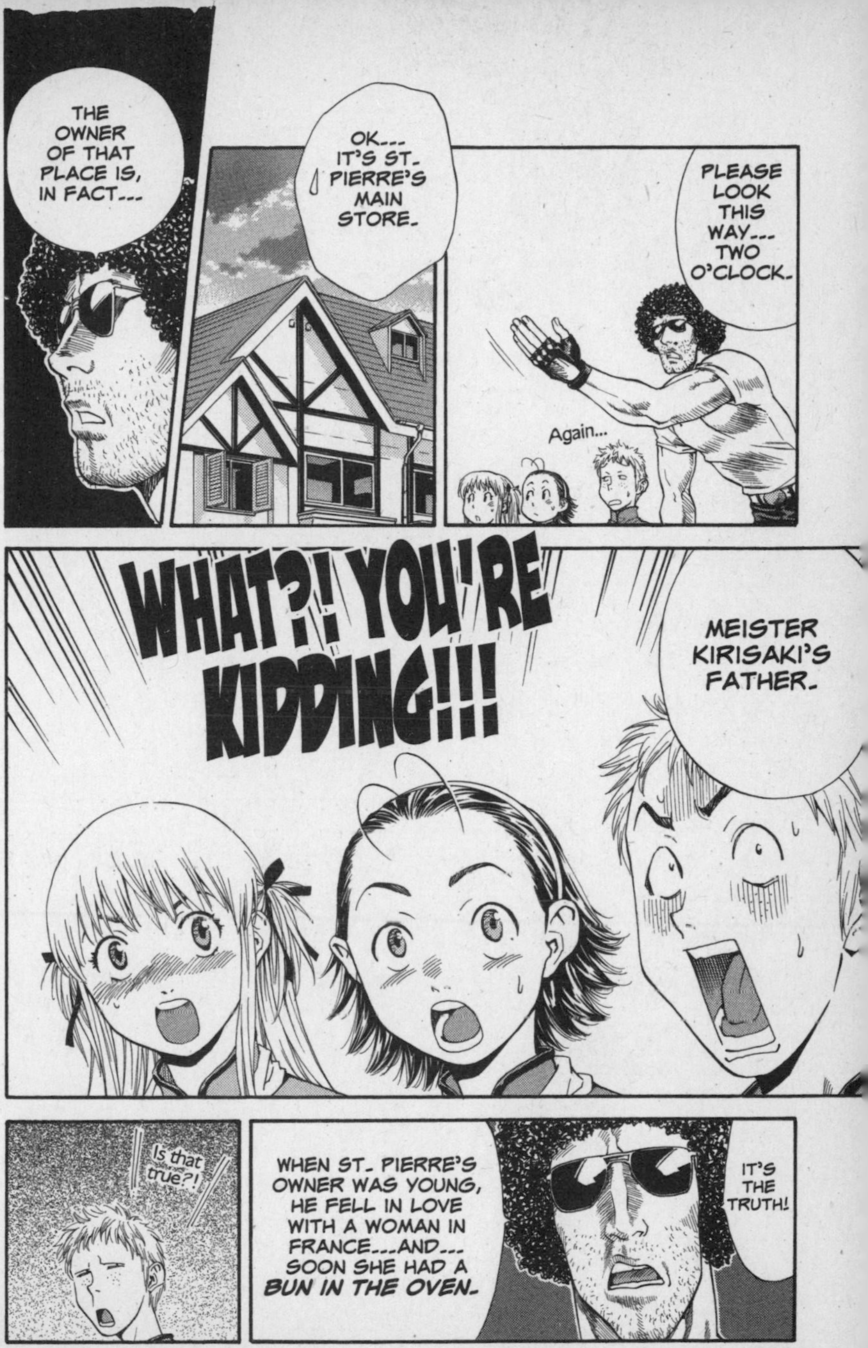
PLEASE LOOK THIS WAY... TWO O'CLOCK.
Again...
OK... IT'S ST. PIERRE'S MAIN STORE.
THE OWNER OF THAT PLACE IS, IN FACT...
MEISTER KIRISAKI'S FATHER.
WHAT?! YOU'RE KIDDING!!!
IT'S THE TRUTH!
WHEN ST. PIERRE'S OWNER WAS YOUNG, HE FELL IN LOVE WITH A WOMAN IN FRANCE...AND... SOON SHE HAD A *BUN IN THE OVEN.*
Is that true?!

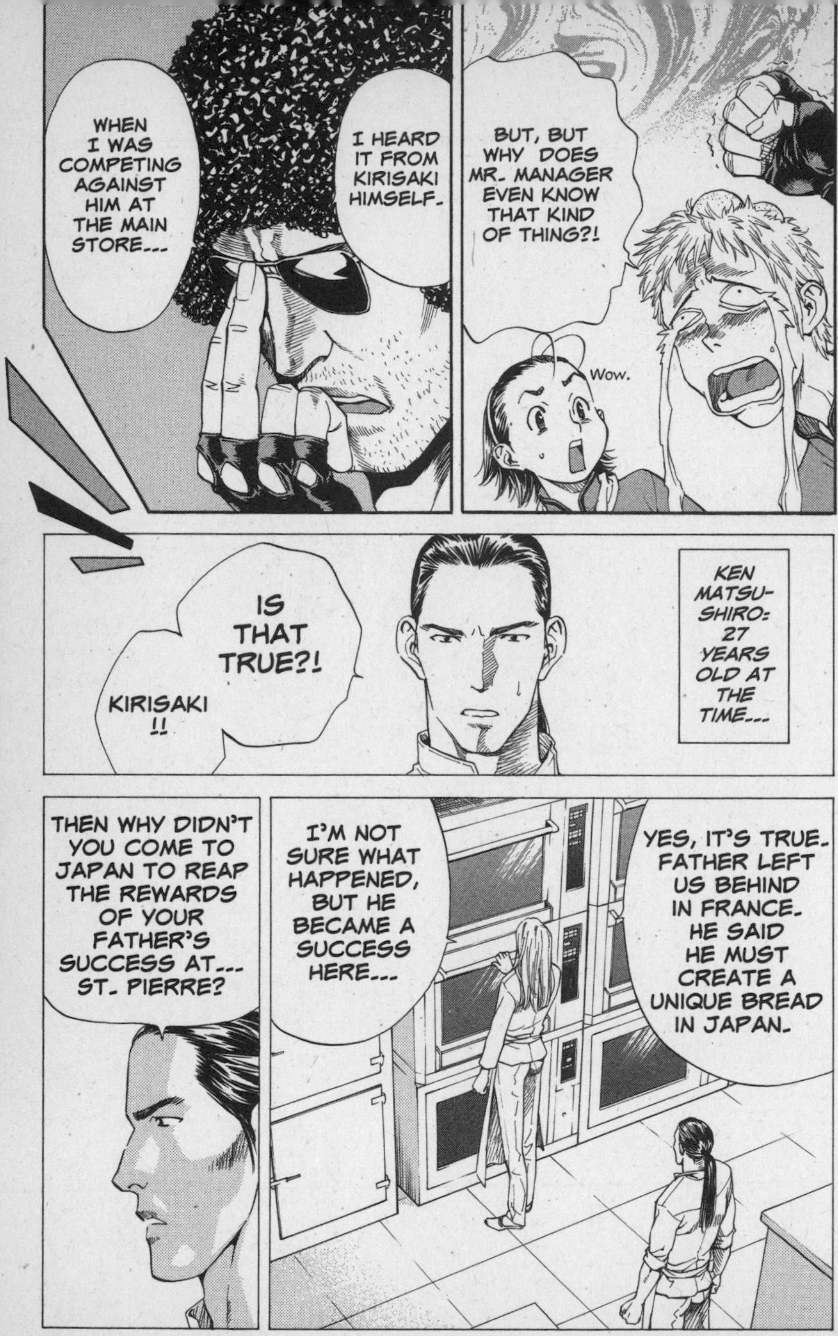
BUT, BUT WHY DOES MR. MANAGER EVEN KNOW THAT KIND OF THING?!
Wow.
I HEARD IT FROM KIRISAKI HIMSELF.
WHEN I WAS COMPETING AGAINST HIM AT THE MAIN STORE...
KEN MATSU-SHIRO: 27 YEARS OLD AT THE TIME...
IS THAT TRUE?!
KIRISAKI!!
YES, IT'S TRUE. FATHER LEFT US BEHIND IN FRANCE. HE SAID HE MUST CREATE A UNIQUE BREAD IN JAPAN.
I'M NOT SURE WHAT HAPPENED, BUT HE BECAME A SUCCESS HERE...
THEN WHY DIDN'T YOU COME TO JAPAN TO REAP THE REWARDS OF YOUR FATHER'S SUCCESS AT... ST. PIERRE?

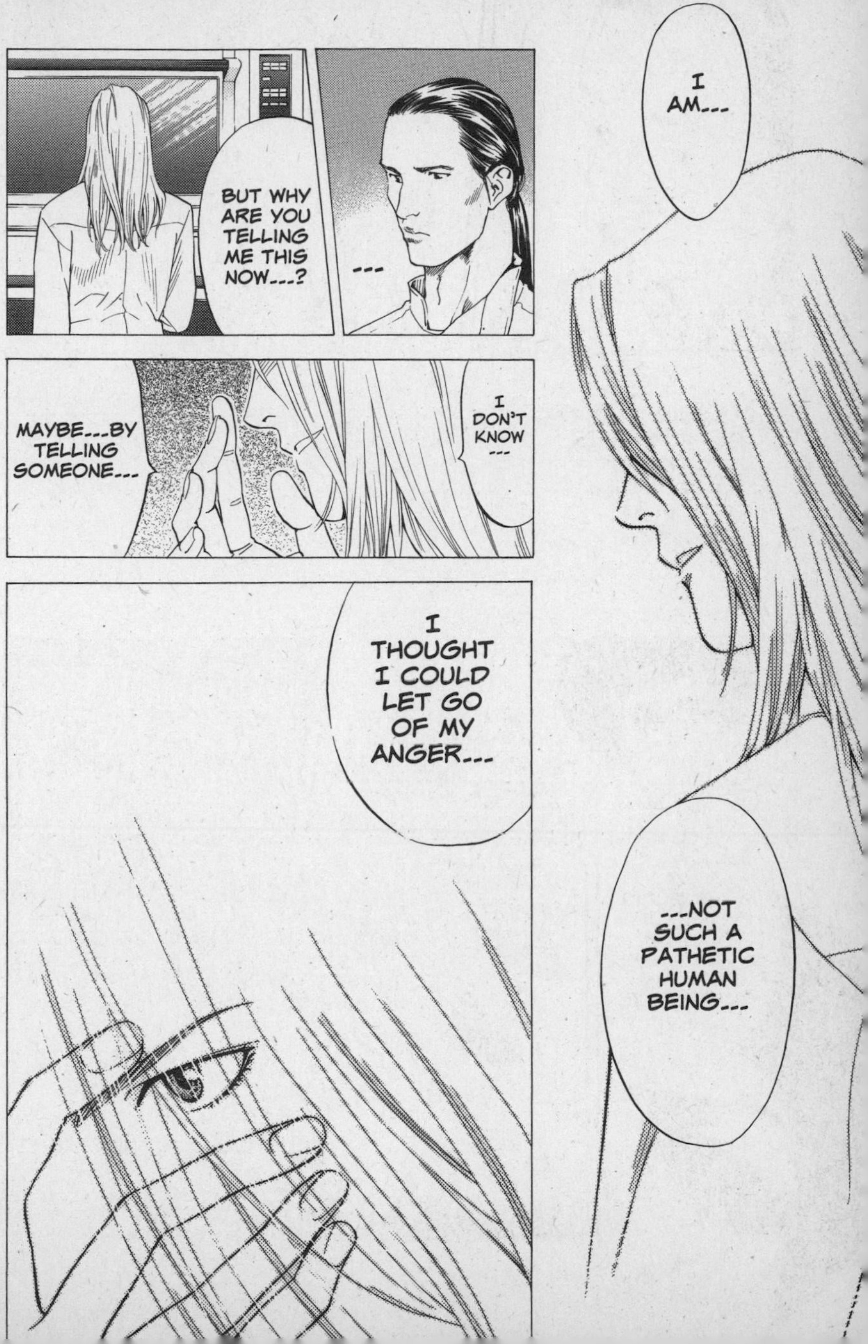
I AM...
...NOT SUCH A PATHETIC HUMAN BEING...
BUT WHY ARE YOU TELLING ME THIS NOW...?
...
I DON'T KNOW...
MAYBE...BY TELLING SOMEONE...
I THOUGHT I COULD LET GO OF MY ANGER...

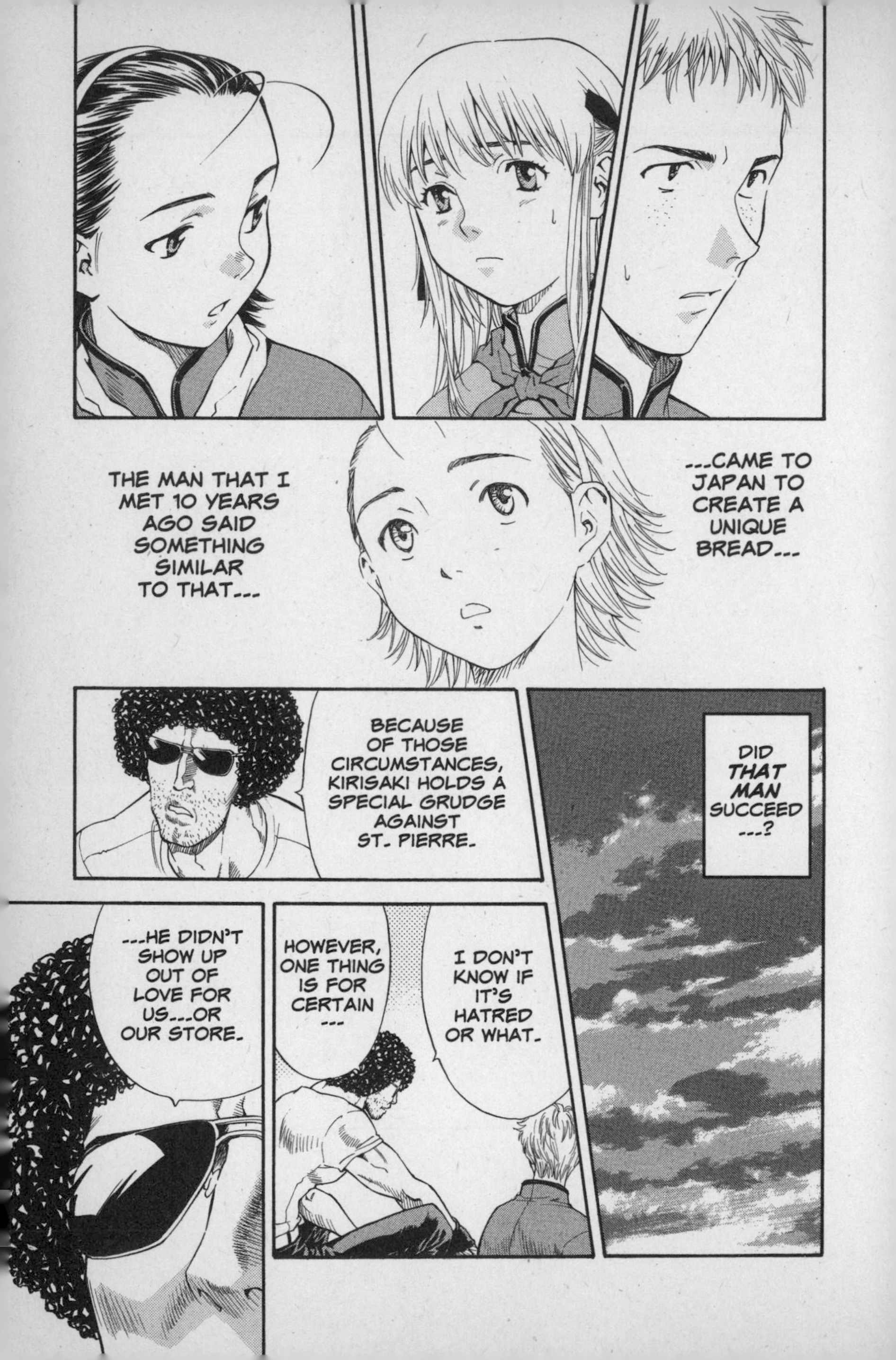
---CAME TO JAPAN TO CREATE A UNIQUE BREAD---
THE MAN THAT I MET 10 YEARS AGO SAID SOMETHING SIMILAR TO THAT---
DID *THAT MAN* SUCCEED ---?
BECAUSE OF THOSE CIRCUMSTANCES, KIRISAKI HOLDS A SPECIAL GRUDGE AGAINST ST. PIERRE.
I DON'T KNOW IF IT'S HATRED OR WHAT.
HOWEVER, ONE THING IS FOR CERTAIN ---
---HE DIDN'T SHOW UP OUT OF LOVE FOR US---OR OUR STORE.

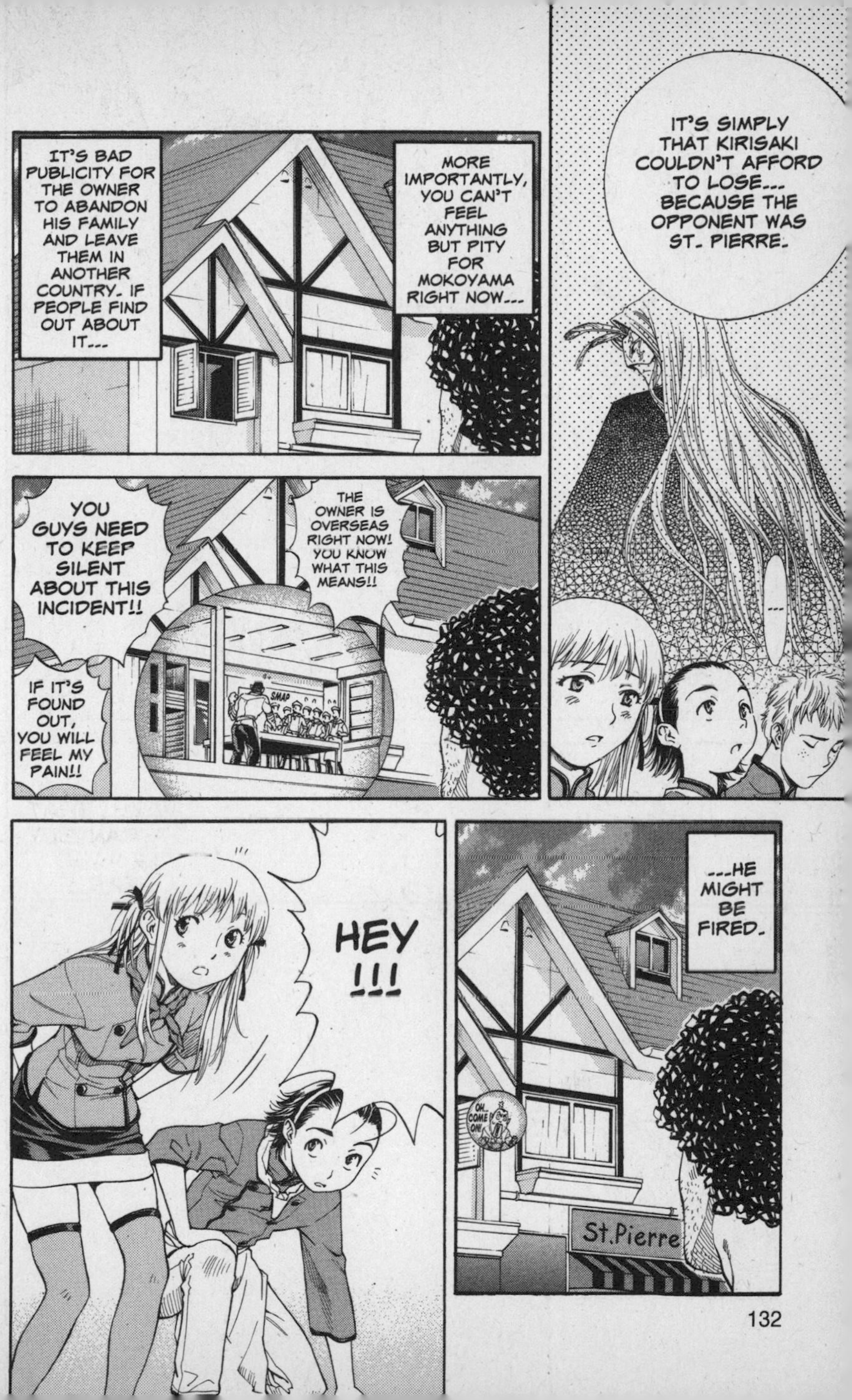
IT'S SIMPLY THAT KIRISAKI COULDN'T AFFORD TO LOSE... BECAUSE THE OPPONENT WAS ST. PIERRE.
...
MORE IMPORTANTLY, YOU CAN'T FEEL ANYTHING BUT PITY FOR MOKOYAMA RIGHT NOW...
IT'S BAD PUBLICITY FOR THE OWNER TO ABANDON HIS FAMILY AND LEAVE THEM IN ANOTHER COUNTRY. IF PEOPLE FIND OUT ABOUT IT...
THE OWNER IS OVERSEAS RIGHT NOW! YOU KNOW WHAT THIS MEANS!!
YOU GUYS NEED TO KEEP SILENT ABOUT THIS INCIDENT!!
IF IT'S FOUND OUT, YOU WILL FEEL MY PAIN!!
SMAP
...HE MIGHT BE FIRED.
OH.. COME ON!
St.Pierre
HEY !!!

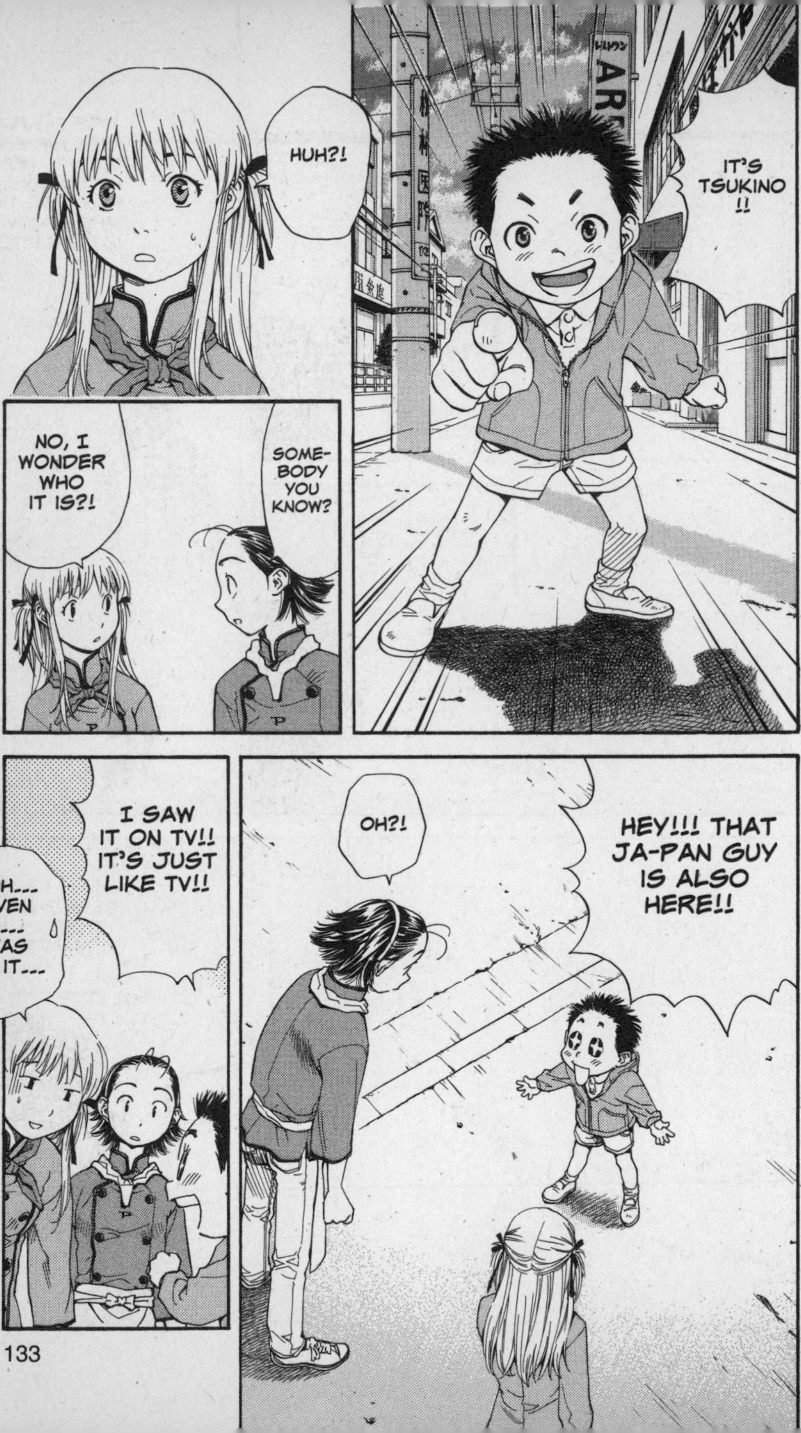
IT'S TSUKINO !!
HUH?!
SOME-BODY YOU KNOW?
NO, I WONDER WHO IT IS?!
HEY!!! THAT JA-PAN GUY IS ALSO HERE!!
OH?!
I SAW IT ON TV!! IT'S JUST LIKE TV!!
AHH... EVEN I... WAS ON IT...

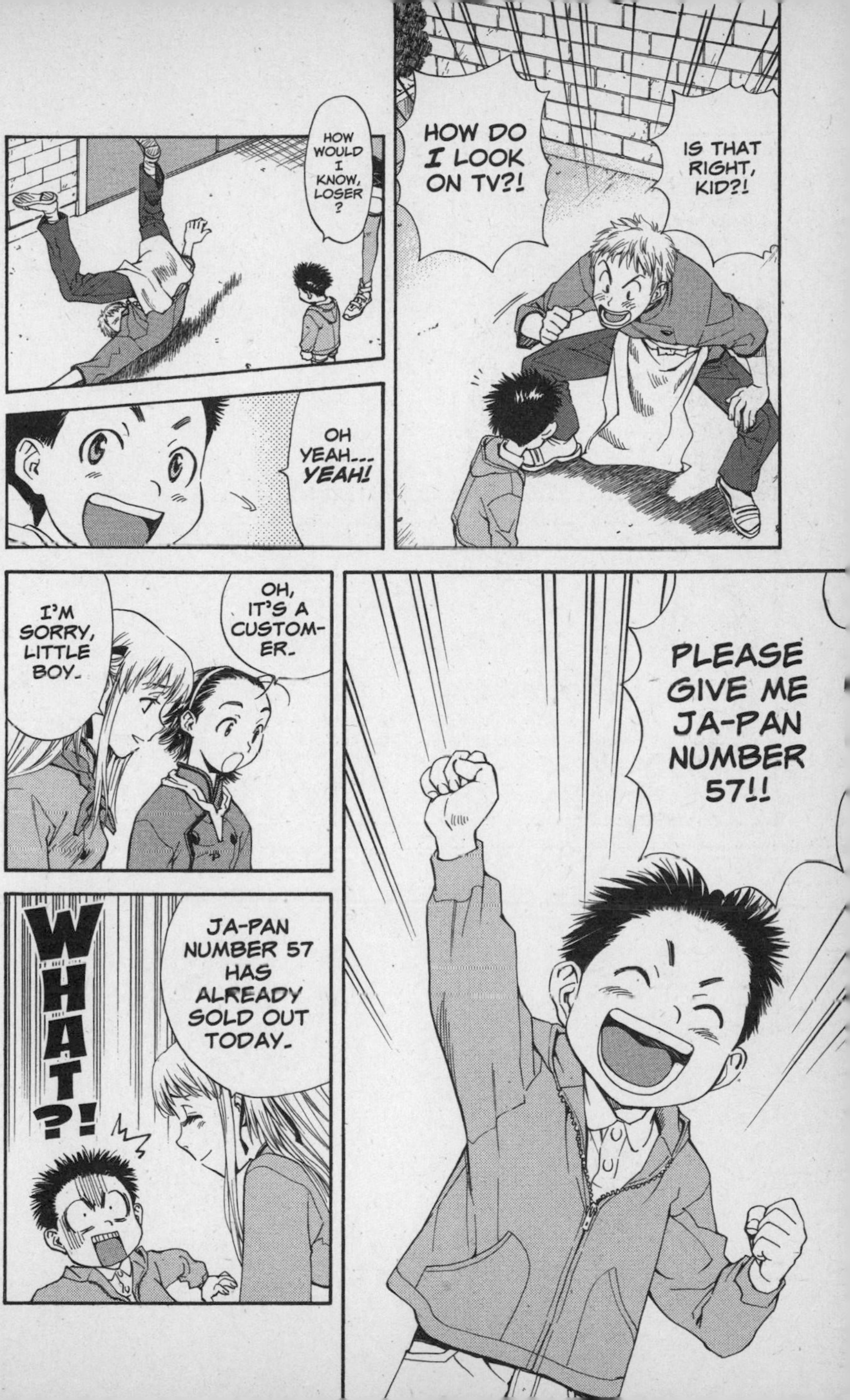
IS THAT RIGHT, KID?!
HOW DO I LOOK ON TV?!
HOW WOULD I KNOW, LOSER?
OH YEAH... YEAH!
PLEASE GIVE ME JA-PAN NUMBER 57!!
OH, IT'S A CUSTOMER.
I'M SORRY, LITTLE BOY.
JA-PAN NUMBER 57 HAS ALREADY SOLD OUT TODAY.
WHAT?!

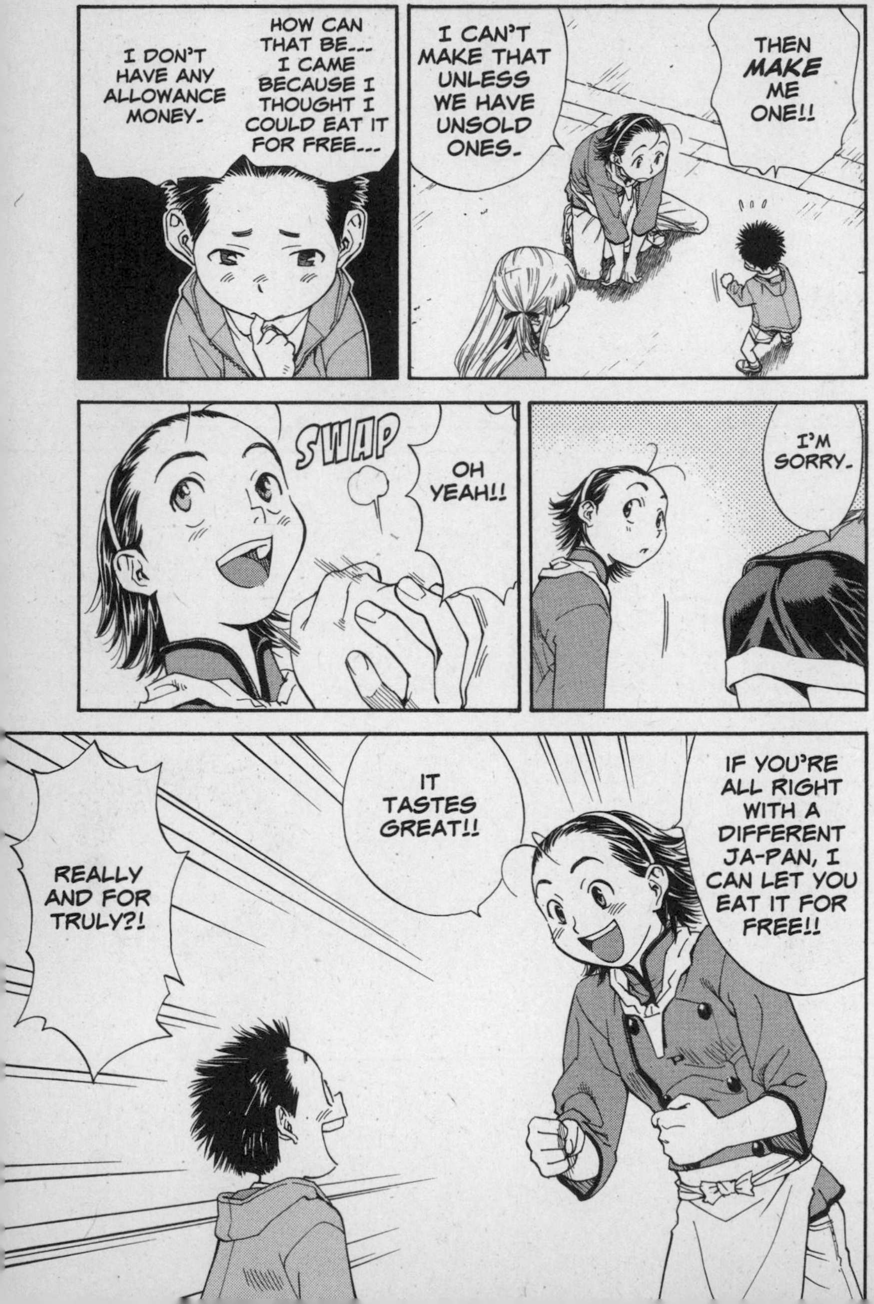
THEN MAKE ME ONE!!
I CAN'T MAKE THAT UNLESS WE HAVE UNSOLD ONES.
HOW CAN THAT BE... I CAME BECAUSE I THOUGHT I COULD EAT IT FOR FREE...
I DON'T HAVE ANY ALLOWANCE MONEY.
I'M SORRY.
SWAP
OH YEAH!!
IF YOU'RE ALL RIGHT WITH A DIFFERENT JA-PAN, I CAN LET YOU EAT IT FOR FREE!!
IT TASTES GREAT!!
REALLY AND FOR TRULY?!

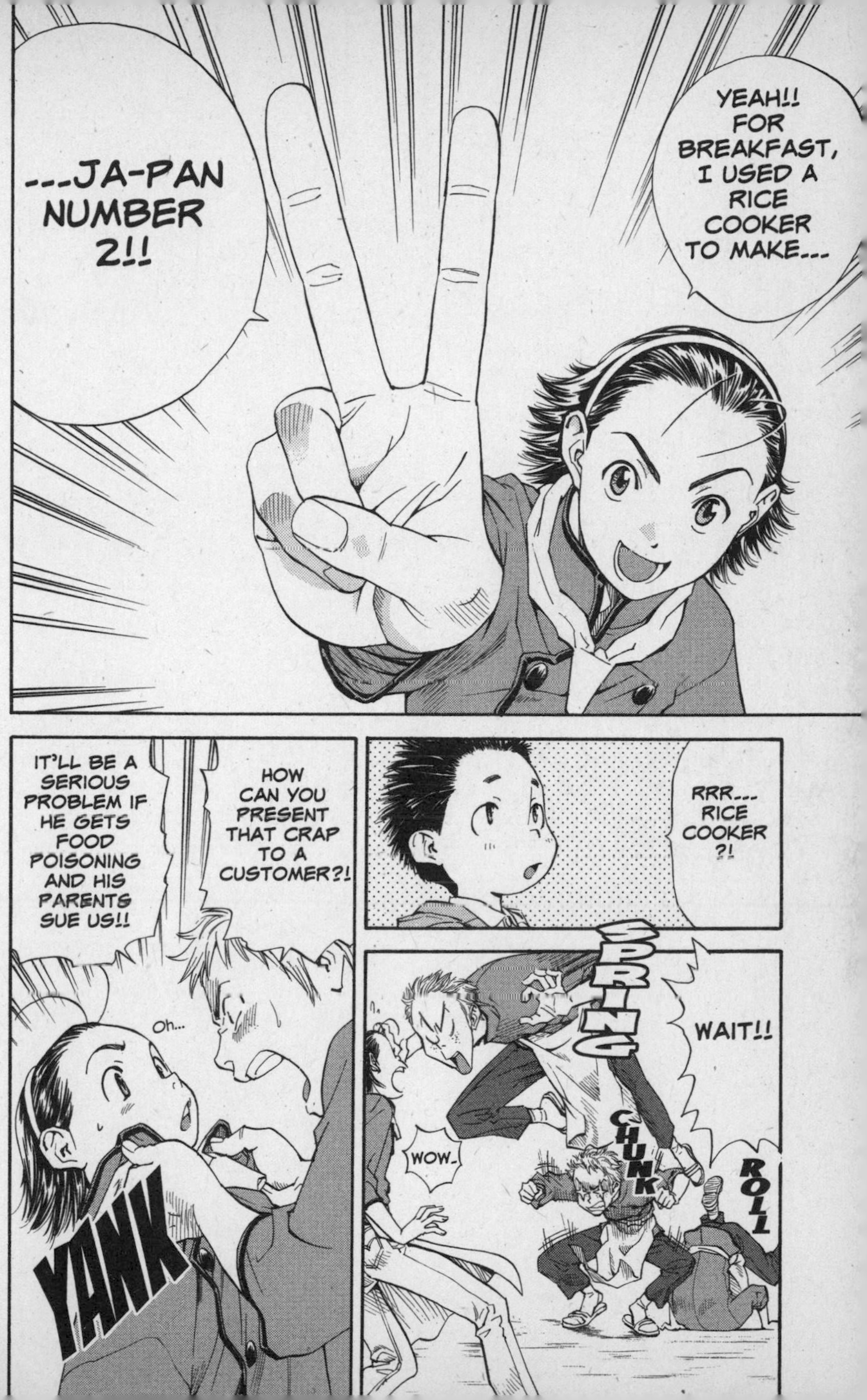
YEAH!! FOR BREAKFAST, I USED A RICE COOKER TO MAKE...
...JA-PAN NUMBER 2!!
RRR... RICE COOKER ?!
WAIT!!
SPRING
ROLL
CHUNK
WOW...
HOW CAN YOU PRESENT THAT CRAP TO A CUSTOMER?!
IT'LL BE A SERIOUS PROBLEM IF HE GETS FOOD POISONING AND HIS PARENTS SUE US!!
Oh...
YANK

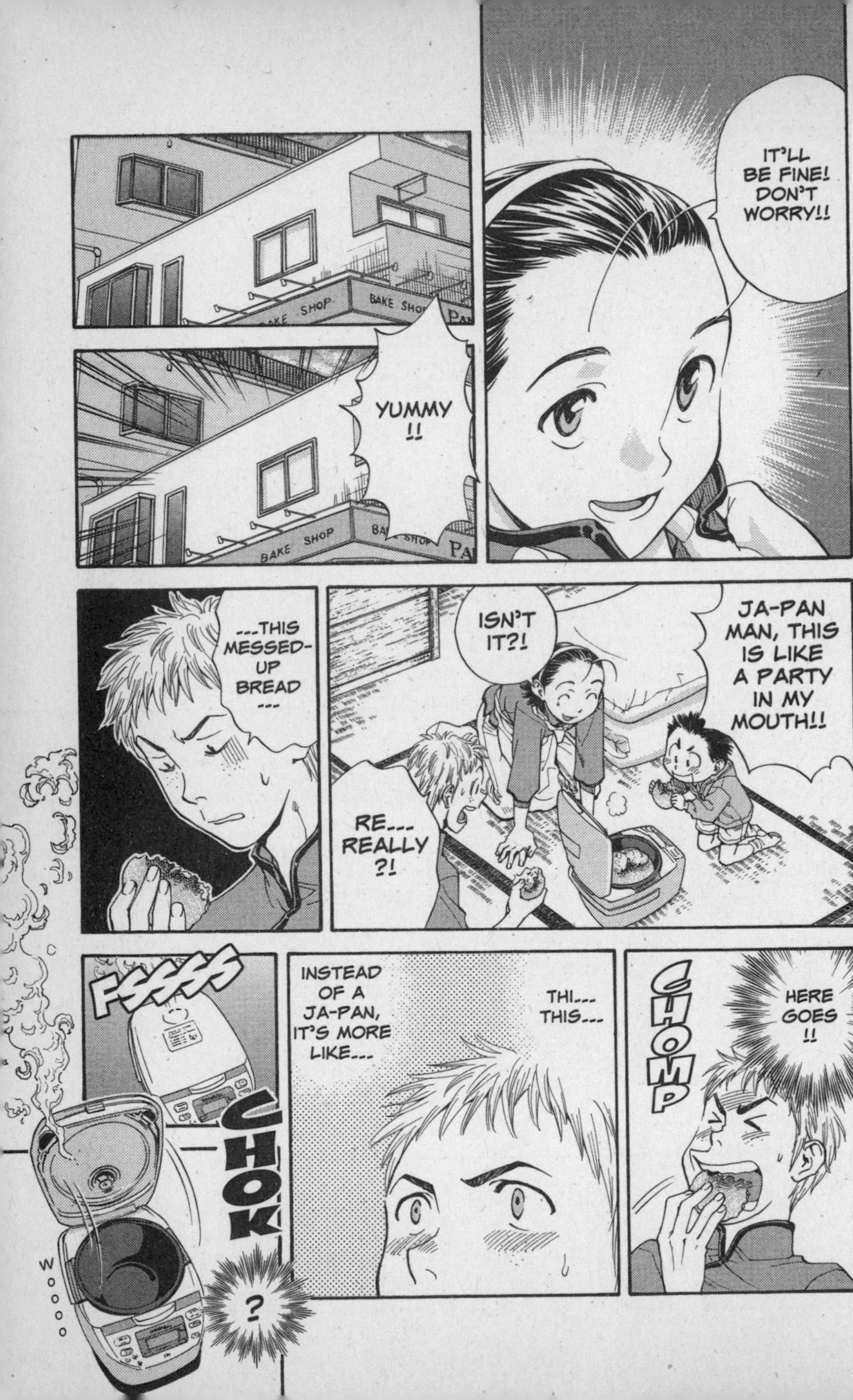
IT'LL BE FINE! DON'T WORRY!!
YUMMY !!
JA-PAN MAN, THIS IS LIKE A PARTY IN MY MOUTH!!
ISN'T IT?!
RE... REALLY ?!
...THIS MESSED-UP BREAD ...
HERE GOES !!
CHOMP
THI... THIS...
INSTEAD OF A JA-PAN, IT'S MORE LIKE...
FSSSS
CHOK
WOOOO
?

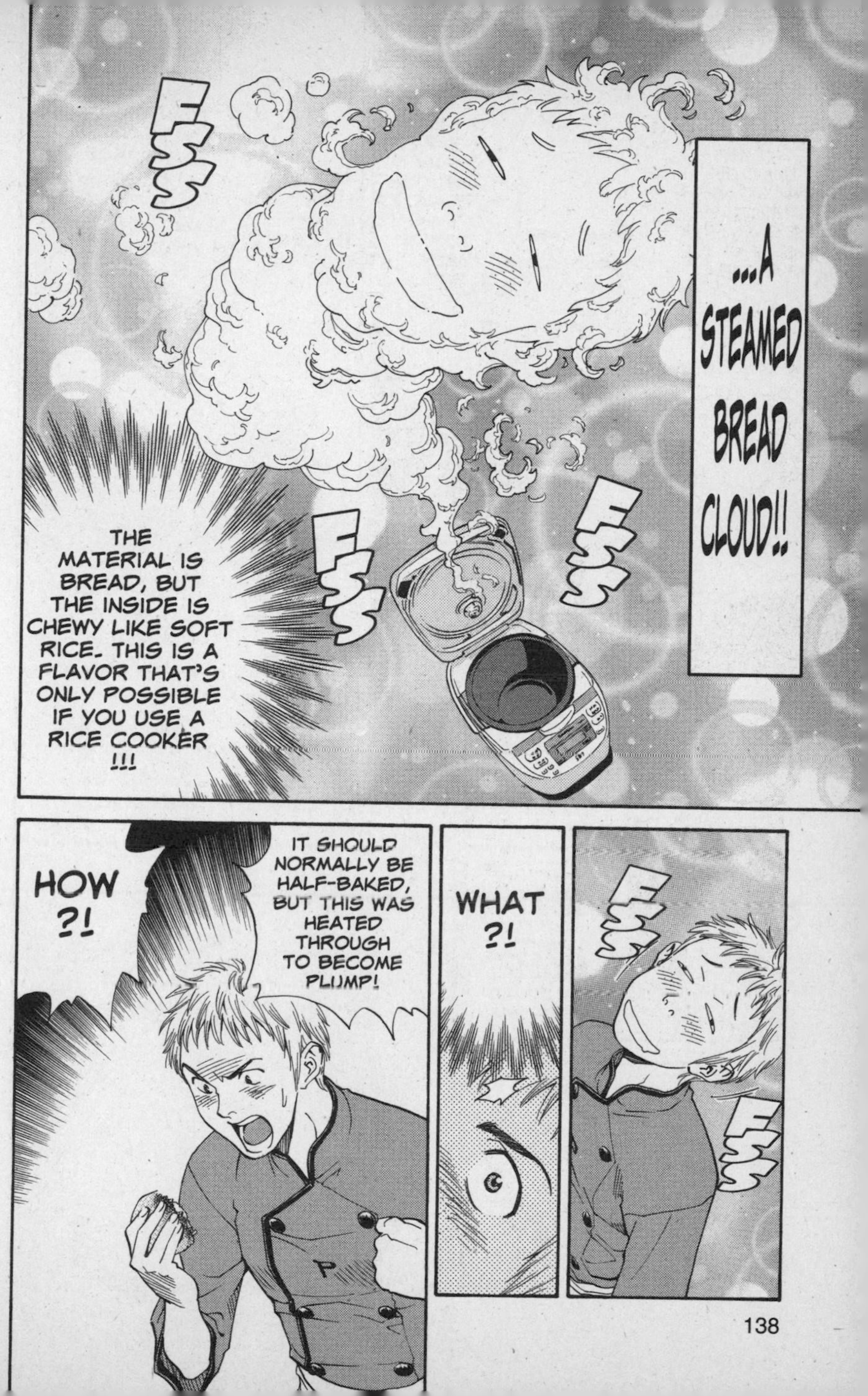
...A STEAMED BREAD CLOUD!!
FSS
FSS
FSS
THE MATERIAL IS BREAD, BUT THE INSIDE IS CHEWY LIKE SOFT RICE. THIS IS A FLAVOR THAT'S ONLY POSSIBLE IF YOU USE A RICE COOKER!!!
FSS
FSS
WHAT ?!
IT SHOULD NORMALLY BE HALF-BAKED, BUT THIS WAS HEATED THROUGH TO BECOME PLUMP!
HOW ?!

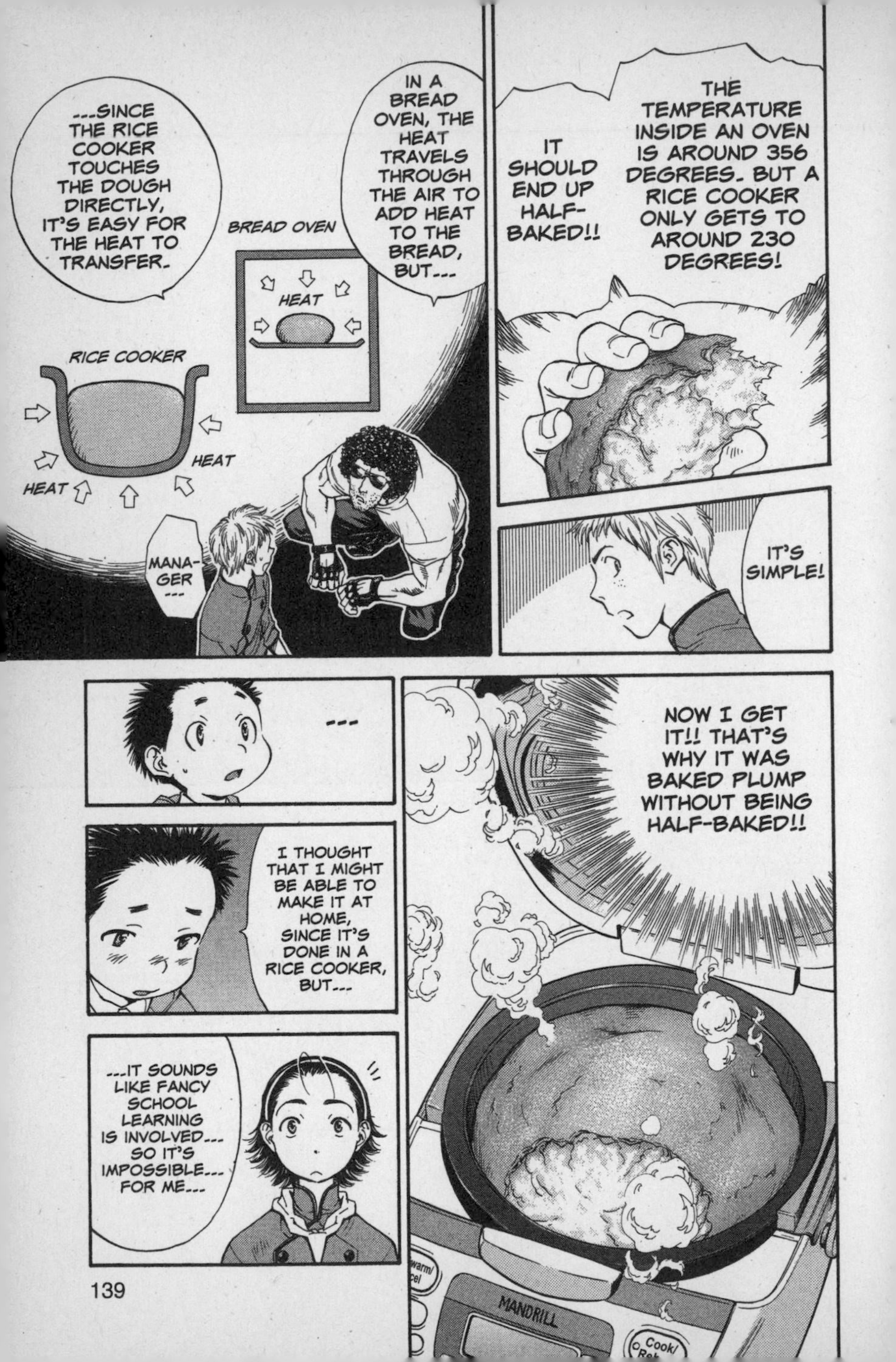
THE TEMPERATURE INSIDE AN OVEN IS AROUND 356 DEGREES. BUT A RICE COOKER ONLY GETS TO AROUND 230 DEGREES!
IT SHOULD END UP HALF-BAKED!!
IT'S SIMPLE!
IN A BREAD OVEN, THE HEAT TRAVELS THROUGH THE AIR TO ADD HEAT TO THE BREAD, BUT...
BREAD OVEN
HEAT
...SINCE THE RICE COOKER TOUCHES THE DOUGH DIRECTLY, IT'S EASY FOR THE HEAT TO TRANSFER.
RICE COOKER
HEAT
HEAT
MANAGER...
NOW I GET IT!! THAT'S WHY IT WAS BAKED PLUMP WITHOUT BEING HALF-BAKED!!
MANDRILL
...
I THOUGHT THAT I MIGHT BE ABLE TO MAKE IT AT HOME, SINCE IT'S DONE IN A RICE COOKER, BUT...
...IT SOUNDS LIKE FANCY SCHOOL LEARNING IS INVOLVED... SO IT'S IMPOSSIBLE... FOR ME...

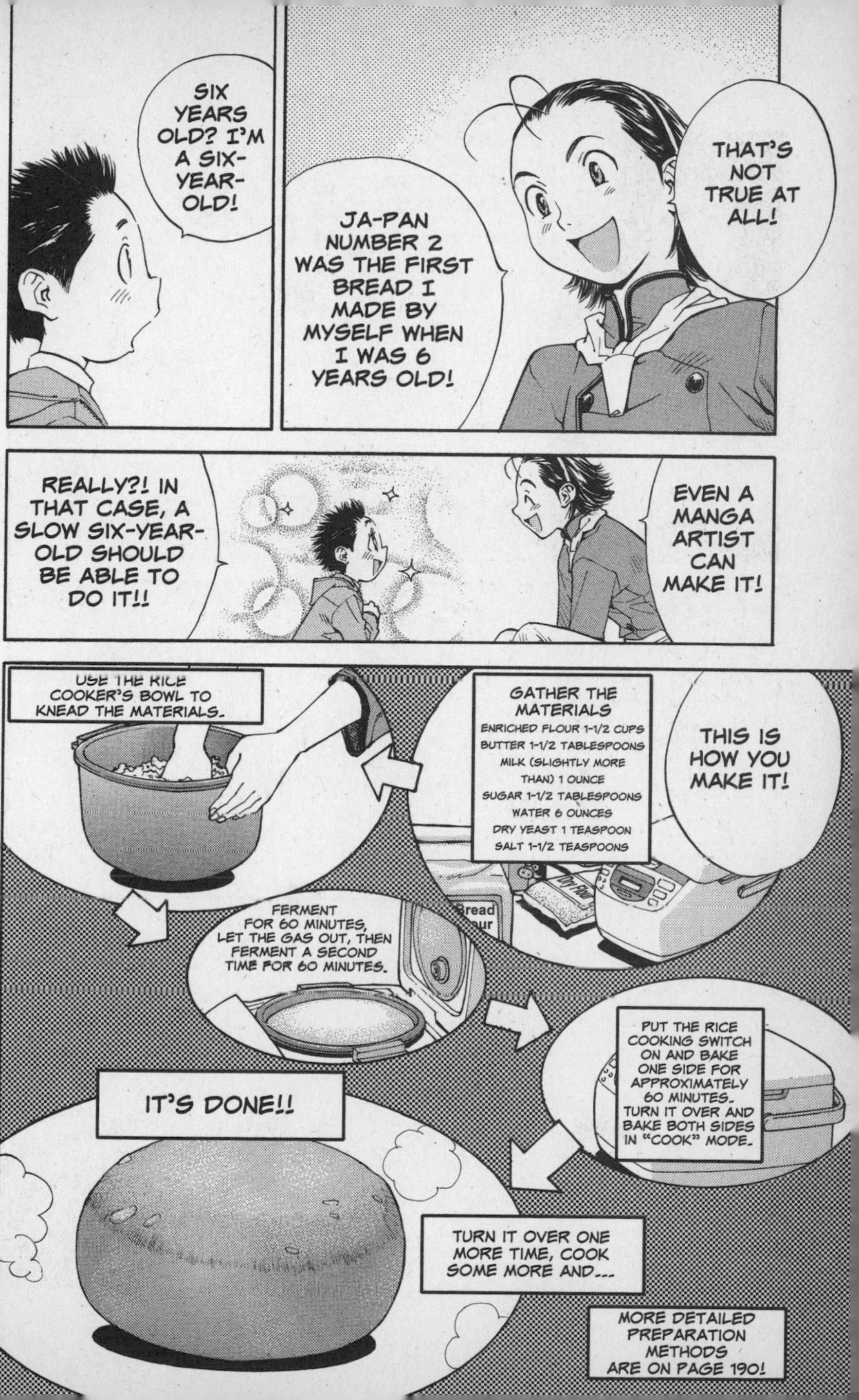
THAT'S NOT TRUE AT ALL!
JA-PAN NUMBER 2 WAS THE FIRST BREAD I MADE BY MYSELF WHEN I WAS 6 YEARS OLD!
SIX YEARS OLD? I'M A SIX-YEAR-OLD!
EVEN A MANGA ARTIST CAN MAKE IT!
REALLY?! IN THAT CASE, A SLOW SIX-YEAR-OLD SHOULD BE ABLE TO DO IT!!
THIS IS HOW YOU MAKE IT!
GATHER THE MATERIALS
ENRICHED FLOUR 1-1/2 CUPS
BUTTER 1-1/2 TABLESPOONS
MILK (SLIGHTLY MORE THAN) 1 OUNCE
SUGAR 1-1/2 TABLESPOONS
WATER 6 OUNCES
DRY YEAST 1 TEASPOON
SALT 1-1/2 TEASPOONS
USE THE RICE COOKER'S BOWL TO KNEAD THE MATERIALS.
FERMENT FOR 60 MINUTES, LET THE GAS OUT, THEN FERMENT A SECOND TIME FOR 60 MINUTES.
PUT THE RICE COOKING SWITCH ON AND BAKE ONE SIDE FOR APPROXIMATELY 60 MINUTES. TURN IT OVER AND BAKE BOTH SIDES IN "COOK" MODE.
TURN IT OVER ONE MORE TIME, COOK SOME MORE AND...
IT'S DONE!!
MORE DETAILED PREPARATION METHODS ARE ON PAGE 190!

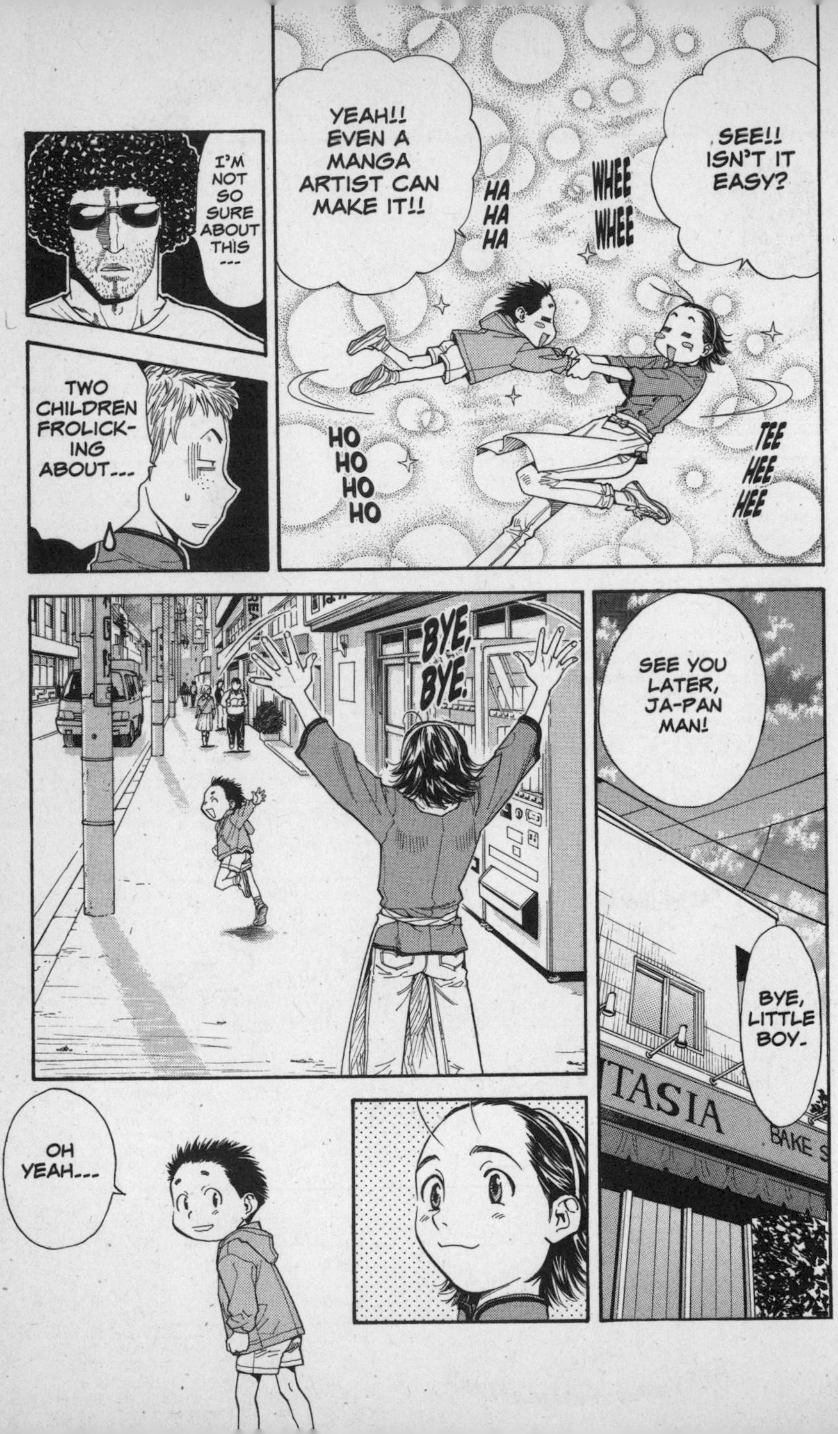
SEE!! ISN'T IT EASY?
WHEE WHEE
HA HA HA
YEAH!! EVEN A MANGA ARTIST CAN MAKE IT!!
TEE HEE HEE
HO HO HO HO
I'M NOT SO SURE ABOUT THIS...
TWO CHILDREN FROLICKING ABOUT...
SEE YOU LATER, JA-PAN MAN!
BYE, LITTLE BOY.
TASIA
BAKE S
BYE, BYE.
OH YEAH...

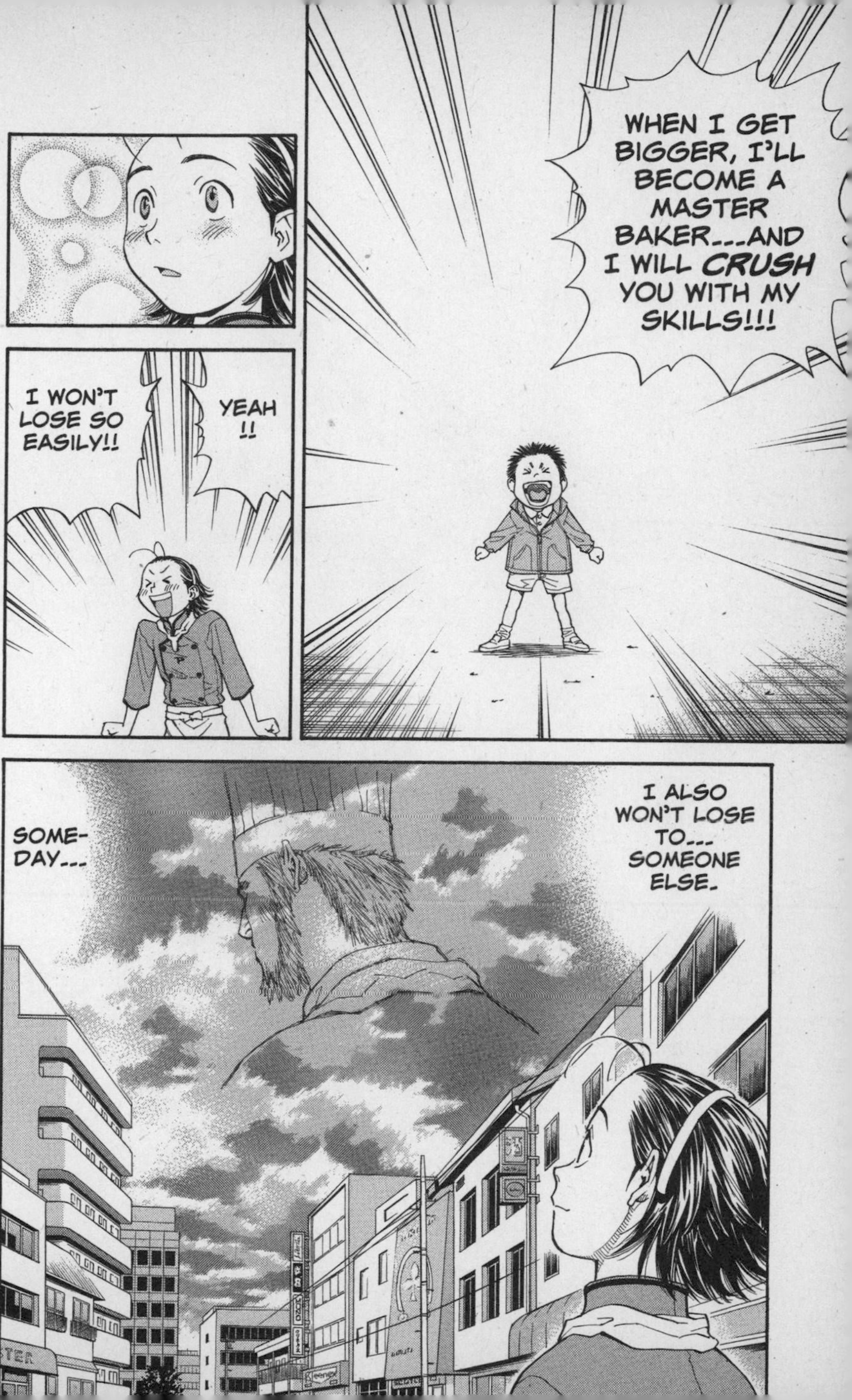
WHEN I GET BIGGER, I'LL BECOME A MASTER BAKER...AND I WILL CRUSH YOU WITH MY SKILLS!!!
YEAH !!
I WON'T LOSE SO EASILY!!
I ALSO WON'T LOSE TO... SOMEONE ELSE.
SOME-DAY...

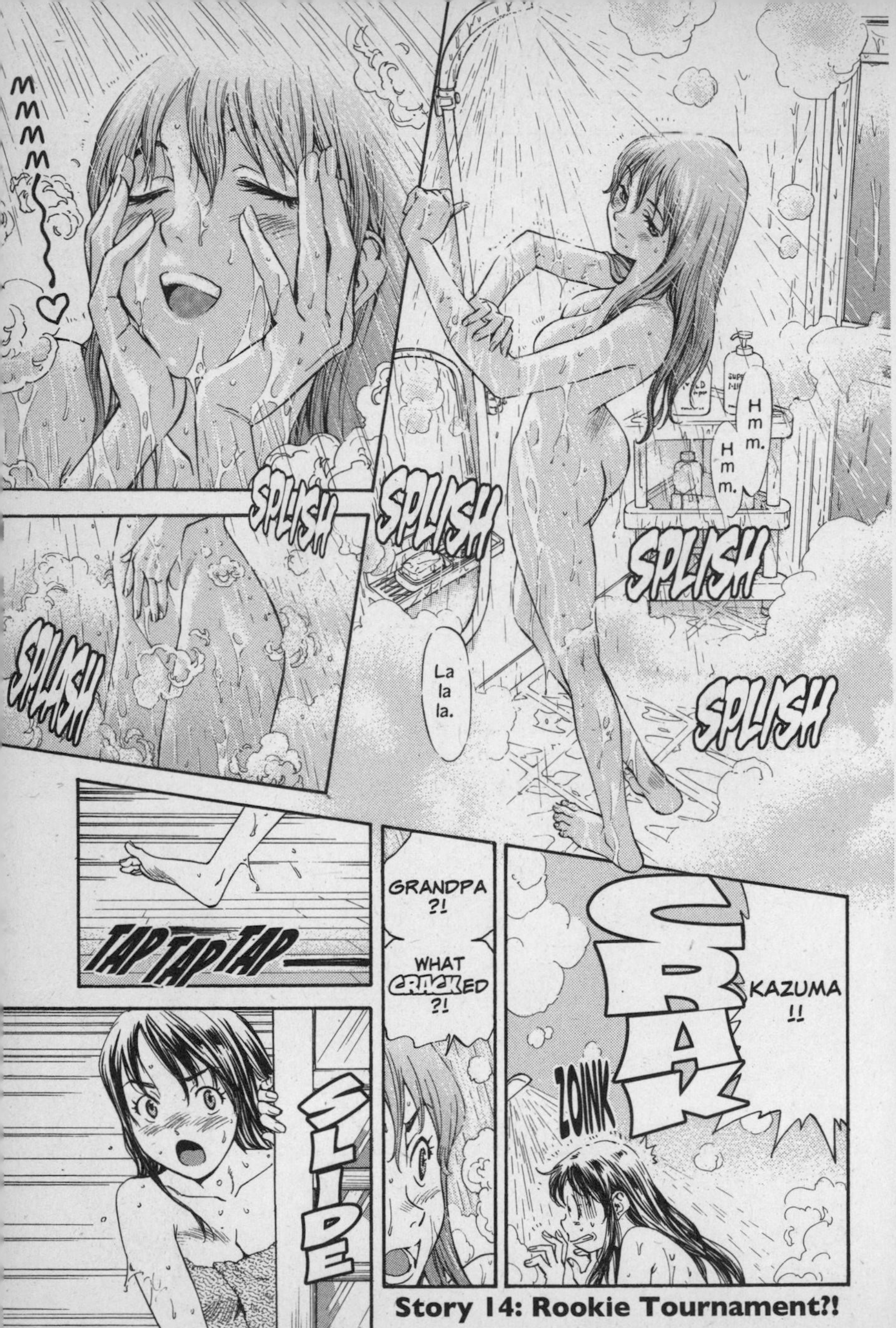
Hmm. Hmm.
SPLISH
SPLISH
La la la.
SPLISH
MMMMM~♥
SPLISH
SPLASH
KAZUMA!!
CRAK
ZOINK
GRANDPA?!
WHAT CRACKED?!
TAP TAP TAP
SLIDE

Story 14: Rookie Tournament?!

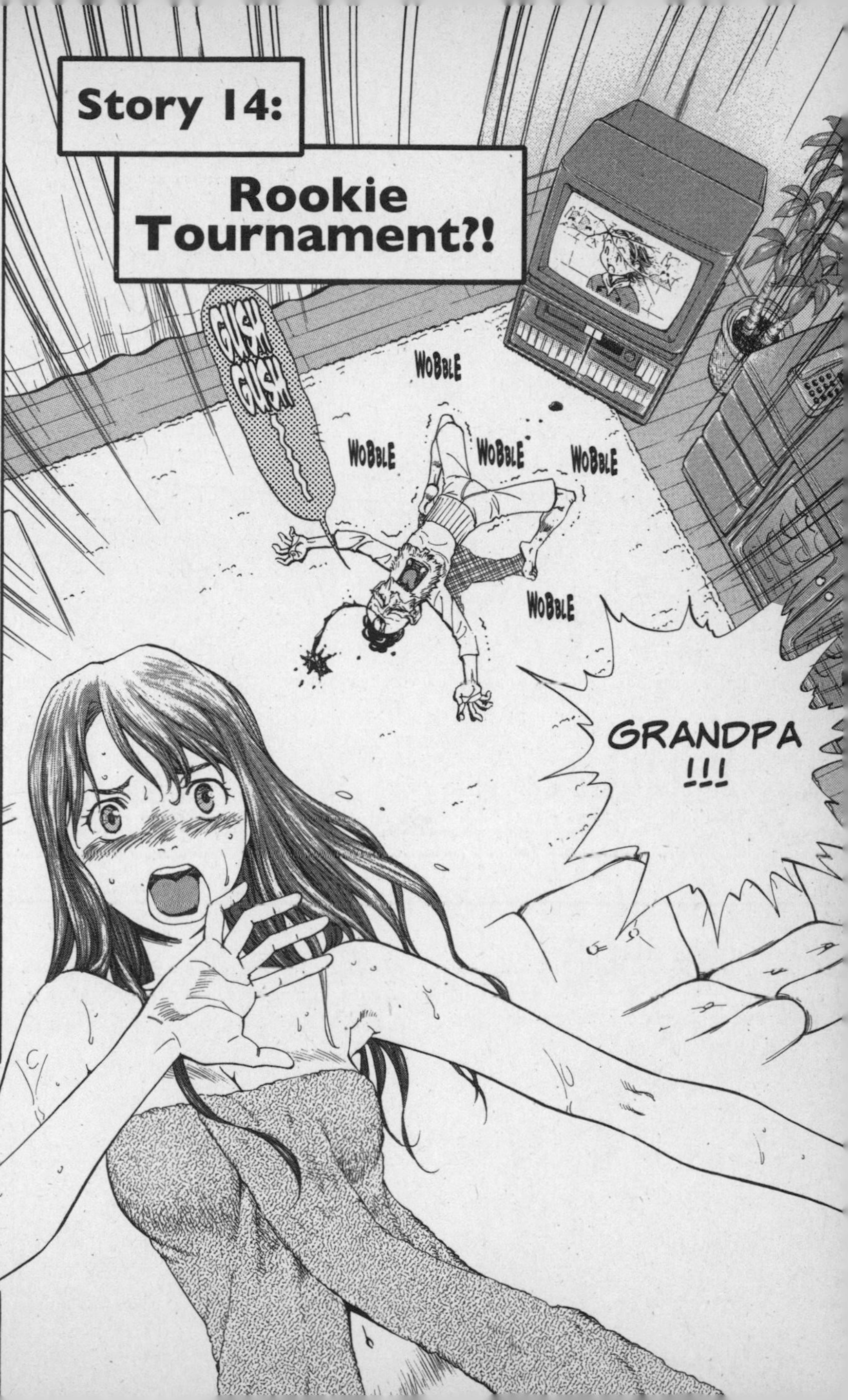
Story 14:
Rookie Tournament?!
GUSH GUSH
WOBBLE
WOBBLE
WOBBLE
WOBBLE
WOBBLE
GRANDPA !!!

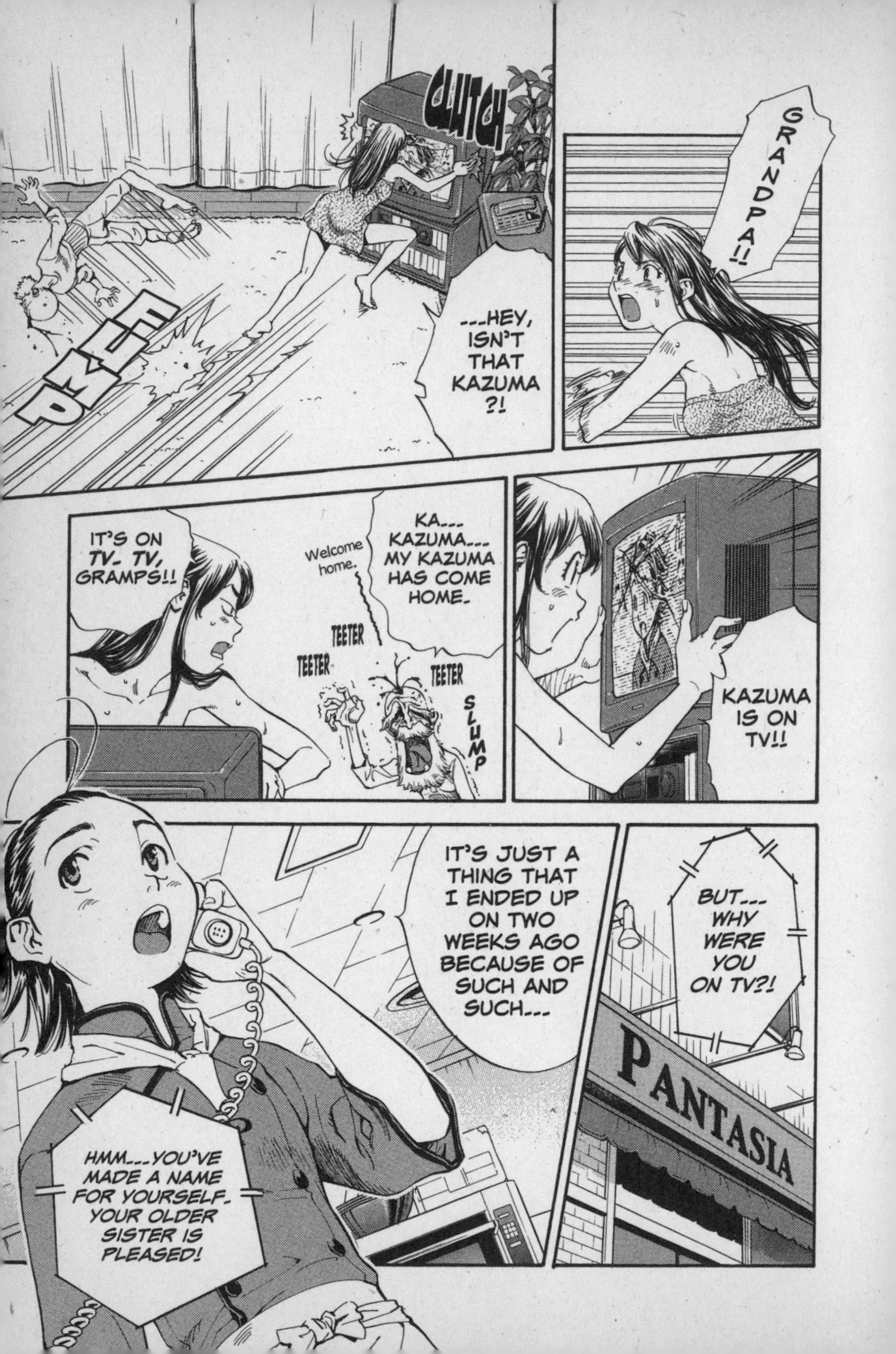
GRANDPA!!
CLUTCH
---HEY, ISN'T THAT KAZUMA ?!
FLUMP
KAZUMA IS ON TV!!
KA--- KAZUMA--- MY KAZUMA HAS COME HOME-
Welcome home.
IT'S ON TV- TV, GRAMPS!!
TEETER
TEETER
TEETER
SLUMP
BUT--- WHY WERE YOU ON TV?!
PANTASIA
IT'S JUST A THING THAT I ENDED UP ON TWO WEEKS AGO BECAUSE OF SUCH AND SUCH---
HMM---YOU'VE MADE A NAME FOR YOURSELF- YOUR OLDER SISTER IS PLEASED!

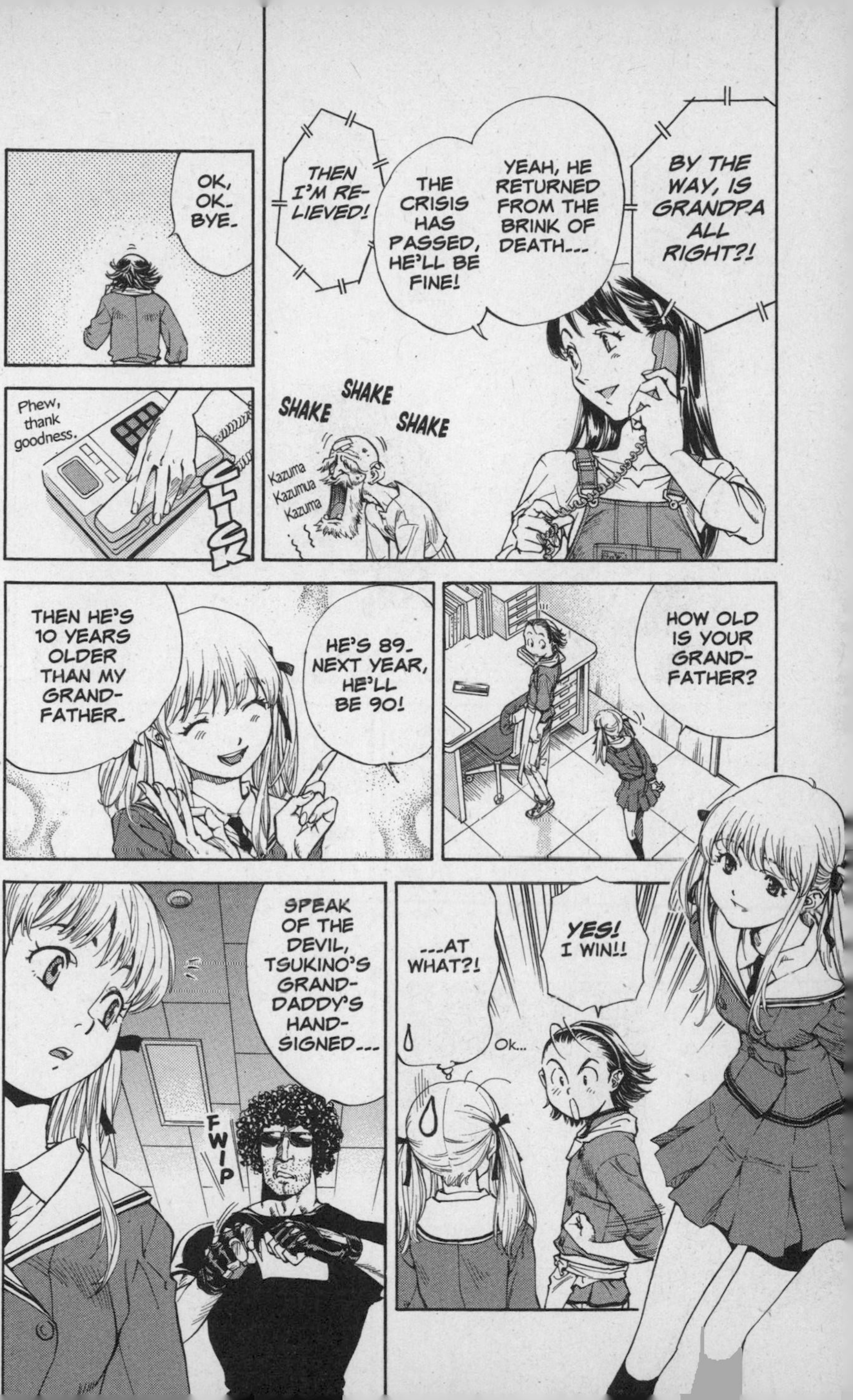
BY THE WAY, IS GRANDPA ALL RIGHT?!
YEAH, HE RETURNED FROM THE BRINK OF DEATH...
THE CRISIS HAS PASSED, HE'LL BE FINE!
THEN I'M RE-LIEVED!
SHAKE
SHAKE
SHAKE
Kazuma Kazumua Kazuma
OK, OK. BYE.
Phew, thank goodness.
CLICK
HOW OLD IS YOUR GRAND-FATHER?
HE'S 89. NEXT YEAR, HE'LL BE 90!
THEN HE'S 10 YEARS OLDER THAN MY GRAND-FATHER.
YES! I WIN!!
...AT WHAT?!
Ok...
SPEAK OF THE DEVIL, TSUKINO'S GRAND-DADDY'S HAND-SIGNED...
FWIP

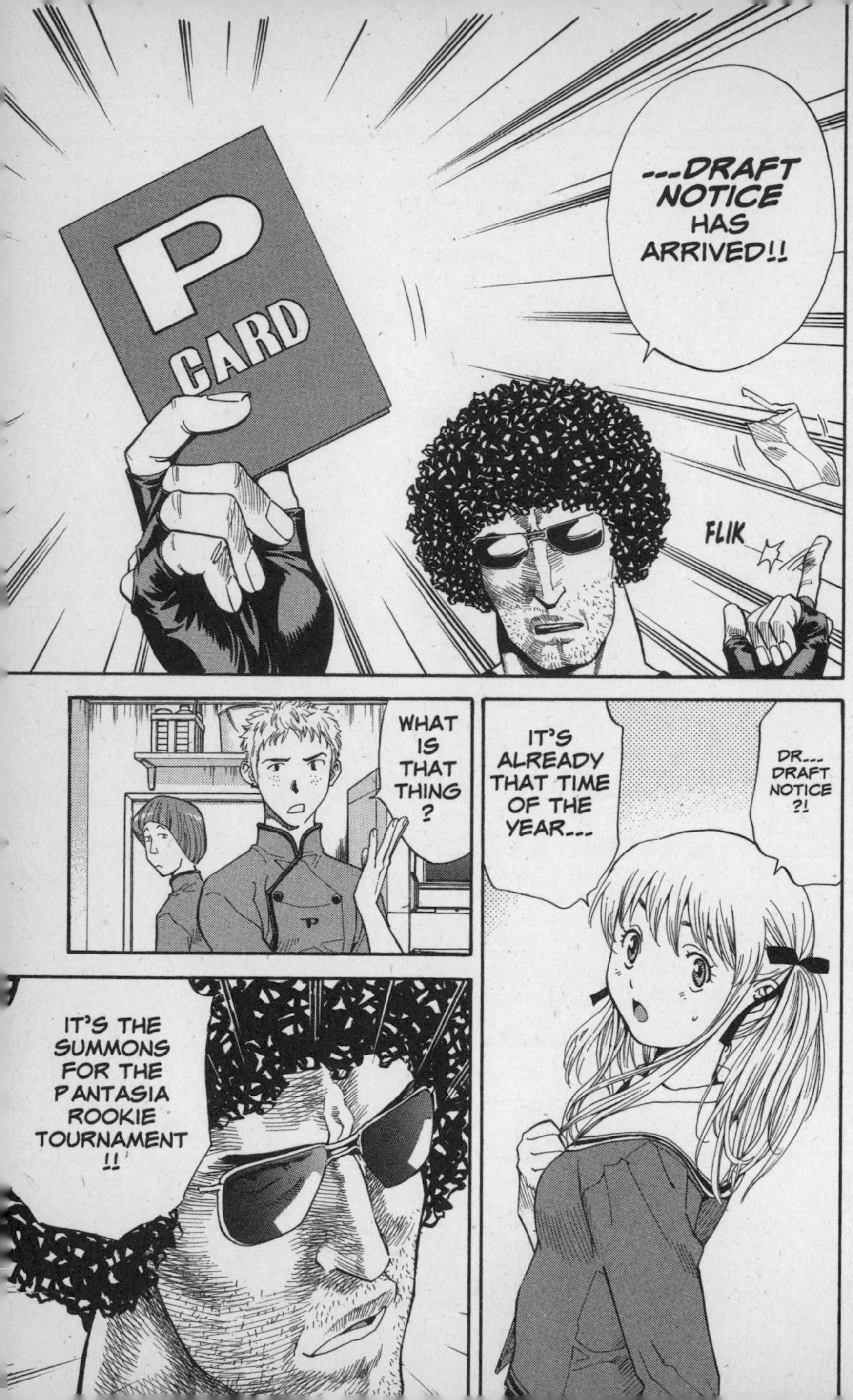
---DRAFT NOTICE HAS ARRIVED!!
FLIK
P CARD
DR... DRAFT NOTICE ?!
IT'S ALREADY THAT TIME OF THE YEAR...
WHAT IS THAT THING ?
IT'S THE SUMMONS FOR THE PANTASIA ROOKIE TOURNAMENT !!

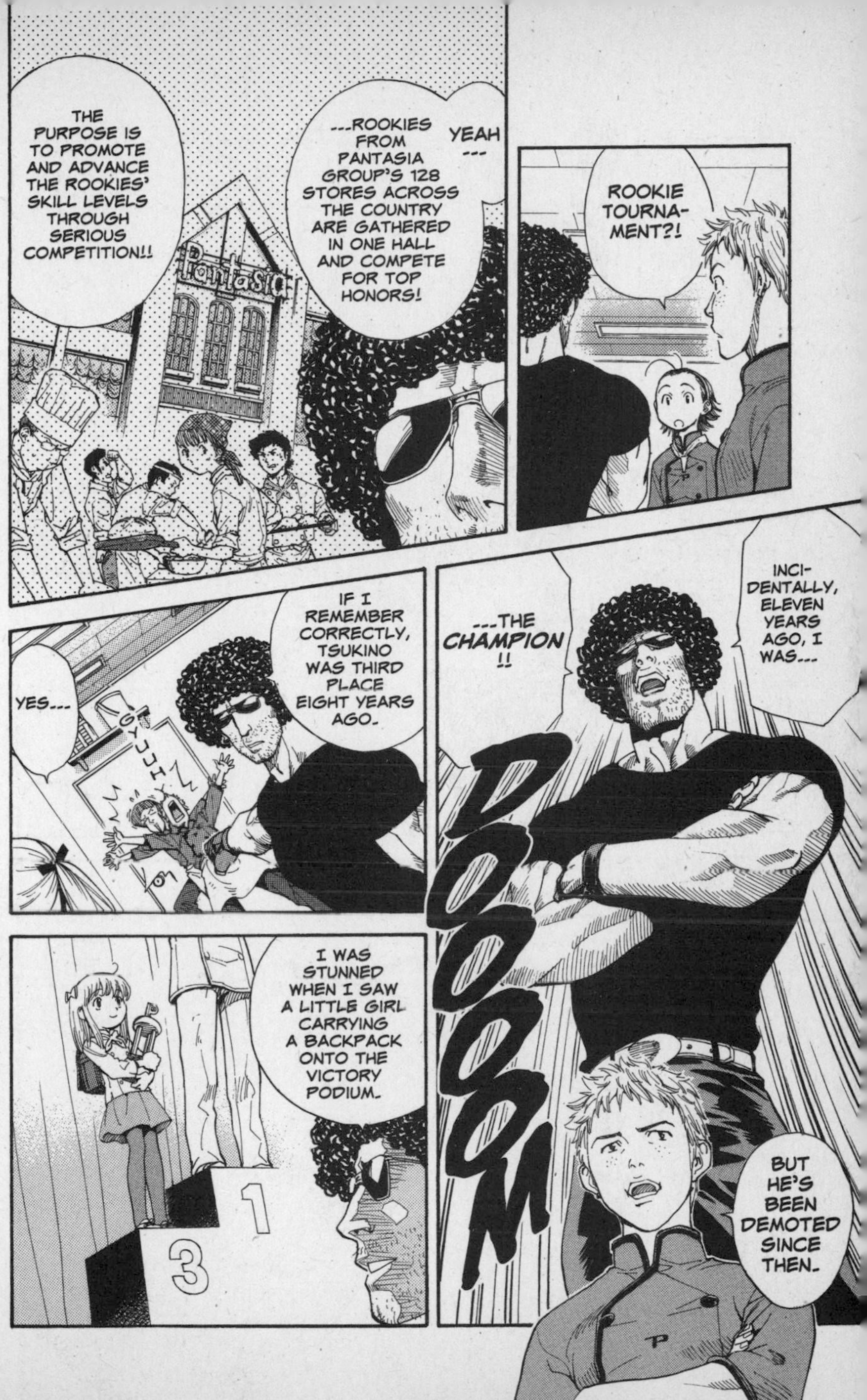
ROOKIE TOURNA-MENT?!
YEAH---
---ROOKIES FROM PANTASIA GROUP'S 128 STORES ACROSS THE COUNTRY ARE GATHERED IN ONE HALL AND COMPETE FOR TOP HONORS!
THE PURPOSE IS TO PROMOTE AND ADVANCE THE ROOKIES' SKILL LEVELS THROUGH SERIOUS COMPETITION!!
Pantasia
INCI-DENTALLY, ELEVEN YEARS AGO, I WAS---
---THE CHAMPION!!
DOOOOOM
BUT HE'S BEEN DEMOTED SINCE THEN.
IF I REMEMBER CORRECTLY, TSUKINO WAS THIRD PLACE EIGHT YEARS AGO.
YES---
GYUUH
I WAS STUNNED WHEN I SAW A LITTLE GIRL CARRYING A BACKPACK ONTO THE VICTORY PODIUM.
1
3

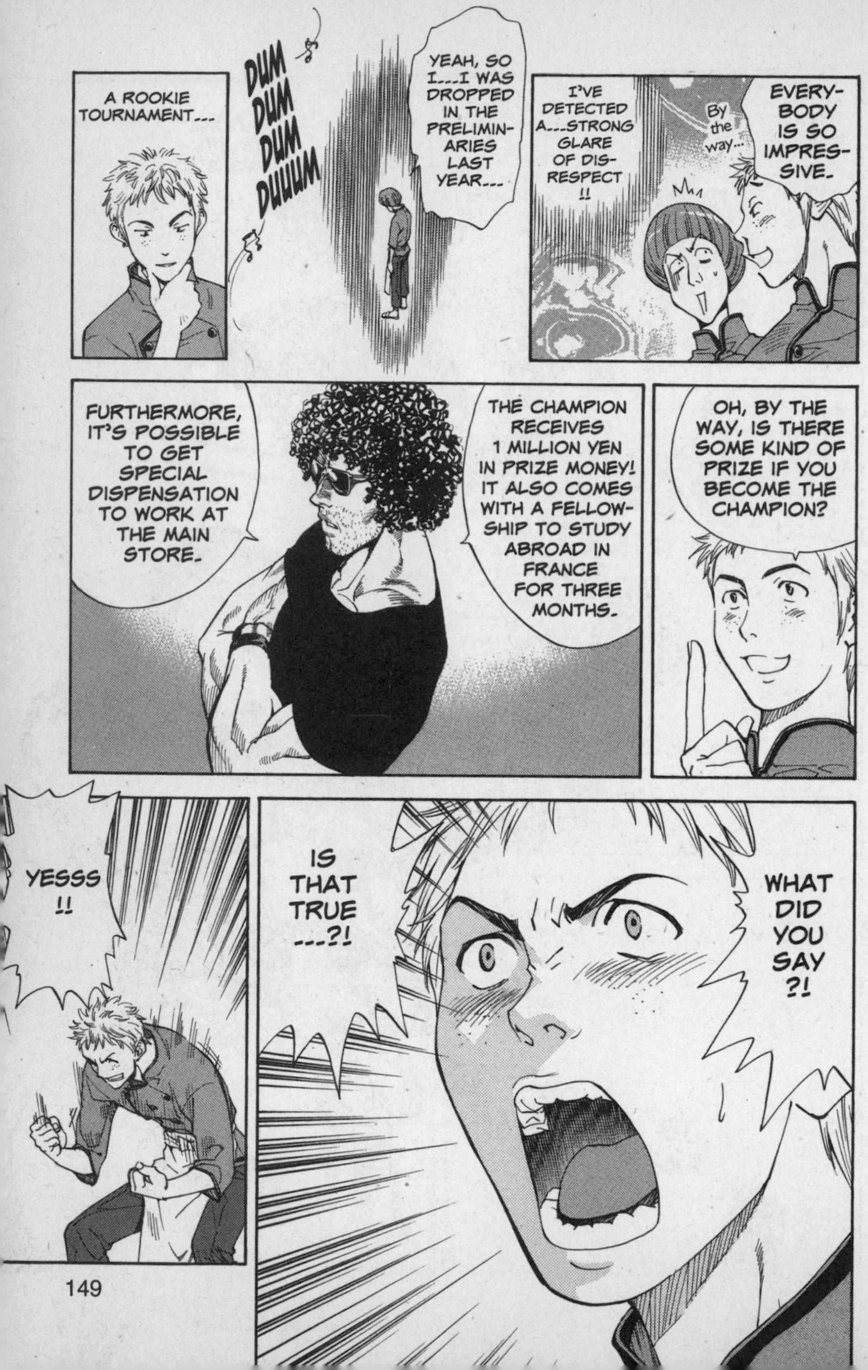

EVERYBODY IS SO IMPRESSIVE.
By the way...
I'VE DETECTED A...STRONG GLARE OF DISRESPECT !!
YEAH, SO I...I WAS DROPPED IN THE PRELIMINARIES LAST YEAR...
DUM DUM DUM DUUUM
A ROOKIE TOURNAMENT...
OH, BY THE WAY, IS THERE SOME KIND OF PRIZE IF YOU BECOME THE CHAMPION?
THE CHAMPION RECEIVES 1 MILLION YEN IN PRIZE MONEY! IT ALSO COMES WITH A FELLOWSHIP TO STUDY ABROAD IN FRANCE FOR THREE MONTHS.
FURTHERMORE, IT'S POSSIBLE TO GET SPECIAL DISPENSATION TO WORK AT THE MAIN STORE.
WHAT DID YOU SAY ?!
IS THAT TRUE ...?!
YESSS !!

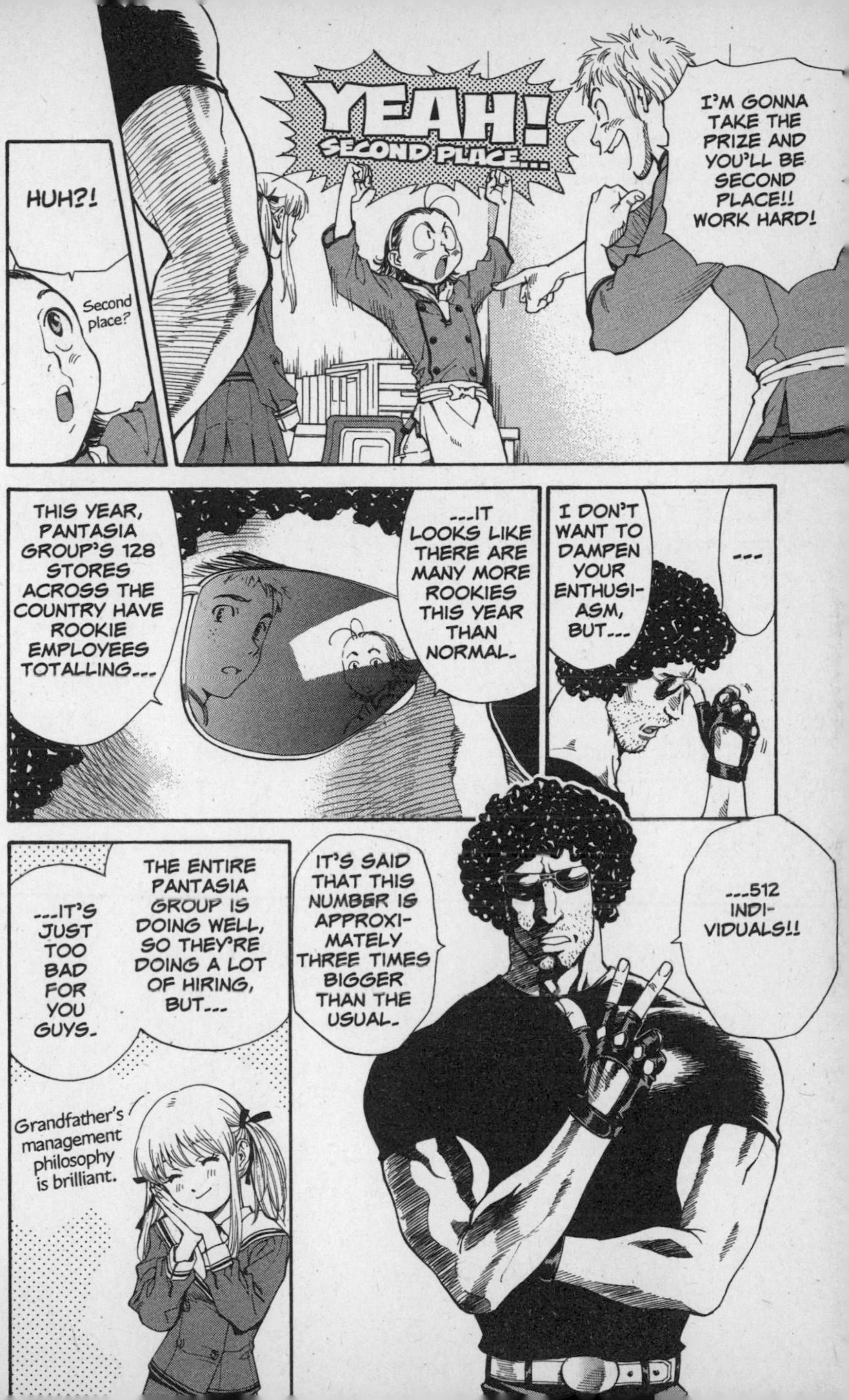

I'M GONNA TAKE THE PRIZE AND YOU'LL BE SECOND PLACE!! WORK HARD!
YEAH! SECOND PLACE...
HUH?!
Second place?
...
I DON'T WANT TO DAMPEN YOUR ENTHUSIASM, BUT...
...IT LOOKS LIKE THERE ARE MANY MORE ROOKIES THIS YEAR THAN NORMAL.
THIS YEAR, PANTASIA GROUP'S 128 STORES ACROSS THE COUNTRY HAVE ROOKIE EMPLOYEES TOTALLING...
...512 INDIVIDUALS!!
IT'S SAID THAT THIS NUMBER IS APPROXIMATELY THREE TIMES BIGGER THAN THE USUAL.
THE ENTIRE PANTASIA GROUP IS DOING WELL, SO THEY'RE DOING A LOT OF HIRING, BUT...
...IT'S JUST TOO BAD FOR YOU GUYS.
Grandfather's management philosophy is brilliant.

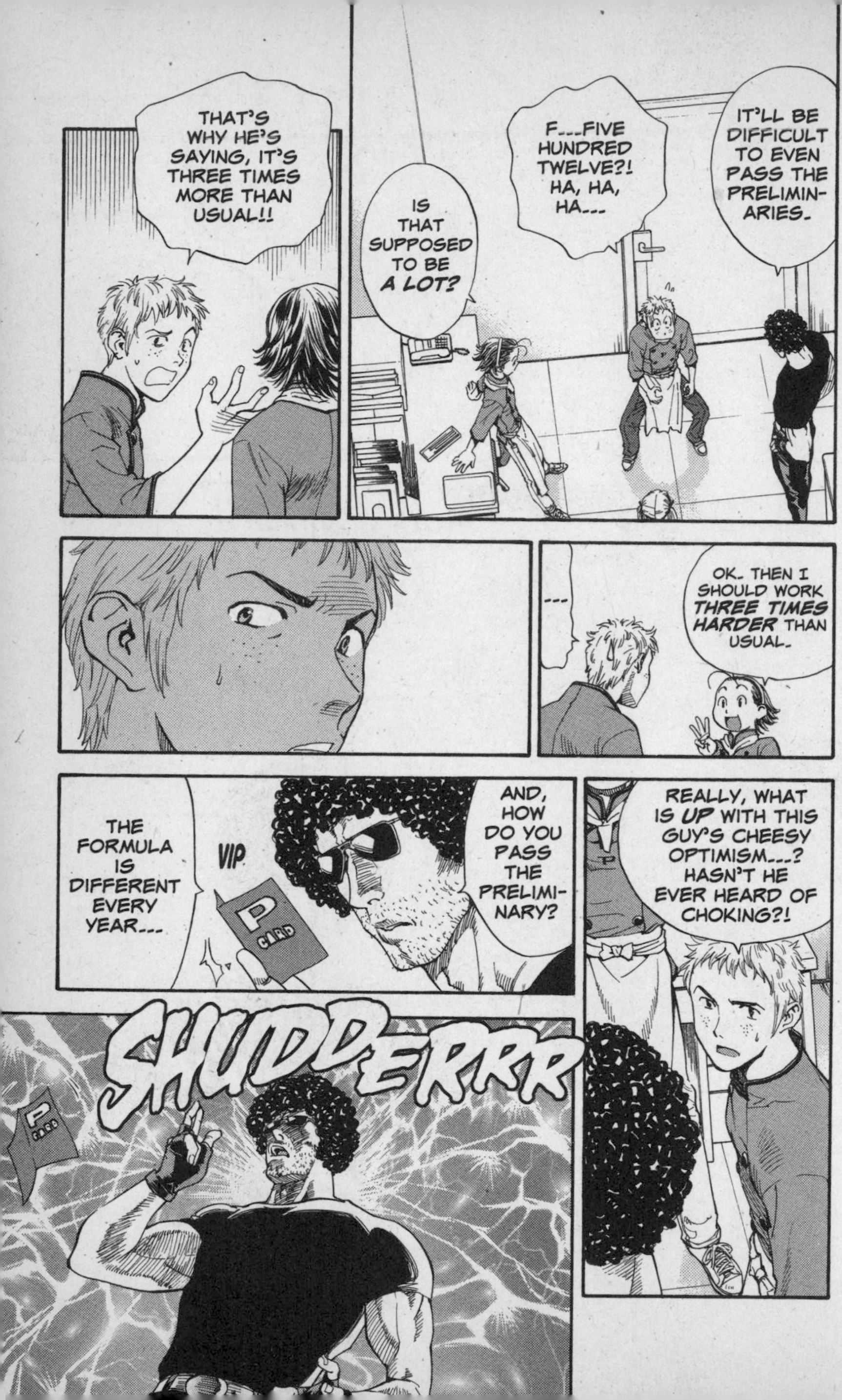
IT'LL BE DIFFICULT TO EVEN PASS THE PRELIMINARIES.
F---FIVE HUNDRED TWELVE?! HA, HA, HA---
IS THAT SUPPOSED TO BE *A LOT?*
THAT'S WHY HE'S SAYING, IT'S THREE TIMES MORE THAN USUAL!!
OK. THEN I SHOULD WORK *THREE TIMES HARDER* THAN USUAL.

REALLY, WHAT IS *UP* WITH THIS GUY'S CHEESY OPTIMISM---? HASN'T HE EVER HEARD OF CHOKING?!
AND, HOW DO YOU PASS THE PRELIMINARY?
VIP
P CARD
THE FORMULA IS DIFFERENT EVERY YEAR---
SHUDDERRR

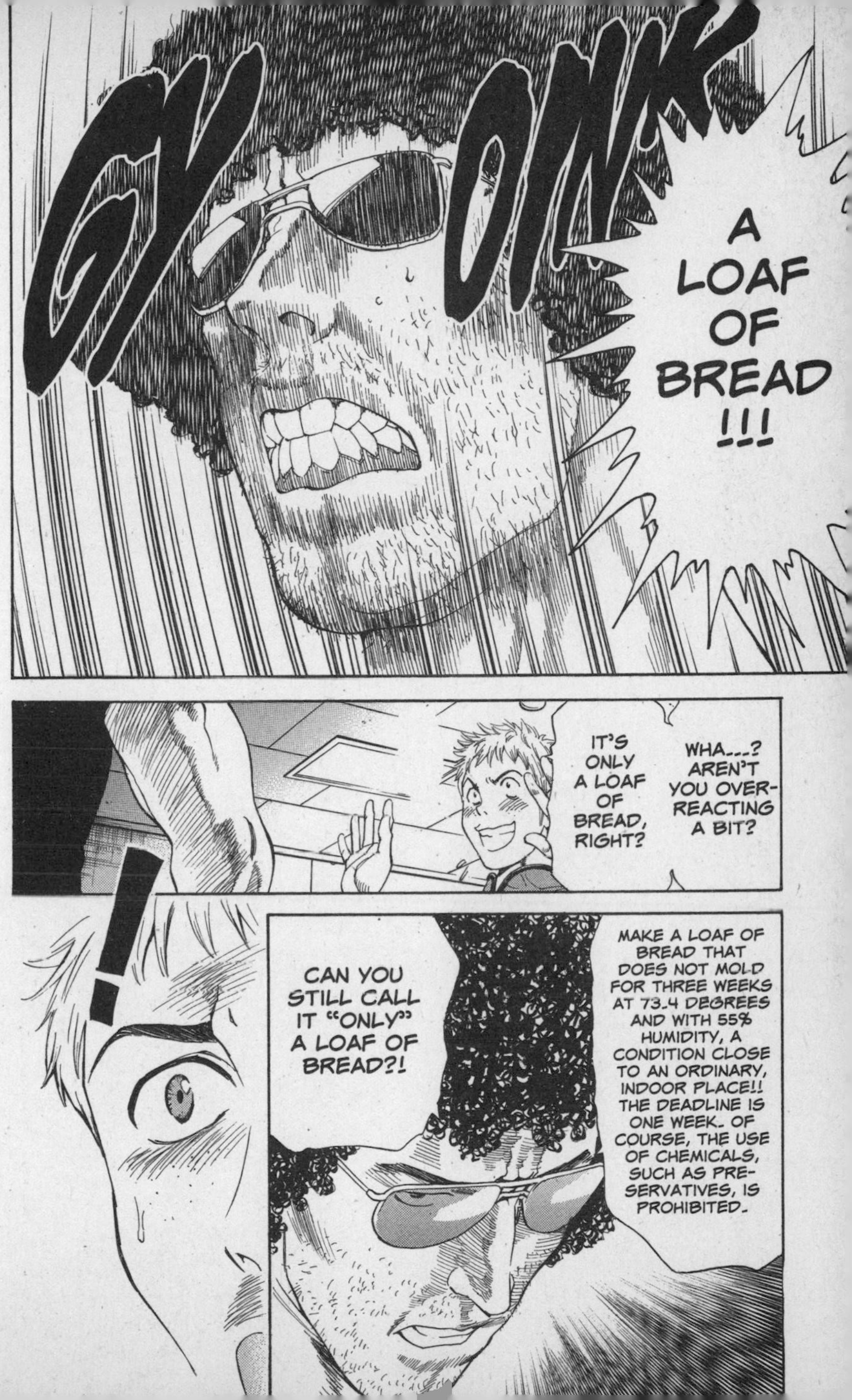
GY-ONK
A LOAF OF BREAD !!!
WHA...? AREN'T YOU OVER-REACTING A BIT?
IT'S ONLY A LOAF OF BREAD, RIGHT?
!
MAKE A LOAF OF BREAD THAT DOES NOT MOLD FOR THREE WEEKS AT 73.4 DEGREES AND WITH 55% HUMIDITY, A CONDITION CLOSE TO AN ORDINARY, INDOOR PLACE!! THE DEADLINE IS ONE WEEK. OF COURSE, THE USE OF CHEMICALS, SUCH AS PRE-SERVATIVES, IS PROHIBITED.
CAN YOU STILL CALL IT "ONLY" A LOAF OF BREAD?!

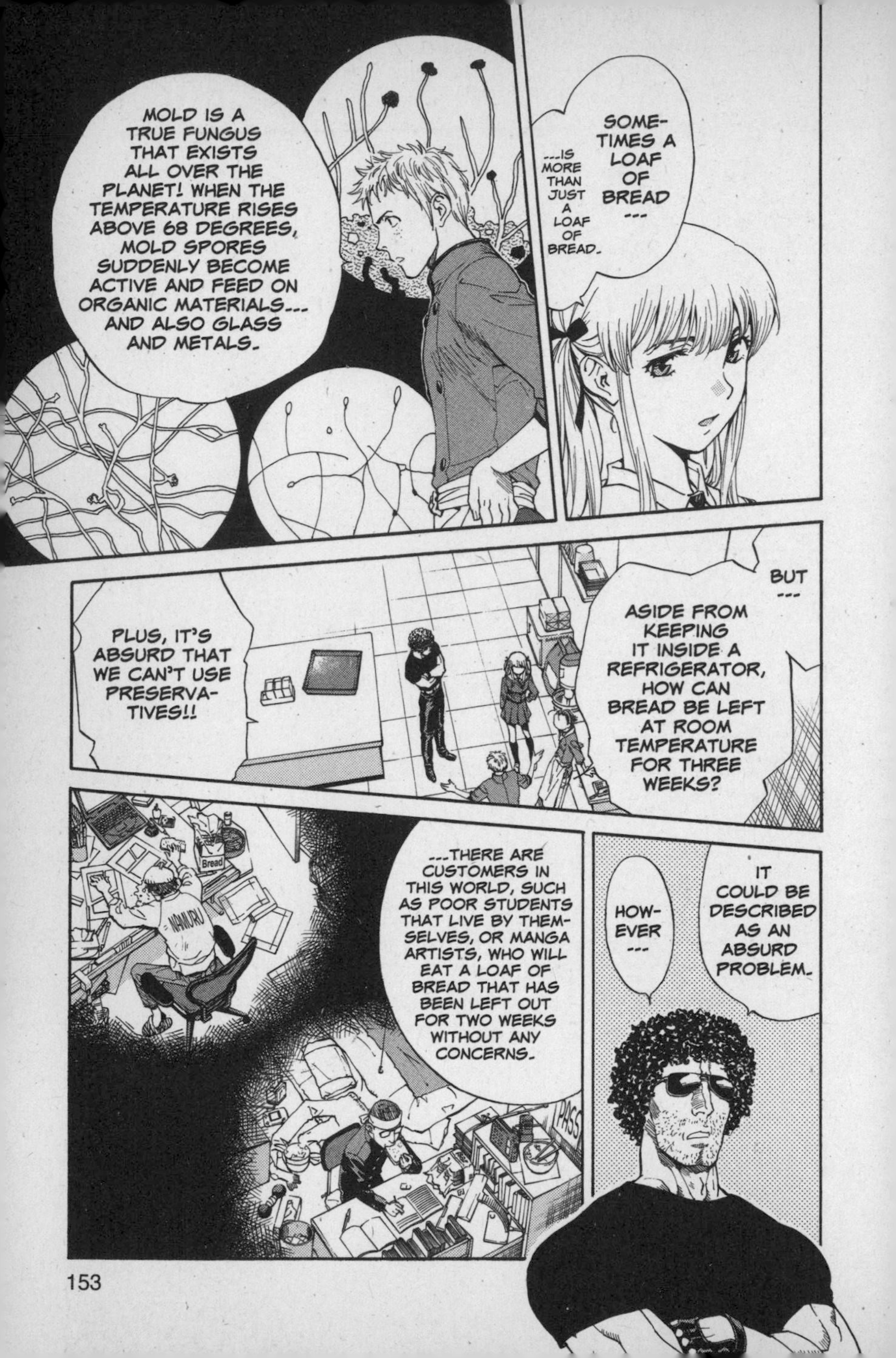

SOME-TIMES A LOAF OF BREAD ---
---IS MORE THAN JUST A LOAF OF BREAD.
MOLD IS A TRUE FUNGUS THAT EXISTS ALL OVER THE PLANET! WHEN THE TEMPERATURE RISES ABOVE 68 DEGREES, MOLD SPORES SUDDENLY BECOME ACTIVE AND FEED ON ORGANIC MATERIALS... AND ALSO GLASS AND METALS.
BUT ---
ASIDE FROM KEEPING IT INSIDE A REFRIGERATOR, HOW CAN BREAD BE LEFT AT ROOM TEMPERATURE FOR THREE WEEKS?
PLUS, IT'S ABSURD THAT WE CAN'T USE PRESERVA-TIVES!!
IT COULD BE DESCRIBED AS AN ABSURD PROBLEM.
HOW-EVER ---
---THERE ARE CUSTOMERS IN THIS WORLD, SUCH AS POOR STUDENTS THAT LIVE BY THEM-SELVES, OR MANGA ARTISTS, WHO WILL EAT A LOAF OF BREAD THAT HAS BEEN LEFT OUT FOR TWO WEEKS WITHOUT ANY CONCERNS.
Bread
NAMURU
PASS

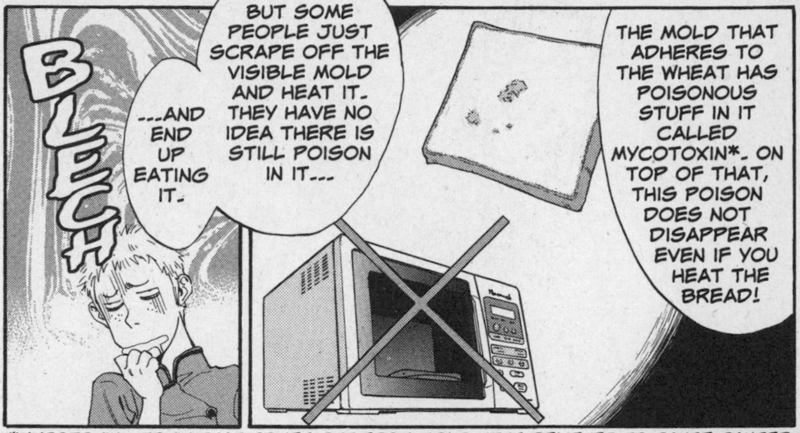
THE MOLD THAT ADHERES TO THE WHEAT HAS POISONOUS STUFF IN IT CALLED MYCOTOXIN*. ON TOP OF THAT, THIS POISON DOES NOT DISAPPEAR EVEN IF YOU HEAT THE BREAD!
BUT SOME PEOPLE JUST SCRAPE OFF THE VISIBLE MOLD AND HEAT IT. THEY HAVE NO IDEA THERE IS STILL POISON IN IT...
...AND END UP EATING IT.
BLECH

*MYCOTOXIN...TOXIN THAT COMES OUT FROM MOLD. IT IS BELIEVED TO CAUSE CANCER.

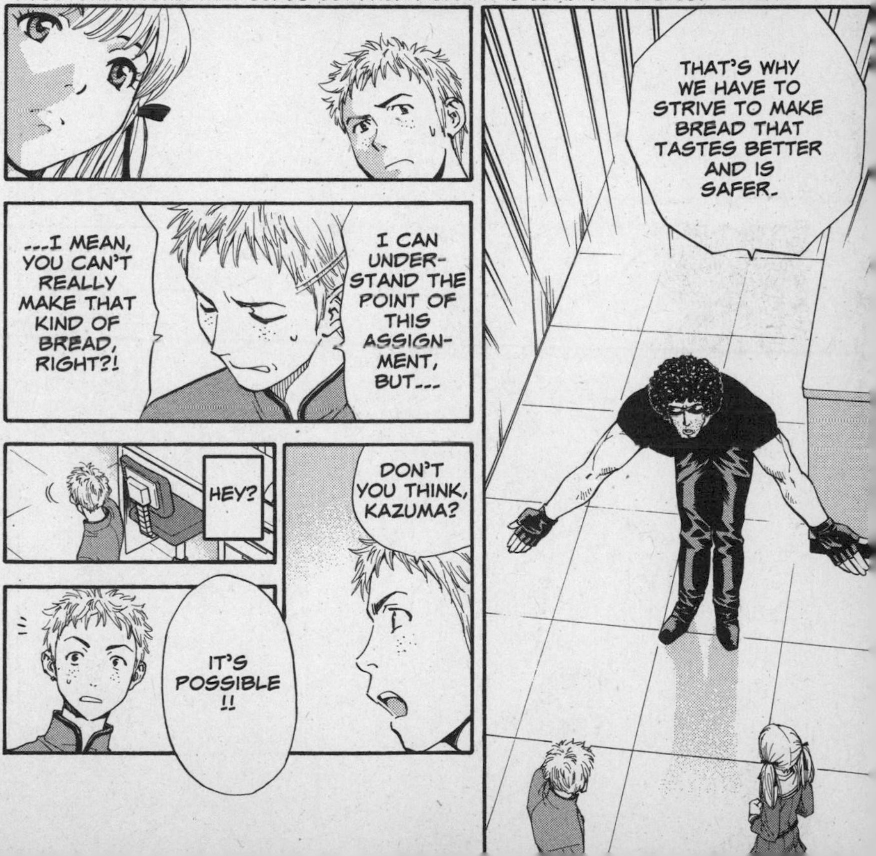
THAT'S WHY WE HAVE TO STRIVE TO MAKE BREAD THAT TASTES BETTER AND IS SAFER.
I CAN UNDER-STAND THE POINT OF THIS ASSIGN-MENT, BUT...
...I MEAN, YOU CAN'T REALLY MAKE THAT KIND OF BREAD, RIGHT?!
DON'T YOU THINK, KAZUMA?
HEY?
IT'S POSSIBLE !!

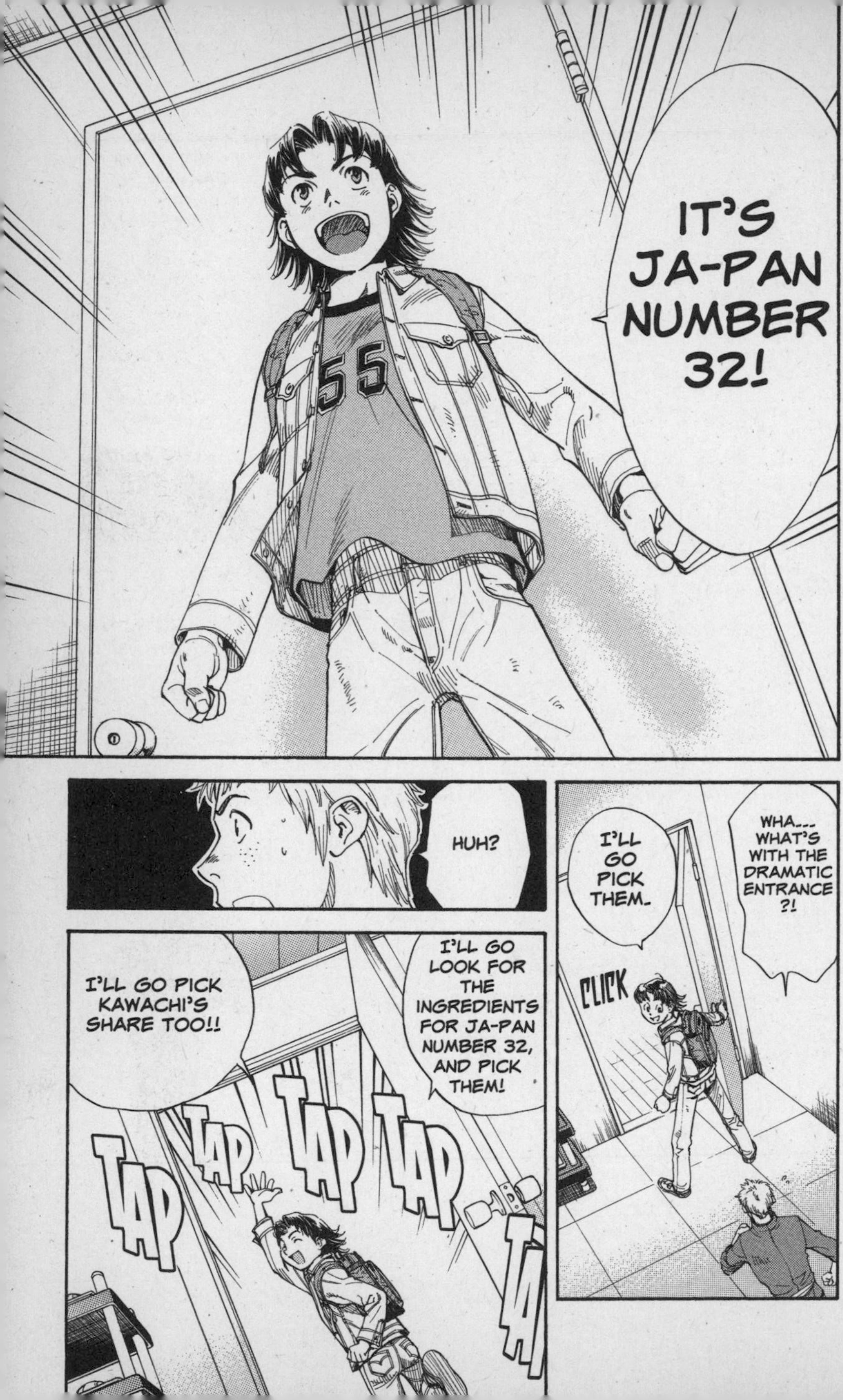
IT'S JA-PAN NUMBER 32!
WHA... WHAT'S WITH THE DRAMATIC ENTRANCE?!
I'LL GO PICK THEM.
CLICK
HUH?
I'LL GO LOOK FOR THE INGREDIENTS FOR JA-PAN NUMBER 32, AND PICK THEM!
I'LL GO PICK KAWACHI'S SHARE TOO!!
TAP
TAP
TAP
TAP
TAP
TA

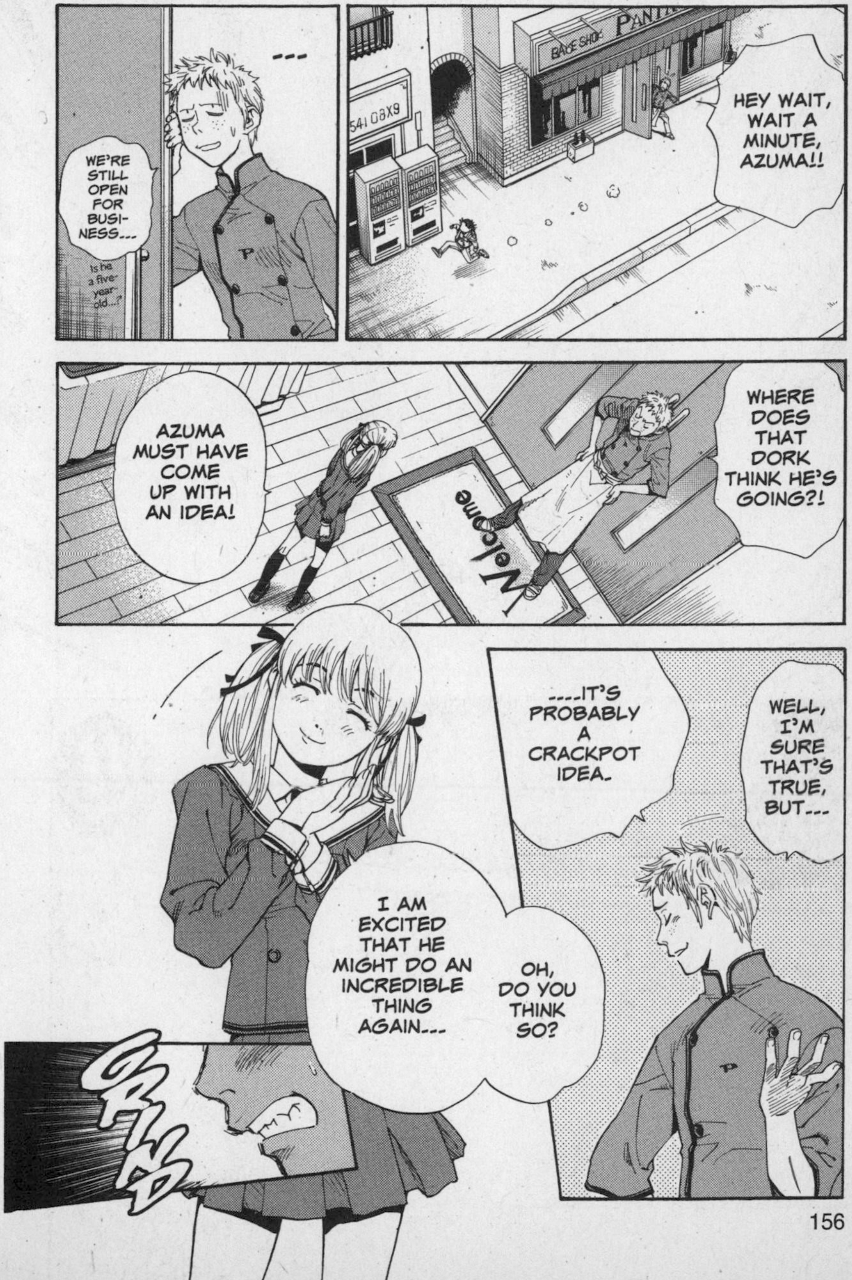
HEY WAIT, WAIT A MINUTE, AZUMA!!
...
WE'RE STILL OPEN FOR BUSINESS...
Is he a five-year-old...?
WHERE DOES THAT DORK THINK HE'S GOING?!
Welcome
AZUMA MUST HAVE COME UP WITH AN IDEA!
WELL, I'M SURE THAT'S TRUE, BUT...
....IT'S PROBABLY A CRACKPOT IDEA.
OH, DO YOU THINK SO?
I AM EXCITED THAT HE MIGHT DO AN INCREDIBLE THING AGAIN...
GRIND

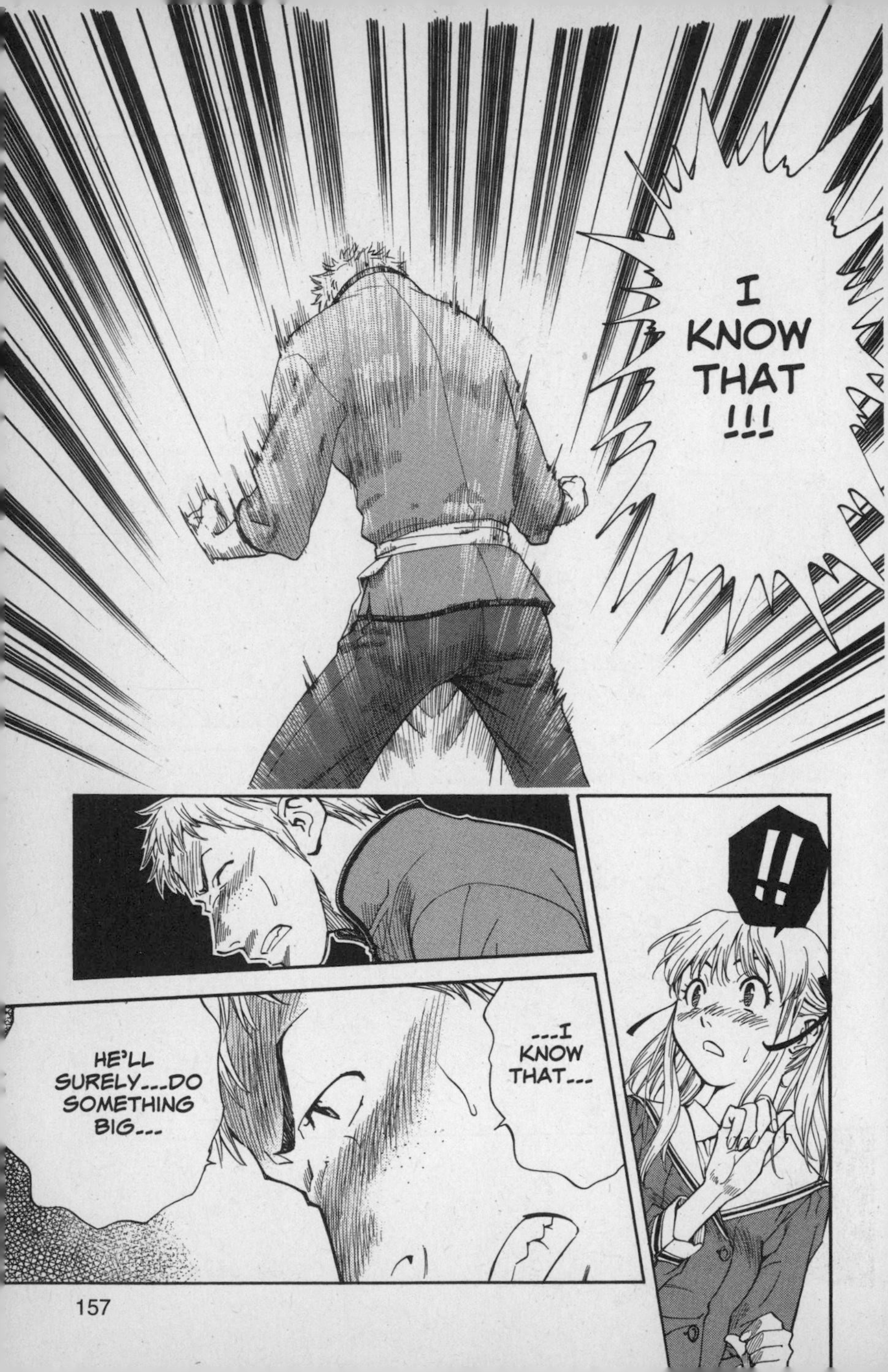
I KNOW THAT!!!
!!
...I KNOW THAT...
HE'LL SURELY...DO SOMETHING BIG...

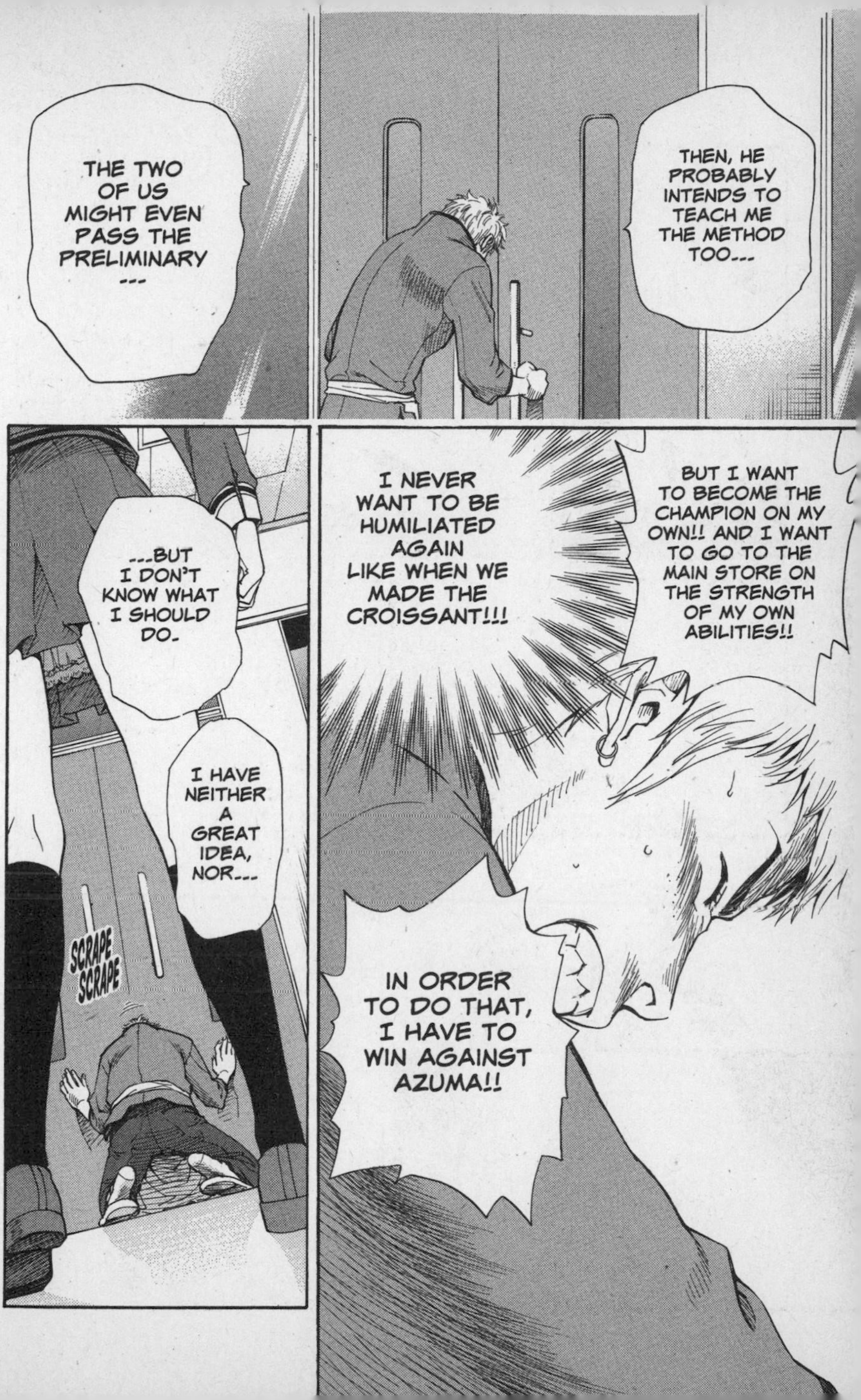
THEN, HE PROBABLY INTENDS TO TEACH ME THE METHOD TOO...
THE TWO OF US MIGHT EVEN PASS THE PRELIMINARY ...
BUT I WANT TO BECOME THE CHAMPION ON MY OWN!! AND I WANT TO GO TO THE MAIN STORE ON THE STRENGTH OF MY OWN ABILITIES!!
I NEVER WANT TO BE HUMILIATED AGAIN LIKE WHEN WE MADE THE CROISSANT!!!
IN ORDER TO DO THAT, I HAVE TO WIN AGAINST AZUMA!!
...BUT I DON'T KNOW WHAT I SHOULD DO.
I HAVE NEITHER A GREAT IDEA, NOR...
SCRAPE SCRAPE

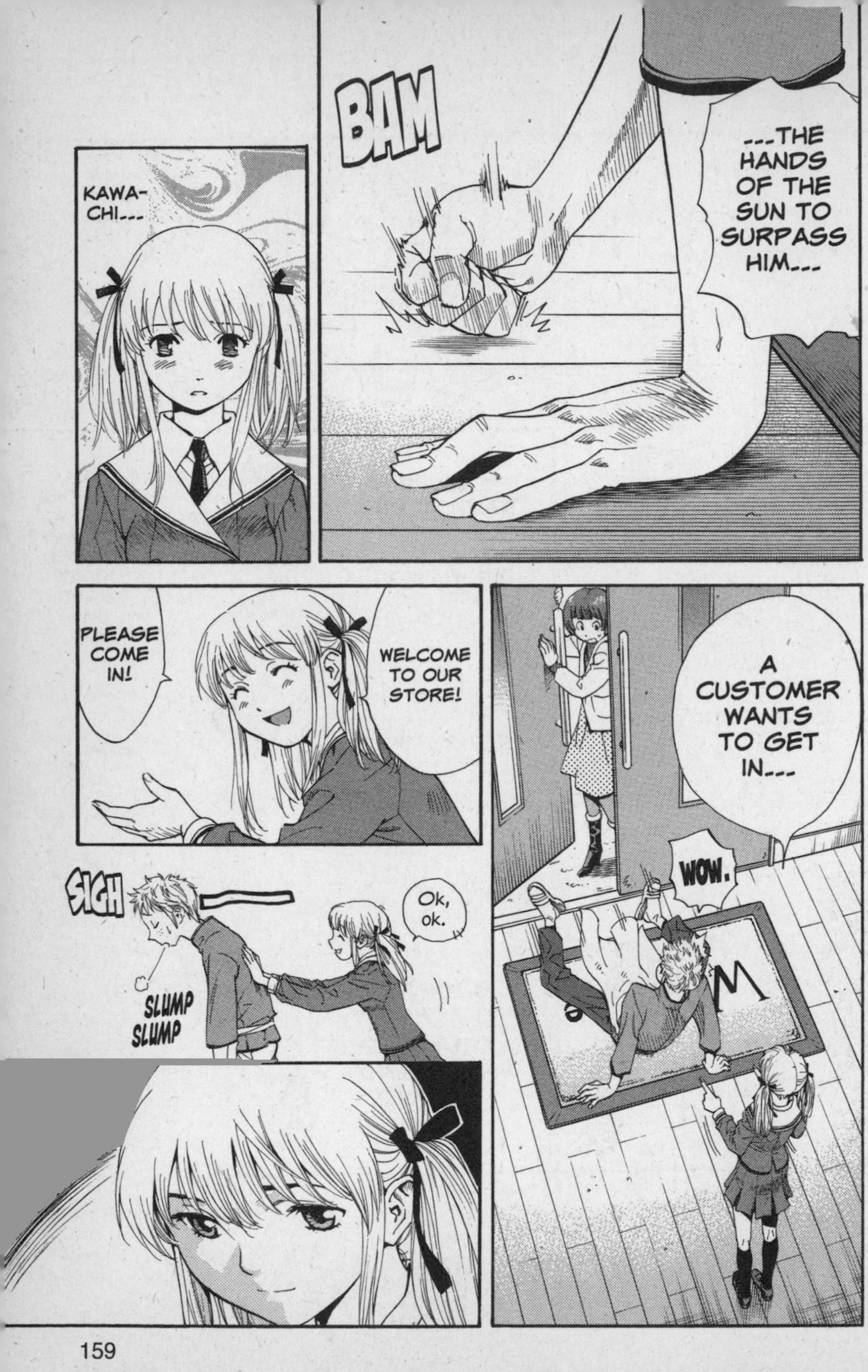
BAM
---THE HANDS OF THE SUN TO SURPASS HIM---
KAWA-CHI!---
A CUSTOMER WANTS TO GET IN---
WOW.
WELCOME TO OUR STORE!
PLEASE COME IN!
Ok, ok.
SIGH
SLUMP SLUMP

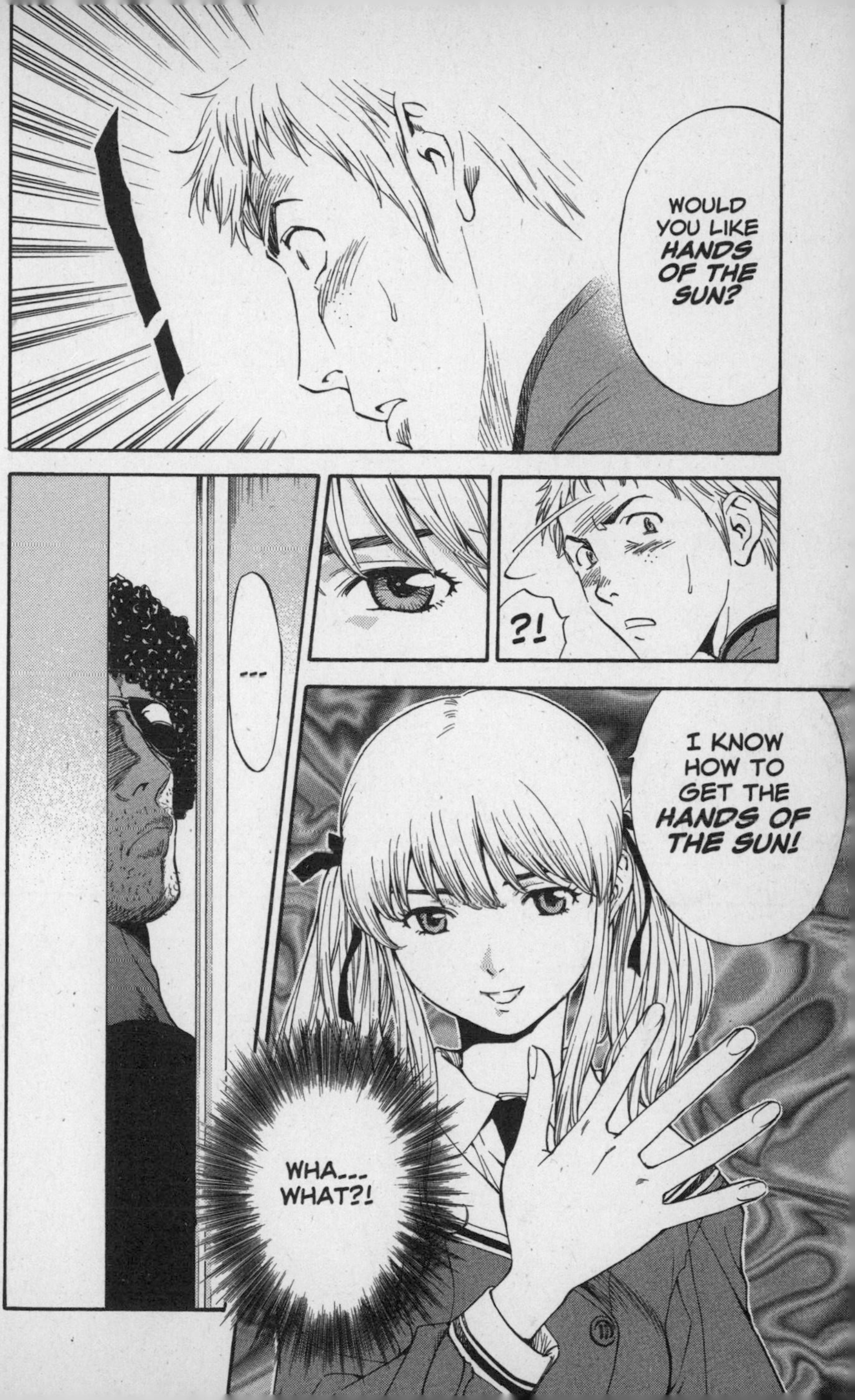
WOULD YOU LIKE HANDS OF THE SUN?
?!
I KNOW HOW TO GET THE HANDS OF THE SUN!
WHA... WHAT?!
...

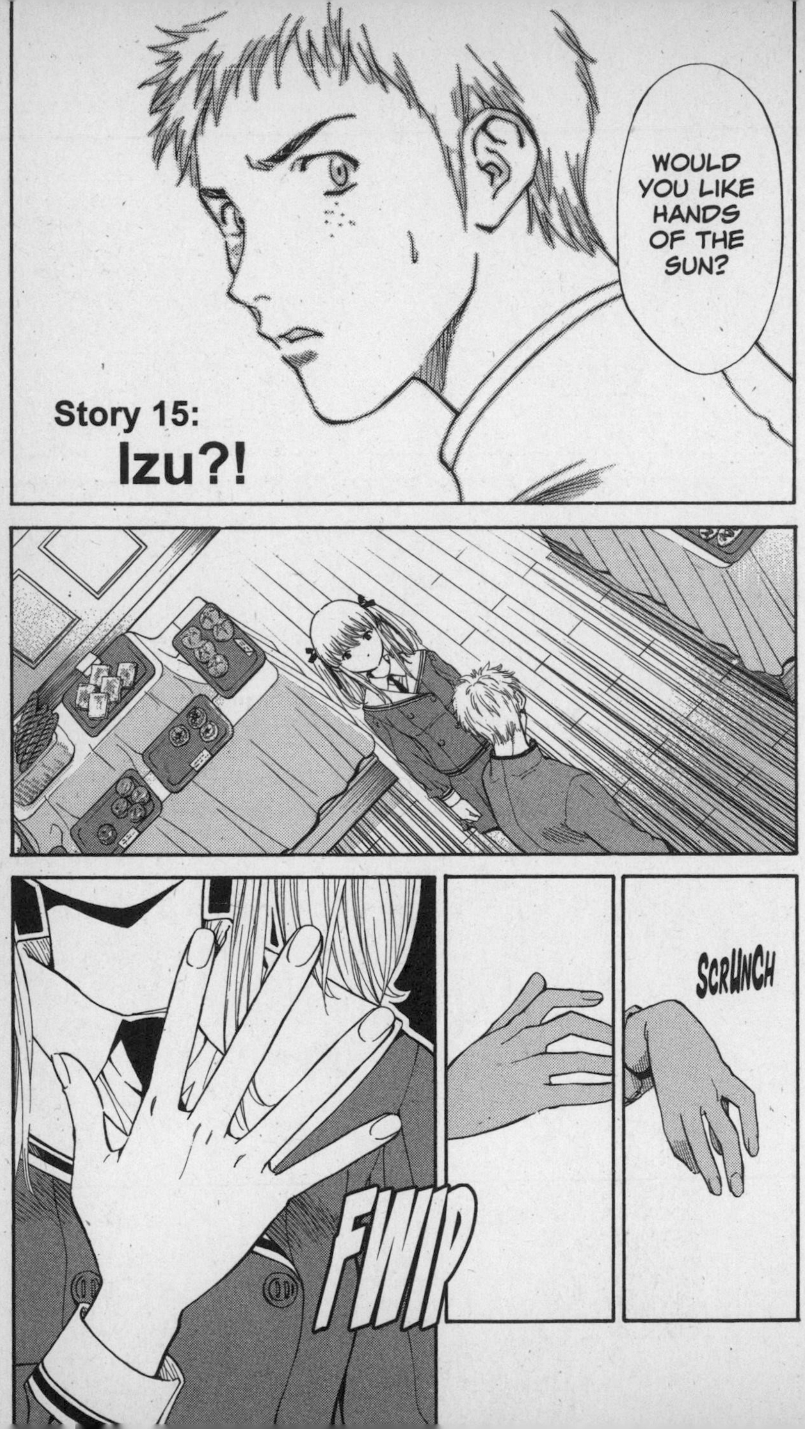
WOULD YOU LIKE HANDS OF THE SUN?
Story 15:
Izu?!
SCRUNCH
FWIP

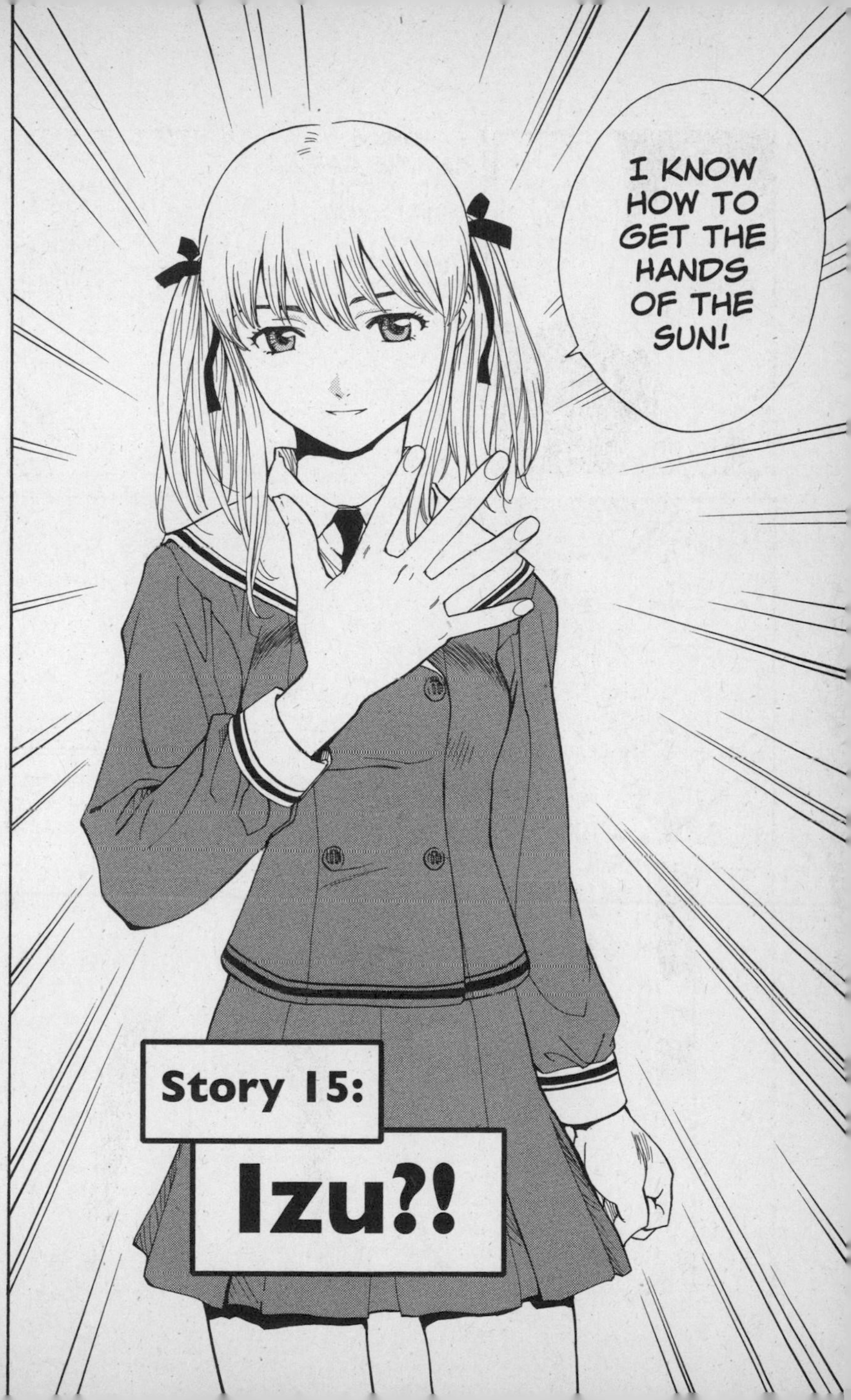
I KNOW HOW TO GET THE HANDS OF THE SUN!
Story 15:
Izu?!

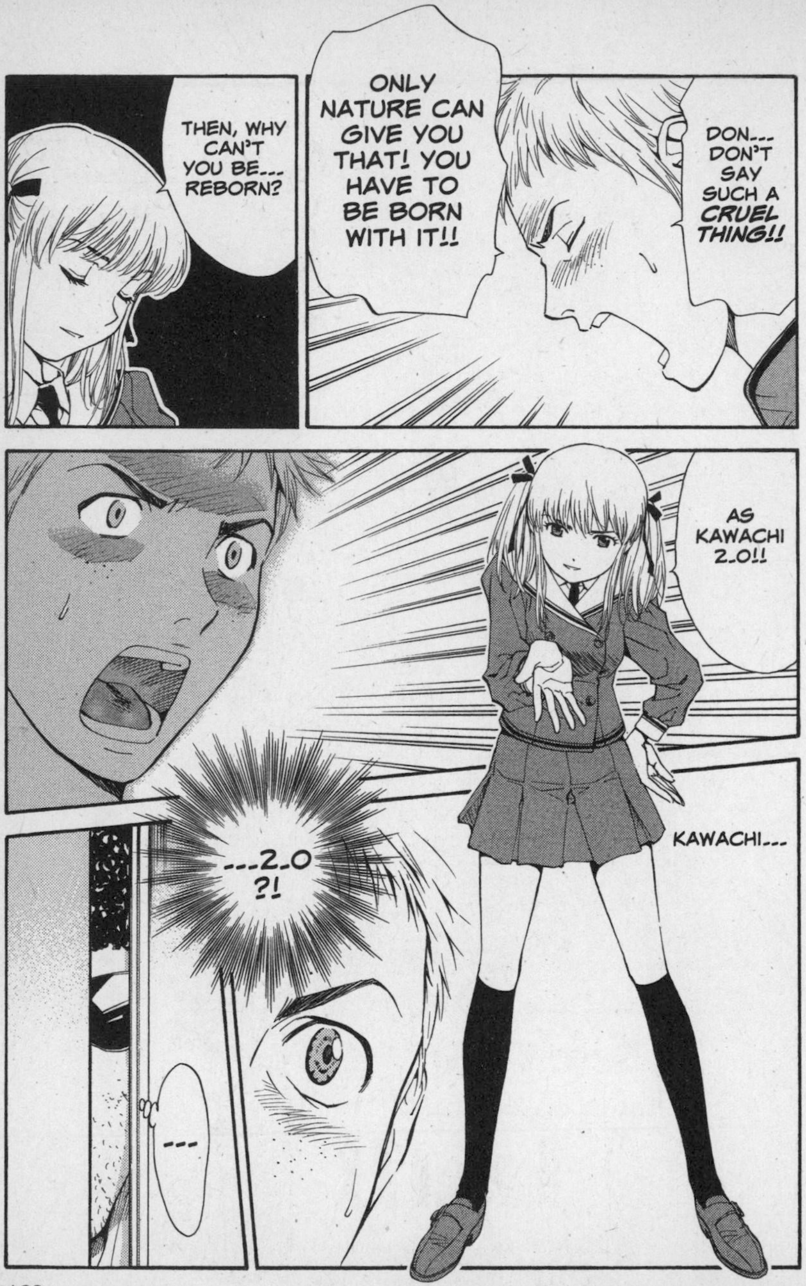
DON... DON'T SAY SUCH A CRUEL THING!!
ONLY NATURE CAN GIVE YOU THAT! YOU HAVE TO BE BORN WITH IT!!
THEN, WHY CAN'T YOU BE... REBORN?
AS KAWACHI 2.0!!
KAWACHI...
...2.0 ?!
...

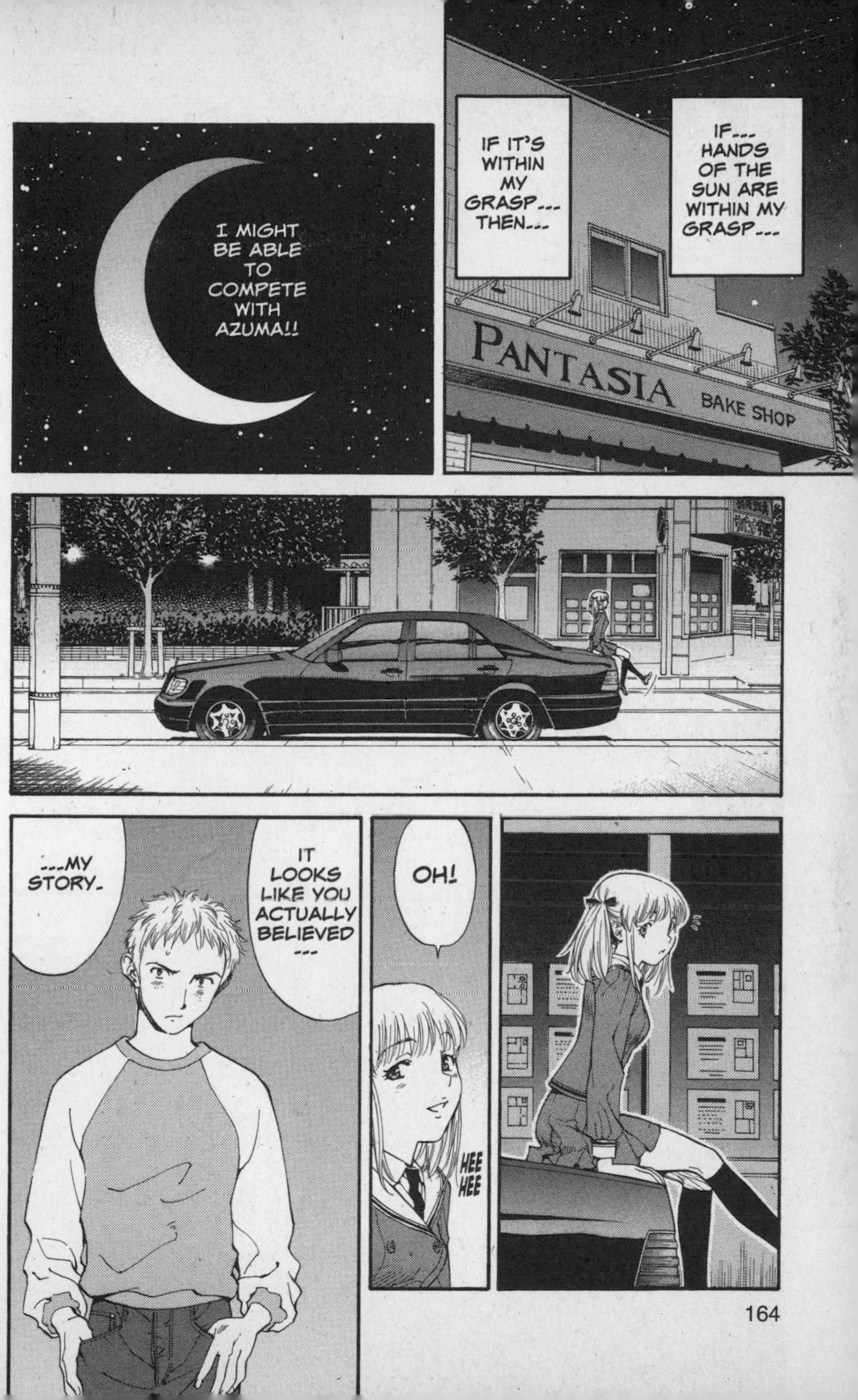
IF... HANDS OF THE SUN ARE WITHIN MY GRASP...
IF IT'S WITHIN MY GRASP... THEN...
PANTASIA
BAKE SHOP
I MIGHT BE ABLE TO COMPETE WITH AZUMA!!
OH!
HEE HEE
IT LOOKS LIKE YOU ACTUALLY BELIEVED ---
---MY STORY.

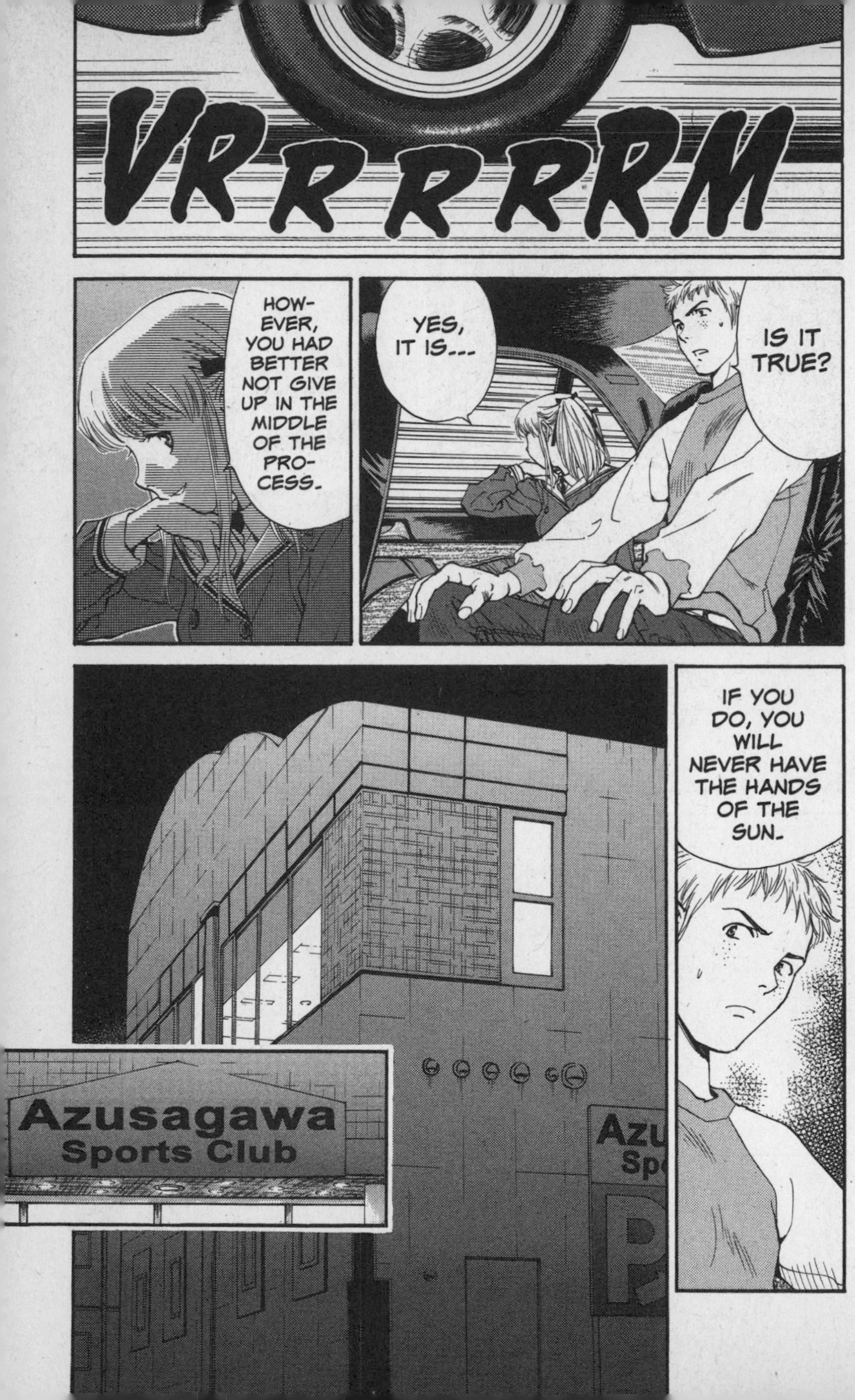
VRRRRRM
IS IT TRUE?
YES, IT IS...
HOW-EVER, YOU HAD BETTER NOT GIVE UP IN THE MIDDLE OF THE PRO-CESS.
IF YOU DO, YOU WILL NEVER HAVE THE HANDS OF THE SUN.
Azusagawa Sports Club

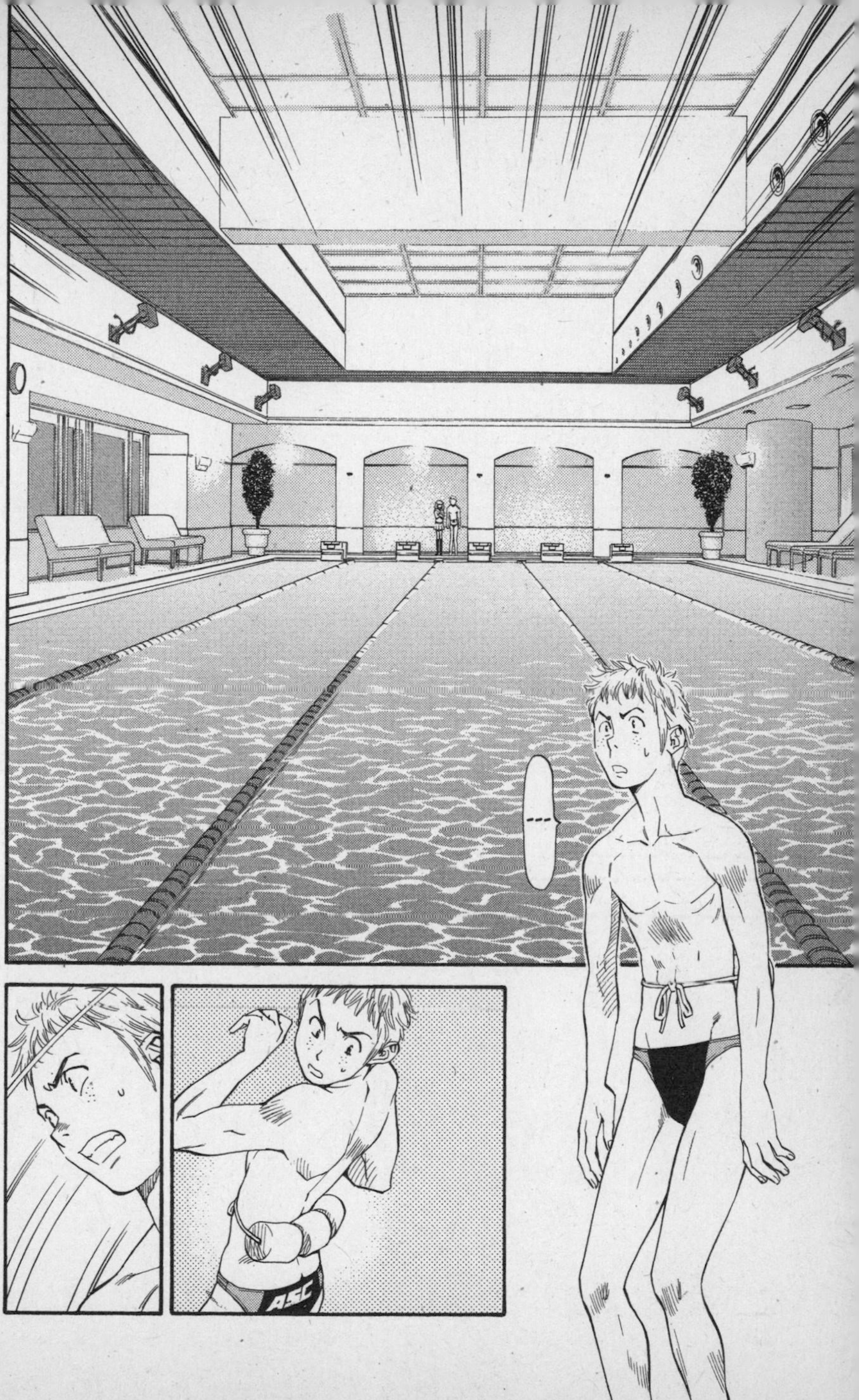
...
ASC

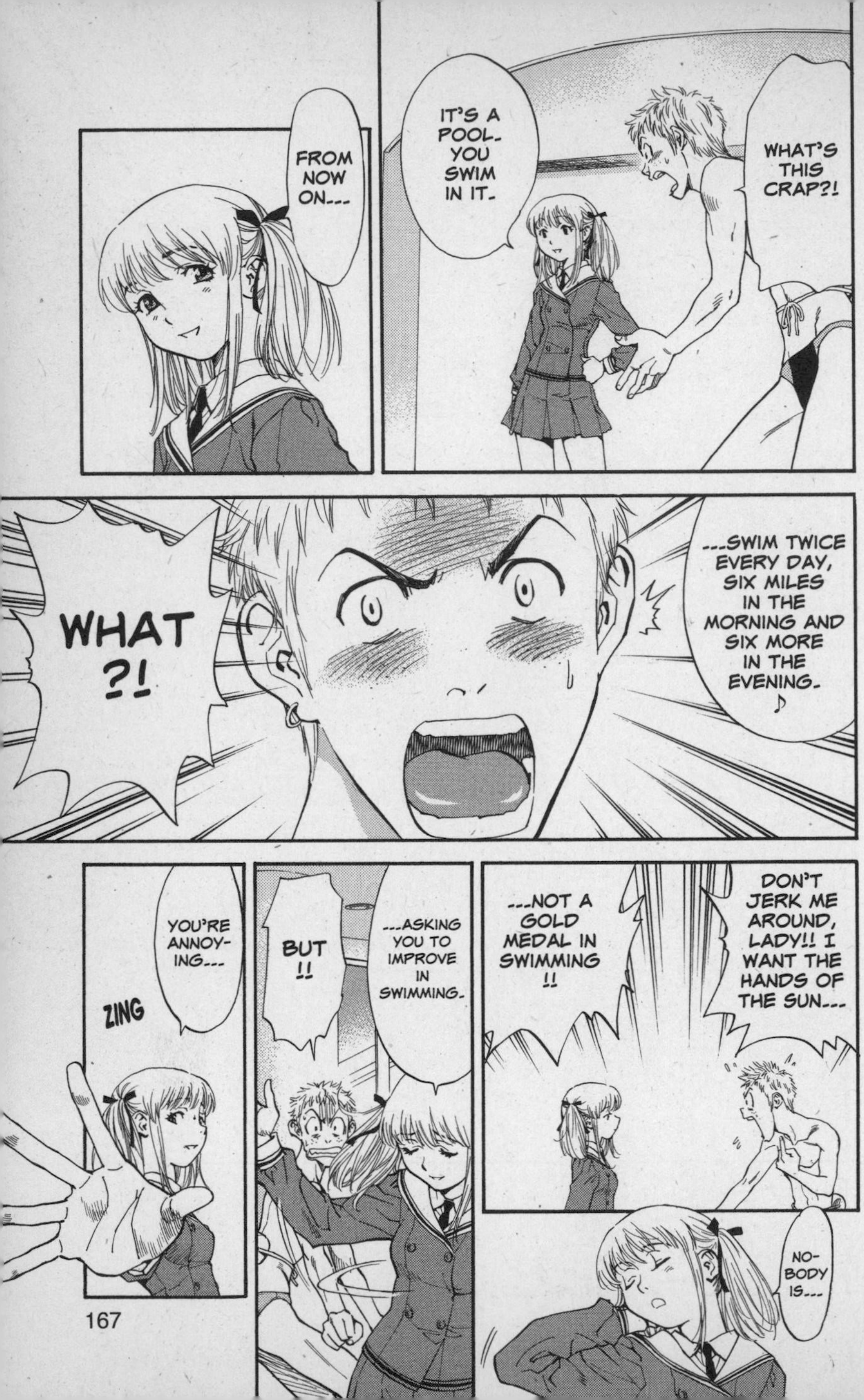
WHAT'S THIS CRAP?!
IT'S A POOL. YOU SWIM IN IT.
FROM NOW ON...
...SWIM TWICE EVERY DAY, SIX MILES IN THE MORNING AND SIX MORE IN THE EVENING. ♪
WHAT ?!
DON'T JERK ME AROUND, LADY!! I WANT THE HANDS OF THE SUN...
...NOT A GOLD MEDAL IN SWIMMING !!
NO-BODY IS...
...ASKING YOU TO IMPROVE IN SWIMMING.
BUT !!
YOU'RE ANNOY-ING...
ZING

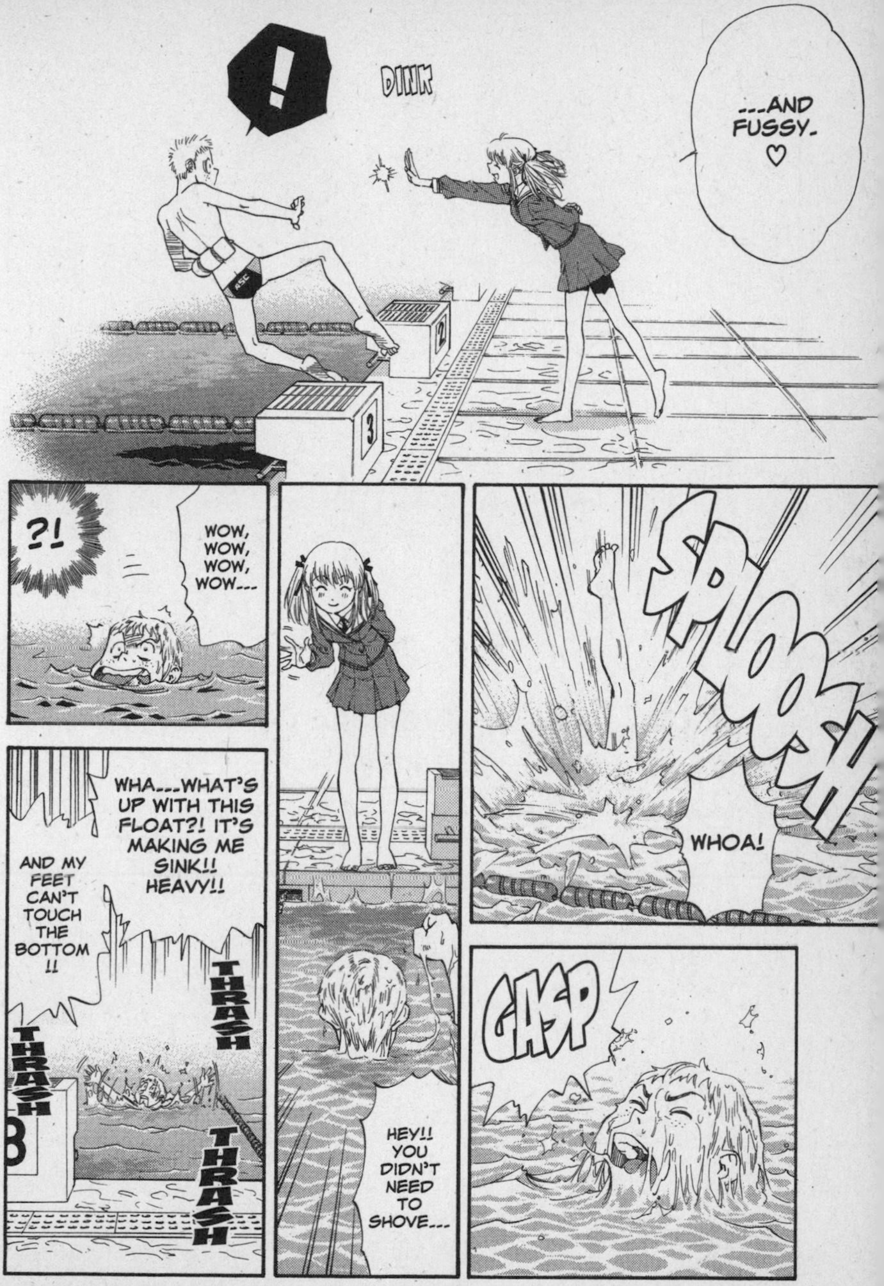
...AND FUSSY. ♡
DINK
!
SPLOOSH
WHOA!
GASP
HEY!! YOU DIDN'T NEED TO SHOVE...
?!
WOW, WOW, WOW, WOW...
WHA...WHAT'S UP WITH THIS FLOAT?! IT'S MAKING ME SINK!! HEAVY!!
AND MY FEET CAN'T TOUCH THE BOTTOM !!
THRASH
THRASH
THRASH

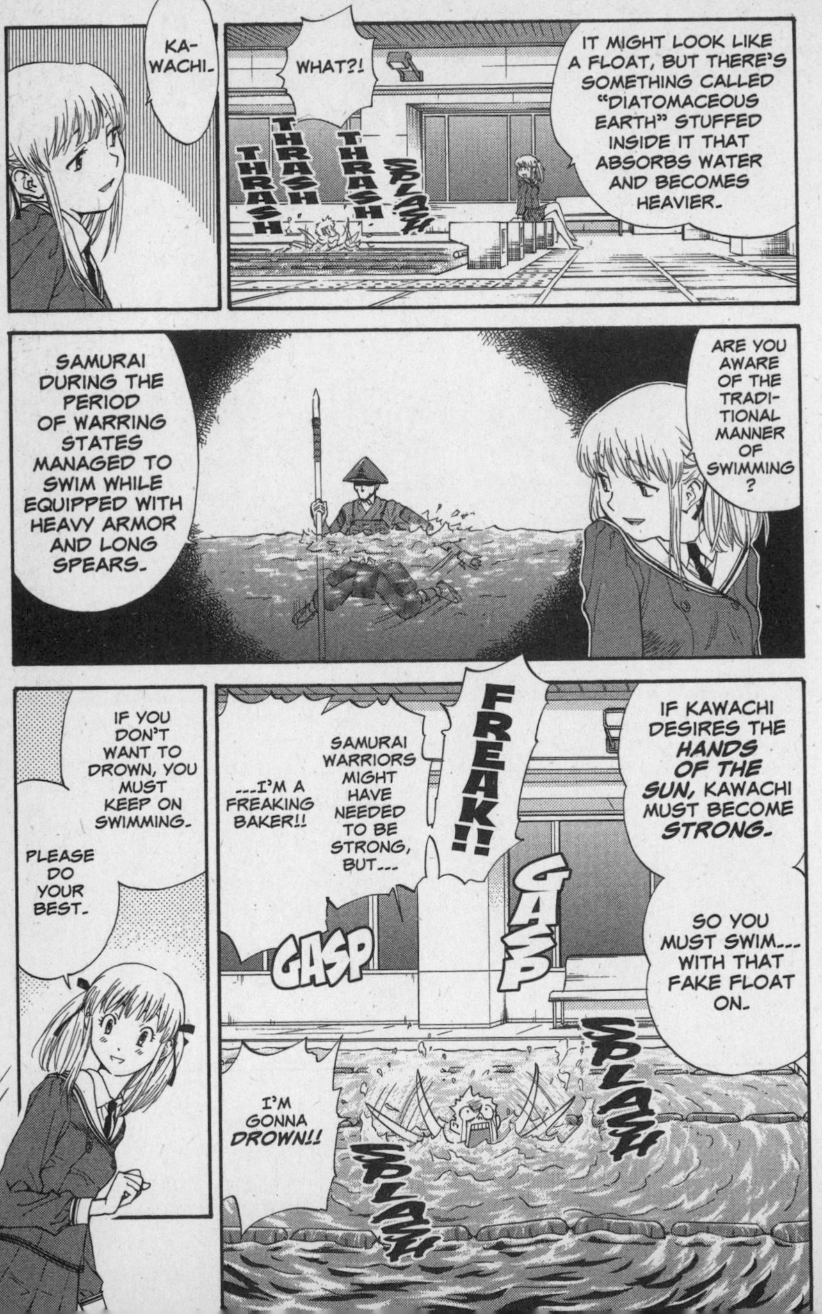
IT MIGHT LOOK LIKE A FLOAT, BUT THERE'S SOMETHING CALLED "DIATOMACEOUS EARTH" STUFFED INSIDE IT THAT ABSORBS WATER AND BECOMES HEAVIER.
WHAT?!
SPLASH
THRASH
THRASH
THRASH
KA-WACHI.
ARE YOU AWARE OF THE TRADI-TIONAL MANNER OF SWIMMING?
SAMURAI DURING THE PERIOD OF WARRING STATES MANAGED TO SWIM WHILE EQUIPPED WITH HEAVY ARMOR AND LONG SPEARS.
IF KAWACHI DESIRES THE *HANDS OF THE SUN*, KAWACHI MUST BECOME *STRONG*.
FREAK!!
SAMURAI WARRIORS MIGHT HAVE NEEDED TO BE STRONG, BUT...
...I'M A FREAKING BAKER!!
SO YOU MUST SWIM... WITH THAT FAKE FLOAT ON.
GASP
GASP
SPLASH
I'M GONNA *DROWN*!!
SPLASH
IF YOU DON'T WANT TO DROWN, YOU MUST KEEP ON SWIMMING.
PLEASE DO YOUR BEST.

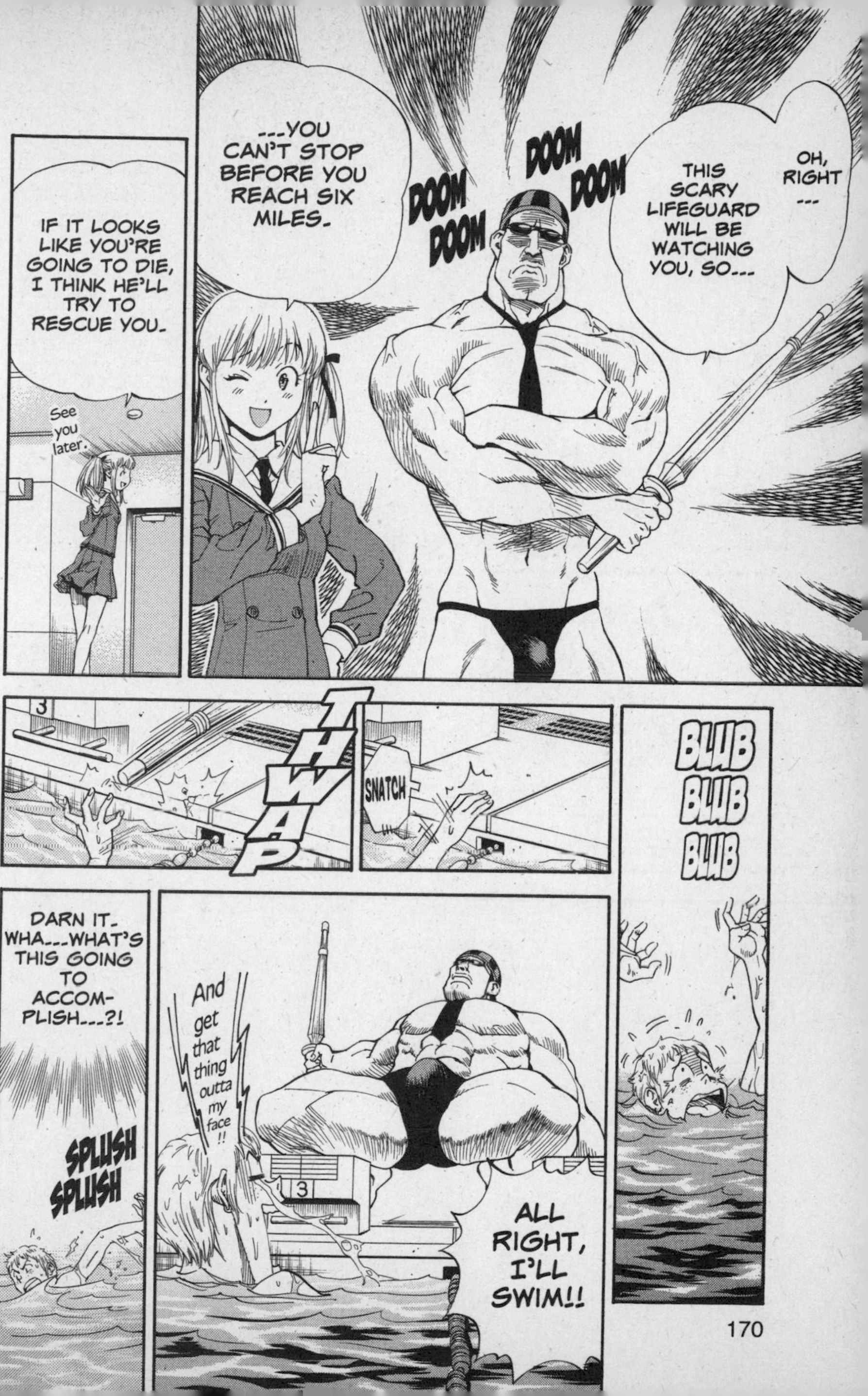
OH, RIGHT ---
THIS SCARY LIFEGUARD WILL BE WATCHING YOU, SO...
DOOM DOOM
DOOM DOOM
---YOU CAN'T STOP BEFORE YOU REACH SIX MILES.
IF IT LOOKS LIKE YOU'RE GOING TO DIE, I THINK HE'LL TRY TO RESCUE YOU.
See you later.
BLUB BLUB BLUB
SNATCH
THWAP
ALL RIGHT, I'LL SWIM!!
And get that thing outta my face!!
DARN IT. WHA...WHAT'S THIS GOING TO ACCOMPLISH...?!
SPLUSH SPLUSH

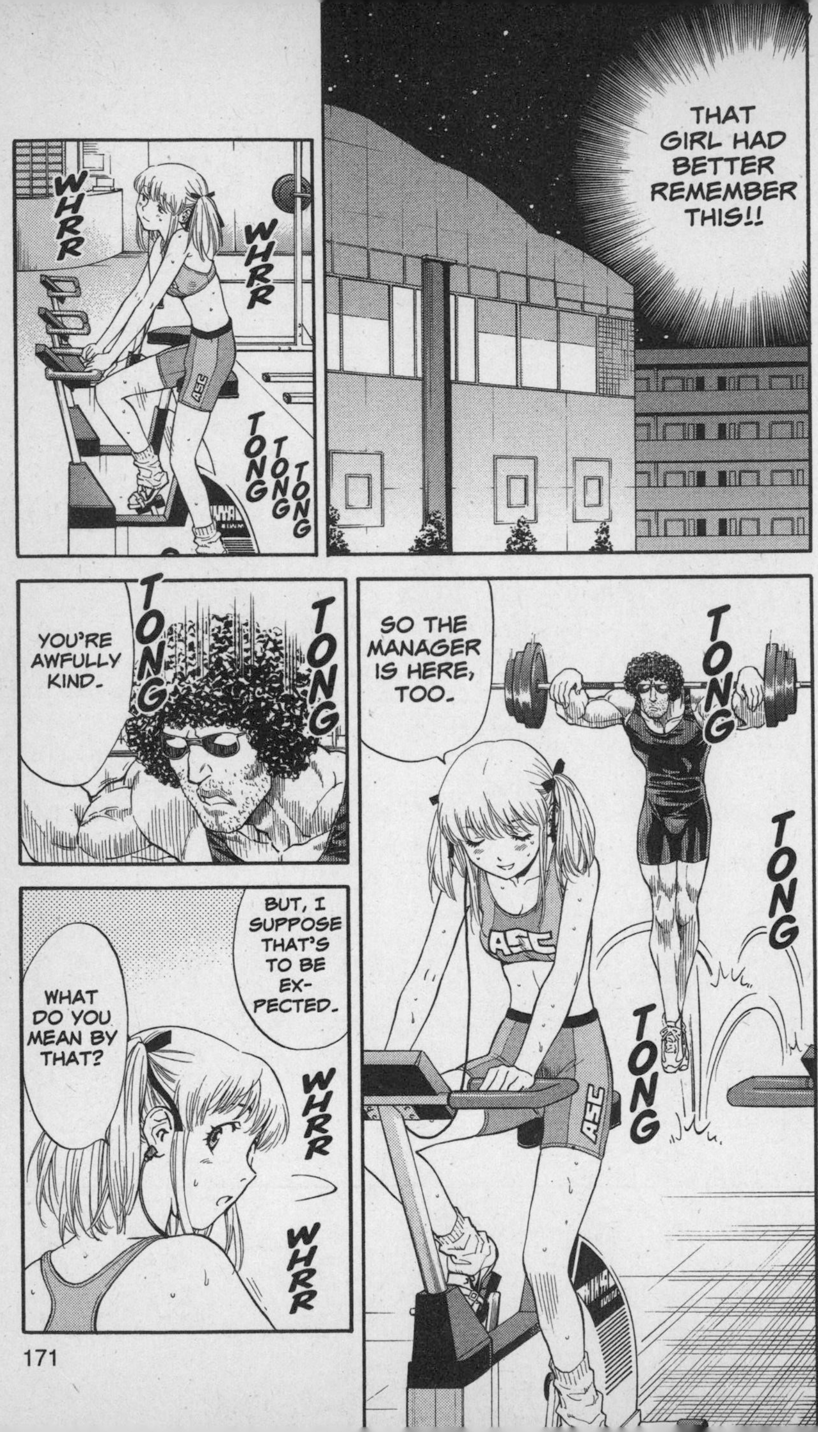
THAT GIRL HAD BETTER REMEMBER THIS!!
WHRR
WHRR
TONG
TONG
TONG
SO THE MANAGER IS HERE, TOO.
TONG
TONG
TONG
TONG
TONG
YOU'RE AWFULLY KIND.
TONG
BUT, I SUPPOSE THAT'S TO BE EX-PECTED.
WHAT DO YOU MEAN BY THAT?
WHRR
WHRR

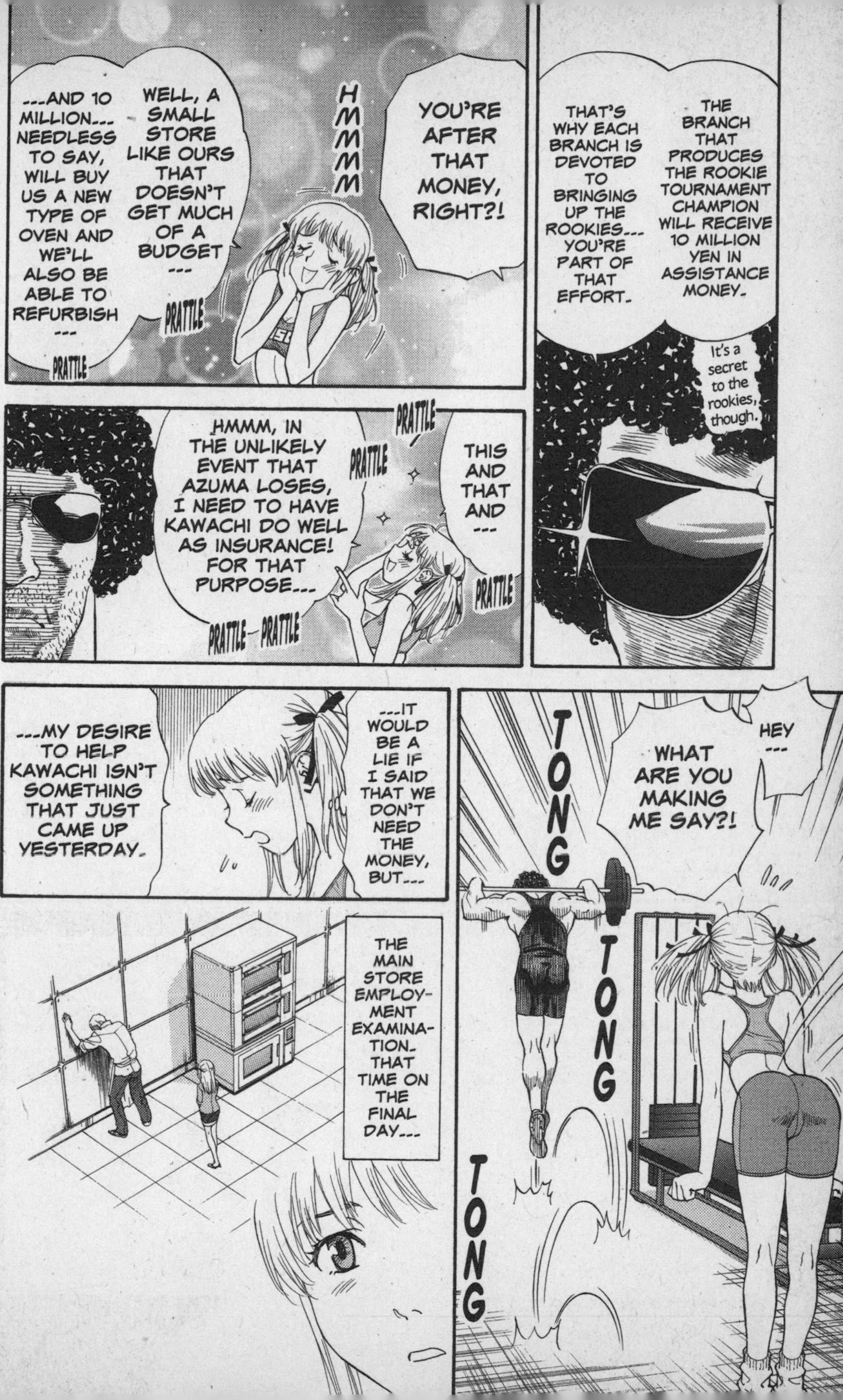
THE BRANCH THAT PRODUCES THE ROOKIE TOURNAMENT CHAMPION WILL RECEIVE 10 MILLION YEN IN ASSISTANCE MONEY.
THAT'S WHY EACH BRANCH IS DEVOTED TO BRINGING UP THE ROOKIES... YOU'RE PART OF THAT EFFORT.
It's a secret to the rookies, though.
YOU'RE AFTER THAT MONEY, RIGHT?!
HMMMM
WELL, A SMALL STORE LIKE OURS THAT DOESN'T GET MUCH OF A BUDGET ---
---AND 10 MILLION... NEEDLESS TO SAY, WILL BUY US A NEW TYPE OF OVEN AND WE'LL ALSO BE ABLE TO REFURBISH ---
PRATTLE
PRATTLE
THIS AND THAT AND ---
PRATTLE
PRATTLE
PRATTLE
HMMM, IN THE UNLIKELY EVENT THAT AZUMA LOSES, I NEED TO HAVE KAWACHI DO WELL AS INSURANCE! FOR THAT PURPOSE...
PRATTLE—PRATTLE
HEY ---
WHAT ARE YOU MAKING ME SAY?!
TONG
TONG
TONG
TONG
---IT WOULD BE A LIE IF I SAID THAT WE DON'T NEED THE MONEY, BUT...
---MY DESIRE TO HELP KAWACHI ISN'T SOMETHING THAT JUST CAME UP YESTERDAY.
THE MAIN STORE EMPLOYMENT EXAMINATION. THAT TIME ON THE FINAL DAY...

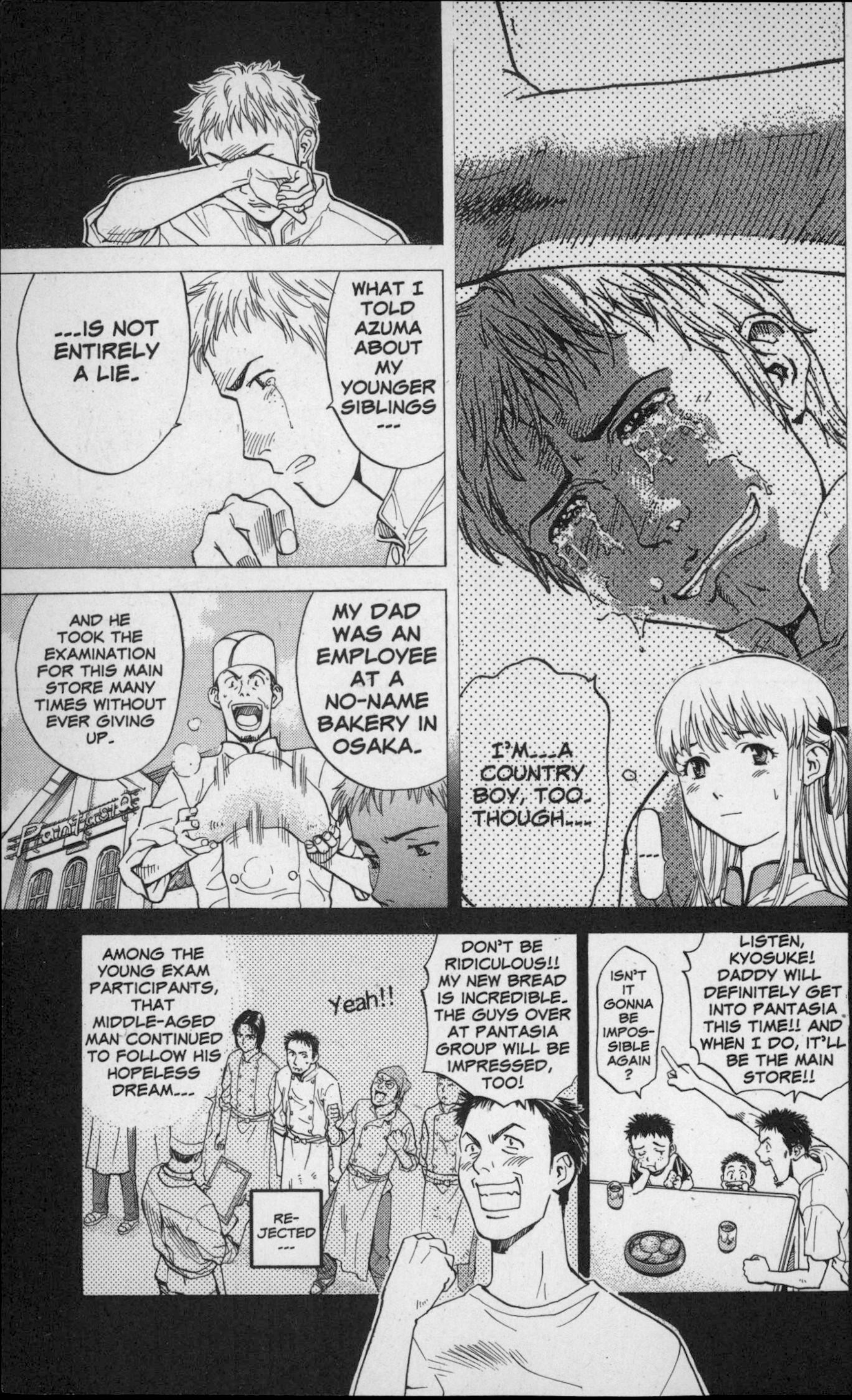
I'M... A COUNTRY BOY, TOO. THOUGH...
...
WHAT I TOLD AZUMA ABOUT MY YOUNGER SIBLINGS ...
...IS NOT ENTIRELY A LIE.
MY DAD WAS AN EMPLOYEE AT A NO-NAME BAKERY IN OSAKA.
AND HE TOOK THE EXAMINATION FOR THIS MAIN STORE MANY TIMES WITHOUT EVER GIVING UP.
LISTEN, KYOSUKE! DADDY WILL DEFINITELY GET INTO PANTASIA THIS TIME!! AND WHEN I DO, IT'LL BE THE MAIN STORE!!
ISN'T IT GONNA BE IMPOSSIBLE AGAIN?
DON'T BE RIDICULOUS!! MY NEW BREAD IS INCREDIBLE. THE GUYS OVER AT PANTASIA GROUP WILL BE IMPRESSED, TOO!
AMONG THE YOUNG EXAM PARTICIPANTS, THAT MIDDLE-AGED MAN CONTINUED TO FOLLOW HIS HOPELESS DREAM...
Yeah!!
RE-JECTED ...

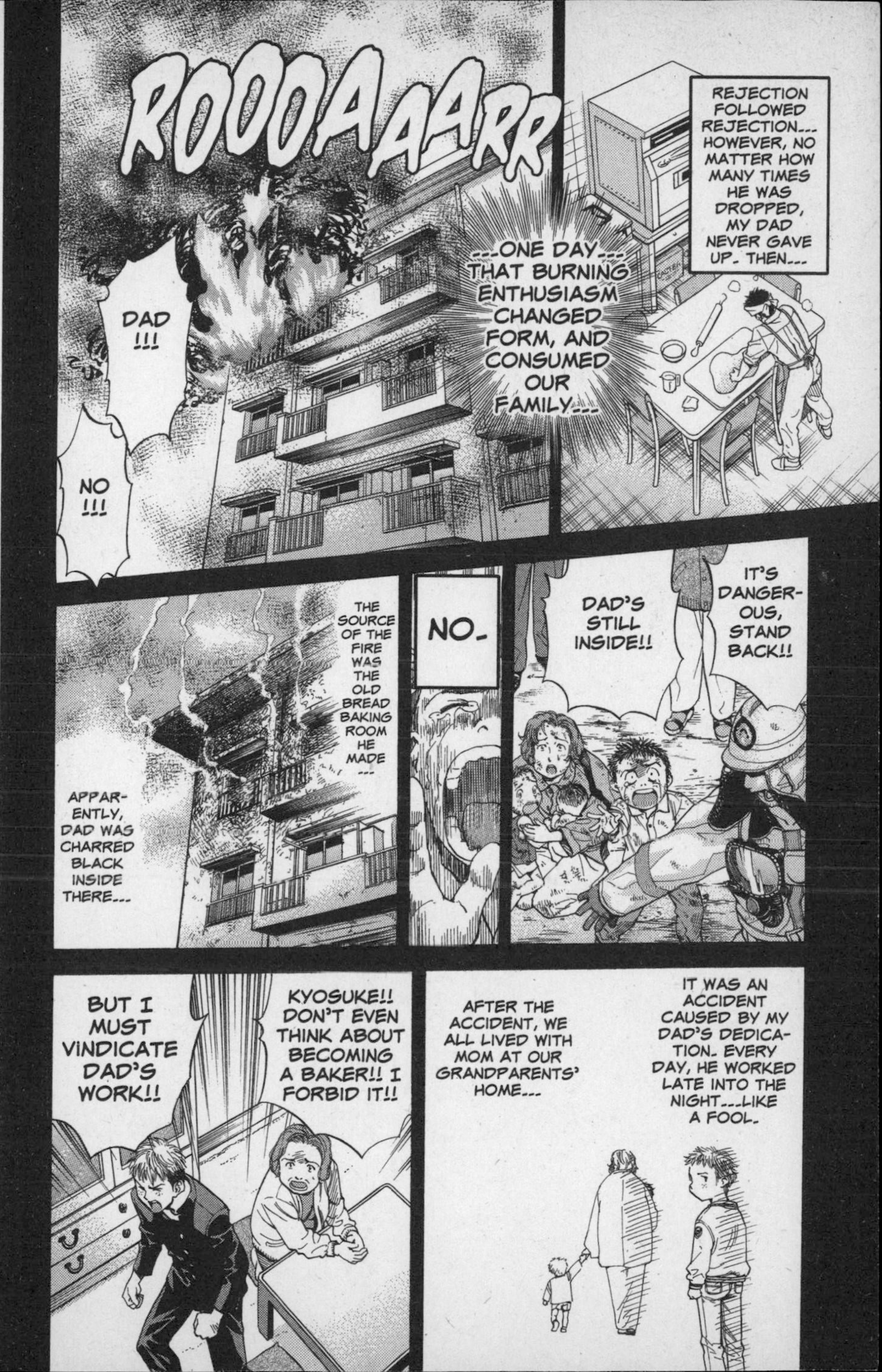
REJECTION FOLLOWED REJECTION... HOWEVER, NO MATTER HOW MANY TIMES HE WAS DROPPED, MY DAD NEVER GAVE UP. THEN...
...ONE DAY... THAT BURNING ENTHUSIASM CHANGED FORM, AND CONSUMED OUR FAMILY...
ROOOAAARR
DAD !!!
NO !!!
IT'S DANGER-OUS, STAND BACK!!
DAD'S STILL INSIDE!!
NO.
THE SOURCE OF THE FIRE WAS THE OLD BREAD BAKING ROOM HE MADE ...
APPAR-ENTLY, DAD WAS CHARRED BLACK INSIDE THERE...
IT WAS AN ACCIDENT CAUSED BY MY DAD'S DEDICA-TION. EVERY DAY, HE WORKED LATE INTO THE NIGHT...LIKE A FOOL.
AFTER THE ACCIDENT, WE ALL LIVED WITH MOM AT OUR GRANDPARENTS' HOME...
KYOSUKE!! DON'T EVEN THINK ABOUT BECOMING A BAKER!! I FORBID IT!!
BUT I MUST VINDICATE DAD'S WORK!!

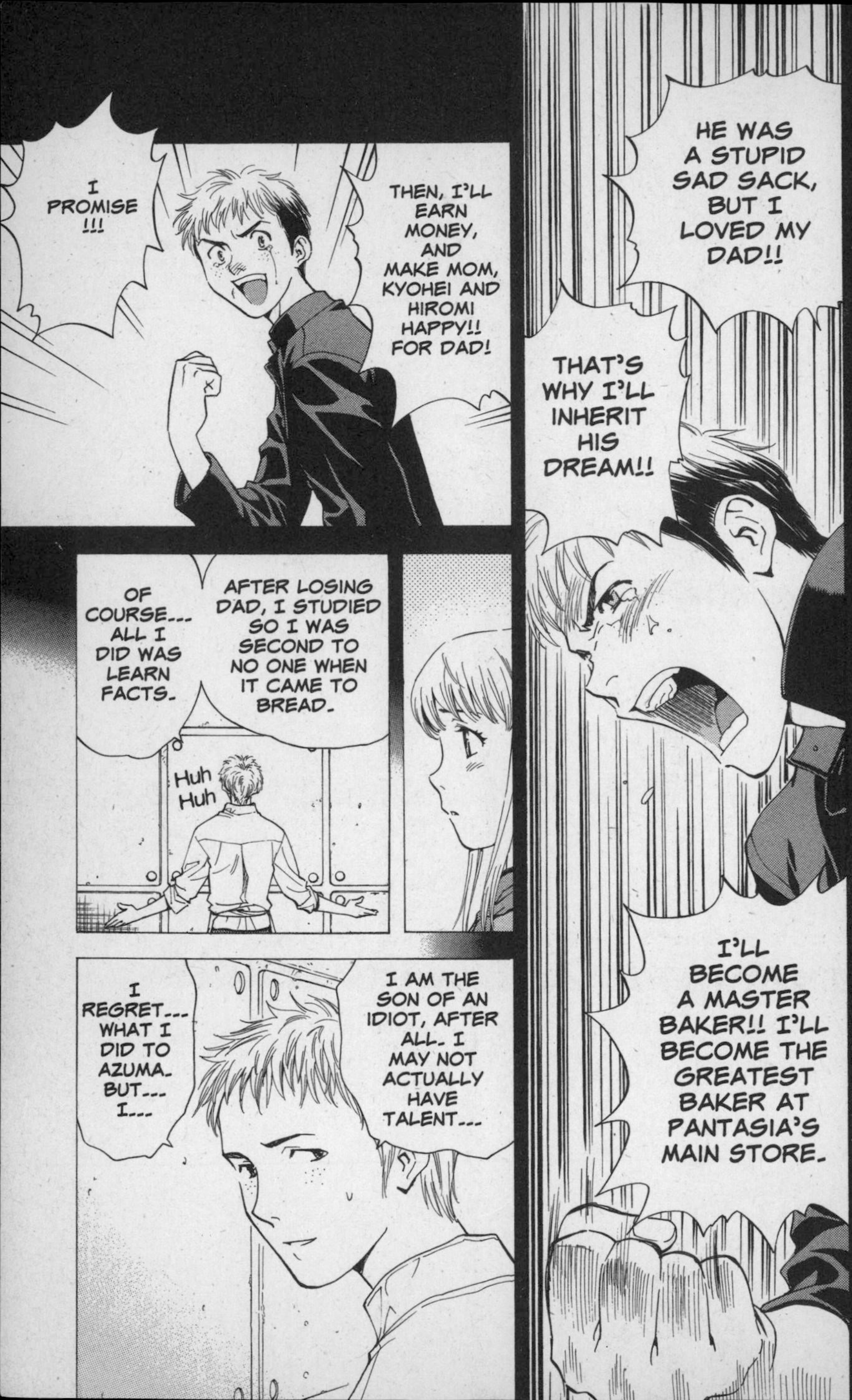
HE WAS A STUPID SAD SACK, BUT I LOVED MY DAD!!
THAT'S WHY I'LL INHERIT HIS DREAM!!
I'LL BECOME A MASTER BAKER!! I'LL BECOME THE GREATEST BAKER AT PANTASIA'S MAIN STORE.
THEN, I'LL EARN MONEY, AND MAKE MOM, KYOHEI AND HIROMI HAPPY!! FOR DAD!
I PROMISE!!!
AFTER LOSING DAD, I STUDIED SO I WAS SECOND TO NO ONE WHEN IT CAME TO BREAD.
OF COURSE... ALL I DID WAS LEARN FACTS.
Huh Huh
I AM THE SON OF AN IDIOT, AFTER ALL. I MAY NOT ACTUALLY HAVE TALENT...
I REGRET... WHAT I DID TO AZUMA. BUT... I...

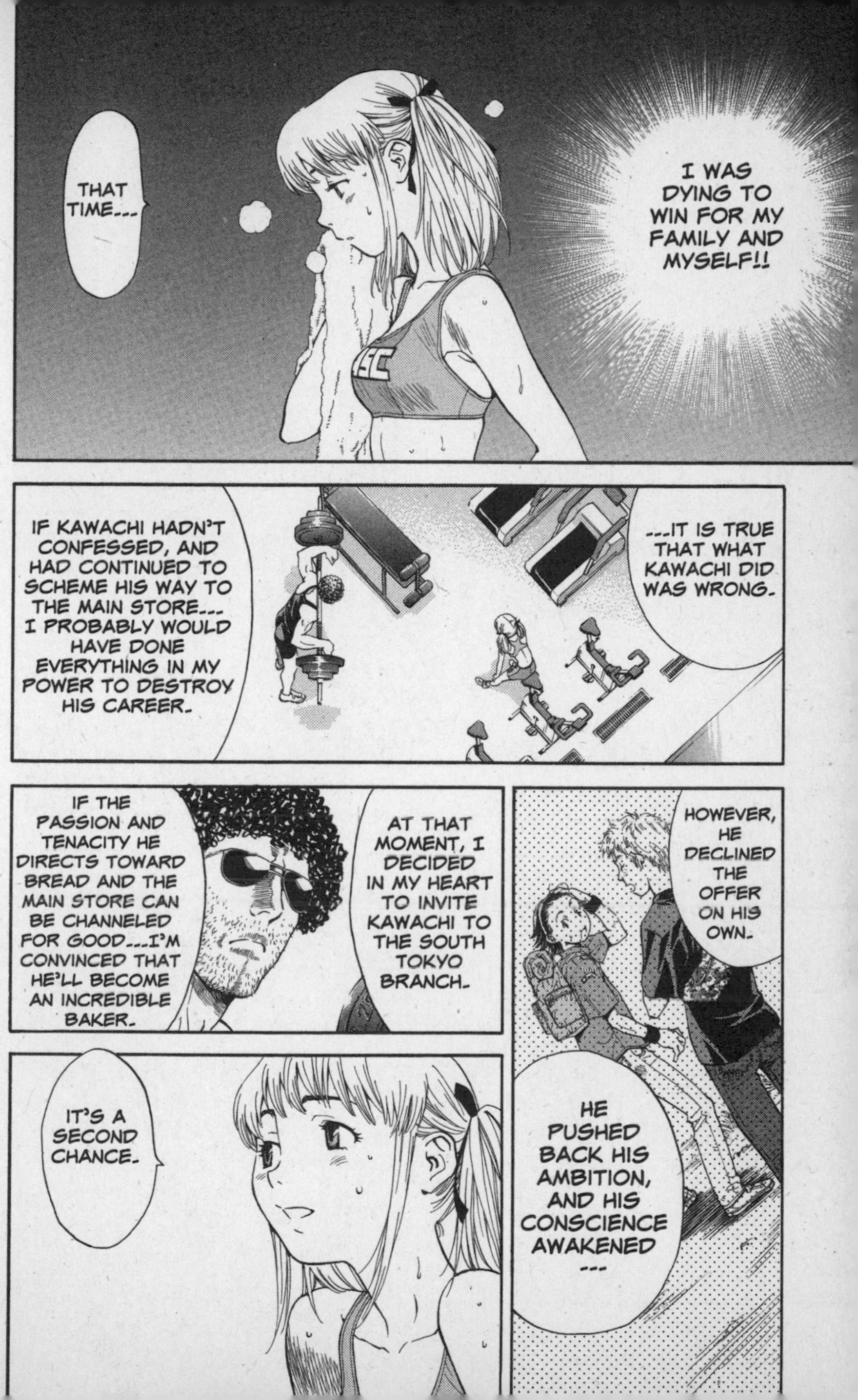
I WAS DYING TO WIN FOR MY FAMILY AND MYSELF!!
THAT TIME...
...IT IS TRUE THAT WHAT KAWACHI DID WAS WRONG.
IF KAWACHI HADN'T CONFESSED, AND HAD CONTINUED TO SCHEME HIS WAY TO THE MAIN STORE... I PROBABLY WOULD HAVE DONE EVERYTHING IN MY POWER TO DESTROY HIS CAREER.
HOWEVER, HE DECLINED THE OFFER ON HIS OWN.
HE PUSHED BACK HIS AMBITION, AND HIS CONSCIENCE AWAKENED ---
AT THAT MOMENT, I DECIDED IN MY HEART TO INVITE KAWACHI TO THE SOUTH TOKYO BRANCH.
IF THE PASSION AND TENACITY HE DIRECTS TOWARD BREAD AND THE MAIN STORE CAN BE CHANNELED FOR GOOD...I'M CONVINCED THAT HE'LL BECOME AN INCREDIBLE BAKER.
IT'S A SECOND CHANCE.

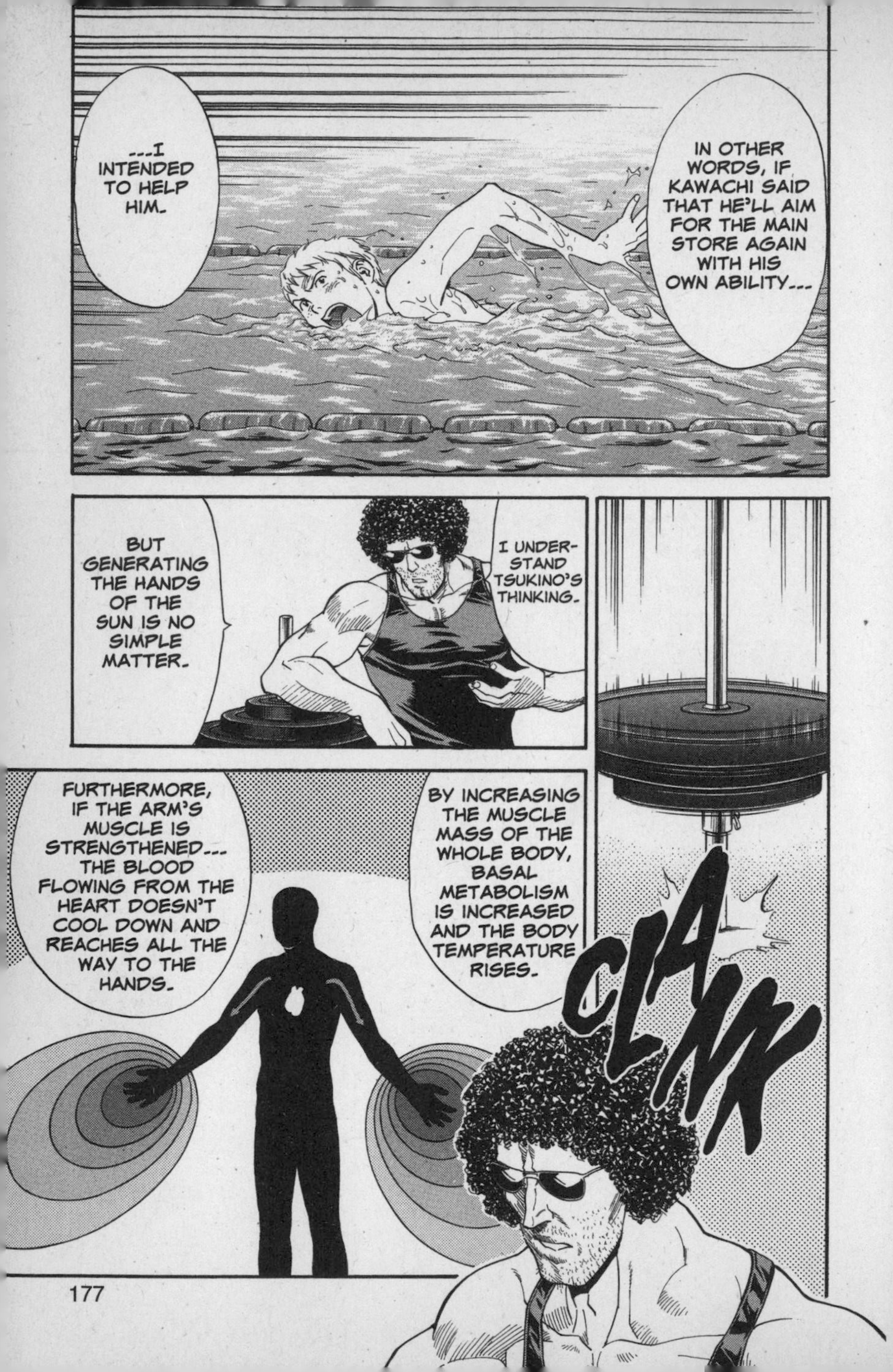
IN OTHER WORDS, IF KAWACHI SAID THAT HE'LL AIM FOR THE MAIN STORE AGAIN WITH HIS OWN ABILITY...
...I INTENDED TO HELP HIM.
I UNDER-STAND TSUKINO'S THINKING.
BUT GENERATING THE HANDS OF THE SUN IS NO SIMPLE MATTER.
BY INCREASING THE MUSCLE MASS OF THE WHOLE BODY, BASAL METABOLISM IS INCREASED AND THE BODY TEMPERATURE RISES.
FURTHERMORE, IF THE ARM'S MUSCLE IS STRENGTHENED... THE BLOOD FLOWING FROM THE HEART DOESN'T COOL DOWN AND REACHES ALL THE WAY TO THE HANDS.
CLANK

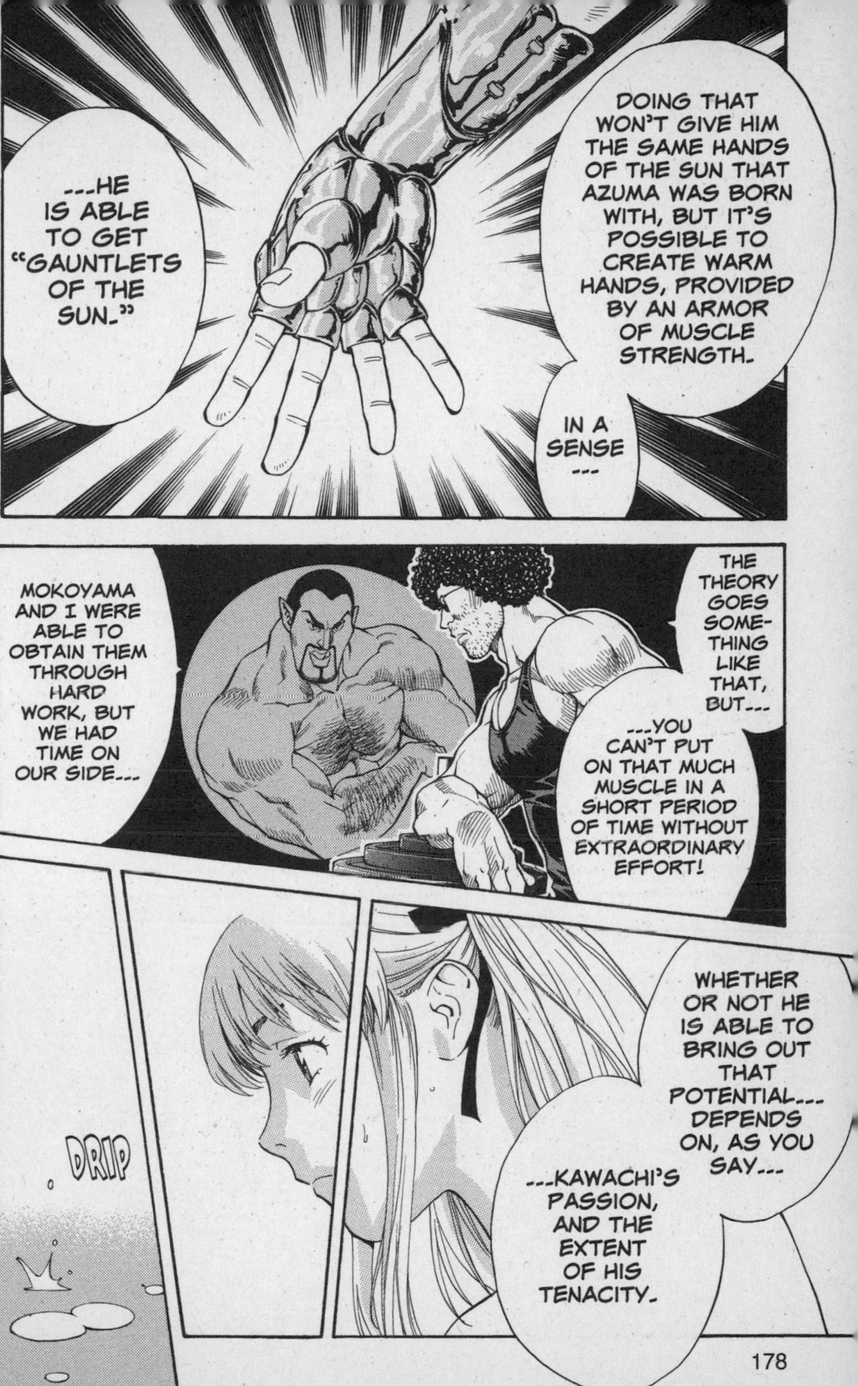
DOING THAT WON'T GIVE HIM THE SAME HANDS OF THE SUN THAT AZUMA WAS BORN WITH, BUT IT'S POSSIBLE TO CREATE WARM HANDS, PROVIDED BY AN ARMOR OF MUSCLE STRENGTH.
IN A SENSE ---
---HE IS ABLE TO GET "GAUNTLETS OF THE SUN."
THE THEORY GOES SOME-THING LIKE THAT, BUT---
---YOU CAN'T PUT ON THAT MUCH MUSCLE IN A SHORT PERIOD OF TIME WITHOUT EXTRAORDINARY EFFORT!
MOKOYAMA AND I WERE ABLE TO OBTAIN THEM THROUGH HARD WORK, BUT WE HAD TIME ON OUR SIDE---
WHETHER OR NOT HE IS ABLE TO BRING OUT THAT POTENTIAL--- DEPENDS ON, AS YOU SAY---
---KAWACHI'S PASSION, AND THE EXTENT OF HIS TENACITY.
DRIP

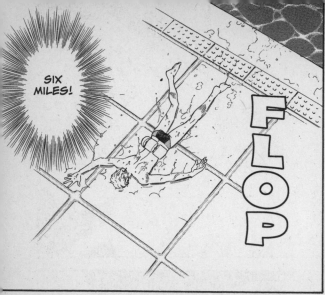

DRIBBLE
SIX MILES!
FLOP
IF... IF I CONTINUE TO DO THIS, I'LL DIE.
HUFF
HUFF
HUFF
HUFF
HUFF
HUFF
HUFF
HUFF
THAT GIRL... IS SHE TRYING TO KILL ME...?!
BUT, I'M AT THE SOUTH TOKYO BRANCH THANKS TO TSUKINO...
I CAN'T IMAGINE THAT SHE'S MAKING ME DO THIS AS A CRUEL JOKE...
HUFF
HUFF
HUFF
SURELY...
SURELY, THERE'S SOME-THING...

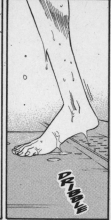

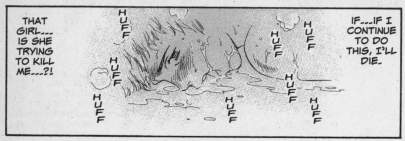

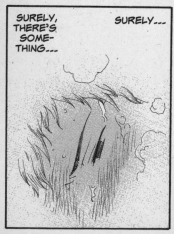

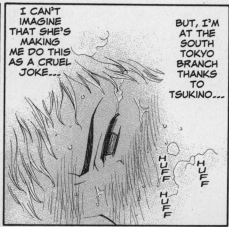

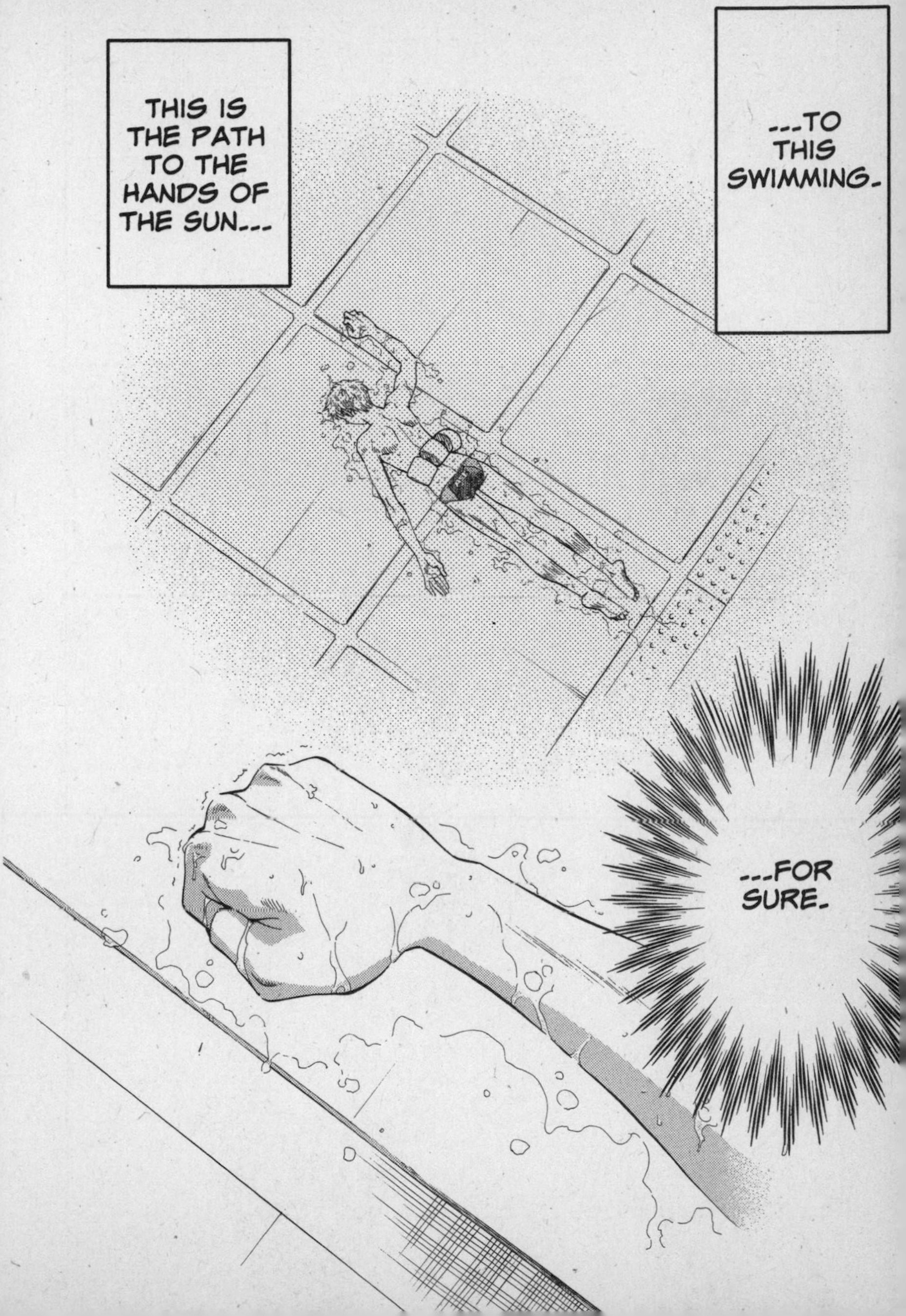
...TO THIS SWIMMING.
THIS IS THE PATH TO THE HANDS OF THE SUN...
...FOR SURE.

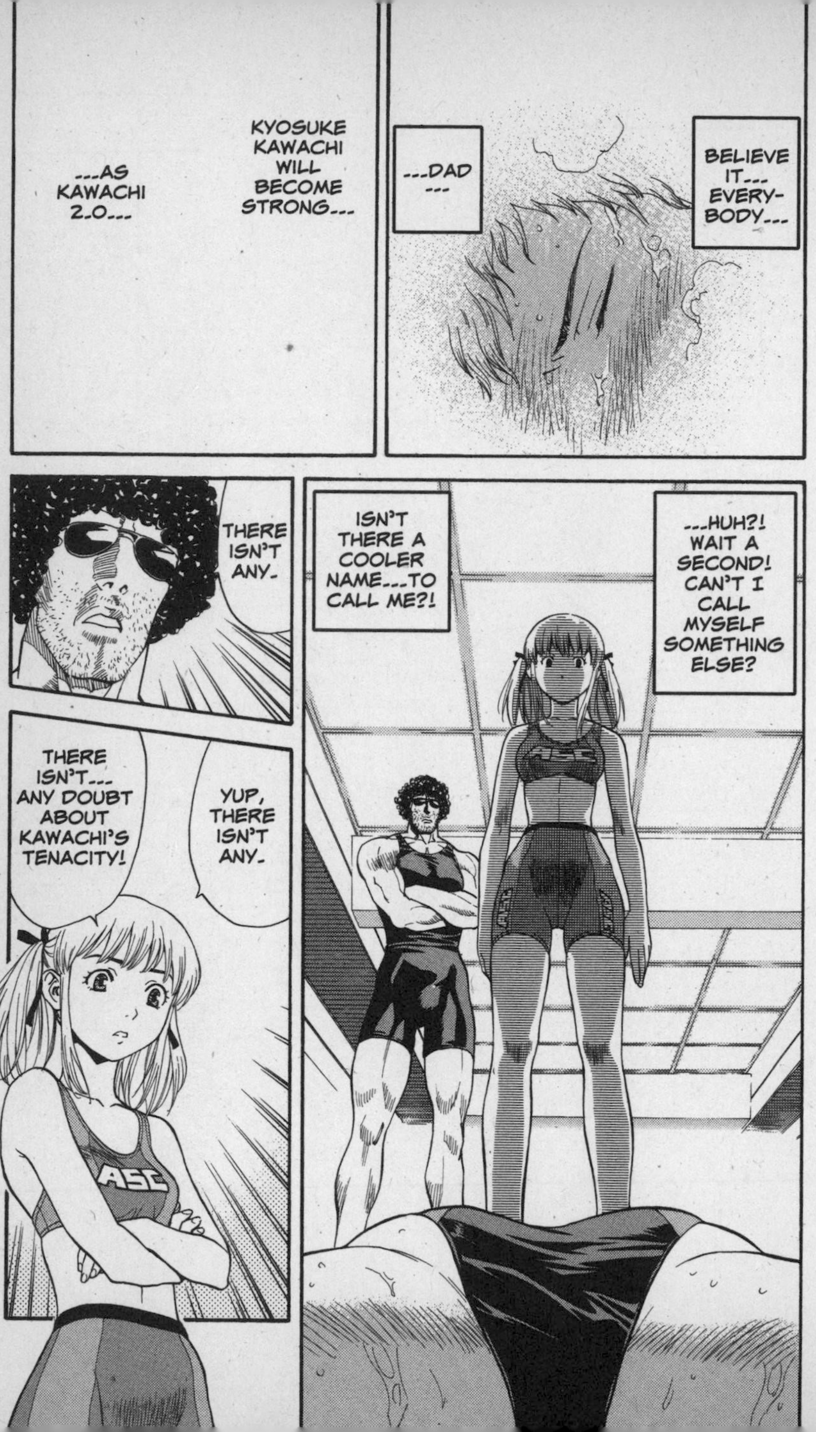
BELIEVE IT... EVERY-BODY...
...DAD ...
KYOSUKE KAWACHI WILL BECOME STRONG...
...AS KAWACHI 2.0...
...HUH?! WAIT A SECOND! CAN'T I CALL MYSELF SOMETHING ELSE?
ISN'T THERE A COOLER NAME...TO CALL ME?!
THERE ISN'T ANY.
YUP, THERE ISN'T ANY.
THERE ISN'T... ANY DOUBT ABOUT KAWACHI'S TENACITY!

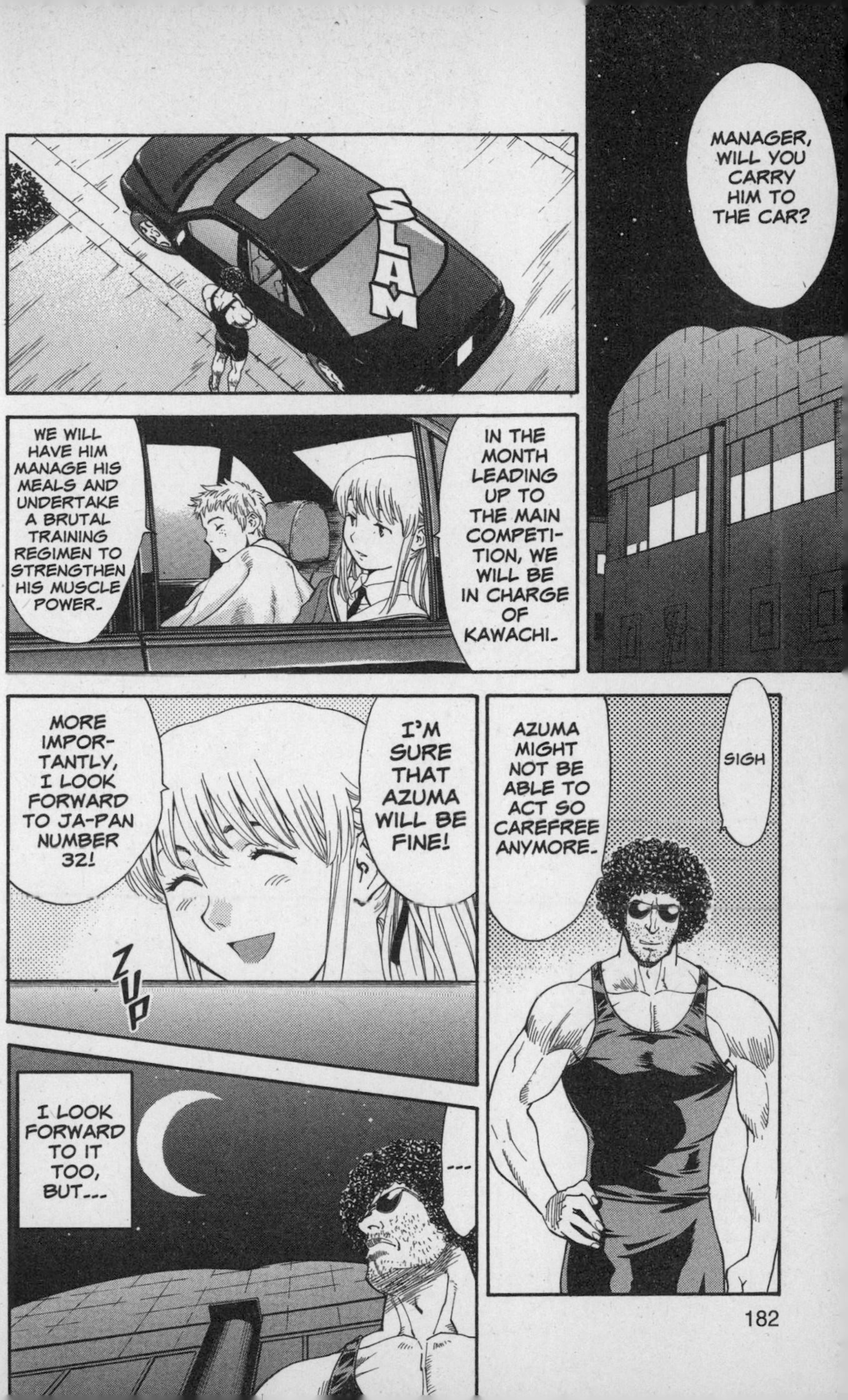

MANAGER, WILL YOU CARRY HIM TO THE CAR?
SLAM
IN THE MONTH LEADING UP TO THE MAIN COMPETITION, WE WILL BE IN CHARGE OF KAWACHI.
WE WILL HAVE HIM MANAGE HIS MEALS AND UNDERTAKE A BRUTAL TRAINING REGIMEN TO STRENGTHEN HIS MUSCLE POWER.
SIGH
AZUMA MIGHT NOT BE ABLE TO ACT SO CAREFREE ANYMORE.
I'M SURE THAT AZUMA WILL BE FINE!
MORE IMPORTANTLY, I LOOK FORWARD TO JA-PAN NUMBER 32!
ZUP
...
I LOOK FORWARD TO IT TOO, BUT...

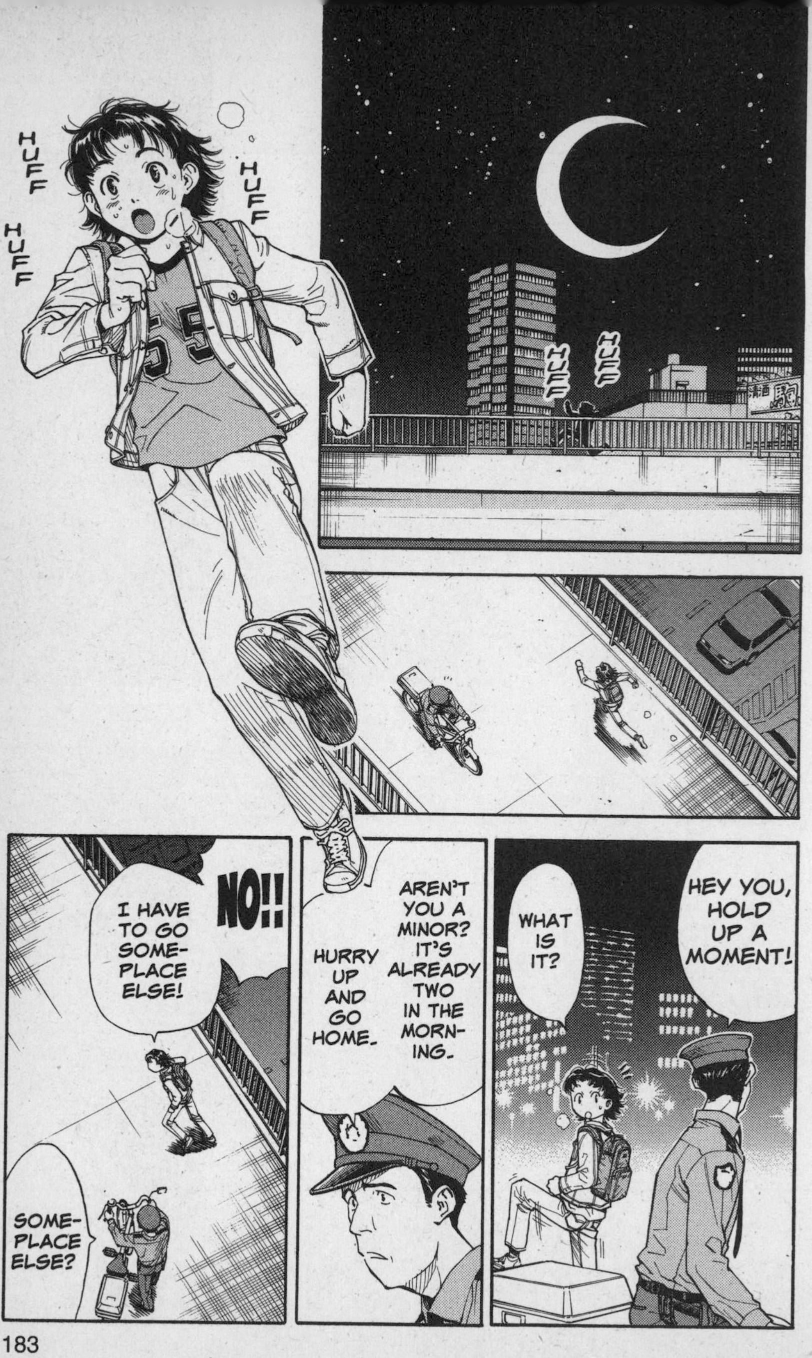
HUFF HUFF
HUFF HUFF
HUFF
HEY YOU, HOLD UP A MOMENT!
WHAT IS IT?
AREN'T YOU A MINOR? IT'S ALREADY TWO IN THE MORNING.
HURRY UP AND GO HOME.
NO!!
I HAVE TO GO SOME-PLACE ELSE!
SOME-PLACE ELSE?

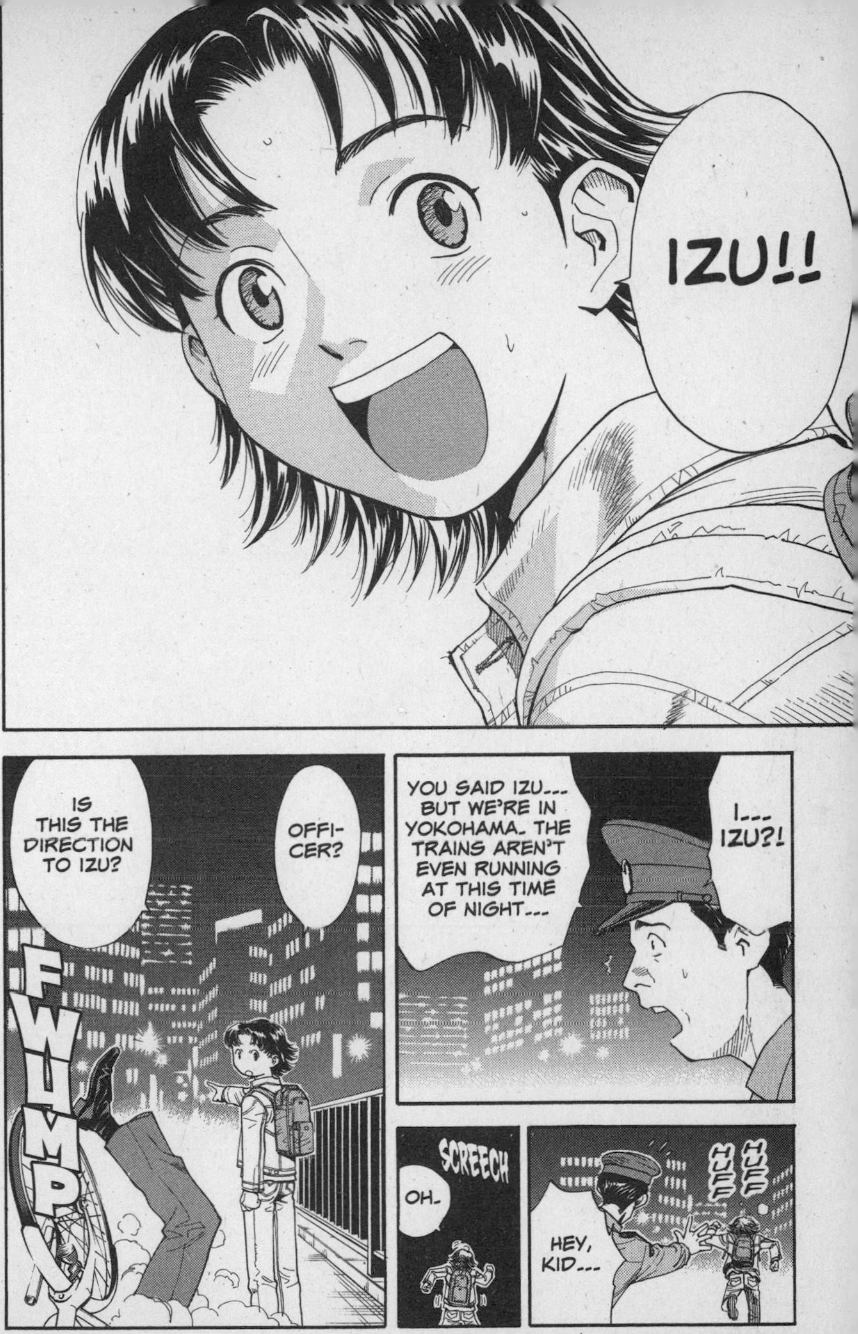
IZU!!
I... IZU?!
YOU SAID IZU... BUT WE'RE IN YOKOHAMA. THE TRAINS AREN'T EVEN RUNNING AT THIS TIME OF NIGHT...
HUFF HUFF
HEY, KID...
SCREECH
OH.
OFFI-CER?
IS THIS THE DIRECTION TO IZU?
FWUMP

TO BE CONTINUED!

Yakitate!! Japan

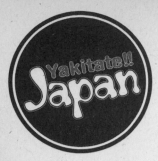

Extra ♥

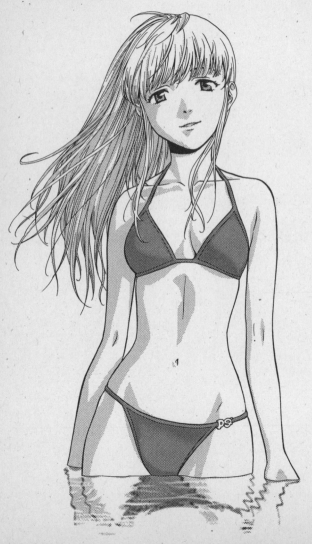

Continued from Volume one!

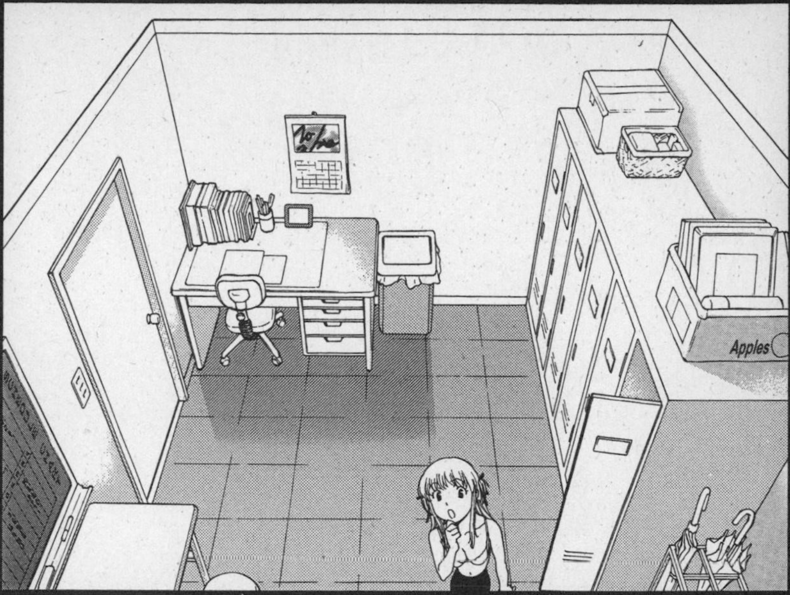
Apples

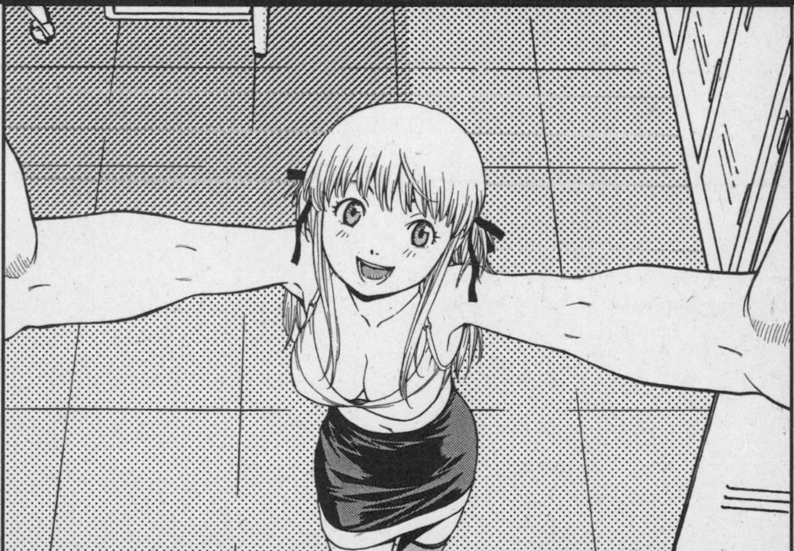

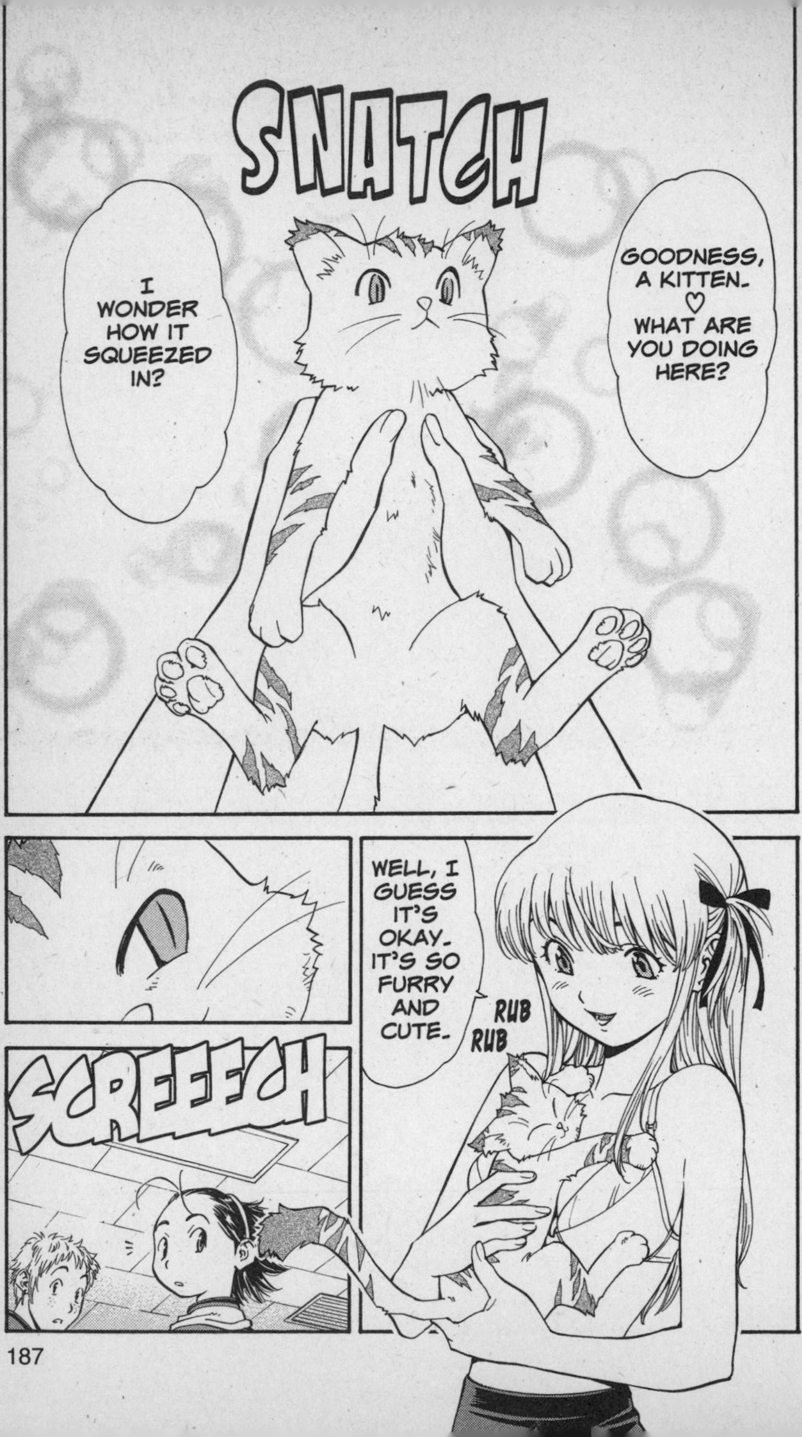
SNATCH
GOODNESS, A KITTEN. ♡ WHAT ARE YOU DOING HERE?
I WONDER HOW IT SQUEEZED IN?
WELL, I GUESS IT'S OKAY. IT'S SO FURRY AND CUTE.
RUB RUB
SCREEECH

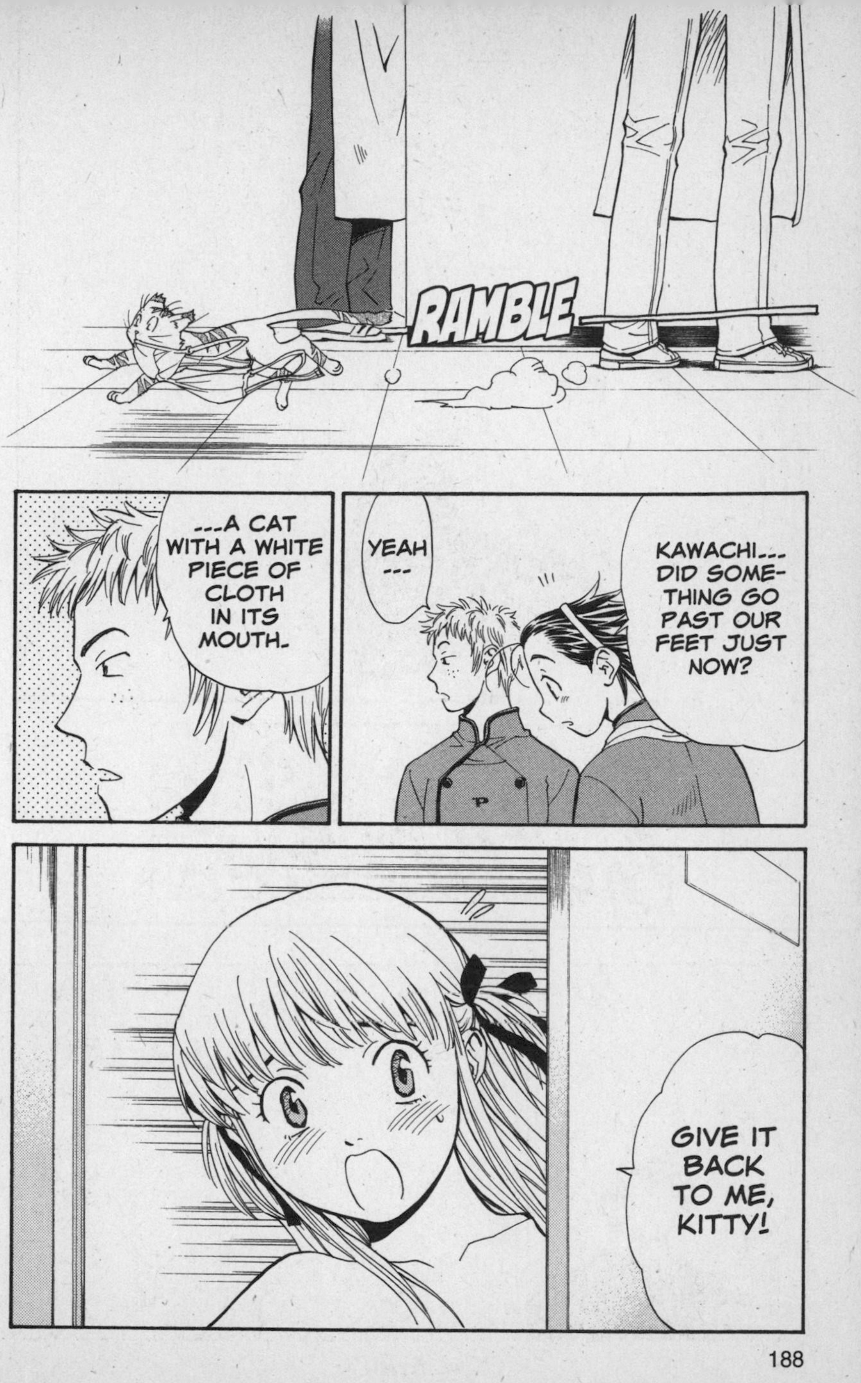
RAMBLE
KAWACHI... DID SOMETHING GO PAST OUR FEET JUST NOW?
YEAH ...
...A CAT WITH A WHITE PIECE OF CLOTH IN ITS MOUTH.
GIVE IT BACK TO ME, KITTY!

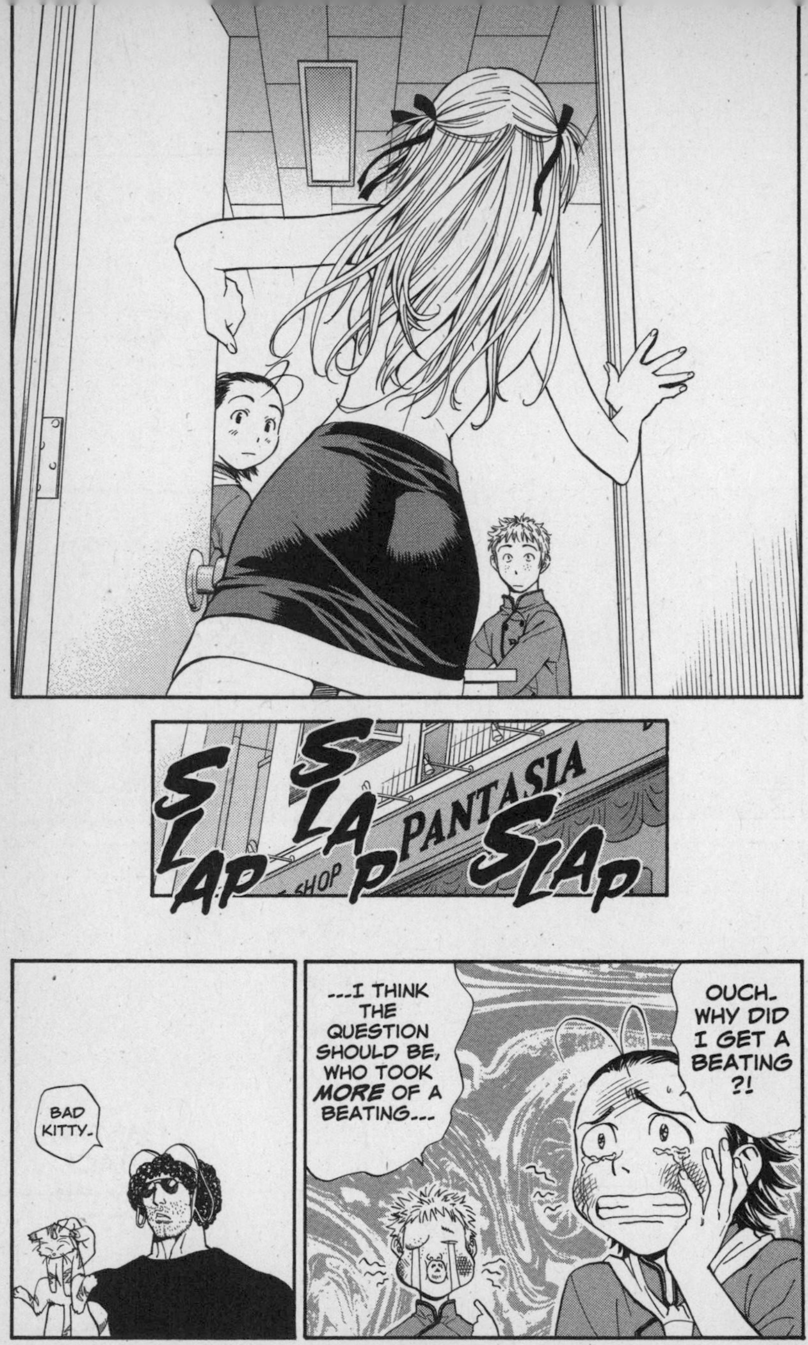
SLAP SLAP SLAP
PANTASIA
SHOP
OUCH. WHY DID I GET A BEATING?!
...I THINK THE QUESTION SHOULD BE, WHO TOOK *MORE* OF A BEATING...
BAD KITTY.

The End♡

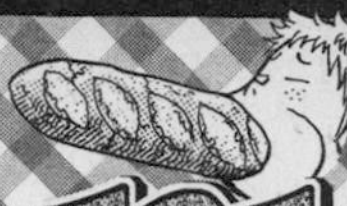

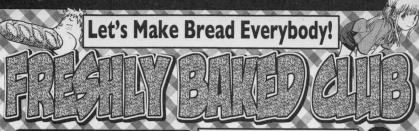

Let's Make Bread Everybody!

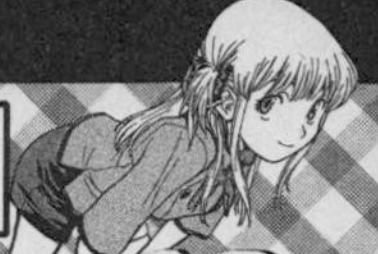

FRESHLY BAKED CLUB

● Ja-pan Number 2 Materials

Enriched Flour – 1-1/2 cups
Salt – 1-1/2 teaspoons
Dry Yeast – 1 teaspoon
Milk – (slightly more than) 1 ounce
Butter – 1-1/2 tablespoons
Water – 6 ounces
Sugar – 1-1/2 tablespoons

There was a saying in the past that a man should not enter the kitchen, but it's the 21st Century now. A man can't survive if he is unable to cook. But cooking can be complicated. That's why today we will present the easy way to make Ja-pan Number 2! It's a great way to surprise your mom, your dad, or your girlfriend. A person who usually doesn't cook should take up this challenge!

You'll be a hit with the ladies! Manly men have to cook in the 21st Century !!

Throw in all the materials and knead it thoroughly. When it's no longer sticky, form the dough into a round shape!

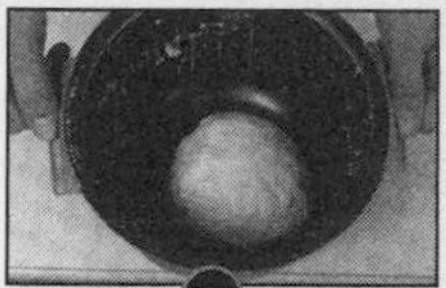

The first fermentation! Leave it in a warm place for 60 minutes, and it will expand to this size. The next step is to pull out the excess gas that built up during fermentation.

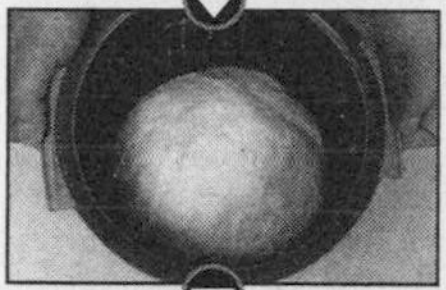

Don't pull out the gas by pushing it—like in the picture on the right. All you need to do is drop the dough from a height of about 50 centimeters.

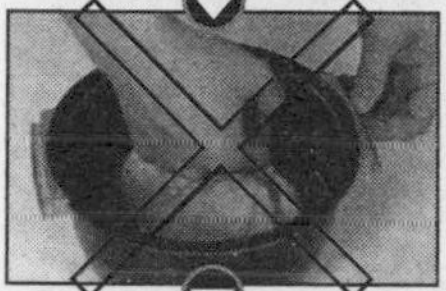

After pulling out the gas, begin the second fermentation (also for 60 minutes), then put the dough into the rice cooker. Now, all you have to do is to close the lid and push the switch!

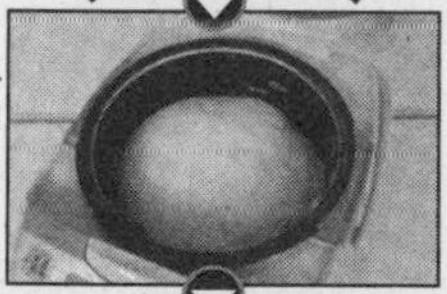

Following the first cooking, turn it over and cook it again. After the second cooking, turn it over again and cook it one more time.

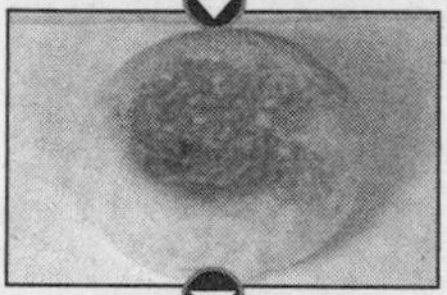

After you cook it three times, it's done! Ja-pan Number 2 is ready to eat: with butter or as is. Now let's make bread, everybody!

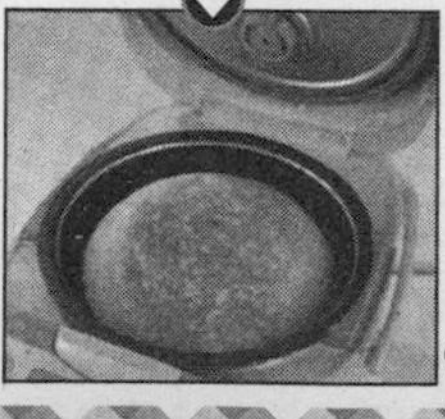

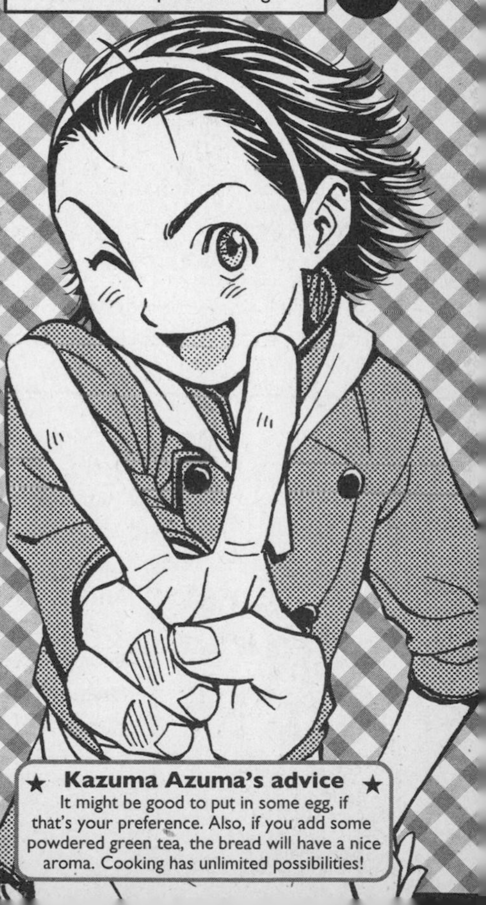

★ Kazuma Azuma's advice ★

It might be good to put in some egg, if that's your preference. Also, if you add some powdered green tea, the bread will have a nice aroma. Cooking has unlimited possibilities!

Freshly Baked!! Mini Information

—— Ja-Pan Number 2 ——

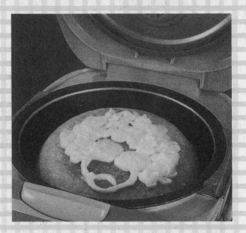

I was surprised by the large number of readers who said they make bread using a rice cooker. I felt very happy as I thought about how people are really reading the story thoroughly. However, there were many people who said that it didn't taste very good...so I will explain a tiny bit here! The most important thing is the temperature at the time of the fermentation. "Firmly maintain the temperature above 86 degrees Fahrenheit and ferment it." If this temperature is not maintained, the fermentation will be insufficient. As you might expect, temperature is vital to bread making!! Please try your best. ♥

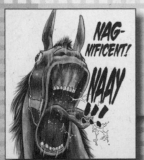

NAG-NIFICENT!

NAAY!!!

YAKITATE!! JAPAN
VOL. 2

STORY AND ART BY
TAKASHI HASHIGUCHI

English Adaptation/Drew Williams
Translation/Noritaka Minami
Touch-up Art & Lettering/Steve Dutro
Cover Design/Yukiko Whitley
Editor/Kit Fox

Managing Editor/Annette Roman
Editorial Director/Elizabeth Kawasaki
Editor in Chief/Alvin Lu
Sr. Director of Acquisitions/Rika Inouye
Sr. VP of Marketing/Liza Coppola
Exec. VP of Sales & Marketing/John Easum
Publisher/Hyoe Narita

Printed in the U.S.A.

Published by VIZ Media, LLC
P.O. Box 77010
San Francisco, CA 94107

10 9 8 7 6 5 4 3 2 1
First printing, November 2006

www.viz.com

store.viz.com

RATED T+ FOR OLDER TEEN

PARENTAL ADVISORY
YAKITATE!! JAPAN is rated T+ for Older Teen and is recommended for ages 16 and up. This volume contains alcohol and tobacco use, crude humor and mature situations.

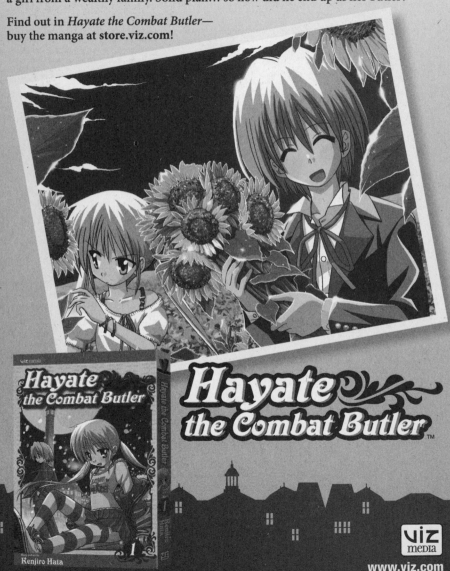

A Comedy that Redefines a

Due to an unfortunate accident, when martial artist Ranma gets splashed with cold water, he becomes a buxom young girl! Hot water reverses the effect, but when blamed for offenses both real and imagined, and pursued by lovesick suitors of both genders, what's a half-boy, half-girl to do?

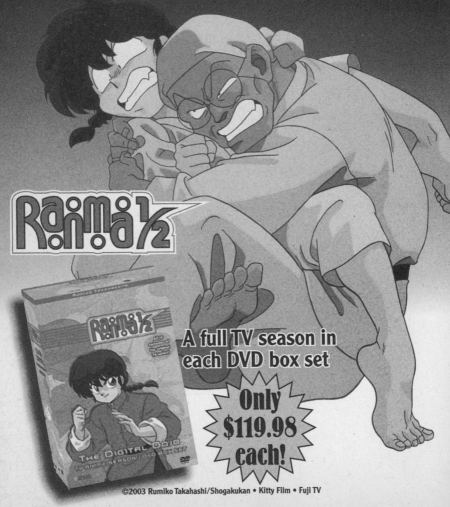

Ranma ½

A full TV season in each DVD box set

Only $119.98 each!

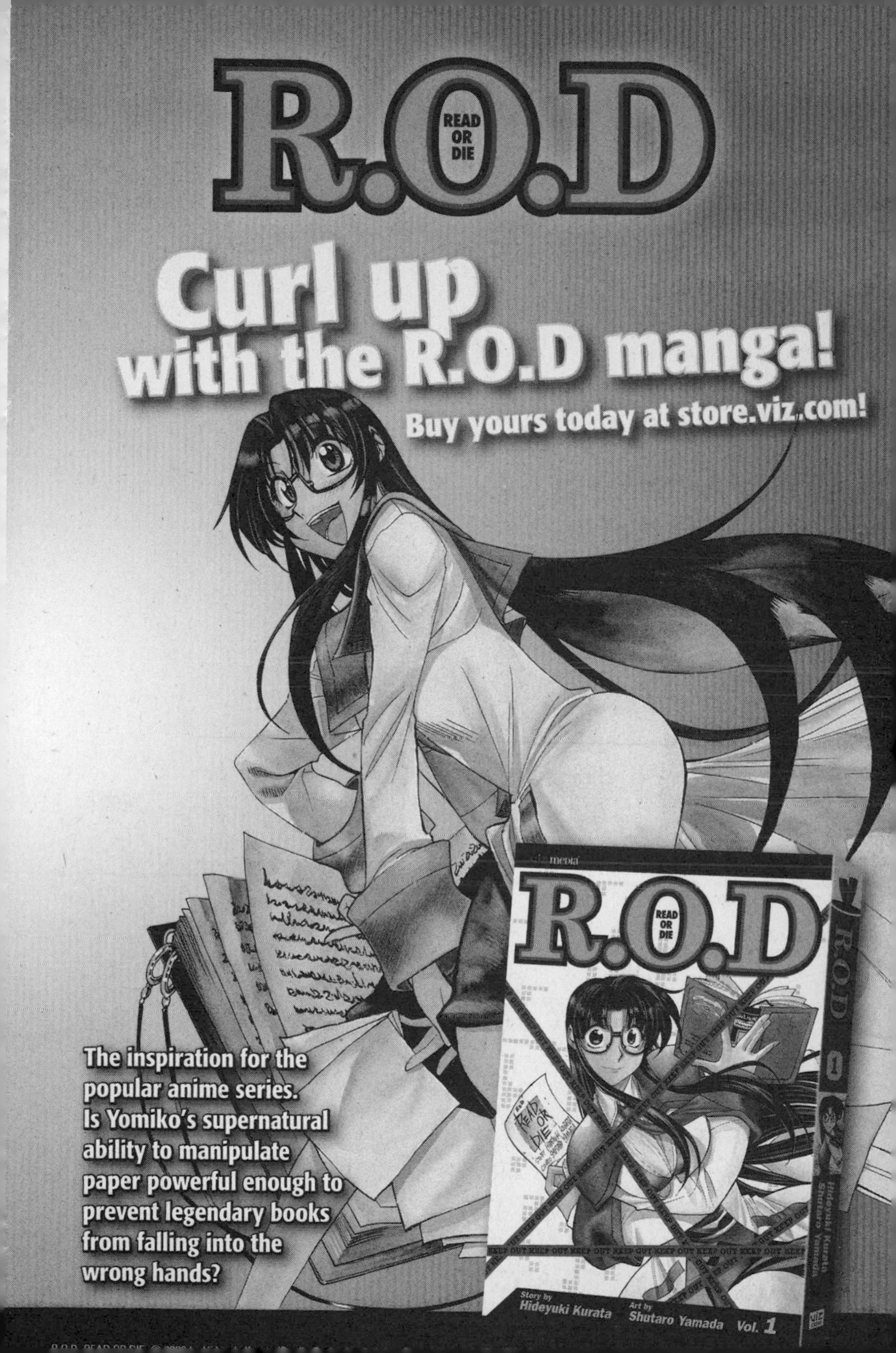
R.O.D
READ OR DIE
Curl up with the R.O.D manga!
Buy yours today at store.viz.com!
The inspiration for the popular anime series. Is Yomiko's supernatural ability to manipulate paper powerful enough to prevent legendary books from falling into the wrong hands?
R.O.D
READ OR DIE
Story by Hideyuki Kurata
Art by Shutaro Yamada
Vol. 1

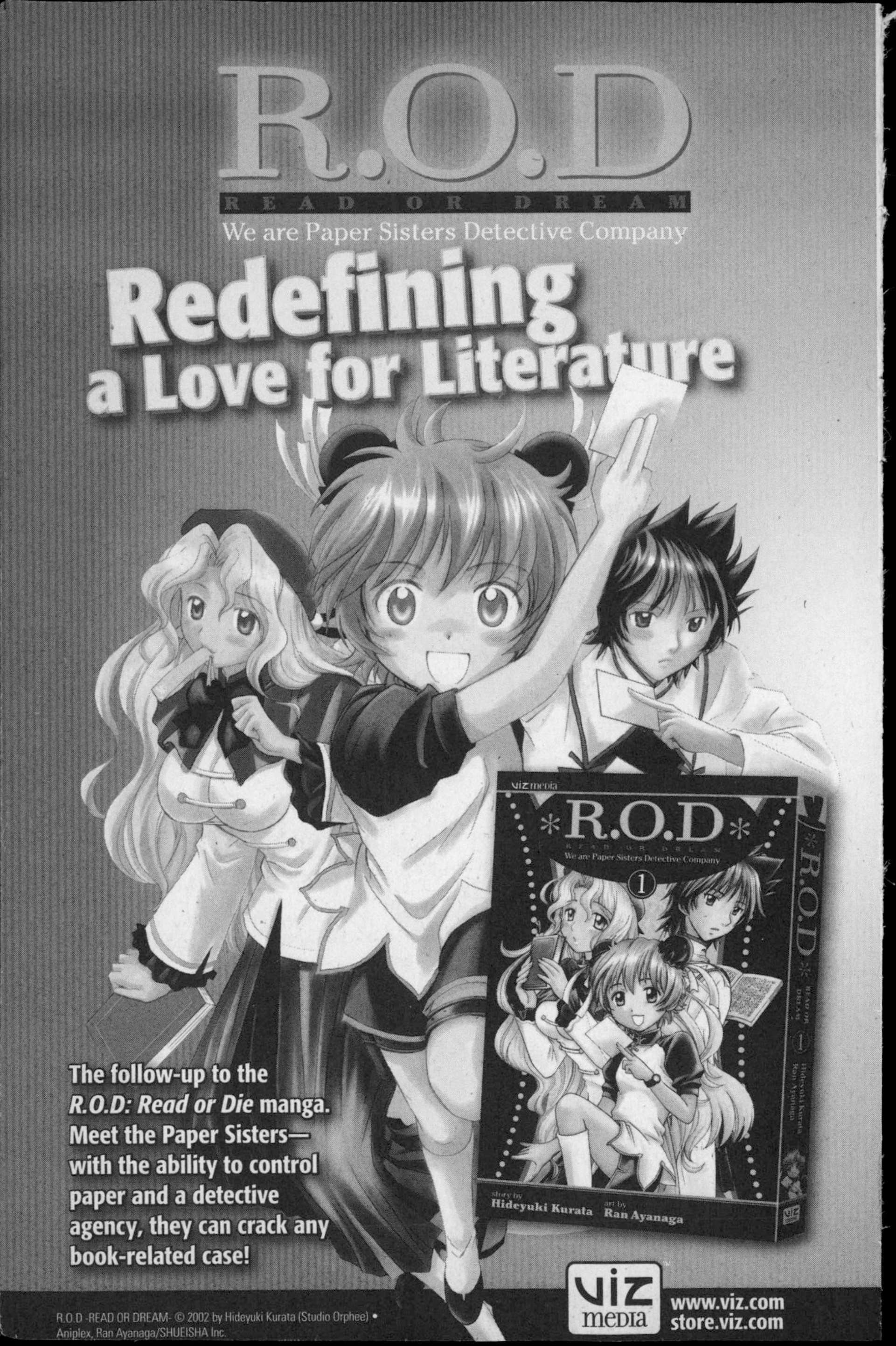
R.O.D
READ OR DREAM
We are Paper Sisters Detective Company
Redefining a Love for Literature
The follow-up to the R.O.D: Read or Die manga. Meet the Paper Sisters—with the ability to control paper and a detective agency, they can crack any book-related case!
viz media
R.O.D
READ OR DREAM
We are Paper Sisters Detective Company
1
story by Hideyuki Kurata
art by Ran Ayanaga
viz media
www.viz.com
store.viz.com
R.O.D -READ OR DREAM- © 2002 by Hideyuki Kurata (Studio Orphee) • Aniplex, Ran Ayanaga/SHUEISHA Inc.

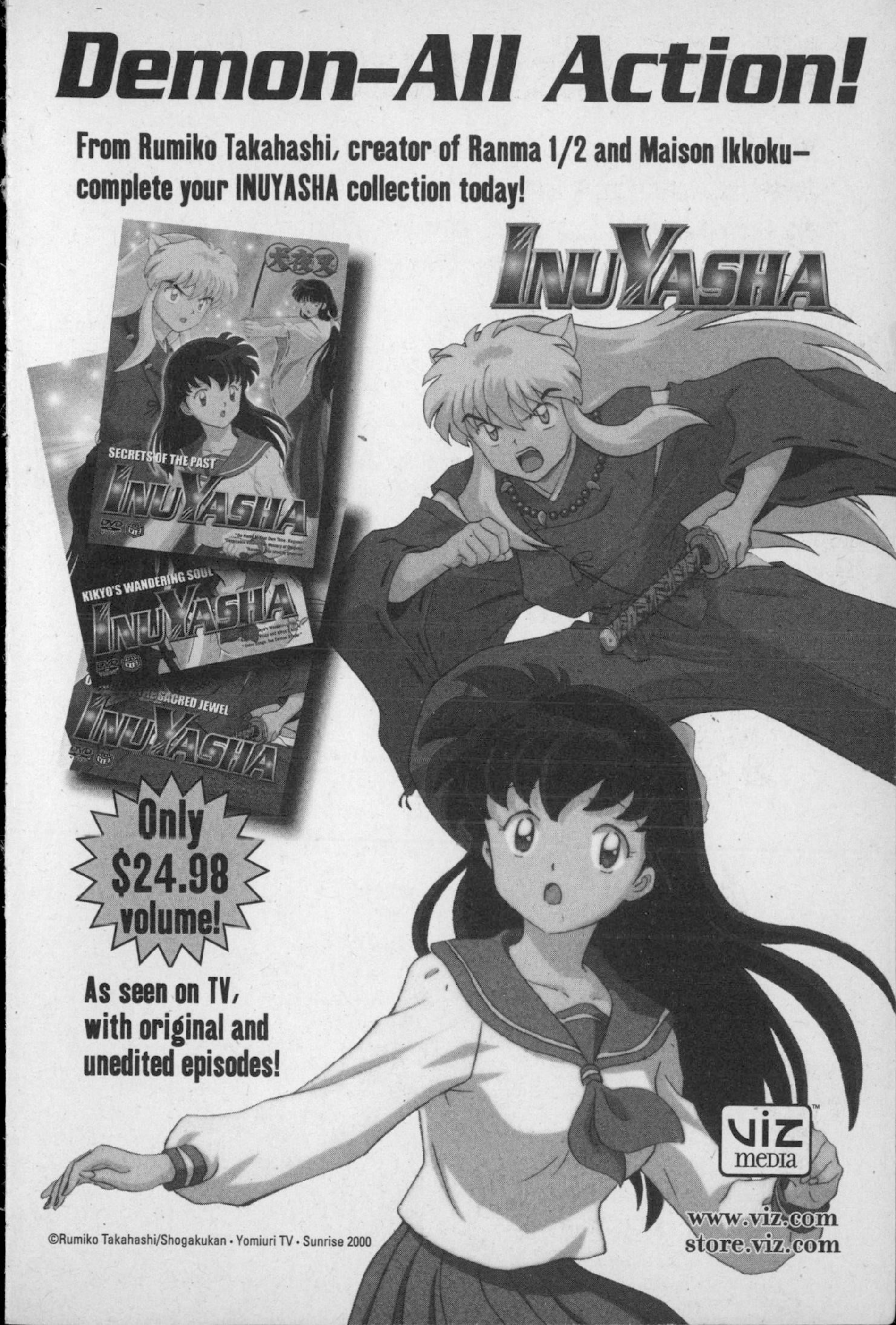

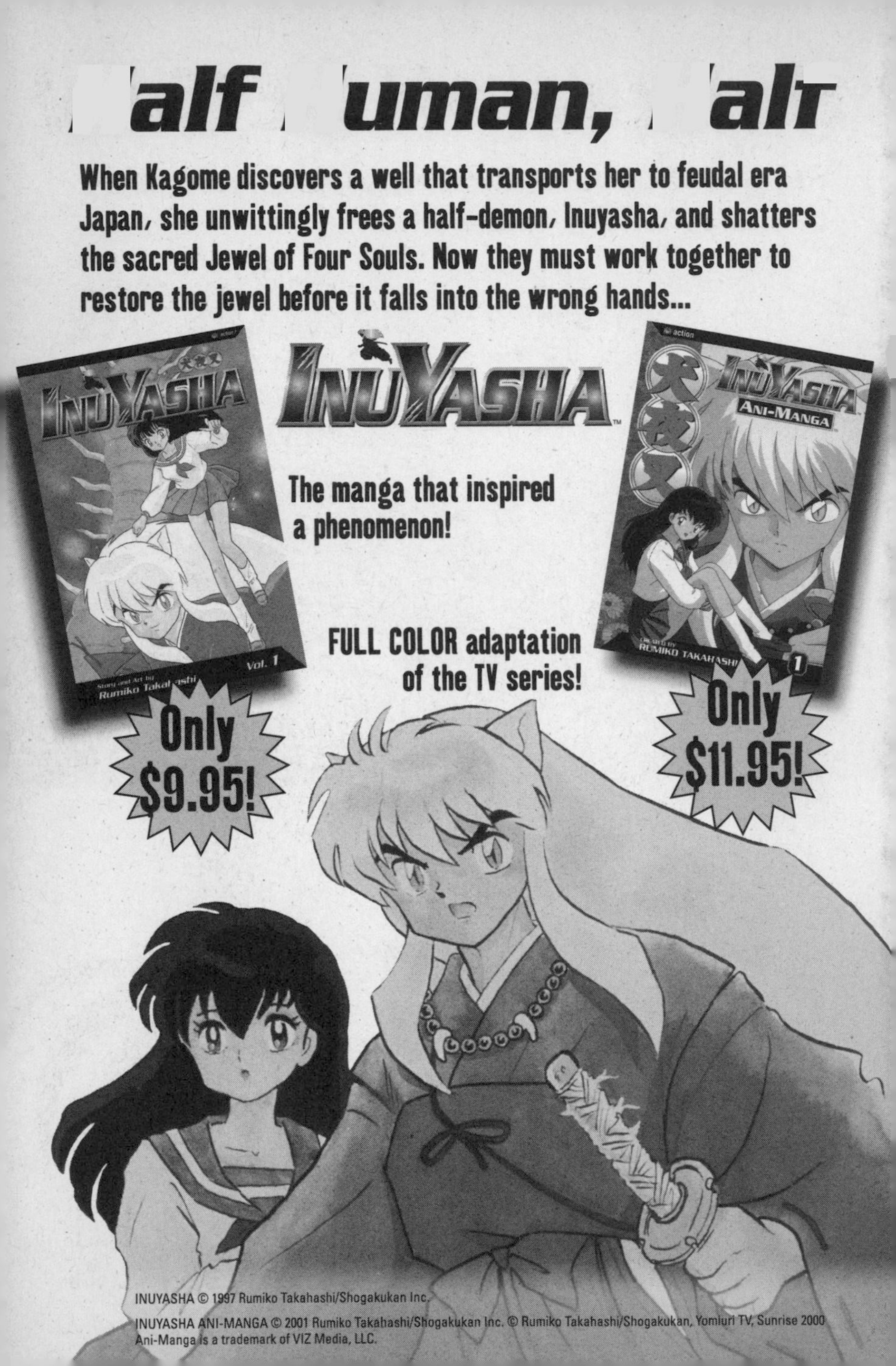

LOVE MANGA?

LET US KNOW W !

AVAILABLE ONLINE. PLEASE VISIT:
VIZ.COM/MANGASURVEY

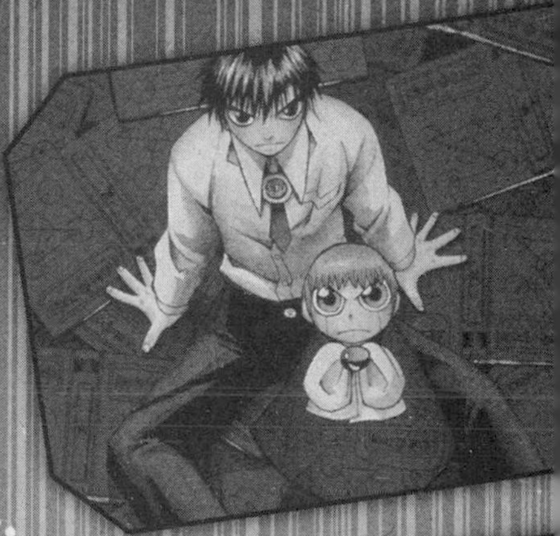

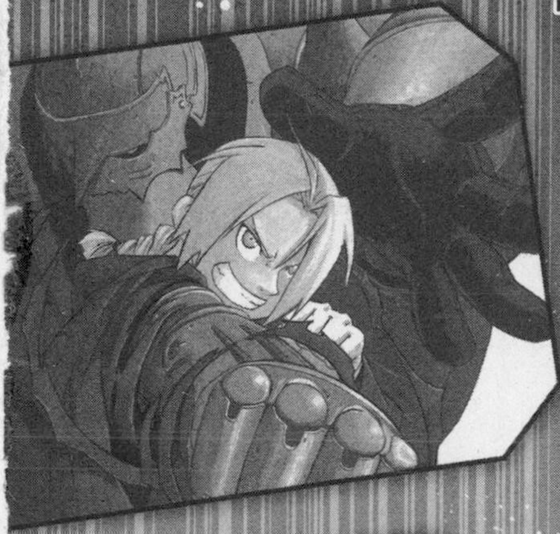

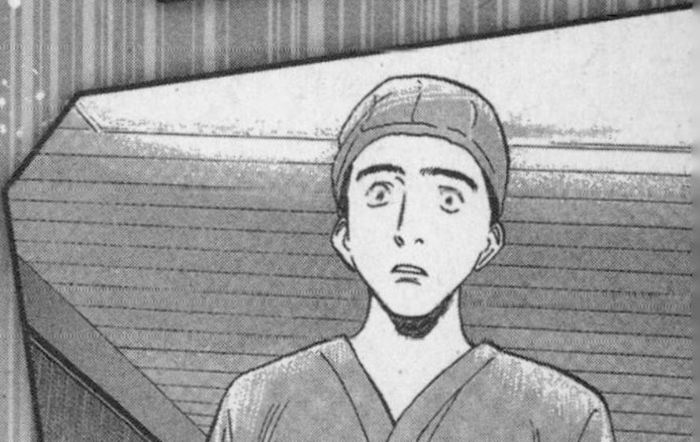

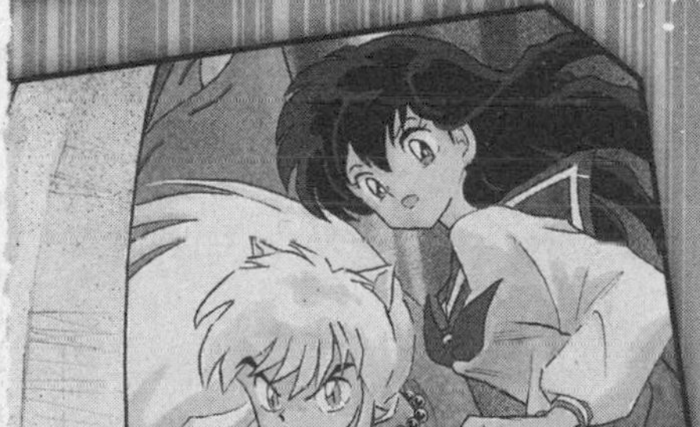

HELP US MAKE THE MANGA YOU LOVE BETTER!

viz media

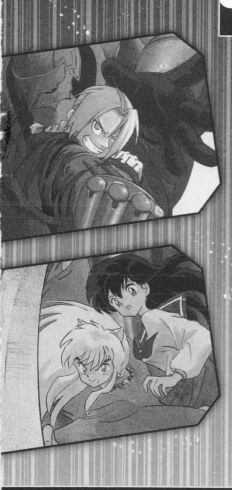

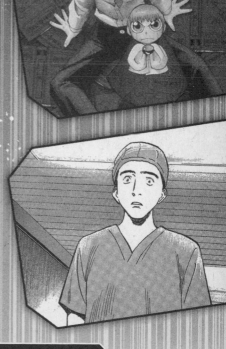